Journey with the Moon

TITHIS IN SPIRITUALITY AND ASTROLOGY

Achala Sylwia Mihajlović

ISBN-13: 978-1-0967-6887-6

CONTENTS

PREFACE

oṁ ajñāna-timirāndhasya
jñānāñjana-śalākayā
cakṣur unmīlitaṁ yena
tasmai śrī-gurave namaḥ

Before I start this book I wish to bow down to my Satguru, Paramahamsa Sri Swami Vishwananda, as without Guru's blessing no work can be complete. Without His inspiration, timeless wisdom and spiritual practices, this book could never come into being.

Secondly, I wish to bow down to the Supreme Goddess, Adi Shakti, who in Her kindness allowed me to have a glimpse of some of Her mysteries. She is the power behind everything, be it outer universe or inner universe. The entire Creation is nothing else but Her playground.

My personal journey with the Moon started already years ago, when for the first time I came in contact with Vedic astrology and the mysteries of Nitya Devis presiding over different lunar phases. But the entire process of writing this book and collecting all the experiences and pieces of information gathered over the years greatly deepened my connection with the tithis. During the entire process of writing this book, I would meditate with Divine Mother in Her exact form, exact yantra and exact mantra every night, while during the day She would somehow guide me to the exact scripture and exact verses, which were hiding the missing pieces of information.

Few people take effort to dive really deeply into the topic of lunar phases – but once you get amazed by their beauty, you will keep coming back to them over and over again. And everytime you will learn something new from them. After all, they are Nitya Devis, "Goddesses of Eternity". Although they are the rulers of Time, their wisdom is timeless and limitless. Not without a reason scriptures say that except Supreme Goddess, nothing and nobody is higher than them. They are the true powers of Time.

The knowledge, which you will find in this book is sacred and it is not only to be read, but also to be meditated on. Nobody can be a greater teacher than your own experience. I hope you will find this journey inspiring.

CHAPTER 1

CELESTIAL DANCE OF SHIVA AND SHAKTI

Eternal dance of Sun and Moon, celestial representatives of Divine masculine principle and Divine feminine principle, Shiva and Shakti, has inspired yogis, *rishis*, astrologers, poets and seers since time immemorial.

"She the Night makes all the worlds sleep. He the Day is verily the waker-up of all."
- Cid-vilasa

He is the giver of light (*Prakasha*), while She is the reflection (*Vimarsha*). Their unique relation, reflecting the sacred relationship between Divine Mother and Divine Father, although one and eternal, keeps manifesting through different moments in time in countless forms. Every relationship is a mere reflection of this eternal relation between the individual and the Supreme. Whenever there is any "I" and any "you" a Divine relationship is formed in one of its unique moods.

Every such a moment, unique with its qualities and celestial rays, represents a different form of relation between Shiva and Shakti, and gives birth to different results. Vedic *rishis* have perceived in their meditation fifteen forms of this universal relationship between Shiva and Shakti, which correlate to fifteen phases of the Moon. They called them *tithis*.

Sacred distances

Tithis are nothing else but solilunar days in Vedic astrology based on the apparent distance between the Sun and the Moon on our sky, which determines Moon phases, as well. All ancient traditions were calling the Sun, the Father, and the Moon, the Mother. In the light of modern science this couldn't be more accurate. The light of the Sun and its warmness is indeed infusing the Earth with creative energy and sustains our life here. But not everyone knows, that without the Moon, most likely there wouldn't be any life on Earth, either. It is our Moon's gravitational influence that helped ensure that Earth's spin axis and climate remained stable over long timescales, which is essential for the life to survive on our planet. As much as the influence of the Sun impregnated the Earth with life, the influence of the Moon preserves it. Thus the influence of Sun is active, masculine and inspiring, while the influence of the Moon is passive, feminine and nourishing.

There is something deep and sacred in the distance between the Sun, the Earth and the Moon, which is already mentioned in Vedas. The diameter of the Sun is about 108 times that of the diameter of Earth. The average distance between the Earth and the Sun is 108 times the Sun's diameter. The average distance from the Earth to the Moon is about 108 times the Moon's diameter. This is actually why the Moon appears the same size as the Sun during eclipses. Dr. Manoj Chalam made a hypothesis, that "the ratio of 108 may be the key to finding planets hospitable to life outside of our solar system" and suggested that we just need to "look toward this same size and distance relationship".

There is an obvious sacredness about number 108. Not without a reason it is mentioned several time in Vedas. It is also a very important number in Vedic astrology. In the science of Jyotish there are 27 nakshatras, 27 lunar mansions working behind the solar zodiac of 12 signs. Each nakshatra has four quarters, called *padas*. This gives 9 quarters per one zodiac sign. 9 x 12 = 108. By dividing the main natal chart into nine parts, we receive so called *navamsha*, the most sacred chart to study in Vedic astrology, which is revealing the true path of our soul in this lifetime. This particular topic is going to become even more interesting, when we will dive deeper into the mysteries of Moon's phases.

Divine romance between Sun and Moon

Sun's brightness is unchangeable. It shines with equal light, regardless of its position on the sky. It doesn't judge. It favours no one. Its *dharma* doesn't change with time. Its only purpose is to shine and to give light. This is why in Vedic astrology Sun is perceived as natural *Atma karaka*, the light of the soul, which stays unchangeable regardless of the different life circumstances and moods of the mind. Sun represents the state of Shiva.

The brightness of the Moon, however, is dependent on the light of the Sun and the distance between them. Moon doesn't have any light on her own – she reflects the light of the Sun. Similarly, our mind doesn't have any brightness on its own. Any brightness manifested through it, is the light of the soul that shines through the veil of *maya* covering it.

Shiva is the Sun, the light of the soul, while Shakti is the Moon, the individual mind, which takes part in a Divine game of life, and is sensitive to different moods of the present moment.

Moon, in Vedic astrology, is our present moment. It alters the eternal burning light of the Sun and turns it into nourishing, motherly love, providing us different qualities in different moments in time, depending on the nakshatra (Vedic constellation) it sits in and its distance from the Sun. Sometimes its capacity to reflect the light of the Sun will be higher, sometimes it will be lower. Sometimes it will be moving away from the Sun, and sometimes it will be moving back towards it. Even though the face of the Moon is always turned towards the Sun, as Earth and Moon are tidally locked, from our earthly perspective sometimes we will perceive the Moon as waxing, and sometimes as waning. Waxing and waning are two main moods of the Divine Mother.

In Vedic astrology the path of waxing Moon and waning Moon was split into 15 lunar days or *tithis* each. Fifteen days of waxing Moon and fifteen days of waning Moon give together a 30-day long soli-lunar month, which is the basis of Vedic calendar.

Bright path and dark path of the Goddess

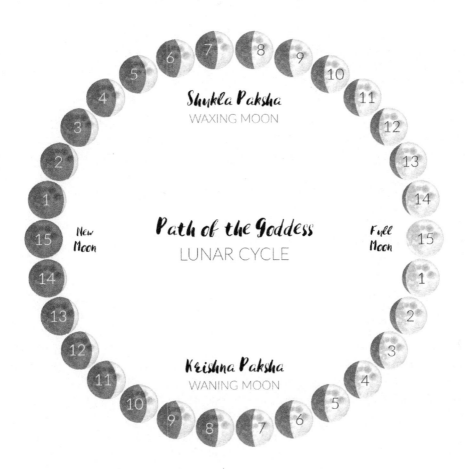

Divine Mother sometimes moves away from Shiva, and sometimes comes back to Him. The Moon sometimes moves away from the Sun, and sometimes comes back to it. Same is with our soul. Although all of us come from the Divine, when we undergo the process of individuation, we move away from our Divine origin to find our true self and realise our individual purpose. Sooner or later, however, the longing to merge back with the Supreme Consciousness awakens in each one of us. If not in this lifetime, then in another. Over and over again countless souls move away from Supreme Consciousness, to rediscover themselves one more time and again return to their Source. It is a Divine romance, which sets whole creation into motion. It is an eternal love story between the soul and its Beloved, which all the *yogis* yearn to have a glimpse of. It is an inborn yearning of each soul. It is the particle of Supreme Goddess within us and a deep longing to be reunited with Her only true Beloved.

As my Gurudev, Paramahamsa Vishwananda, has beautifully said: "Nothing in this universe exists without Love, as all is the Lord Himself and His Love is constantly in movement."

When the Moon moves away from the Sun, when the Goddess moves away from Shiva to rediscover Herself, to understand Her purpose and to reflect Shiva's light into the outer world in its full glory, the Moon is waxing. In Vedic astrology we call it *Shukla paksha* – the bright fortnight. In *Shukla paksha* Goddess becomes curious about the world and understanding Her true potential. She wishes to interact, to play, to manifest, to communicate and to bestow Her boons. She looks towards the outside. With each of Her steps She discovers a new quality (*kala*) within Herself. Yet, as She becomes brighter and brighter, She moves away from the Sun, Her true Beloved. She enters the material world. The fullness of individuality can be learned only from the distance. And being so, in every relationship some distance is needed for the self-discovery to happen, as well.

When the Goddess finally realises fullness of Her potential during the Full Moon, a peak moment, when She is at maximum distance from the Sun and when She reflects the fullness of light; when Her desires become satiated and there is nothing else to fulfill, no more light to be reflected, the Divine longing awakens in Her heart. She starts to long and cry for Her Beloved Shiva. With each of Her tears She loses some of Her brightness. With each of Her steps, She moves one step closer to Her Beloved. She realises that She has been distanced from Her origin, and She yearns to come back to it. She abandons all the brightness of the external world and becomes more introvert and more humble. She slowly detaches Herself from each of Her qualities gained on Her way in *Shukla paksha*, so She can reunite again with Shiva on the New Moon day, when She merges back completely into Him. When Goddess is returning to Her Beloved, the Moon is waning. We call it *Krishna paksha* – the dark fortnight.

Like that, each and every month, the Goddess moves away from Shiva and returns back to Him. She distances Herself from the Source, to reunite with it again. One lunar month is a complete cycle of Her sacred journey of self-discovery. And, as the Mother represents our mind itself, She takes us all on that journey with Her. Wherever She moves, She holds us in Her lap. She is the present moment, which holds us closely to its bosom - like a loving mother would do.

On Her way through the sky, when She forms fifteen different dance positions with Shiva, the Supreme Consciousness, and manifests fifteen different moods and fifteen different qualities of light, She assumes fifteen different aspects. Sometimes She will be more playful, sometimes She will be more strict. Sometimes She will bring us happiness, sometimes sadness. Like a wise mother She will teach us the story of life, so we can become fit to rediscover our own life's purpose. Sometimes we would embrace those lessons with an open heart, but sometimes we would reject them, according to our personal likes and dislikes. No wonder that highest Goddess always holds in Her hands *pasha* (the noose representing our likes and attachments) and *ankusha* (the goad representing our dislikes). If we choose to focus on Her supreme beauty instead of our likes and dislikes, leaving them both in Her hands and accepting with a childlike trust that the present moment is always bringing us exactly what we need, nourishing us like the Divine Mother in many different ways, we can live our life happy and contented, surrendered to the will of the Divine and noticing Her blessings, even if they come in the form of apparent adversities. If we could notice the Divine in every single moment of life, in every single situation, mood or living being, that would be nothing smaller than enlightenment. That would be the Full Moon of the soul.

That is the true meaning of *atithi devo bhava* or "guest is God". When we greet each "guest", be it human, animal, emotion, thought or life experience, with the same accepting, loving and humble attitude, this is when our inner Moon is healthy. That is why the word *tithi* is derived from *atithi*, meaning "a guest" – as it reveals, how we welcome things in life.

My personal journey with the Goddess

My personal experience with the Goddess wasn't an easy one. There were many things that were experienced on the way, which are going to stay forever only between me, Her and my Gurudev. She was the one, through whom I got attracted to Vedic astrology. I never had any interest to learn how to predict future or read charts. In the science of Jyotisha I was seeking something much deeper and much more beneficial for the individual soul's development: to understand what the present moment is bringing me and which Divine lessons the universe is sending me, so I can become a better human being.

On spiritual path it is very easy to fall prey to our pride and stay blind to our own faults and mistakes. But the stars will never lie. Whenever you will make a mistake, they will always reveal this to you with astonishing clarity. They will try, over and over again, to bring you to the right path - like the Divine Mother, who never loses faith in Her child. This is why certain basic knowledge of astrology is something that is of great help to any person on spiritual path, as a valubale tool for introspection. Understanding lunar cycles and qualities of different lunar days, does not only teach us more about the sacred relationship between Spirit and Nature. In fact, it reveals us something very profound about our personal relationship with the Divine.

Studying the lunar phases was the very first thing I ever approached in Vedic astrology, when I started my journey with Jyotisha some years ago. The beauty of eternal goddesses of the lunar phases, Nitya Devis, was always attracting me, and I always yearned to learn from them more and more. The more I meditated with them, the more I learned from them about myself. This humble book is the result of my *sadhana*. Yet, this little information present here is just a drop in an ocean, of what is still to be discovered and what is still to be known. After all, those eternal goddesses, guardians of time, are infinite in their nature. From our earthly perspective we can grasp just a glimpse of their beauty and sacred meanings.

The Mother doesn't expect much from Her child. To meditate with Her only an open heart is needed. Each and every single day I would sit for a while with one of those goddesses, whose lunar phase was active at the moment, imaginening myself on Her lap, as my Gurudev taught me to meditate with Divine Mother. With some of Her manifestations I would feel more comfortable and safe, while being with other forms of Divine Mother was sometimes more challenging for me. The more I meditated with each of Her forms, the more I understood my relationship with Her, as well as Her inner and outer qualities; and the more I started to notice, how each of Her forms manifests in the outer world.

I have learned a lot about myself on the way. The most powerful lesson from the Mother was the lesson of humility and surrender. Once you find yourself in Her lap, with some of Her forms, with which you might not resonate so well, and once you realise, that She is this very present moment itself and there is no running away from here, it automatically makes you more humble. It makes you realise, that surrender is the only right thing to do. And in surrender itself, so much sweetness and so many blessings are hidden. Once you get over your likes and dislikes and embrace, what the Divine Mother in the form of present moment has to offer, there is something magical happening. But it is not something, which should be described in words. It is something to be experienced in the depth of one's own soul. If this would be something, that could be grasped in words, our great *rishis* and seers would have already written whole scriptures about it.

My Gurudev wrote so beautifully on 15 November 2017: "Some secrets are secrets because they are sacred, which means one has to find them out by one's own efforts and sacrifices. It is not a problem to tell them as they are usually very simple, but only fiery intelligence, determination, will and longing will be able to reveal them. People are generally lazy and even as much as they get from Masters, saints, scriptures and Guru, they take it for granted and it is only taking, which means that there is no transformation and sharing, giving back in other form."

Hence, this little book is not going to be about me or my personal experiences. Personal experience is the real "secret" of any teaching – but it is something to be experienced in the chamber of one's own heart, on individual level. Instead, it is going to be an invitation for you to go on this sacred journey with Divine Mother with your own efforts and understand yourself on a much deeper level. In our times, when we have became so self-centered with our attention running constantly towards the outside, the biggest blessing we can get from Jyotisha, the science of time, is how to reconnect with the natural forces around us and their sacred cycles – not to abuse it, but to learn how to go with Nature's sacred flow, instead of opposing it. Out of all the things the science of astrology can bless us with nowadays, there is nothing higher or more sacred than the possibility to rediscover ourselves and our inner *you*-niverse – over and over again. To become *whole* again.

CHAPTER 2

IN THE DUAL WATERS OF THE MIND

Each moment in time is said to have five limbs, according to Vedic astrology: *vara* (week day), *nakshatra* (the constellation, which the Moon dwells in), *tithi* (lunar day or phase of the Moon), *karana* (half of tithi) and *yoga* (angular relationship between the Sun and the Moon). Each of those limbs correlates to one of the five elements or *tattwas*: earth, water, fire, air and ether. *Tithis*, the lunar days, belong to water element or *jala tattwa*, like the Moon itself. How wondrous, that this book allowed itself to be published only when Saturn entered Purvashadha nakshatra - the lunar mansion of Cosmic Waters.

In Vedic astrology Moon represents our mind and the way it is able to receive the light of the present moment. It is defined by its ability to receive - which is why the Moon is associated with Divine Mother in almost every culture. Divine Mother represents our ability to receive the impregnating light of the present moment; She is the inner fertility of our mind, as well as qualities it tends to get pregnant with and give birth to.

As the Moon causes tides in huge water bodies on our planet, so it causes tides within us, depending on its phase or *tithi*. Although the light is one, its reflection undergoes constant changes. Imagine the Sun reflected in the sea. Depending on how current waves are shaping the surface of the sea at the moment, such will be the shape of reflected Sun. Like the waves on the surface of the ocean are ever changing and cyclic in nature, so our mind constantly undergoes different changes and experiences different moods and emotions. This is why the purpose of any *yogic* practice is to still those waves, to still this mind, so the Divine light may reflect in it in its purest form.

Studying the *tithis* allows us to understand our own inner cycles and helps us to comprehend, why certain emotions or feelings tend to emerge on certain days, and what exatly does the Divine try to communicate to us through them. Our soul is in a constant dialogue with the Supreme Consciousness. But when the mind becomes callous and refuses to receive certain Divine messages, which might be unpleasant to our ego, we block this sacred communication on our end and thus become more and more disconnected from life itself.

Although this is going to be the book on Vedic astrology and understanding the patterns behind sacred lunar cycles, my highest intention and wish, above all, is to help you, who are reading this, to unblock the natural flow of water element within you and to help you in opening up more for receiving the light of the present moment – as there are many secret blessings hidden in it.

Dual nature of water element

Jala tattwa, water element is connected to *svadhishthana*, sacral chakra in our energy body. It is all about relationships, exchange of energy, emotions, feelings, beliefs, hopes and duality. It is about where we chose our energy to flow, what we allow ourselves to receive, and how much we are able to simply surrender. Water element is all about the quality of our relationship with the world around us. Every experience is some sort of relationship. And the experience itself is said to be Shakti.

All relationships are dual in nature. There has to be some "you" and there has to be some "me". Whatever happens between those two is called a relationship. Differentiation is inevitable for a relationship to happen. As it is beautifully explained in *Garland of Letters*: "By 'differentiation' is meant the polarisation of Consciousness into subjective (*Prakasha* - light) and objective (*Vimarsha* - reflection) aspects. The Self sees another."

In a way, every relationship is a metaphor of this eternal relation between the Sun and the Moon, *Prakasha* and *Vimarsha*, consciousness and reflection. Sometimes you are the one giving some sort of light to others, sometimes you are the one receiving and reflecting it. There is always somebody giving and somebody receiving. Healthy balance between those two results in a healthy relationship. This is why studying the lunar phases will reveal us a lot about our relationships as well.

Water itself is also dual in its nature. On Northern hemisphere its motion is clockwise, while on Southern hemisphere it flows counterclockwise. The sea rises and falls. Similarly, in lunar cycle, clockwise motion and the rise is connected to *Shukla paksha*, the bright fortnight of waxing Moon, which stands for evolution, expression of the self and creation, while counterclockwise motion and fall is connected to *Krishna paksha*, the dark fortnight and waning Moon, which represents involution, returning back to our center and destruction. This is why *Krishna paksha* is often wrongly considered as "inauspicious time", as the Moon becomes weaker during the dark fortnight and it is connected with counterclockwise motion in tantric worship. Even though *Krishna paksha* may indeed bring more challenges on material level and requires much more effort to overcome obstacles during its time, from the perspective of spiritual development it is actually even more auspicious than *Shukla paksha* – as during *Krishna paksha*, the Moon, or the mind, is slowly "dying" to reunite with the Divine. It is looking towards the Divine and moving towards the Divine in the process of involution of consciousness, to rediscover its true origin.

This is why people born in *Shukla paksha* or bright fortnight, are usually more extravert and more concerned with the matters of the world and their own creative self expression, while people born in *Krishna paksha* are usually more introvert and their awareness is turned more towards the inside. Both qualities in excess can cause certain misbalance. *Shukla paksha* Moon can easily become too materialistic and too overwhelming with its presence, while *Krishna paksha* Moon can become too closed up or even develop low self-esteem and weakness. By knowing, whether we were born under the dark Moon or bright Moon, we can understand and accept our destiny on a much deeper level, and reflect the exact quality of the Divine, which yearned to be manifested through our life in a constructive way. Not everyone's purpose is to shine the light into the external world. Some people's purpose is to meet this light deep within them. Evolution and involution are equally important in the development of consciousness.

The Divine romance

According to Vedic thought, this whole universe, with its intricate creations, patterns and cycles, is just the manifestation of Cosmic *lila*, the game of the Divine. It emerged from one Supreme Consciousness, one Cosmic "I", which yearned to express itself over and over again, through countless "you"s to experience the greatest Cosmic miracle: Love. It is an eternal Divine romance manifesting itself over an over again. Every relationship ever existing is just a dim reflection of the sublime relationship between the soul and its eternal Beloved.

Shiva, although complete in His fullness, yearned to see His reflection, and so the creation took place. Shakti became His first and the most perfect reflection. Upon receiving Shiva's light She became pregnant with all creation and gave birth to every single "you". *Kamakala vilasa* speaks beautifully about Her:

"She the Primordial Shakti who excells all and who in Her own true nature is eternal, limitless Bliss, is the seed of all the moving and non-moving things which are to be, and is the pure mirror in which Shiva experiences Himself."

Garland of Letters furtherly explains: "A handsome King looking at his reflection in a mirror which is before him knows 'I am he who is thus reflected.' So the Supreme Lord looking at His own Power within Himself knows His own Self as 'I am all (*Paripurno'ham*)', that is, the whole or Perfect 'I.' This is the union of *a* = Śiva and *ha* = Śakti. A + ha = *aham* or 'I.'"

Thus, each one of us is a particle of this Divine romance. Every "I" is a small fragment of an infinite fractal of Shiva's and Shakti's Divine dance.

God always looks towards us, as His very glance sustains our life - like the light of the Sun sustains the life on Earth. He patiently waits for us to remember Him and start our journey towards Him (which for most of us can take up to lifetimes). If in this lifetime you have the grace to be a spiritual seeker and search for the Divine, you can be sure that He was already seeking you before for countless of your earthly lives. He is always looking for us and He is always few steps ahead of us. It is us, who are only sometimes looking for Him.

This fundamental truth, which was often repeated by my Gurudev, became to me even more obvious, when I started to meditate deeper on the *tithis*, sacred phases of the Moon. In *Shukla paksha*, the bright fortnight, when you look at the sky, it will seem as if the Sun (Shiva) is running after the Moon (Shakti), and the Moon is moving away from the Sun. The individual consciousness separates itself from the Supreme Consciousness for the sake of creation, evolution and understanding its individual life purpose – while the Divine is running after it. In *Krishna paksha*, however, it looks as if Moon (individual self) runs back towards the Sun (Supreme Consciousness) – but the Sun does not run away from it. Sun moves very slowly when compared to the Moon, one degree a day, to make sure the Moon will catch up and the union on the New Moon day will happen. This in itself reveals us a lot about the nature of the Sun, representing the Supreme Consciousness in our solar system. Even though the soul can sometimes forget about the Divine, God never forgets about the soul. He always provides us light on our path - but whether we are able to receive or not, depends on our own free will. Our ability to receive is the only little bit of free will that is there for us.

In *Shukla paksha*, when Moon becomes brighter and brighter, the Sun shines secretly behind it, giving it its light and blessings. As the Moon moves away from the intense heat of the Sun, it becomes more and more capable of understanding its own creative power and inner potential. But during bright fortnight the Moon has the Sun behind it from our earthly perspective. Similarly, when everything goes well in our life and when we keep receiving blessings from the universe, we easily forget about God and turn our back to Him. This is one of the reasons, why things, which are auspicious in the eyes of the world, like *Shukla paksha* is traditionally considered to be, are not necessarily always auspicious for the development of the soul.

During *Krishna paksha*, however, when Moon starts its journey back to the Sun, it loses some of its brightness, which symbolises detachment from false identity and pride. The Moon faces the Sun during the dark fortnight and moves closer to its intense heat, blinded by its brightness. During *Krishna paksha* Sun shines directly into Moon's face, and the Moon slowly surrenders and becomes more humble with every step. This is why *Krishna paksha* might not necessarily be so "pleasant" for the mind, as lots of karma is getting burned on the way. Yet, things, which are pleasant for the mind, and things, which bring true pleasure to the soul, are often completely opposite. The mood of the Goddess in *Krishna paksha* is intense longing for Her eternal Beloved, and She will do anything to reunite at least some part of you with the Higher Consciousness. She will remove all the obstacles from your path to the Divine and take away from you all that takes you away from Him. This is why traditionally in tantra it is said that Goddess in bright fortnight is Lalita Tripurasundari, the most beautiful in the three worlds, the benevolent goddess of creation, while in the dark fortnight She assumes a form of Mother Kali, the dark goddess of destruction, which is completely naked. As Kali, She represents the death of the ego. Yet, in both fortnights, She is still the very same Shakti, the same loving Mother, who is performing each of Her actions only for the benefit of Her child.

In *Shukla paksha*, when the Moon moves away from the Sun, when Shakti moves away from Shiva, the Sun would need to go clockwise in zodiac to catch up with the Moon, therefore its rays are following the Moon in the clockwise direction. In *Krishna paksha*, on the other hand, the Sun would need to go counter-clockwise through the zodiac to meet the Moon, therefore its rays are following the Moon in the counterclockwise direction. This is one more reason, why in Sri Vidya tradition we always worship the fifteen eternal goddesses, which represent fifteen phases of the Moon, in a clockwise manner during *Shukla paksha* and counterclockwise manner during *Krishna paksha*. In some traditions, however, there is only counterclockwise way of worshipping the Nitya Devis, goddesses of the phases of the Moon, as it is connected with involution and diving deeper within ourselves in the process of meditation, freeing ourselves from the illusions of the outer world.

CHAPTER 3

CONSCIOUSNESS FULL OF NECTAR

ॐ पूर्णमदः पूर्णमिदं पूर्णात्पुर्णमुदच्यते
पूर्णस्य पूर्णमादाय पूर्णमेवावशिष्यते ॥

oḿ pūrṇam adaḥ pūrṇam idaḿ pūrṇāt pūrṇam udacyate
pūrṇasya pūrṇam ādāya pūrṇam evāvaśiṣyate

- Isha Upanishad

That is *purnam* (full of Divine consciousness) and this is *purnam*. You are full and I am full. This is Divine and that is Divine. This is perfect and that is perfect. From that, which is full, Divine and perfect, only something that is full, Divine and perfect can be manifested. Fullness always remains full, Divine and perfect. If you take a little bit of fullness away from the fullness, it will still remain full. Divine. And perfect.

That is the secret of life.

This mysterious verse, which is holding a deep secret of understanding the true nature of this world and the true nature of ourselves, comes from *Isha Upanishad*. Mahatma Gandhi had said once so beautifully, that even if all the Vedas would perish, but only this verse would remain, it would be enough for the Vedic culture to survive.

When we realize that all is pervaded by Divine consciousness and we acknowledge its presence in everybody and everything, this is when we start to live a truly enlightened life. When we accept everything that comes as perfect, and when we accept everything that we lose as perfect, we start to truly live in the present moment, in the heart. We become *whole*.

This Divine ability to embrace the fullness of life, to nurture a heart connection with reality, the way it is, recognizing the fullness and the Divinity in every object, person and situation that we meet, lies deep within our hearts. It is our true nature. We were not created to worry about petty things, nurture our petty fears or fall a prey to our petty desires. We were created to *love life* in its multitude of forms and to enjoy the eternal interaction between our soul and the Divine, no matter which shape does it take at the moment.

The essence of life

"O Soma, Pavamana, bless us, so that we may live,
with that bright milk of thine which hath been brought from heaven."
- Rig Veda

One of the names of the Moon, as he is often addressed in the Vedas, is Soma or Pavamana. *Soma* means "the nectar of life", while *pavamana* means "flowing clearly". It indicates the true, higher nature of our mind, which was created to "flow clearly", channeling the "milk from heaven", becoming pregnant only with the Divine inspiration and rejoicing in the "nectar of life". Whenever this pure flow of Divine energy is interrupted in our mind by our own likes and dislikes, we also lose the ability to rejoice in the essence of life: bliss or *ananda*.

Dr David Frawley has written so beautifully:

"*Soma* is a spiritual principle, an aspect of the infinite and a key to immortality. In the state of meditation, the brain and mind naturally secrete a special type of *soma* or nectar of peace and contentment, which reflects this spiritual *soma*. Ultimately *soma* is the bliss of all existence, the *ananda* through which the universe is created and into which it must return. It is this *soma* or *ananda* that is the *prima materia* or ultimate substance behind the entire world."

This pure state of mind, in which *soma*, the nectar of life, gets awakened and relished, is also symbolised by two open lotus flowers, which Moon-god is holding in his hands. Open lotuses do not only represent the awakening of Divine consciousness within us, but also the purity of the soul. Lotus flowers grow in mud, yet they rise above the mud they come from, they pierce through the surface and blossom to become the most magnificent of all flowers. Once they are fully blossomed, no matter how much water falls on them, they do not hold even a single drop. Due to this unique quality of lotus flower it was for ages glorified as a symbol of purity of the mind.

Similarly, our consciousness grows in a mud of mundane vibrations. Yet, once we start to work on our spiritual progress, we slowly rise above the density of earthly vibrations, and our consciousness slowly blossoms to manifest its true form and spread its hidden fragrance of bliss. This bliss, which is the very essence of who we truly are, is what *soma* stands for.

The enlightened mind

The word *soma* is derived from *sa-uma*: *sa* meaning "with", *uma* meaning "tranquillity, resplendence, light". Uma is also one of the names of Shakti. She received the name "Uma" after Her long penance to get Shiva as Her husband, when Her body started to glow and reflect Shiva's light due to Her spiritual power and devotion. *Soma is thus the name of the higher nature of our mind: the enlightened mind, which is tranquil and full of light.*

Saumya, an adjective derived from *soma*, beautifully describes the qualities of such an enlightened mind: placid, happy, gentle, auspicious, likeable, cheerful, peaceful, lovely, resembling the moon, mild, cool, balanced, moist and full of nectar.

Soma is the mythical nectar of immortality, the very essence of life, which is pure bliss, *ananda* - the delight of the soul. "*Soma*, the Cheerer, yields whate'er the heart finds sweet", say the words of the rigvedic hymn. This seeking of *soma*, "the juice of life" is inherent in every soul. We all seek some kind of happiness and bliss in life, and in our own way, each of us is trying to squeeze the juice out of life to enjoy it to the fullest. Yet, with distracted mind, our happiness never lasts forever. We seek bliss in perishable things of the material world, constantly running from one thing to another, but we fail to recognise the true essence of life hidden within us.

The true essence of life is the Divine Soul, the *atma* pervading the whole universe. The Supreme Self is "the taste of the water, the fragrance of the earth, the sound in the ether, the heat of the fire and the light of the Sun and the Moon", as proclaims Lord Krishna in Bhagavad Gita. It is the unique quality and the true essence of everything, what is the highest and best in all things.

Interestingly, this *soma*, this nectar of life, was hidden on the Moon, according to Hindu mythology. Similarly, the very nectar of life, the sweetness of life is hidden within our own mind. What an unparalleled cosmic joke is that: restlessly we seek the sweetness and joy of life in everything around us, while it is hidden deep, deep within us.

The mind starts to rejoice in *soma*, in its true nectar, once it starts to perceive the true essence, the Divinity, in everything around it. It is the conscious effort we need to make to train our mind to see and honour the Divine present in every aspect of creation: in every person, in every object, in every life situation. It

15

requires some patience, humility and detachment. This magical moment, when your mind perceives the Divinity, or what is the highest and best in something, you are able to truly appreciate it and it brings a true bliss to your mind. In that very moment you relish the essence of life.

The harmonious flow of *soma*, which is invoked through so many hymns of Rig Veda, is nothing else, but invoking the purity of our mind and harmonious flow of consciousness, which in its purest state perceives everything as equal, Divine and full. This is why *soma* was called a drink of gods, a heavenly offering. Yet, to be able to perceive the one, true essence of the universe in everything around us, firstly we need to reach the essence of our own nature within us. This happens on the deepest level through the process of scientific meditation practice, such as Atma Kriya Yoga.

Dr David Frawley, once again, had put it so accurately in words:

"Cultivating *soma* means cultivating the fuel of devotion, receptivity, love and surrender. It means increasing the power to feel, dissolve, merge and become one with all. We must eventually realize that all things are offerings to the Divine light of awareness within us. Then there will be nothing that is not *soma* for us."

Sixteen qualities of nectar

"In the waxing fortnight kalas shoot and expand; in the waning fortnight they shrink and small become. They who can know the mystery of kalas sixteen, may well reach the Feet of the Lord of glory indescribable."
- Thirumanthiram

There is one *soma* and one Moon. Yet, it has sixteen different qualities or *kalas*, which change according to the current Moon phase. Fifteen *kalas*, *amrita* (nectar), *manada* (pride), *pusha* (nourishment), *tushti* (contentment), *pushti* (comfort), *rati* (passion), *dhrti* (courage), *shashini* (swiftness), *candrika* (moonlight), *kanti* (beauty), *jyotsna* (halo), *sri* (opulence), *priti* (love), *angada* (self-sacrifice) and *purna* (fullness) belong to this world and correspond to each of the phases of the Moon. Sixteenth *kala*, however is beyond the boundaries of the space, time and material perception. It is perceived only in deep meditation. It is called *purnamrita* – "nectar of fullness". It stands for the Goddess Herself in Her purest, unaltered form.

These sixteen *kalas* correspond directly to the sixteen *kalas* of an avatar or an enlightened soul and sixteen qualities of Lord Krishna, such as: *daya* (compassion), *dhairya* (patience), *kshama* (forgiveness), *nyaya* (justice), *nirapeksha* (impartiality), *niraskata* (detachment), *tapasya* (penance), *aparajita* (invincibility), *dhanashila* (generosity), *saundaryamaya* (beauty), *nrityajna* (best of dancers), *sangitajna* (best of singers), *nitivati* (good judgement), *satyavati* (truthfulness), *sarvajnata* (omniscience) and *sarvaniyanta* (control over everything).

On the first day of *Shukla paksha*, first day after New Moon, one *kala* arises in the Moon – one quality of light is reflected. One taste of nectar gets manifested. On the second day, one more *kala* joins the Moon, strengthening its light and making the taste of its nectar sweeter. Similarly, during bright fortnight *kalas* arise in the Moon one by one, making it brighter, sweeter and more full, until all the fifteen worldly *kalas* shine in their fullness during the Full Moon night – when the Goddess manifests in Her fullness.

In *Krishna paksha*, on the other hand, on the first day after Full Moon, one *kala* leaves the Moon. The same *kala* that awakened as the first one in the Moon on the first day of *Shukla paksha* is going to be the first one to leaves Moon during *Krishna paksha*. Being so, each *kala* dwells with the Moon for full fifteen days. *Kalas* continue to leave the Moon, one by one, during the dark fortnight until the Moon loses all its light and taste during the New Moon, when it merges with the Sun – when lower self merges with Supreme Self and offers back to it all its qualities.

Similar thing happens on spiritual path. In the first place, we are usually attracted to spirituality because of some of qualities of Divine Light, which we would like to "gain". In such a state of mind we are discovering ourselves and our own light, but we are still a bit selfish and we still look for our own benefit. But the more our mind matures, the more we realise, that on true spiritual path it is never about gaining anything – it is just about surrendering everything to the Divine.

It is said that each *tithi*, lunar day and each of the fifteen manifestation of the Goddess Herself has two aspects: *Prakashamsa*, which rules the day portion of the *tithi*, and *Vimarshamsa*, which rules the night portion of the *tithi*. At night the Goddess in one of Her fifteen forms collects the nectar reflecting some of its qualities, while during the day She releases it, so it can recharge us. During the night nectar is replenished by Soma or the Moon, while during the day the nectar is burned or consumed by Agni or Surya. Being so, the main quality of the Moon and moonlight is to make things grow (*rohana shakti* of Rohini nakshatra), while the main qualitiy of the Sun is to burn things (*dahana shakti* of Krittika nakshatra). Therefore our life itself is a metaphor of Vedic fire sacrifice, in which *soma*, the sacred nectar of life is offered to the sacred fire.

One *Krishna paksha* and one *Shukla paksha* form a 30-day lunar cycle. 12 lunar months form a 360-day lunar year. Multiplied by two (the day and night aspects of the *tithis* or Nitya Devis, lunar goddesses) we have 720 aspects of Goddess in each lunar year. 720 different moods and 720 different love stories to be experienced during a year. This way the fifteen Goddesses rule the day, the night, the days, months, seasons and the years. Furthermore, each aspect of Supreme Goddess rules 100 *nadis* in our energy body. This way they rule 72000 *nadis* or energy channels in our subtle body and influence them differently during different lunar phases.

Like Swami Sivananda explained beautifully: "The lunar days influence the function of the *nadis* (astral energy channels). It should be born in mind that the Moon exercises a powerful influence over the human mind. In the *Purusha Sukta* you will find the statement: *candrama manaso jatah* – the Moon is born of the mind of the *Virat Purusha* or Cosmic Being. In the cosmos, the Moon is controlled by the Cosmic Mind. The individual mind being a speck of the cosmic mind has therefore a connection with the Moon, and being only a speck it feels controlled by the Moon. When the Moon waxes and wanes, its connection with the mind also fluctuates and thus, there arises a sympathetic reaction in the mind. Hence, the relationship between the flow of the breath and the lunar days."

Sixteen *svaras* of Sanskrit alphabet

Where there is light, there is also a vibration. Light and sound always go hand in hand in a complex process of creation. Each of the sixteen celestial qualities of the Moon and its sixteen rays corresponds to one of the sixteen *svaras* or vowels of Sanskrit alphabet: *a, ā, i, ī, u, ū, ṛ, ṝ, ḷr, ḹr, e, ai, o, au, aṁ* and *aḥ*. Interestingly, in all the tantras and Jyotish works vowels are always connected to the qualities of the Sun, as they represent pure consciousness. Vowels are the true *shakti* and true life of any lanuage - as no language can function without vowels or *svaras*. Like Sun gives the light to the Moon, so it gives the Moon its sixteen vowels or vibrations, one by one – each corresponding to different qualities of *soma*, the Divine nectar.

Lunar day	Tithi (Vedic name)	Kala	Svara
First	*Pratipad*	*daya* (compassion)	a अ
Second	*Dvitiya*	*dhairya* (patience)	ā आ
Third	*Tritiya*	*pusha* (nourishment)	i इ
Fourth	*Caturti*	*tushti* (contentment)	ī ई
Fifth	*Panchami*	*pushti* (comfort)	u उ
Sixth	*Shashti*	*rati* (passion)	ū ऊ
Seventh	*Saptami*	*dhrti* (courage)	ṛ ऋ
Eight	*Ashtami*	*shashini* (swiftness)	ṝ ॠ
Ninth	*Navami*	*candrika* (moonlight)	ḷr ऌ
Tenth	*Dashami*	*kanti* (beauty)	ḹr ॡ
Eleventh	*Ekadashi*	*jyotsna* (halo)	e ए
Twelfth	*Dvadashi*	*sri* (opulence)	ai ऐ
Thirteenth	*Trayodashi*	*priti* (love)	o ओ

| Fourteenth | *Caturdashi* | *angada* (self-sacrifice) | au ओ |
| Fifteenth: Full Moon / New Moon | *Purnima/Amavasya* | *purna* (fullness) | aṁ अं |

As per *Vishnu Purana* it is the Sun, through one of its rays named *sushumna* ("the most subtle one"), that nourishes and revives the Moon throughout *Shukla paksha*. Is it a coincidence, that this very ray of the Sun, which nourishes the Moon with its light, has the same name like the central and innermost channel in our energy body, through which our consciousness is rising, throug the ladder of the chakras, to meet with its Supreme Beloved at the top of the head, in *sahasrara chakra*? I doubt so.

These sacred 16 vowels associated with 16 *kalas* of the Moon, come from the Sun itself and represent the most subtle manifestation of sound vibration. Unique vibrations of these 16 vowels are directly connected to *vishuddha*, throat chakra in our energy body. Each of them dwells on one of the petals of this chakra, which symbolically represents 16 *nadis*, energy channels connecting in this important energy cenre. Being so, each of the sixteen *svaras*, sixteen sacred vowels, energises this energy center in our subtle body (this concept was describing in detail in my previous book, *Discovering Youniverse*).

It is said that Shiva manifests Himself as Mrityunjaya, "the conqueror of death" in *vishuddha chakra*, while Goddess manifests Herself as Amriteshwari, "the goddess of nectar or immortality". It is believed that close to our pineal gland dwells *amrita kalasha* or "pot of nectar", from which a drop of nectar falls to the base of the mouth, rejuvenating the soul each sunrise. It is as if one dies each night, when one goes to sleep and is reborn next morning by the nectar that drips down the throat at dawn. Shiva in the form of Mrityunjaya gives new life each morning after the daily death of nightly sleep. Each day thus is like a fresh cycle of creation and destruction, with the creative process commencing with the materialization of sound.

Yogis, who consciously practise *khechari mudra* under the guidance of a Guru, like it is done in many traditions of *kriya yoga*, make a conscious effort to protect this Divine nectar from unnecessary waste and being burnt by the digestive fire, to rejuvenate their bodies. Being so, the sixteen qualities of the Moon or the nectar, are not just some metaphor to describe some intangible state of mind. For the *yogis* deeply immersed in their spiritual practice it is a very tangible experience and a real nectar, which can be relinquished and tasted by the senses.

Thus, the sacred cycles of the Moon do not only reveal to us all the different "tides" and patterns in our consciousness, but have a very tangible effect on the biorhythms of our body as well.

CHAPTER 4

BIORHYTHMS OF THE MOON

The changing phases of the Moon have an obvious effect on human body. Similarly like the gravitational pull of the Moon affects large water bodies on our planet, it has even stronger effect on living organisms, which are, at least in case of humans, made up to 60% of water. Our body recognises the lunar phases and reacts to them differently, which was proved by several scientific experiments. It is not a new thing, that crime rate is the highest on Full Moon, when the water in our body is the most disturbed, while there is the biggest number of suicides on New Moon, when we naturally feel more apathic. This might be also the reason why New Moon is said to be ruled by ancestors or "the dead" in Vedic astrology. People with urinary retention problem also notice the biggest problems with their condition on New Moon days, when water element has its smallest activity – while on Full Moon days we would naturally go more frequently to the toilet. This is also why it is greatly recommended to always keep your body well hydrated around New Moon time.

Yet, apart from these obvious connections between the natural rhythms of our body and changing phases of the Moon, there are also much deeper and much more spiritual connections between the flow of energy in our subtle bodies and the *tithis*. Understanding them can be greatly helpful in understanding our own sacred biorhythms on a deeper level and can even help us to heal our own body, by adjusting it to harmonious rhythm of Nature Herself.

Moon cycle and menstrual cycle

By nature women are lunar, and therefore connected in the most intimate way with the changing phases of the Moon. If we would be in ideal harmony with nature, then we would menstruate around New Moon and ovulate around Full Moon – which is even proven in scientific research as the most common timing for a woman to menstruate. Moon is connected with Shakti, the Supreme Goddess, and a woman, being Her miniature, does not only experience the changes of Her moods on a much deeper level, but her body itself reflects all the births and rebirths the Goddess goes through during Her journey throughout lunar month. Therefore observing the different phases of the Moon and getting in touch with their fifteen different goddesses is of much higher importance for the women, as it can help them to understand themselves on a much deeper level – and discover the Divinity hidden on each and every step on this sacred journey with the Goddess.

There is also one well-known treatment for women suffering from issues with irregular menstrual cycle, which is said to work miracles. Specialists say that if you take one tablespoon of flax seed oil a day during *Shukla paksha*, and one tablespoon of evening primrose oil during *Krishna paksha*, it will naturally reconnect your body to its natural cycle and align it with the phases of the Moon, which will also result in less painful menstruations. This type of knowledge was widely known in the past and lunar cycles were greatly honoured, especially by the women. In our times, when we are slowly moving more and more away from Nature, going back to so simple remedies can seem to us akin to miracle – but is barely reconnecting our body to its natural cycle.

Sun and Moon in our breath

Shiva Svarodaya, an ancient treatise on the science of breath, a sacred dialogue between Shiva and Parvati, reveals that different phases of the Moon and different *tithis* have different effects on our breath or *svara* as well. It is believed that whenever our breath follows its natural pattern, tuned to the changing phases of the Moon, health and prosperity are the result. This is why majority of scientific meditation techniques, such as Atma Kriya Yoga, keep as their priority stabilisation of the breath and bringing it back to its natural pattern.

On the two sides of *sushumna*, main energy channel in our subtle body, run two important energy channels from the bottom of our spine, which are finishing in our nostrils. They are called *ida* and *pingala*.

Ida is the lunar channel and whenever it is active, the nourishing qualities of the Moon are activated in our energy body, inspiring us to do all auspicious activities, such as learning, meditation or taking important decisions. Whenever Moon channel, *ida nadi*, is active, it will make each and every action grow and flourish and it will brings us success, as we are then in naturally more peaceful and balanced state of mind.

Pingala is the solar channel and whenever it is active, the burning qualities of the Sun become activated in our energy body, inspiring us to take action, do our work or remove, "burn" all the impurities. Whenever Sun channel, *pingala nadi*, is active, it will bring its burning effect into our actions. Therefore it is not recommended for undertaking any auspicious task. It is best to use this intense energy for physical exercise, doing our work or some sort of purification process or healing.

As *ida* and *pingala nadis* finish their course in our nostrils, they become active at different parts of the day, depending on our breathing pattern. Whenever our breath is stronger in our left nostril, *ida nadi* is activated and the Moon is more active in our energy body. Whenever it is strong in our right nostril, then *pingala nadi* is activated and the Sun is more active in our energy body. Just by observing our breath we can very easily determine, whether Moon or Sun are more active at the moment in the microcosm of our body, and thus easily understand, in which activities are we receiving more support at the moment.

In ancient times there was a whole science based on making predictions based only on the observation of one's own breath during the time of receiving a question (*prashna*). Shiva explains to Parvati that "astrologer without the knowledge of *svara* is like a body without life". In our hectic times, when we have become so disconnected from Nature, our body and our breath itself, this ancient practise became completely forgotten.

Soli-lunar breathing pattern

In a healthy body the breath changes every hour. For one hour it should be more active in the left nostril, *ida nadi*, and for one hour it should be more active in the right nostril, *pingala nadi*. If you take a little bit of time to observe this patterns during a day, you will clearly notice this altering happening in a harmonious cycle. Whenever this cycle is disturbed in any manner, when *ida* or *pingala* become more dominant, due to the breath dwelling for too long in one of the nostrils, some sort of illness is inevitable. Awareness of it and conscious altering of the breath to another nostril can act as one of the most powerful remedies. No wonder that all the ancient *kriya yoga* techniques are so focused on rectifying our breathing pattern. Healthy breath, results in healthy body and quite literally has the power to change our destiny.

But, how to determine, which exact nostril should be active in exact moment in time? *Shiva Svarodaya* explains, that on specific *tithis* an exact *nadi* needs to be active at sunrise. For example, on *Pratipad tithi*, the first lunar day in *Shukla paksha*, *ida nadi* is supposed to be active at sunrise, which means that the flow of the breath should be stronger in left nostril. On the first lunar day of *Krishna paksha*, however, *pingala* should be active at sunrise – flow of the breath should be stronger in right nostril. If *ida* must be active at sunrise, then one hour after sunrise, *pingala* should become more active. One hour after that *ida* should be active again. Like that during a day the strength of the flow of the breath should change from one nostril to another every hour. This is said to be the most healthy breathing pattern, as it regulates our own breath and tunes it to the mood of the day, or *tithi*.

NADI TO BE ACTIVE AT SUNRISE DURING DIFFERENT TITHIS

Tithi	Nadi in Shukla Paksha	Nadi in Krishna Paksha
Pratipad (1)	ida	pingala
Dvitiya (2)	ida	pingala
Tritiya (3)	ida	pingala
Caturti (4)	pingala	ida
Panchami (5)	pingala	ida
Shashti (6)	pingala	ida
Saptami (7)	ida	pingala
Ashtami (8)	ida	pingala
Navami (9)	ida	pingala
Dashami (10)	pingala	ida
Ekadashi (11)	pingala	ida
Dvadashi (12)	pingala	ida
Trayodashi (13)	ida	pingala
Caturdashi (14)	ida	pingala
Purnima/Amavasya (15)	ida	pingala

Tithis and the breath

The intimate connection between the *tithis*, fifteen phases of the Moon in each *paksha*, and the breath, is very obvious both in Vedic astrology and old tantric scriptures. It is said that each *tithi* is 1440 breaths long. Being so, one lunar fortnight (*paksha*) is 21600 breaths - which is the number of a whole sacred breathing cycle. In one fortnight there would be 10800 breaths taken during the day (which are solar) and 10800 breaths taken during the night (which are lunar). Through the thread of the breath itself the fifteen phases of the Moon, fifteen *kalas*, fifteen manifestations of Goddess, time, space and human being are intimately interconnected.

In Sri Vidya tradition time is breath. Even our modern science confirms that there is an exact maximum number of breaths we can take during a lifetime – this is why breath, which is chaotic or too fast, influenced by the negative emotions, is quite literally going to bring us closer to death. Due to stressful lifestyle of modern life our breathing pattern had become completely hectic. If we were to believe statistics, an average human being makes 960 (!) breaths an hour, which is not very far away from 1440 – which, according to the scriptures, should be the total amount of breaths *a day*. This gives one inhalation and one exhalation per minute. No wonder that the secret of one of the animals, which lives the longest, a tortoise, is a very slow breathing pattern: one breath per 3-4 minutes. Not without a reason all the great enlightened masters keep repeating us, that our breath itself is a secret connection between our individual self and the Divine.

Fifteen lunar points in our energy body

According to ancient *siddha* medicine, which is said to be older than Ayurveda itself, there are fifteen lunar points in our energy body, through which our life force is travelling during different phases of the Moon. These are called lunar *marma* points. It is said that during each respective *tithi* the rejuvenating energy of the Moon (*soma*) is entering our body through these exact points. It is believed that by massaging these points on their respective lunar days or even just by meditating on them (some of them are corresponding to exact chakras in our energy body), we can greatly increase the flow of vital energy in our body and speed up all healing processes.

This flow of energy is different in the body of a man and a woman. In the body of man the energy starts its flow in the beginning of *Shukla paksha* from the right big toe, and then moves day by day up to the top of the head and skull roof on Full Moon day (*adhipati marma*), while in *Krishna paksha* it moves in reversed order: from top of the head to the left big toe, where it ends on New Moon. In the body of a woman this order is reversed: it starts from the left big toe and finishes with the right big toe.

Treating these lunar points on exact lunar days is a fascinating concept in *siddha* medicine and it can potentially act as a powerful healing remedy, especially if a person born on exact lunar day experiences any *tithi dosha* ("flaw" caused by less auspicious position of lunar day or its resonance with other factors in a birth chart).

MARMAS ACTIVE DURING DIFFERENT TITHIS (MAN)

Tithi	Shukla Paksha	Krishna Paksha
Pratipad (1)	right big toe	third eye (*sthapani*, corresponding to third eye chakra)
Dvitiya (2)	top of the right foot (*talahridaya*)	under the left eye
Tritiya (3)	right ankle (*gulpha*)	palate (*sringataka*)
Caturti (4)	counterpoint of *indrabasti marma* on the front of the right shinbone	point in front of the left ear
Panchami (5)	middle of the right thigh (*amai marma*)	pit of the throat (corresponding to *vishuddha chakra*)
Shashti (6)	*basti* (corresponding to sacral chakra)	*hridaya* (corresponding to heart chakra)
Saptami (7)	*nabhi* (navel, corresponding to solar plexus chakra)	*urumi marma* (solar plexus point)
Ashtami (8)	*urumi marma* (solar plexus point)	*nabhi* (navel, corresponding to solar plexus chakra)
Navami (9)	*hridaya* (corresponding to heart chakra)	*basti* (corresponding to sacral chakra)
Dashami (10)	pit of the throat (corresponding to *vishuddha chakra*)	middle of the left thigh (*amai marma*)/ *manipura*
Ekadashi (11)	point in front of the right ear	counterpoint of *indrabasti marma* on the front of the left shinbone
Dvadashi (12)	palate (*sringataka*)	left ankle (*gulpha*)
Trayodashi (13)	under the right eye	top of the left foot (*talahridaya*)
Caturdashi (14)	third eye (*sthapani*, corresponding to third eye chakra)	right big toe
Purnima / Amavasya (15)	*adhipati marma* (highest point on the skulll)	---------

MARMAS ACTIVE DURING DIFFERENT TITHIS (WOMAN)

Tithi	Shukla Paksha	Krishna Paksha
Pratipad (1)	left big toe	third eye (sthapani, corresponding to third eye chakra)
Dvitiya (2)	top of the left foot (talahridaya)	under the right eye
Tritiya (3)	left ankle (gulpha)	palate (sringataka)
Caturti (4)	counterpoint of indrabasti marma on the front of the left shinbone	point in front of the right ear
Panchami (5)	middle of the left thigh (amai marma)	pit of the throat (corresponding to vishuddha chakra)
Shashti (6)	basti (corresponding to sacral chakra)	hridaya (corresponding to heart chakra)
Saptami (7)	nabhi (navel, corresponding to solar plexus chakra)	urumi marma (solar plexus point)
Ashtami (8)	urumi marma (solar plexus point)	nabhi (navel, corresponding to solar plexus chakra)
Navami (9)	hridaya (corresponding to heart chakra)	basti (corresponding to sacral chakra)
Dashami (10)	pit of the throat (corresponding to vishuddha chakra)	middle of the right thigh (amai marma)/ manipura
Ekadashi (11)	point in front of the left ear	counterpoint of indrabasti marma on the front of the right shinbone
Dvadashi (12)	palate (sringataka)	right ankle (gulpha)
Trayodashi (13)	under the left eye	top of the right foot (talahridaya)
Caturdashi (14)	third eye (sthapani, corresponding to third eye chakra)	right big toe
Purnima / Amavasya (15)	adhipati marma (highest point on the skulll)	---------

Tithis and the chakras

According to Sri Yukteshwar, different chakras get activated during different *tithis*, too. *Shukla paksha* is connected with the energy rising from the *muladhara chakra* to the crown center, *sahasrara*, while *Krishna paksha* is connected with the descent of energy and consciousness back to *muladhara chakra*, following the sacred path of rising an descending of *kundalini shakti*, the Supreme Goddess in the macrocosm of our body, the Divine spark itself. The flow of energy in different chakras in our energy body resembles in an obvious way the flow of vital energy through the *marma* points in our physical body as described above.

CHAKRAS ACTIVE DURING DIFFERENT TITHIS

Tithi	Shukla Paksha	Krishna Paksha
Pratipad (1)	muladhara	ajna
Dvitiya (2)	muladhara	ajna
Tritiya (3)	svadhishthana	vishuddha
Caturti (4)	svadhishthana	vishuddha
Panchami (5)	svadhishthana/manipura	anahata/vishuddha
Shashti (6)	manipura	anahata
Saptami (7)	manipura	anahata
Ashtami (8)	anahata	manipura
Navami (9)	anahata	manipura
Dashami (10)	anahata/vishuddha	svadhishthana/manipura
Ekadashi (11)	vishuddha	svadhishthana
Dvadashi (12)	vishuddha	svadhishthana
Trayodashi (13)	ajna	muladhara
Caturdashi (14)	ajna	muladhara
Purnima/Amavasya (15)	sahasrara	muladhara

Now, if we try to superimpose this model on the zodiac signs, we can notice some astonishing patterns. This concept was, again, explained much more in detail in my previous book, *Discovering Youniverse*.

PANCAMI   DASHAMI

CATURTI TRITIYA	SHASHTI SAPTAMI	ASHTAMI NAVAMI	EKADASHI DVADASHI
DVITIYA PRATIPAT CATURDASHI TRAYODASHI	*Rashi Chakra*		TRAYODASHI CATURDASHI PRATIPAT DVITIYA
DVADASHI EKADASHI	ASHTAMI NAVAMI	SHASHTI SAPTAMI	TRITIYA CATURTI

AMAVASYA   PURNIMA

DASHAMI   PANCAMI

First thing we can immediately notice is that those *tithis*, which fall partially in one chakra, and partially in another, which is *Pancami* (fifth lunar day) and *Dashami* (tenth lunar day) in *Shukla paksha* and *Krishna paksha*, fall exactly in the *gandanta* zones of the zodiac or nakshatras ruled by Mars, which are the most vulnerable points in the whole zodiac chart. With *Amavasya* (New Moon) and *Purnima* (Full Moon) falling exactly in the middle of zodiacal *muladhara chakra* and *ajna chakra*, it makes the cycle complete.

This pattern is not a coincidence. Even in *Brihat Parashara Hora Shastra* the last portions of *Panchami, Dashami* and *Purnima* or *Amavasya tithis* (which are *Purna tithis*) were called *tithi gandanta*. Many other secrets can be understood through this holistic approach. In the next chapters, when we will slowly start to analyse the qualities of different Nitya Devis, fifteen eternal goddesses of the *tithis*, their moods and secret meanings, some connections will become more obvious. In fact, this model can be very helpful not only in understanding the biorhythms of the Moon, but a whole natal chart can be superimposed on it, revealing hidden moods of every planet, and their intricate relationships – for nothing in the universe is just a separate entity. Everything is connected and interwoven together. Every "this" is in relationship to some "that".

Tithis, elements and gunas

Each lunar day is also connected to one of the five elements, which our body is made of, and which are governing its different moods - as well as to one of the three *gunas* or modes of Nature. *Kamakala vilasa* states:

"There is only one Supreme Maheshwara, whose name is *Prakasha* ("light") and the name of whose Shakti is *Vimarsha* ("reflection"). She is called *Nitya* ("eternal") by the wise. She the Devi whose name is *Vimarsha*, becomes fivefold as Ether (*akasha*), Air (*anila*), Fire (*Saptarcih*), Water (*Salila*) and Earth (*Avanih*). By the increase of *gunas*, one by one, She reaches the number of the *tithis* (fifteen). The Devi who is *Vimarsha* (*Vimarsha-rupini*) is known as the sixteenth (*Shodashi*). The Highest Goddess, Parameshwari, who is Maha Tripurasundari undergoes these sixteen forms, the last of which is Citra."

Thus, two fundamental forces in the universe, elements and *gunas*, play together in the form of *tithis*, fifteen different moods of the Divine Mother, forming ever-changing stream of Time. It is said that no other form of the Goddess, apart from Tripurasundari Herself, is higher than those fifteen Goddesses of lunar days.

In Vedic astrology, the *tithis* ruled by specific elements have their additional names, reflecting the results of Moon combining with each element. Whenever a *tithi* is in the mode of fire, it is called *Nanda* ("happiness"), as it helps us to obtain happiness and pleasure, as well as supports us in social encounters, entertainment, creativity and art. They are connected to *dharma* or action performed on material level. *Tithis* in the mode of earth are called *Bhadra* ("lucky"), as they support us in business and help us to attain success and prosperity. They are connected to *artha*, or accumulation and seeking stability. *Tithis* in the mode of ether are called *Jaya* ("victorious") as they help us in overcoming obstacles, competitions, examinations, debates and attaining success. They are connected to *kama* or fulfilliment of desires. *Tithis* in the mode of water, however, are called *Rikta* or "empty" – as they are related to purification, demolition, destruction, cleaning and removing negativities. They are connected to *moksha* or liberation. And the last group of *tithis*, connected to element of air is called *Purna* or full – they are meant only for completing something, harvesting or education, as well as for reaching final fulfillment.

Similarly, people born on any of those lunar days will manifest bright and dark qualities of elements connected to those *tithis*. *Nanda tithis* connected to element of fire always carry a danger of overindulgence and indicate the need to control their desires, as well as their anger. *Bhadra tithis* connected to earth element indicate a strong danger of pride or too much focus on the body or appearance. *Jaya tithis* connected to ether are always connected with the danger of losening one's boundaries too much. *Rikta tithis* are very special, as they are connected to element of water, like all the *tithis* in *Panchang* and Moon itself. Too much of water quality present in *Rikta tithis* may often make people born on those lunar days too focused on themselves and may cause them have lack of understanding and respect towards other people's emotions and boundaries. This is why people born on fourth, ninth and fourteenth lunar day must be especially careful not to cross other people's boundaries and they need to work a bit more harder to be more understanding and accepting towards other people's limitations and emotions. *Purna tithis*, on the other hand, as they are connected to element of air, indicate a danger to be sometimes a bit too ungrounded, indecissive, and stuck in their own drama, ignoring good advices of others, without possibility to move forward.

TITHIS AND THEIR ELEMENTS

Element	Name	Tithis
Fire	*Nanda*	*Pratipad (1), Shashti (6), Ekadashi (11)*
Earth	*Bhadra*	*Dvitiya (2), Saptami (7), Dvadashi (12)*
Ether	*Jaya*	*Tritiya (3), Ashtami (8), Trayodashi (13)*
Water	*Rikta*	*Caturti (4), Navami (9), Caturdashi (14)*
Air	*Purna*	*Panchami (5), Dashami (10), Amavasya/Purnima (15)*

The element of the *tithi* however, does not only say something about you, but also about the way you form your relationships with others. Afterwards, *tithi* in itself is a relationship between the Sun and the Moon, which is why in *Panchang* we are saying that *tithis* are ruled by water element, connected to our second chakra: our emotions, our culture, our sensitivity and the way we respect the boundaries of others.

People born on fiery *tithis* (1, 6, 11) will always seek in their relationships the feeling of energy, vitality, passion and focus. They are looking for partners, who have clear goals in their life and who are able to take action. This is why these people also need to be very careful, when they are choosing their own goals in life. Whenever you look at a chart of a person, who is born on *Nanda tithi*, ruled by element fire, you should additionally have a look at the state, which their 10th house is in (house of our action and goals), as any affliction to the 10th house in their birth chart will have a very strong impact on their overall emotional state.

People born on earthly *tithis* (2, 7, 12), on the other hand, are rather seeking stability and affection in their relationships. They are always looking for emotional nurturing and attention from their partners. Their weakness is that sometimes they mighty be emotionally quite needy or... too attached to their or their partner's outer appearance. They love beautiful fragrances and aromatherapy can be of great help for them. They suffer emotionally if 12th house in their birth chart is in any way afflicted, as in such a case it is inviting too much of unstable energies into their lives and forces them to let go of some attachments, which they are not ready to let go of yet.

People born on the *tithis* of ether (3, 8, 13) are always looking in their relationships, above all, for an exchange of energy. They love to socialise with people and they expect the same thing from their partners. If they somehow end up with a partner, who doesn't have so strong need to socialise with others, they might feel hurt. As element of ether is also connected to throat chakra, people born on any of the *Jaya tithis* need to choose their words and their company a bit more carefully. These people will suffer emotionally if their 11th house in their birth chart, which stands for social circles, is in any way afflicted.

People born on watery *tithis* (4, 9, 14) are usually not that much focused on others as on themselves. They are often withholding or even surpressing their emotions and affection. Sometimes they might find it hard to express themselves emotionally. They are like raincloud, which is withholding water for a very long time. But once the rain pours, it pours out completely – just for one person. When they give themselves to somebody, they give themselves completely to the person. They stick with one partner for a very long time and they feel very disturbed, when a relationship, to which they gave themselves completely, suddenly finishes. Even though people born on *Rikta tithis* may sometimes seem a bit reserved in the outside, deep inside they are extremely sensitive and emotionally vulnerable, which makes it easy to hurt them. This people suffer additionally if the first house in their birth chart is afflicted, as it additionally weakens their already vulnerable self. And as the element of water also stands for the sense of taste and all the food we eat, people born on *Rikta tithis* must be particularly careful about their diet and the quality of the food they are eating, as it will deeply affect their consciousness. They must be vegetarian by any means, and they need to be particularly careful to never eat food, which is spoiled or contaminated in any other way.

People born on the *tithis* of air element are mostly seeking from others sensitivity and respect towards their boundaries. They are particularly disturbed when their personal boundaries are crossed in any way. Quite interesting to think about it, when you realise, that only all the *Purna tithis* (or *tithis* of air element) are placed exactly on *gandantas* or nakshatra of Mars in the above diagram of superimposing the *tithi mandala* on *rashi mandala* and *chakra mandala*. Thus, boundaries are very important for all the people born on the *tithis* of air element. Also in a romantic relationship they do not like when their boundaries are broken too fast – they like to go slowly into any relationship, without rushing. They feel particularly disturbed if their partners are saying something inapriopriate in the bigger group of people, which reflects diplomatic qualities of Vayu, the presiding deity of air element. And, similarly like it is for Vayu, their inner feeling of freedom and independence is extremely important for them. *Purna tithi* natives will feel emotionally disturbed if there is any affliction to their ninth house, standing for moral code and boundaries.

Tithis and modes of Natures

Additionally, the cycle of fifteen *tithis* is divided into three *gunas*. First group of five *tithis* (1-5) is connected to *guna* of *rajas* (passion, activity, creativity), next group of five *tithis* (6-10) is connected to *guna* of *tamas* (ignorance, darkness, stagnation) and last group of five *tithis* (11-15) is connected to *sattwa guna* (purity, spiritual awakening). Like this, each element contains the *tithi* of each of the three *gunas*, symbolising its different modes. And, similarly like in *rashi chakra*, whenever there is a transition from one *guna* to another, which happens in the beginning of every *tithi* of fire and end of every *tithi* of air element, this short transition period is called *tithi gandanta*.

Element / Guna	Rajas	Tamas	Sattwa
Fire	*Pratipad (1)*	*Shashti (6)*	*Ekadashi (11)*
Earth	*Dvitiya (2)*	*Saptami (7)*	*Dvadashi (12)*
Ether	*Tritiya (3)*	*Ashtami (8)*	*Trayodashi (13)*
Water	*Caturti (4)*	*Navami (9)*	*Caturdashi (14)*
Air	*Panchami (5)*	*Dashami (10)*	*Purnima / Amavasya*

Lunar days and stages of consciousness

Additionally, each lunar day is also connected to some stage of consciousness. There are four main stages of consciousness as described in Vedas: *jagrat* (waking state), *svapna* (dreaming state), *sushupti* (deep sleep state) and *turiya* (spiritual awakening). *Tithis* in number of sixteen are equally divided among these four. First four *tithis* (1-4) are connected to waking state, next four (5-8) to dreaming state, another four (9-12) to deep sleep state and last four (13-16) to state of spiritual awakening. Furthermore, as explained by Swami Sivananda, each of these four groups is subdivided into four different stages once again. Therefore some form of each of these four states appears within each of those states – like dreaming state can appear even when we are awake, yet lost in our thoughts and imagination.

State of consciousness	Subdivision	Tithi
Jagrat (waking state)	Jagrat (waking state)	Pratipad (1)
	Svapna (dreaming state)	Dvitiya (2)
	Sushupti (deep sleep)	Tritiya (3)
	Turiya (spiritual awakening)	Caturti (4)
Svapna (dreaming state)	Jagrat (waking state)	Panchami (5)
	Svapna (dreaming state)	Shashti (6)
	Sushupti (deep sleep)	Saptami (7)
	Turiya (spiritual awakening)	Ashtami (8)
Sushupti (deep sleep)	Jagrat (waking state)	Navami (9)
	Svapna (dreaming state)	Dashami (10)
	Sushupti (deep sleep)	Ekadashi (11)
	Turiya (spiritual awakening)	Dvadashi (12)
Turiya (spiritual awakening)	Jagrat (waking state)	Trayodashi (13)
	Svapna (dreaming state)	Caturdashi (14)
	Sushupti (deep sleep)	Purnima / Amavasya
	Turiya (spiritual awakening)	beyond time

Understanding these subtle connections between different *tithis* and stages of consciousness they govern, can give us far deeper insights into their meaning. During the first five *tithis* our energy is the most *rajasic*, as we are in waking state, performing our activities in physical reality. *Ekadashi*, on the other hand, eleventh lunar day and the first sattwcic *tithi*, which is considered to be the best time for spiritual practice and fasting, falls exactly in the deep sleep portion of deep sleep quarter, denoting the time, when our mind is the most absent – which is the best time for direct contact with God, as we are not going to be obstructed by our own mind on that day. Additionally, if we fast on that day and spend it in prayer, reducing our bodily activities to minimum, we can have a direct vision of the Lord dwelling in our heart, as explained by Swami Sivananda.

Similarly each and every single *tithi* has its special qualities and supports different activities, by activiating different stages of consciousness, elements, *gunas*, *chakras*, *swaras* and energy channels.

Resonance with different cycles of Time

Moon phases have a very profound effect on our consciousness, emotional state and physical body. But lunar cycle is not the only natural cycle, which is affecting our consciousness. Days of week, nakshatras, months and even different seasons influence us greatly, as well – and all of them have their own, unique qualities. *Tithis*, too, will resonate differently with different days of week, nakshatras and even months. In the chapters dedicated to each respective lunar day and its presiding Goddess you will find the tables showing, how each lunar day resonates with different nakshatras and/or weekdays. You will find the most popular *muhurta yogas*, as well as some of less known combinations, which can be found in some of the *Puranas*. Some of those combinations will be more auspicious, while some of them will be less auspicious. The ones, which are particularly auspicious, will be marked in **bold**.

One interesting thing, which you will notice, when it comes to *muhurta yogas* produced with the *tithis*, is that their names will be strongly related to fire sacrifice. In the past, choosing the right *muhurta* or the right timing was, indeed, used mostly by *brahmins* or priests, to choose the most auspicious time for performing a fire sacrifice and worshipping the Divine. The deeper, esoteric meaning behind fire sacrifice is explained by Bhagavan Krishna Himself in Bhagavad Gita.

Yajna or fire sacrifice, is nothing else, but symbolic offering of lower self to the Supreme Self. According to Lord Krishna, every action can become an act of sacrifice. Every action can become a fire sacrifice, if we only perform it with an attitude of detachment from the fruits of our actions and treat it as offering to the Divine. Every action has some fire in it, and thus every action is some sort of fire sacrifice. But whether our sacrifice is pure and whether we worship with it the Highest Self or our lower ego - that is the question. When we perform all our actions with pure heart, keeping the Divine as our highest objective, such actions will naturally purify us, as Lord Krishna said in the Gita:

"All these performers who know the meaning of sacrifice become cleansed of sinful reactions, and, having tasted the nectar of the results of sacrifices, they advance toward the supreme eternal atmosphere."

Thus, acting in the world with an attitude of sacrifice and fulfilling our sacred duty with detachment from the fruits of our actions, leads us to tasting the true *soma* or the true fulfillment in life.

Muhurta yogas help us to predict, how different lunar days, in combination with different nakshatras and weekdays, support us in performing this inner fire sacrifice, or, in other words, how they support us in performing auspicious actions. They inform us, if our inner *yajna kund*, or *manipura chakra*, the seat of fire within us, will be pure or polluted on that day – and depending on that, we can determine the potential outcome of our actions undertaken on that very day.

Two auspicious *yogas*, which are formed on every lunar day and are produced from the combination of *tithi* (lunar day) and *vara* (weekday or solar day), are called **siddha yoga** ("combination of accomplishments") and **amrita yoga** ("combination of nectar"). *Siddha yoga* ensures that our actions will bring good results or will bring us accomplishment, while *amrita yoga* ensures that "nectar" or satisfaction will be the result of our actions on such days. Even more powerful *siddha yoga* can be also produced due to combination of *tithi*, *vara* and nakshatra. Such *siddha yoga* is much more powerful, as on those days all three factors will give us the power to accomplish things in life.

Another auspicious combination of *tithi*, *nakshatra* and weekday is called **suta yoga**. *Suta* literally means "to extract". This combination is connected to pressing stones used to extract *soma*, the herbal nectar offered as oblation in Vedic fire ceremony. Similarly, *suta yogas* are greatly auspicious, as they give us the power to extract "nectar" of fulfillment from life and derive satisfaction from our efforts.

There are also five different inauspicious combinations of *tithi* and weekday: **dagdha yoga** ("burnt combination"), **visha yoga** ("poisonous combination"), **hutashana yoga** ("combination of fire as oblation eater"), **krakacha yoga** ("combination of a saw") and the most rare **samvartaka yoga** ("combination of dissolution").

Whenever *dagdha yoga* happens, due to some combination of *tithi* and weekday, our inner fire has a tendency to burn things too much. Things might get easily out of control on such days, as well as we may literally feel an inner burnout. We won't only feel stressed and agitated inside, but we might feel that our efforts and work load is literally burning our life force.

A very similar feeling may appear in us during *hutashana yoga* – with a little difference, that this planetary combination will literally consume all our efforts, due to what they might become futile. *Hutashana* is one of the names of fire god, when he assumes his form as oblation eater. It is very much advised to keep a healthy dose of detachment, when it comes to the fruits of our actions, on the days when this *yoga* occurs. Reading Bhagavad Gita will be a good remedy, if taking some important action on such a day is unavoidable. Also, both during *dagdha yoga* and *hutashana yoga*, you might like to make sure that your body is well hydrated.

Visha yoga is a bit more dangerous than two previous *yogas*, as it is the combination that produces a "poison" or adverse results. On the days, when *visha yoga* is produced, we need to be especially careful, when it comes to our emotions and our internal state. We might have a higher tendency to be a bit stingy on those days, as well as bitter emotions from the past may return and "poison" our inner space. We might also experience an unpleasant encounter with other people's "poisons". Even more severe *visha yoga* can be created by exact combinations of *tithi*, *vara* and nakshatra.

Krakacha yoga is much more dangerous than previous combinations. Interestingly, it happens, whenever the number of the *tithi* (lunar day) and *vara* (weekday) adds up to 13. It is said that this combination has the power to "cut" all other positive influences. It always brings some "cuttings" and endings into our life. It also makes us naturally less sensitive, which is why it may sometimes make us behave in quite unpleasant way towards other people.

Samvartaka yoga, the last of five inauspicious *yogas* formed by specific combination of *tithi* and weekday, is the most severe of all of them, and the rarest one, too. It can happen only when *Pratipad tithi* (first lunar day) falls on Wednesday or when *Saptami tithi* (seventh lunar day) falls on Sunday. *Samvartaka* means "the destroyer". It is both the name of the fire, which destroys everything at the end of creation, as well as the name of clouds of dissolution, sent at the end of each great cycle of Time to submerge the world in the causal waters. *Samvartaka yoga* produces destruction, chaos and invokes all endings into our life. Such days are better to be avoided for undertaking any important actions.

Combination of certain *tithis* and nakshatras may also produce such inauspicious *yogas* as *ashubha yoga* ("inauspicious combination"), *visha yoga* (more severe "poisonous combination") or highly inauspicious *vinasha yoga* ("combination of destruction").

Now, it may also happen quite often, that more *yogas* will be produced at the same time. Sometimes both auspicious *yoga* and inauspicious *yoga* can happen simultaneously. Days, which have so mixed influences will also bring mixed results. For example, combination of *amrita yoga* ("combination of nectar") and *visha yoga* ("combination of poison") can, indeed, bring us some satisfaction, but it may be achieved through impure or "poisonous" means – or may bring with itself some "poisonous" side effect. For example, imagine achieving some great success in life, while at the same time some person dear to you becomes jealous. That is one way how mixture of "nectar" and "poison" can manifest. Similarly, if *dagdha yoga* ("burnt combination") and *siddha yoga* happen simultaneously, you may, indeed, accomplish something important on that day, but the price for that will be "burnout" of your life force.

Through studying the resonance of different *tithis* with different nakshatras and weekdays, we can learn not only much more about each exact lunar day, but we also get to really *feel*, how our inner *soma* (Moon, water element within us) reacts with the fire of our everyday actions.

And so, on every lunar day there is a lot to observe. On every day Goddess in the form of the Moon will be in different mood and in different state of mind. Her changing moods will affect in various ways our breathing, consciousness, elements, *gunas* and flow of energy in our subtle body - and depending how Her sacred cycle will overlap with other cycles of Time, some very specific results will be experienced.

CHAPTER 5

MUSIC OF THE SKIES

Every day the Moon is at some exact distance from the Sun, moving away from it during *Shukla paksha* or moving back to it during *Krishna paksha*. Being so, Sun and the Moon are "pressing" the cosmic wheel of zodiac in exact points, like a cosmic instrument, which is then forced to produce different sound vibrations. The question is: how it would actually *sound*?

Being a musician myself, I was always fascinated by *musica universalis* or harmony of the spheres. Each and every day planets are in some relation to each other, which can be easily translated into some mathematical ratios – and every mathematical ratio can be translated into actual music.

Similarly like every music interval is defined by its mathematical ratio, we can read and hear some exact intervals from the very same ratios created by exact distance between Sun and Moon during different *tithis*. And, if you understand the music, at least a little bit, you will be able to clearly notice, that while some *tithis* will be forming harmonious and pleasant intervals, others will be forming rather irritating sounds. Just by analysing these simple sound relations between Sun and Moon you can learn a lot about the *tithis*, even without studying any Jyotish scripture before. Music explains it all, without using any words – as it is the only science, which translates mathematics and geometry into *feelings*. And *tithis*, lunar days, are all about the feelings.

Tithis in the wheel of Time

In *Rashi chakra*, the zodiacal wheel of time, which has 360 degrees, each *tithi* or lunar day is 12 degrees long. When the Sun is conjuct on the very same degree with the Moon, that is the end of *Amavasya tithi* or New Moon. Therefore, whenever the distance between the Sun and the Moon is 0 to 12 degrees counted clockwise, it is *Pratipad tithi* or first lunar day of *Shukla paksha*, bright fortnight. Whenever this distance will be between 12 to 24 degrees counted clockwise it would be *Dvitiya tithi* or second lunar day of *Shukla paksha*. In similar way we would count all the *tithis* of *Shukla paksha*, one by one, 12 degrees by 12 degrees, until the Moon will reach the distance between 168 and 180 degrees from the Sun, which is a Full Moon or *Purnima tithi*. Then, when the distance between the Sun and the Moon is between 180 and 192 degrees it is already the first day of *Krishna paksha*, dark fortnight: *Pratipad tithi*. Then we continue to count the *tithis* again, one by one, 12 degrees by 12 degrees, until the Moon reaches the distance between 348 to 360 degrees from the Sun (counted clockwise), which is *Amavasya tithi* or New Moon again.

Celestial music of Sun and Moon

In *Rashi chakra*, the zodiacal wheel of Time, which has 360 degrees, each *tithi* or lunar day stands for some exact distance between Sun and Moon and some exact ratio between them. As individualisation is the process of *Shukla paksha*, so in *Shukla paksha* we will be taking Moon (individual self and the mind) as a reference point and the base sound, original unison, 0 or 360th degree, from which we will count all the music intervals. Similarly, in *Shukla paksha* music intervals will be gradually rising, until they reach perfect octave or perfect opposition. In *Krishna paksha*, on the other hand, when the process of surrendering and purifying the self becomes more prominent, we will be taking Sun (Supreme Self) as a reference point and the base sound, from which we will count all the music intervals. Similarly, in *Krishna paksha* all the intervals will be descending.

Be it music or movement of our bioenergy in our subtle body, *Shukla paksha* is always connected to ascending energy, while *Krishna paksha* is always connected to descending energy. Growing energies of the Moon will be always more prominent in bright fortnight, while burning energies of the Sun will be always more prominent in dark fortnight.

In the table below you will find all the ratios connected to different *tithis*, and the music intervals, which they form assigned to them. If you already know a little bit about the lunar days, you will quickly notice, that these lunar days, which are considered more auspicious in Vedic astrology, will also form more harmonious sounds – while the ones, which are considered less auspicious will form less harmonious sounds. Additionally, the *tithis*, during which Sun and Moon are forming more irritating sounds, will have naturally more active energy, while the *tithis*, which are connected to more harmonious intervals, will be naturally more passive. Irritating sounds are always seeking fulfillment or some other way of resolving their tension, which naturally leads to action – while sounds, which are already very harmonious do not have this inner motivation, as they feel contented within their current state. This is why they are more passive and less inclined to take action.

There is an explanation for that even in ancient Vastu Shastra or the science of building sacred spaces. Entire Vastu Shastra is based on the science of sacred geometrical relationships or ratios. But it is never about finding the ratio or sacred *ayadi* number, which is "just perfect" – there always must be some remainder left, like *prasadam* after offering a food to a deity. It is this remainder or this "disharmonious" sound that makes things grow, evolve and live. Because when something is already perfect, there will be no growth and no evolution. If something is complete in itself, nothing is left over, there is an end to it – something has come to conclusion. But if there is a remainder, there is no end to it. This is why the *tithis*, which will be forming more harmonious intervals, will be naturally more passive, too – and this is also why *Purna tithis* ("full" lunar days, ruled by air element) are naturally more passive, as well, especially *Purnima* or Full Moon. Because if something is already complete, there is no need to take any action – there is no friction, no tension, no remainder.

In this way, just by observing different sounds connected to different *tithis*, you can already understand and *feel* a lot about the nature of this lunar day.

And, if we would like to take it one step further, these are not only the *tithis*, which can be translated into music. All planets are forming some sort of intervals and some sort of relationship with each other. The model of understanding the *tithis* through music can be applied to any other planetary relationship – and the accuracy of the results might surprise you.

Personally, I was experimenting a lot with assigning a sort of *tithi* to each planet in the charts. I would just take any planet in the chart and count its distance from the Sun, in exactly the same way, how I would count the *tithi*. Afterwards I would check the form of a Goddess presiding this sacred relationship between the Sun and that planet – and many times I was astonished, how accurate were the results. You can understand a lot about the internal mood and emotion of any planet just by experimenting with this concept. After all, all planets are in a way "remainders" of our Sun – in the same way, how everything in the universe is in some relation to the Supreme Self.

RATIOS AND MUSIC INTERVALS FORMED IN SHUKLA PAKSHA

Tithi	Ratio range	Music interval
Pratipad (1)	360:348 to 360:360	from unison to minor second
Dvitiya (2)	360:336 to 360:348	minor second (360:337.5 = 16:15)
Tritiya (3)	360:324 to 360:336	between minor second and major second
Caturti (4)	360:312 to 360:324	major second (360:320 = 9:8)
Panchami (5)	360:300 to 360:312	minor third (360:300 = 6:5)
Shashti (6)	360:288 to 360:300	from minor third (360:300 = 6:5) to major third (360:288 = 5:4)
Saptami (7)	360:276 to 360:288	major third (360:288 = 5:4)
Ashtami (8)	360:264 to 360:276	perfect fourth (360:270 = 4:3)
Navami (9)	360:252 to 360:264	augmented fourth
Dashami (10)	360:240 to 360:252	diminished fifth
Ekadashi (11)	360:228 to 360:240	perfect fifth (360:240 = 3:2)
Dvadashi (12)	360:216 to 360:228	from minor sixth (360:225 = 8:5) to major sixth (360:216 = 5:3)
Trayodashi (13)	360:204 to 360:216	from major sixth (360:216 = 5:3) to minor seventh (360:192 = 15:8)
Caturdashi (14)	360:192 to 360:204	from minor seventh (360:192 = 15:8) to major seventh (360:202.5)
Purnima (15)	360:180 to 360:192	from major seventh (360:192 = 15:8) to perfect octave (360:180 = 2:1)

RATIOS AND MUSIC INTERVALS FORMED IN KRISHNA PAKSHA

Tithi	Ratio range	Music interval
Pratipad (1)	360:180 to 360:192	from perfect octave (360:180 = 2:1) to major seventh (360:192 = 15:8)
Dvitiya (2)	360:192 to 360:204	from major seventh (360:192 = 15:8) to minor seventh (360:202.5 = 16:9)
Tritiya (3)	360:204 to 360:216	from minor seventh (360:192 = 15:8) to major sixth (360:216 = 5:3)
Caturti (4)	360:216 to 360:228	from major sixth (360:216 = 5:3) to minor sixth (360:225 = 8:5)
Panchami (5)	360:228 to 360:240	perfect fifth (360:240 = 3:2)
Shashti (6)	360:240 to 360:252	diminished fifth
Saptami (7)	360:252 to 360:264	augmented fourth
Ashtami (8)	360:264 to 360:276	perfect fourth (360:270 = 4:3)
Navami (9)	360:276 to 360:288	major third (360:288 = 5:4)
Dashami (10)	360:288 to 360:300	from major third (360:288 = 5:4) to minor third (360:300 = 6:5)
Ekadashi (11)	360:300 to 360:312	minor third (360:300 = 6:5)
Dvadashi (12)	360:312 to 360:324	major second (360:320 = 9:8)
Trayodashi (13)	360:324 to 360:336	between major second and minor second
Caturdashi (14)	360:336 to 360:348	minor second (360:337.5 = 16:15)
Amavasya (15)	360:348 to 360:360	from minor second to unison

Music of the *tithis* and Indian ragas

Being a musician myself, this model of understanding the *tithis* was for me like a missing ingredient to really *feel* them and understand their secrets on a much deeper level. The descriptions of fifteen Nitya Devis, fifteen goddesses of the lunar phases, which stand for fifteen different moods of the Divine Mother (which you will find in the next chapters of this book) are greatly influenced by this simple knowledge of musical interactions between the Sun and the Moon. Take it one step further, and you can quite literally translate any relationship, planetary or human, into music.

Interestingly, in *ragas*, melodic modes of classical Indian music, each and every single note, being the base for different music intervals, has a certain quality assigned to it, as well as planet governing it, which in itself reveals how closely music is interconnected with Vedic astrology - and how they were perceived as one in the past. Music is truly the only science that bridges the time, space and geometry, allowing us to understand their interactions on a much deeper level. It was Pythagoras who said: "There is geometry in the humming of the strings, there is music in the spacing of the spheres."

Let us have a closer look at each sound of Indian *raga* and see how they were connected with the planets in Vedic astrology – and how does this overlap with different intervals formed by *tithis*.

The first note in Indian *raga* is called **shadja**. It is the defining base note of the scale, from which all other intervals are created. Perfect unison happens here, as well. This is why it is called *shadja* or "giving birth to six" other sounds. This note is ruled by Mercury, who is also the lord of our first breath and our throat chakra. Mercury is also the only planet, which is completely neutral - being neither male nor female.

The second note in *raga* is called **rishabha**: "great one" or "courageous one". It is the first note emerging from perfect unison and arising from the first, original sound – and being so, it is connected to Mars, the planet of taking action. As *rishabha* sounds a bit irritating in regards to first, original sound, so it resembles the qualities of Mars: dynamism, impatience, tension, stress or even nervousness. It is action-oriented, bold and courageous. In ascending mode of *raga* it will be the first sound to ascend, while in descending *raga* it will be the last sound leading to the union of *unison*. This sound will be created during last four days in *Krishna paksha* and first four days in *Shukla paksha* – which is why these lunar days are quite action oriented and very much connected with our ambitions in life. They are also the bringers of transformation.

The third note in Indian *raga* is called **gandhara** or "sweet-sounding". It is the first note which sounds harmonious in regards to first, original sound. It is also the sound, which determines the character of the *raga* – it determines, whether *raga* will be more joyous (major) or sad (minor). As this sound has such an important role in determining the overall character of the *raga*, no wonder that it is assigned to the Sun, who stands for our very Self and personality in Vedic astrology. This sound will be created during *Panchami*, *Shashti* and *Saptami tithis* in *Shukla paksha*, and *Navami*, *Dashami* and *Ekadashi* during *Krishna paksha*.

The fourth note in *raga* is called **madhyama** – "middle one" or "moderate one". Harmonious *madhyama* would produce the first perfect interval from the original sound: perfect fourth. And since this interval awakens a feeling of peace in a listener, it is ruled by the Moon, who is a natural *karaka* of our peace of mind - as Moon rules natural fourth house (Cancer). Interestingly, perfect fourth is the only music interval, which will be created by Sun and Moon during the same *tithi* in both *pakshas*: *Ashtami*, the middle *tithi*, when there will be always exactly half of the Moon visible on the sky.

The fifth note in Indian *raga* is called **panchama** – "the fifth one". This note is used to finetune different instruments and, when harmonious, it creates another perfect interval with the base sound: perfect fifth. Similarly, in Vedic astrology, the planet, which is "finetuning" us, and bringing us back on the right track, is Saturn – and so, Shani is ruling *panchama* sound. Even the *tantric yantra* of Saturn is just a single line, while his birth nakshatra is Revati according to *Vayu Purana* – which reflects his capacity to straighten everything up and bring us back to the right path. The most harmonious manifestation of this sound and perfect fifth interval will happen between Sun and Moon on *Shukla Ekadashi* and *Krishna Panchami* – which is why these two lunar days are considered especially auspicious.

The sixth note in Indian *raga* is called **dhaivata** or "Divine one" – since it is an overtone of *gandhara* and can be heard by a sensitive person already when *gandhara* is being played. Due to the "Divine" nature of this sound it was associated with Jupiter, the Guru of gods – who stands for our receptivity and sensitivity to absorb the Divine knowledge. This sound will be created during *Krishna Chaturti* and *Shukla Dvadashi*, which are very auspicious days, as well.

And the seventh note in Indian *raga* is called **nishada** or "outcaste". In Sanskrit, *nishadati* literally means "to suffer" or "to be afflicted". It is the sound, which in ascending *raga* represents the last friction before reaching the state of perfect octave – and since the passion for union and release of energy is so strong in this sound, it is ruled by passionate Venus. This sound will be created during last three days before Full Moon and first three days after Full Moon – which is why it is said that due to so passionate nature of these lunar days, we should avoid making any important decisions or starting any important projects around this time.

It is all about sacred relationships

I still remember one beautiful evening, during the process of writing this book, when I attended the concert of great Indian violinist, Anupriya Deotale, which Croatia had an honor to host. The concert was opened with a soulful rendition of *raga Jyoti*, "the *raga* of light", which immediately took all the participants into a meditative state. With my eyes closed I was enjoying the music. I was observing and feeling in my inner space all the little tensions and ecstasies derived from certain musical notes coming together or detaching from each other. Some sounds were bringing joy, other sadness. Some were bringing more peace, and some were bringing more excitement. And I remember thinking at that time: "Wow. This is exactly how planets are influencing us – through changing influences and changing vibrations."

Problems start only when we start to focus exclusively on one note in the Cosmic *raga* and we miss the rest of the Cosmic masterpiece. But if we would take a simple step back and really *hear* and *feel*, what the Universe is trying to sing to us through our own life's story, we might just stand in amazement.

Imagine, if you would play in orchestra. Sometimes, if you practice just your own part, without listening to the entire piece before, you might think: "That doesn't really sound nice. There is nothing special in it." But if you expand your consciousness a little and hear all the other instruments playing around you, you would become amazed, how everything fits together perfectly, and how invaluable is every contribution to this Cosmic masterpiece called Life.

CHAPTER 6

DANCE OF TIME IN KALACHAKRA

When diving deeper and deeper into the science of lunar days ruled by Nitya Devis or *kala-shaktis*, "the powers of Time", it is essential to understand in the first place, what is *Kalachakra*: "the wheel of Time". Different lunar days presided by different *shaktis*, who are fifteen parts of the continuum of consciousness, are said to be dancing through the wheel of Time, with each breath bringing us closer to our final destination. This is why the knowledge of *Kalachakra*, in Vedic astrology, is most often utilised to predict dangers, diseases or death coming our way – because the wheel of Time is at the same time the wheel of destruction. After all, is there anything that scares people more than inevitable flow of Time? This is why *Srimad Bhagavatam* says:

"The influence of God is felt in the world as the Time factor, which causes fear to the false ego."

Every breath and every second is taking us closer to our final journey. With the help of *Kalachakra* we can predict quite accurately all the blockages of energy or life force coming our way, as well as understand on a deeper level, which activities or directions are better to be avoided on certain days.

To describe in detail the greatness of Kalachakra and all its uses in Vedic astrology, another book would need to be written on that topic. Even though scriptures such as *Prasna Marga* or *Jataka Parijata* describe the flow of energy in *Kalachakra* just in couple of verses, in Tibetan tradition there is an entire scripture dedicated just to *Kalachakra*, called *Kalachakra Tantra*. In this book I will not go into details of all the different uses of *Kalachakra* in Jyotish, but I will stick to what is useful and insightful, when it comes to understanding the movement of energy on different lunar days.

Dance of Yogini

According to *Prasna Marga*, Yogini is a fearful feminine form of Time. She brings end to everything. Adorned in garments red like twilight, having red eyes, with a sword to cut and end everything, She is a dangerous form of Time. Whichever direction She is dwelling in, She brings there death – literally or symbolically.

Kalachakra is sometimes also called a dance of Yogini, as it helps us in determining, from which side the danger may come during different moments in time. Each of the eight planets (Ketu excluded) are residing in eight directions of *Kalachakra*, as shown in the diagram below. It is said that through those exact directions planetary energies may manifest in the most destructive way. *Tithis* ruled by those planets will make Yogini dwell in this exact direction.

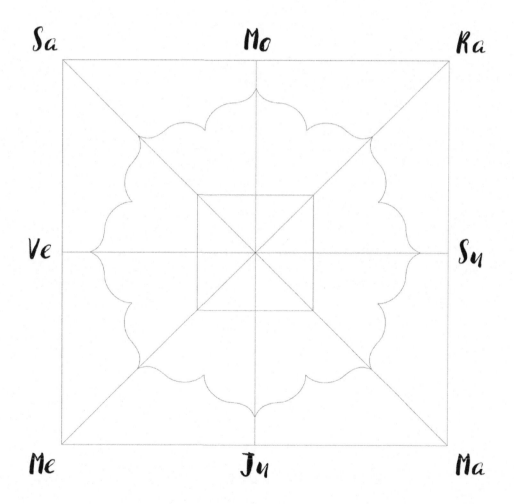

For example, on *tithis* ruled by Sun (*Pratipad* and *Navami*), the Yogini or the danger will come from the East. As Eastern direction is presided by Indra in Vedic tradition, the king of heavens, it clearly denotes that on lunar days co-ruled by Sun, we might experience some issues related to authority, power, position, father, ego, image or individuality. Also, travelling towards the East or facing East for too long may cause us some troubles – especially if our birth chart is already vulnerable for such planetary influence. If this would additionally "clash" with the movement of our individual life force in our individual *Kalachakra* (which will not be discussed in this book due to the vastness of this topic), it may cause more serious problems or even a disease. In fact, the entire science of *Kalachakra*, being a dynamic concept is nothing else but studying the movement of different *pranas* of objective Time and analysing their resonance with our individual timing and movements of our inner life force. Personal *Kalachakra* is like our fully personalised Cosmic Clock. Mastering the deeper understanding of *Kalachakra* requires some time, practice and diligent observations – but once you master it, you can very accurately predict, how the outer influences are going to affect your inner universe.

Planetary co-rulers of different lunar days

Lunar phases or *tithis* are governed by Nitya Devis or fifteen different forms of the Supreme Goddess, who are also called "powers of time". Yet, each *tithi* also has its planetary co-ruler, who will not only tell us about some exact qualities of each lunar phase, but will be also very helpful in making some predictions. Planetary co-rulers of the *tithis* are derived from the science of *Kalachakra* – and being so, each *tithi* will be connected not only with one of the eight planets, but also with one of the directions.

Planetary co-rulers, similarly like the directions associated with them, will be revealing us mostly the shadow qualities of each lunar day. Planetary co-rulers in a way "eclipse" the Divine qualities of the *tithi* and its ruling Goddess. When you understand, which exact qualities need to be overcome in your mind (which is what *tithi* lord is telling you about) in order for the healthy flow of energy to manifest in your life (which is represented by the Goddess of each *tithi*), you can start to manifest the best version of yourself.

Tithi lord or planetary co-ruler reveals us how we utilise the water element or the emotions in our life. The planet, which is your *tithi* lord, becomes the carrier of water element and carrier of emotion in your natal chart. Wherever it dwells in a chart, it is a direct manifestation of this exact form of Goddess or Nitya Devi.

The quality of your emotions or flow in life will depend mostly on the placement of your *tithi* lord. *Tithi* lord present in water signs (Cancer, Scorpio or Pisces) is excellent and reveals very pleasant emotions or *soma* flowing harmoniously. In earthly signs (Taurus, Virgo or Capricorn) the flow of emotions won't be bad either. In airy signs (Gemini, Libra or Aquarius) the natural flow of emotions might be already a bit disturbed. But with *tithi* lord in fiery signs (Aries, Leo or Sagittarius) the person might experience really intense, transformative emotions and certain emotional shocks, as well – especially in the sphere of relationships, as this sphere of our life is mostly affected by the *tithis*. Such person will need to consciously work on uplifting the energies of one's water element with the help of remedies such as keeping one's body well hydrated, daily meditation to increase inner flow of *soma* or getting in touch with the form of Goddess presiding over one's birth *tithi*.

Apart from the sign, occupied by the *tithi* lord, it is always important to check, if the *tithi* lord has any company or receives any aspects – as it may significantly change the entire story.

Lunar day	Tithi (Vedic name)	Planetary co-ruler	Direction
First	*Pratipad*	Sun	East
Second	*Dvitiya*	Moon	North
Third	*Tritiya*	Mars	Southeast
Fourth	*Caturti*	Mercury	Southwest
Fifth	*Panchami*	Jupiter	South
Sixth	*Shashti*	Venus	West
Seventh	*Saptami*	Saturn	Northwest
Eight	*Ashtami*	Rahu	Northeast
Ninth	*Navami*	Sun	East
Tenth	*Dashami*	Moon	North
Eleventh	*Ekadashi*	Mars	Southeast
Twelfth	*Dvadashi*	Mercury	Southwest
Thirteenth	*Trayodashi*	Jupiter	South
Fourteenth	*Caturdashi*	Venus	West
Fifteenth	*Purnima*	Saturn	Northwest
Fifteenth	*Amavasya*	Rahu	Northeast

Kalachakra and *Digchakra*: Wheel of Time and Wheel of Directions

People, who are familiar with Vastu Shastra, will surely notice that in *Kalachakra* the directions are presided by different planets than in *Digchakra* or "wheel of direction". Similarly like *Kalachakra* can be compared to wheel of destruction and transformation, so *Digchakra* is connected to wheel of creation and manifestation. Yet, the way, how they overlap each other is very significant and we can derive from it very profound spiritual knowledge.

On the picture below you can see the planets presiding different directions in *Kalachakra* (outer square) superimposed on the planets presiding different directions in *Digchakra* (inner square), as taught in Vastu Shastra:

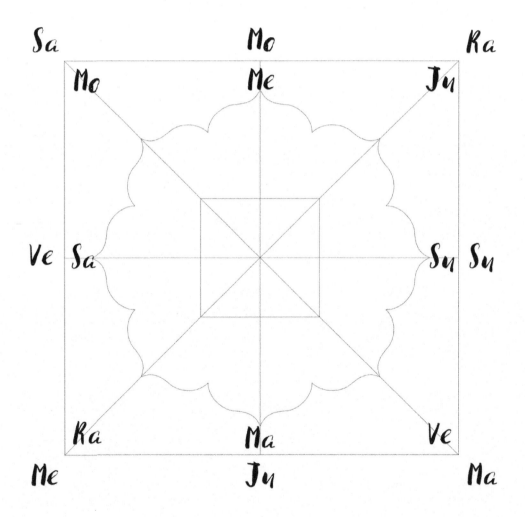

As *Kalachakra* represents the wheel of Time and cycle of destruction, while *Digchakra* represents the wheel of Direction and cycle of creation, so the planets residing in exact directions of *Digchakra* will act as remedies for the planets residing in the same direction of *Kalachakra*.

In this way, if we look at Southeast direction on the picture above, we can read from it that increasing the loving and compassionate energies of Venus (*Digchakra*) is a natural remedy for fiery, short-tempered and nervous energies of imbalanced Mars (*Kalachakra*). This is why people born on *tithis* ruled by Mars (*Tritiya* or *Ekadashi*) will need to consciously work on controlling their martian energies and uplifting their venusian qualities.

In similar way, the energy of self-motivated, hard-working and active Mars will act as a naturally remedy for overly optimistic, overly philosophical, indecisive or even lazy energies of imbalanced Jupiter (South). Jupiter, on the other hand, with its strong drive towards spirituality and receptivity to learn something new, will act as a natural remedy for ungrounded, chaotic and eccentric Rahu (Northeast). Rahu, with his ability to think out of the box, will act as a natural remedy for imbalanced Mercury, which can sometimes become a bit too stiff and calculative (Southwest). Mercury, on the other hand, with his bright intellect, ability to think logically regardless of the circumstances and the power of discrimination will act as a natural remedy for overly emotional Moon (North). The moisture and water element of Moon will naturally counteract the energies of imbalanced Saturn, which may have a tendency to dry everything up (Northwest). Saturn, on the other hand, with his self-discipline and restrictive energies, will help in controlling over-indulgent Venus.

The only planet, which becomes a remedy for itself, is the Sun – as the only remedy for imbalanced ego or self-esteem, can be a connection to the Soul, which is symbolised by Sun, as well.

In this way, combination of *Digchakra* and *Kalachakra* can become extremely helpful in finding the right remedy for a person – especially if the person is experiencing some of the negative effects of his/her birth *tithi*. Even without applying exact remedies, just knowing our "primary mistake" and being aware of the right direction to overcome it, is already a tool, which can help one greatly in one's own spiritual development.

It can be also a very interesting self-analysis tool. If some "friction" happens to you in life on exact lunar day, it is worthy to check, which planet is usually causing "problems" on that *tithi* and the energy of which planet might be the potential solution. Once you practice this on your own example, even to resolve the most simple life situations, and once you observe this sacred dance of Time in your own life, something will surely change within you – and as a side effect you will also become much more intuitive about choosing the right remedy for the right person in your Vedic astrology practice.

CHAPTER 7

NITYA DEVIS – GODDESSES OF ETERNITY

In tantric tradition, inner continuum of consciousness is identical with external continuum of eternal Time. Microcosm is indentical with macrocosm. Different stages of consciousness are reflected in the outer world as different phases of the Moon, representing different moods of Shakti - which affect our breathing, state of consciousness, movement of energy in our subtle body and the water element in our physical body. These sixteen stages of consciousness are sometimes called *kala-shaktis*, "powers of Time" or *atmikas*, "soul particles". But they are mostly called Nitya Devis – Goddesses of Eternity.

Fifteen Nitya Devis are presiding over a mystical inverted triangle, which represents the *yoni* or the creative womb of the universe. Goddesses of fiery *tithis* are presiding over its corners, while all other Nitya Devis are placed in between them on the arms of the triangle. Sixteenth Nitya Devi, who is said to dwell right in the center of this mystical triangle, is Lalita Tripurasundari Herself – the Highest Goddess representing the hidden factor acting behind all the phases of the Moon and all the changing moods of Time: *Prakriti*, Nature Herself.

Lalita means "playful one", while Tripurasundari means "the most beautiful in all the three worlds". She represents the playfulness of our consciousness, which takes part in the *lila* of life – and the enchanting beauty of *maya*, the illusion. Being a playful Goddess, She represents the desire of our soul to experience all the different moods of life, symbolised by Nitya Devis, Her own manifestations. While the light of the Sun (Shiva) is unchanging in its love for Moon, the Moon (Shakti) is always fickle, and so its phases are symbolising many different moods it undergoes. Through those very changes, through this playful dance of Time, the story called Life is happening. Through Nitya Devis, or the powers of Time, eternal love story between Shiva and Shakti, Soul and its Beloved, is manifested in the world. Nitya Devis represent the different flavours of this eternal love story.

Each of the Nitya Devis has very specific attributes, which reflect Her mood and Her qualities, as well as powers manifested in the present moment. Some of them are more gentle, while others are fierce. Some have just one head and two arms, while others have many heads and many arms, symbolising their complex nature. Even the attributes, which they are holding in their arms will be of great importance, when it comes to interpretation of their cosmic influences. Some of them might hold just a flower or sugarcane bow, while others will be well equipped with weapons.

Interestingly enough, if you add up the number of all the arms of all fifteen Nitya Devis, you will get to 108 – which stands not only for the sacred ratio between our Sun, Moon and Earth, but also for 108 nakshatra *padas*, 108 qualities of the soul, into which the entire wheel of zodiac is split. From the exact number of arms, which each Nitya Devi has, we will also derive the connection between each lunar day and similar qualities reflected by respective nakshatras connected to it. (See the table below.)

TITHI AND NAKSHATRA CONNECTION

Goddess	Number of arms	Nakshatra connection
Kameshwari (1)	6	Ashwini, first two *padas* of Bharani
Bhagamalini (2)	6	last two *padas* of Bharani, Krittika
Nityaklinna (3)	4	Rohini
Bherunda (4)	8	Margashirsha, Ardra
Vahnivasini (5)	8	Punarvasu, Pushya
Vajreshwari (6)	4	Ashlesha
Shivaduti (7)	8	Magha, Purva Phalguni
Tvarita (8)	4	Uttara Phalguni
Kulasundari (9)	12	Hasta, Citra, Svati
Nitya (10)	12	Vishakha, Anuradha, Jyeshtha
Nilapataka (11)	10	Mula, Purvashadha, first two *padas* of Uttarashadha
Vijaya (12)	10	last two *padas* of Uttarashadha, Shravana, Dhanishta
Sarvamangala (13)	2	first two *padas* of Shatabhisha
Jwalamalini (14)	12	last two *padas* of Shatabhisha, Purva Bhadrapada, Uttara Bhadrapada, first two *padas* of Revati
Citra (15)	2	last two *padas* of Revati

Each Nitya Devi will be also connected to some vowel or *swara*, from which another nakshatra connections may be derived – as sixteen vowels of Sanskrit alphabet are connected with the nakshatras from Revati to Punarvasu, according to the model presented in *Discovering Youniverse*. Additionally, as each lunar day is governed by some combination of *tattwa* (element) and *guna* (mode), we can also find different nakshatras, which are governed by the same element-*guna* combination. The same *tattwa-guna* combination will always produce similar results.

It is very important to add that in the entire book elements are assigned to the nakshatras exactly, how they are assigned in the *Puranas* and other scriptures (such as *Shiva Swarodaya*), as this is not only the most ancient system, but it also proved to bring me the best results in my personal Vedic astrology practice. In this system nakshatras are split into four groups, which gives us seven nakshatras of fire (Bharani, Krittika, Pushya, Magha, Purva Phalguni, Vishakha, Purva Bhadrapada), seven nakshatras of earth (Rohini, Anuradha, Jyeshtha, Uttarashadha, Abhijit, Shravana, Dhanishta), seven nakshatras of air (Ashwini, Margashirsha, Punarvasu, Uttara Phalguni, Hasta, Citra, Swati) and seven nakshatras of water (Ardra, Ashlesha, Mula, Purvashadha, Shatabhisha, Uttara Bhadrapada, Revati).

Each Goddess of Eternity or Nitya Devi will also have Her sacred mantra, *yantra*, vowel, *kala* of the Moon, direction, favourite colours, secret tantric name, secret *yogini* and secret syllable of Sri Vidya mantra. Into some of these topics I will not go into details in this book, as this is the sort of knowledge, which you need to get directly from a Guru.

Yantras or sacred geometric diagrams of Nitya Devis are particularly interesting, as they allow us to understand the nature of each lunar day and its natural flow of energy on a much deeper level. You can think of these *yantras* as of geometric representations of the flow of energy on this exact lunar day. Or, if it is a *yantra* connected with your birth *tithi*, you can think of it as a geometric representation of your own mind. Simpler *yantras* will be representing more easy-going energies, while more complex *yantras* will represent more complex energies. Similarly, *yantras* with more round shapes will have more harmonious flow of energy, while *yantras* with sharper angles will be connected to more strict forms of the Divine Mother. Every element of each *yantra* is also presided by several *shaktis* or abstract powers, which can help us to understand on even deeper level the energy of each Nitya Devi and Her lunar day.

These *yantras* can be of great help in one's personal *sadhana* and they can also act as remedial measures. This will be described in detail in Chapter 24.

16 secret forms of Shiva

Apart from sixteen Nitya Devis, there are also sixteen secret forms of Shiva described in some of the older Vastu scriptures, such as *Mayamatam*. Even though these forms of Shiva are not directly connected to fifteen lunar days, once you study their features and symbols, the connection becomes obvious. As Goddess is changing Her mood during different lunar phases, even Shiva Himself is changing His mood a bit.

These forms are Sukhasana ("the one comfortably seated"), Kalyana ("married one"), Umaskanda ("the one with Uma and Skanda"), Vrisharudha ("the one mounted on a bull"), Tripurantaka ("the one who finished Tripura"), Nirritha (also known as Nataraja, "king of dance"), Chandrashekhara ("the one adorned with crescent Moon"), Ardhanarishwara (half Shiva, half Shakti), Harihara (half Shiva, half

Vishnu), Chandeshanugraha ("the one preparing a bow"), Kamari ("destroyer of desire"), Kalanasha ("destroyer of impurities"), Dakshinamurti ("embodiment of South direction", Shiva in the form of a Guru), Bhikshatanamurti ("the one in the form of a beggar"), Kankalamurti ("the one with a skeleton") and Mukhalinga – Shiva in His formless form as a *lingam*: form beyond all forms and all modes of Nature.

Tithi devatas – other deities presiding over lunar days

In strictly astrological scriptures you won't find much information on Nitya Devis or different forms of the Divine Mother presiding over different lunar phases. Instead, you will find *tithi devatas*, who are gods, for whom these *tithis* are sacred. What will be a bit confusing, however, is that in every scripture you will find different *tithi devatas*. Having looked through *Brihat Samhita*, *Muhurta Cintamani*, *Narada Purana*, *Agni Purana*, *Uttara Kalamrita* and *Bhavishya Purana*, I have seen completely different gods prescribed to the same lunar days. Why is that so?

The difficulty with understanding the *tithis* lies in their very element: water. *Tithis* represent how water flows in our life and how emotions manifest in our life. This is why some of the scholars of older times and perhaps even ancient *rishis* simply failed in accurate "categorisation" of lunar days. Because, in reality, how can you, *really*, categorise emotion? Emotion is like water - it has no shape of its own. But its very movement gives, in time, a shape to *everything*. This is also from where comes the difficulty in proper understanding of the *tithis* – as to truly understand them, you need to *feel* the emotion, which is produced by them.

This is also the major difference between the energy of the *tithis* and the energy of the nakshatras. Nakshatras are always presided by the same deities, whichever scripture you will take. Their categorisation is much easier, as they are ruled by objective Saturn – main planet, which creates our objective reality and tells us about objective truth. This is why each nakshatra is presided by exact god, who has exact qualities, both postive and negative, as well as exact mythological stories connected to him.

When it comes to *tithis*, however, everything is subjective – as they are ruled by subjective Moon. This is why you cannot grasp their energy so easily just by assigning some deity to it. In a way, all scriptures failed to do that. Because emotion in its very nature is *feminine*. This is why in tantric tradition lunar phases are presided by Nitya Devis or abstract forms of the Divine Mother, who represent some of Her qualities, powers, moods and states of consciousness.

In tantric tradition nothing is supposed to be *understood* – everything is supposed to be *felt* and *experienced*. None of Nitya Devis had ever left their post of guardian of Eternity; none of them had ever incarnated on Earth, so there are no stories about them, like in case of other gods – and a very limited scriptural knowledge, present only in some of the tantric scriptures. But by meditation on their images, *yantras* and *mantras* you can get much closer to them – and closer to understanding the real nature of each *tithi* than ever before. Because when you start to *feel* the *tithi*, this is when you start to truly understand it.

This is why in this book there will be very small attention given to *tithi devatas*, even though they will be mentioned. But the ones, who will truly unveil for us the mysteries of each *tithi* will be Nitya Devis – Goddesses of Eternity.

CHAPTER 8

KAMESHWARI – GODDESS OF LOVE
PRATIPAD – FIRST LUNAR DAY

kameśvari jaganmata satcitananda vigrahe

grahanarcam imam pritya prasida parameśvari

"O Goddess of Love, Mother of the world, embodiment of conscious bliss, Highest Goddess, be pleased with my worship and Love."

- Devi Kshama Prarthana Stotram

Kala	Element	Planet	Guna	Yogini	Vowel
amrita (nectar)	fire	Sun	rajas	East	a

Stage of consciousness	Divine quality	Deity (Muhurta Cintamani)	Deity (Varahamihira)	Nakshatra connection	Form of Shiva
waking (waking)	daya (compassion)	Agni	Brahma	Ashwini Bharani	Sukhasana

Shukla Paksha

Nadi: ida
Chakra: muladhara
Interval: smaller than minor second
Deity (Narada Purana): Brahma
House from the Sun: 1 or 2

Krishna Paksha

Nadi: pingala
Chakra: ajna
Interval: bigger than major seventh
Deity (Narada Purana): Durga
House from the Sun: 7 or 8

Kameshwari, the first Nitya Devi occupying the bottom corner of the mystical triangle, denoting Her fiery nature and fire element She is ruling, is considered also the highest among the lunar Goddesses – the direct manifestation of Goddess Tripurasundari Herself. She represents rising from sleep, the very first stage of the waking state of consciousness, as well as the first rays of the Sun. She is the creative force of the universe in its purest form, with Brahma Himself (the creator and progenitor of mankind) co-ruling *Pratipad tithi* with Her. She is the one, who brought Manmatha (Cupid) back to the world, after Shiva burned him to ashes – and thus, She had restored fertility and life to the world. Her name means "Goddess of Desire" or "Goddess of Love". She is the intensity of *rajas*, *guna* of passion. Her syllable in Sri Vidya mantra is *ka*, the mantra of desire and creation, while *yogini* associated with Her is Kama-karshini, "the one attracting all desires or all love". Along with Kameshwara (Lord Shiva, Her counterpart), Goddess Kameshwari is creating countless worlds.

Whenever there is the first ray of the Moon after *Amavasya*, this is Kameshwari. Whenever there is the first shadow on the Moon after *Purnima* this is Kameshwari. She is always the first to start a new cycle. In *Shukla paksha* She is the desire of the Self to manifest its wishes into the world, while in *Krishna paksha* She is the desire of the Soul to return to its origin. Whatever our true desire is, Kameshwari makes it emerge on the surface of our consciousness and makes us aware of its existence.

Kameshwara, interestingly, is also one of the names of Kubera, god of prosperity, increase and fulfillment of material desires. Even the quality of this *tithi* is *vriddhi*, to increase all things – because it is on this day, first day after New Moon, that the Moon slowly starts to increase in its light.

Goddess Kameshwari clarifies our doubts, dispells all confusion and makes us see the truth, so we can make the right decision. With Sun being the planet of Her *tithi*, She makes visible all that is hidden. She gives form to all that is formless. She brings all secret desires to daylight, in order for us to fulfill them or purify our consciousness out of them. And as our desires define our personality to a very big extent, ultimately She helps us to understand ourselves on a much deeper level and guides us closer and closer to the core of our Soul - if we just allow ourselves to be guided by Her.

Kameshwari is the friction of the desire emerging on the surface of consciousness, which in its essence is fully satisfied. It is the first inharmonious sound emerging from unison of union between Shiva and Shakti during the New Moon, and the first inharmonious sound descending from the perfect octave of Full Moon. It is like buzzing of a honey-bee, which is looking for nectar. Its very message is: "Something is not full. Something is still to be fulfilled. Something is still to be completed. Some new Love story is yet to be experienced." Although this very yearning, the very desire itself takes us away from the perfect state of completion and fulfillment, experienced during the New Moon or Full Moon, ultimately, it is also the beginning of our journey towards fulfilling ourselves on yet another level. In immature mind, however, the influence of Goddess Kameshwari can be experienced only on the level of never-ending material desires.

Her tantric name in *64 Yogini Namavali* is Sarva-shakti or "the power behind everything". From material perspective desire is the power, which creates the world and makes it running. From spiritual perspective, it is Love, the refined form of desire that is the basis of all. Similarly, Goddess Kameshwari, in Her lower octave, is the Goddess of never-ending desires. But Her true Self is Goddess of Love. It is the powerful gravity of Divine Love that She stands for. Not without a reason a Divine quality of Lord Krishna associated with this lunar day is *daya* – compassion, the most refined and the most unconditional form of Love.

My Gurudev often speaks so beautifully about Love and how it is misunderstood in our times. On the New Moon in Vishakha nakshatra, 17 November 2017, Guruji wrote:

"It is simply amazing to observe these two types of gravity: the gravity of this world, which gives one endless pain and suffering, and the gravity of Love, which gives one endless Bliss.

The laws of Nature show that gravity, as a force, is weaker compared to forces in the atom, where the nuclear force is present. Then what is Love and what kind of gravity does Love have? Gravity means holding something close to the body of gravity, which means that a specific body has the power to attract another body, and we know that Love is an attractive force. It is the most powerful force but, at the same time, it is the lightest phenomenon; so much so, that we do not notice Love. We do not notice that Love itself has a higher speed than light, whose speed can be measured. But what about the speed of Love? Do we notice when we fall in love and how quickly that happens? Do we notice how Love makes us stronger than we usually are in our everyday lives or stronger than we usually think we are? Do we notice how much more creative we are due to the Love force? More focused, more happy, more satisfied, more actually *our Self*? Why we do not notice these things? It seems that Love is very, very fast and its gravity acts in a direction other than what we are used to experiencing, since it is opposite to the gravity we know so well!

The greatest quality of Love's gravity is that Love attracts us to God, to the Realisation of the ultimate reality, to the Realisation of our true nature and our relationship with Him.

It is important to understand in which way the gravity of Love is different from the gravity that we know in this world. For the gravity in this world, we do not have to do anything. It is simply there and will keep us together whether we know it or not. The gravity of this body, mind and ego, and the gravity of negativity, *tamas*, and laziness offer themselves for free and we are the 'happy' owners of them, or, better to say, they own us. But for the gravity of Love, one must put in a certain effort to be pulled by Love towards Love and more Love and the reality of Love. One must let go of all the heavy things that one carries inside, because although the gross body looks the heaviest, actually it is our thinking, which is usually negative, constantly judging, selfish and ignorant, that is heavier than the physical body.

In order to be pulled towards the gravity of Love, one must let go of this kind of thinking and of all these things that have the kind of mass that pulls one towards the gravity of matter. Once we are pulled by the gravity of Love, we will start rising higher and higher, far away from the density of ignorance and forgetfulness, and we will realise how Love is lightest of the lightest and we will know the real Light of life. Understanding these two gravities is up to each one, as well as to decide which gravity one really wants."

Love is one of the most powerful forces in the world. Similarly, the presence of Kameshwari Devi is so powerful, that even if you glance at Her *yantra* just for a few minutes, your thoughts will get clarified and you will understand better, which decision to take or what is the true desire of your heart. Her presence is purifying everything around just like the fire burns all the impurities. Her power is such, that even right now, at this very moment, when I started to write about Her, She has revealed me something very deep about myself. I bow to the feet of Goddess Kameshwari, who is the cause of all creation and who guides everybody towards the light of truth.

Meditation with Goddess Kameshwari

Hue: lustrous red like ten milion rising suns
Number of heads: 1
Number of eyes: 3
Number of hands: 6
Right hands: 5 flowery arrows, *ankusha*, cup filled with nectar
Left hands: sugarcane bow, *pasha*, *varada mudra*
Garments: red
Ornaments: bright crown of rubies, throat ornament, necklaces, waistchains, rings on Her feet and hands, crescent Moon (*kala*) on Her head

There is a beautiful description of Kameshwari, as well as other Nitya Devis, in *Tantraraja*. As the first Goddess to be worshiped in lunar cycle, She is lustrous red like ten milion rising suns. Her light dispells all the darkness for those, who are humble, and blinds those, who are proud. She is adorned with red silk, bright crown of rubies and various ornaments set with precious gems, such us throat ornament, necklaces, waistchains and rings on Her feet and hands. A crescent Moon (*kala*) adorns Her head – like the first ray of the Moon after New Moon. Her face is lit up with a soft smile and Her eyes are merciful.

Kameshwari Devi has 3 eyes, like all the Nitya Devis (which symbolises their awakened consciousness), and 6 arms. In Her right hands She carries (starting from the top) five flowery arrows, *ankusha* (goad) and cup made of gems filled with nectar. In Her left hands She carries sugarcane bow, *pasha* (noose) and *varada mudra* – a gesture of bestowing boons.

Pasha, ankusha, five flowery arrows and sugarcane bow are atributes of Lalita Tripurasundari Herself. *Pasha* or noose represents our attachments or likes, which bind us to the world of illusion – it represents *raga* or passion, things we run after. *Ankusha* or elephant goad, symbolises *dwesha* or repulsion - all the things that we repell from our life and try to run away from. Being so, *pasha* and *ankusha* symbolise our likes and dislikes, the major duality of the mind, which produces desire itself. Sugarcane bow, *ikshu danda*, symbolises our mind, *manas*, the matrix of all desires. It is said that a string of that bow is made of bumble bees, which represents our never ending desires, and other "buzzing" thoughts and emotions, which keep our mind away from our highest goal. Mind, which is free of passion and repulsion and in which the constant "buzzing" of the bees of our thoughts and desires is stilled, is sweet in its nature, as it becomes full of *soma*, the Divine nectar. Flowery arrows, *pancha bana*, symbolise our five senses, through which our desires are experienced.

Tantraraja gives also a much deeper meaning of five flowery arrows in the hands of Goddess Kameshwari. It associates them with five results of desire itself, which are *madana* (desire), *unmadana* (longing maddening), *dipana* (kindling), *mohana* (enchanting) and *shoshana* (wasting). Goddess Kameshwari reminds us through the five arrows in Her hands, that each and every desire has its price; fulfillment of each and every desire is connected with some waste of energy – especially, when it comes to sexual desire. Although She is often approached for fulfillment in sexual life, She reminds us that sexual activity is always connected with some sort of waste of life energy.

Goddess Kameshwari is, indeed, sexual energy itself. She is the one, who controls sexual desires, as well as the Mother of five Kamadevas, gods of desire, who are said to be Her five senses, *jnanendriyas*. Their names are: Kamaraja (yellow-hued "king of desire"), Manmatha (white-hued "agitator of the mind)", Kandarpa (red-hued "inflamer"), Makaraketana (purple-hued "god, whose banner is Makara or a crocodile") and Manobhava (blue-hued "mindborn god"). These five gods, five children of Goddess Kameshwari, are intimately connected with the powers of five flowery arrows in Her hands. They have two eyes and arms each, they are of smiling countenance and each carries sugarcane bow and flowery arrows. *Tantraraja* says that they are the ones, who agitate the world. They exist in the souls of all beings and in the form of all things. Since Cupid lost his physical body, when Shiva burned it to ashes, he became Ananga, "bodiless one" – and the one, who dwells in the body of everybody and everything.

Saundarya Lahari beautifully praises Lalita Tripurasundari in the form of Kameshwari, or Mother of Cupid: "Oh daughter of the snow-clad Himalaya mountain! Kamadeva, the God of love, has only a bow made of arrows, with its string comprised of a cluster of honeybees, and arrows barely five. The spring season (periodical and undependable) is his assistant and the southern breeze, his war-chariot. Yet, with such frail equipment, bodiless and alone, Manmatha conquers the entire Universe, having obtained some favour through Thy benign side-glance."

With Her left hand in *varada mudra*, Goddess Kameshwari assures us, that She will grant us all our wishes, as well as reminds us to choose them wisely. One of Her names is *Kamada* or "the one, who fulfills all desires".

Cup made with gems filled with nectar is not without significance, as well. After all, Goddess Kameshwari rules over the first *kala* of the Moon, called *amrita*, or the nectar. She represents our mind's inborn desire to seek for sweetness, for *soma*, for the juice and nectar of life. Immature mind will seek the nectar of life in the perishable pleasure of this world and fulfillment of its petty desires. The mind purified by the fire of spiritual practice will look inwardly instead and seek the true fulfillment in the Self itself - which is symbolised by Devi Kameshwari and the light of the Sun She represents.

Kameshwari is, indeed, *mulagni* itself, the sacred fire of the Sun hidden like the fire in embers in our *muladhara chakra*. This very *mulagni* is the cause of aroosal of our desires, with sexual desire as the primary one. Yet, this very *mulagni* also has the power to purify us from all the lower qualities, if we endure its intense heat and firmly decide to focus on the light of the Self. It can lead us to perishable "sweetness" of the world, or the nectar of true spiritual satisfaction within ourselves, which cannot be substituted by anything, what external world has to offer. Therefore in *Shukla paksha*, Goddess Kameshwari is connected to energy of *mulagni* rising from *muladhara chakra*, while in *Krishna paksha* She is connected to the energy of consciousness and awareness of the Self, descending from *ajna chakra* and enlightening us on its way.

Numerology: 1

Chandogya Upanishad says: "In the beginning there was only one Being, and that Being thought, 'I want to be many'." The first *tithi* is connected with number 1. There is only one Sun, one Moon and one Soul. Therefore number one stands for the Self itself, from which everything else emerges. It is a silent indication that all people born on *Pratipad tithi* should look more towards seeking fulfillment in their true Self rather than in fulfillment of their countless desires. Even the form of Shiva connected to *Pratipad tithi* is Sukhasana or "the One seated comfortably". Shiva is always absorbed in His own true Self and complete in Himself, without the need for anything else to complete Him. True feeling of comfort in life comes from understanding "Nothing else is needed. This present moment is full in itself", while each desire comes from a thought: "Something is missing. Something is incomplete." Indeed, shadow side of people born on *Pratipad tithi* is that sometimes they have too many desires and are too much occupied with their personal comfort – which inevitably leads to certain feeling of dissatisfaction, as the bigger are our expectations, the greater the disappointment. Sometimes they also tend to be too self-centered or may seek too much attention from others. Their personal energy tends to run a lot towards the outside, and due to that can be greatly wasted, as well. The become easily excited, but also easily disappointed.

Similarly, in first chapter of *Bhagavad Gita*, Arjuna is also very self-centered. He acts, thinks and talks from the perspective of his lower self. He stands in front of the battlefield, made visible in front of his eyes, and he is not ready to fight – because he doesn't see a bigger picture. He is too preoccupied with the external world. Similarly, *Pratipad tithi* natives sometimes tend to be too preoccupied with the outer perception of things (as energies of Goddess Kameshwari make everything clear and visible on that day), due to what they fail to see a bigger picture. Reading the first chapter of *Bhagavad Gita* could be greatly therapeuthic for them.

Yogini in *Kalachakra*: East

On *Pratipad tithi* the danger comes from the East. It is said that we should avoid travelling into that direction during the first lunar day in any of the two *pakshas*. It carries, however, a much deeper, spiritual meaning. As Goddess Kameshwari helps us to understand our own truth and strengthens our ability to see the reality clearly, as well as helps to become more aware of our true wishes, She also warns us not to abuse Her power for fullfilment of egoistic desires – as Eastern direction is connected in *Kalachakra* with the Sun and god Indra. Danger that comes along with the abuse of the energy of the Sun, is inflated ego and pride, which can make us blind for the truth – like Indra Himself was blinded by his opulence and several times fallen a prey to his own desires. Not without a reason Kameshwari is described in *Tantraraja* as being "lustrous like ten milion rising suns". The very same creative energy, which can make us blossom and see the truth, can also inflate our desires to such an extent, that they will completely blind us and move us away from our path.

Goddess Kameshwari warns us to focus during Her *tithi* not on Her light itself, but rather on the areas of our life it brightens up. A torch is for us not to focus on its light and get blinded by it, but it is for us to see more clearly; for the darkness to get dispelled. The light of the torch is not to be blamed, if our eyes get burned. It is our focus that is to be blamed. Meditation on the *yantra* of Kameshwari Devi brings this focus to our consciousness.

On 18 November 2018, which was *Shukla Pratipad*, my Gurudev, Paramahamsa Vishwananda, has published this profound message, which is so much in tune with the message of Kameshwari Devi:

"In order to advance spiritually, one needs knowledge. And spiritual knowledge is always described symbolically like a torch that dispels the darkness of ignorance. But the tricky thing about knowledge and a torch is that, instead of observing the space we illuminate with the torch, we focus on torch! The torch becomes more important than its purpose and use! And instead of a way to help us to see, it actually blinds us!"

Kameshwari always brings us light during Her *tithi*. And there is always a lesson that comes with that. If we are attentive enough, we can understand this lesson and learn something profound about ourselves. But if our ego will blind us, we will repell the message and focus on our petty desires instead.

East is also the direction, which has the capacity to fulfill all our wishes. Whenever you have an intention and pray facing East direction, your capacity to attract the object of your desire becomes higher. Yet, during Her *tithi*, Goddess Kameshwari also warns us, that we need to be very careful about what we desire, as "the danger comes from the East" – our very own wishes can sometimes be the cause of our misfortune. If we pray to Goddess Kameshwari on *Pratipad tithi*, first lunar day, with full devotion and humility, She will enlighten us about which of our desires are good for our growth, and which are not. But to be ready to receive Her guidance, we need to firstly abandon our ego and the attitude of "knowing better". We need to overcome the negative qualities of the Sun and East direction, represented by Indra, the guardian of Eastern direction.

People born on *Pratipad tithi* may sometimes have a tendency to act a little bit too selfishly, when it comes to fulfillment of their desires – or they might have had abused their power for fulfillment of their desires in previous lifetimes. This is another reason, why they might sometimes feel so dissatisfied in this life. Lack of ability to fulfill their desires in this lifetime, while feeling them strongly, becomes their penance. If there is any affliction to *tithi rashi* or *tithi* lord, they might also sometimes have a tendency to play a role of a victim or feel like everything is their fault. It is believed that Moon-god apologised and repented for kidnapping Tara, wife of Brihaspati, on *Pratipad tithi* – which is why *Pratipad tithi* natives may sometimes also have a tendency to apologise for everything, especially if there is any affliction to their *tithi* lord or *tithi rashi*. In such cases, Sun, instead of being egoistic, reaches another extreme, which is low self-esteem. Finding some healthy balance between those two extremes is of great importance for *Pratipad tithi* natives.

Shaktis of Goddess Kameshwari

Different *shaktis* or powers of Goddess Kameshwari dwell in the different places of Her *yantra*. A huge *bindu* or circle in the center symbolises Goddess Kameshwari Herself and Her powerful presence, as well as unrestrained source of energy. Five petals around it symbolise Her aforementioned five flowery arrows and five results of desire associated with them: *madana* (desire), *unmadana* (longing maddening), *dipana* (kindling), *mohana* (enchanting) and *shoshana* (wasting). Interestingly, five-petalled flower is also a well known symbol of Venus in Vedic astrology, the planet of passion and desire. 8 year long Venus cycle observed from Earth creates this beautiful flower pattern, so similar to the five flower petals in the middle of Goddess Kameshwari's *yantra*:

8 flower petals around them, which distrubute the *shaktis* of desires to the 8 directions of the world, are ruled by *shaktis*: Ananga-kusuma ("the flower of the Cupid/bodiless one"), Ananga-mekhala ("the girdle of the Cupid/bodiless one"), Ananga-madana ("the desire of the Cupid/bodiless one"), Ananga-madantura ("the governer of the desire or bodiless one"), Mada-vegini ("the impulse of desire"), Bhuvana-pala ("the protector of the world"), Shashi-rekha ("the line of the Moon") and Gagana-rekha ("the line of the space"). Perhaps these 8 petals stand for the 8 years of the cycle of Venus, as well.

The sixteen petals enclosing them, traditionally worshipped with sixteen vowels or *swaras* before recitation of their names are occupied by *shaktis*: Shraddha ("faith"), Priti ("love"), Rati ("passion"), Dhriti ("courage"), Kanti ("beauty"), Manorama ("enchantress of the mind"), Manohara ("captivator of the mind"), Manoratha ("heart's desire"), Madanonmadini ("the enchantress of the Cupid"), Mohini ("enchantress"), Dipani ("enkindler"), Shoshani ("waster"), Vashankari ("attractor"), Sinjini ("tinkling one"), Subhaga ("fortunate one"), Priya-darshana ("pleasant to look at"). They represent all the qualities, which the power of desire or Love brings with itself. As some of them are also very similar to the *kalas* of the Moon phases, they might perhaps denote, as well, the sixteen different ways, how desire manifests itself during different *tithis*.

These sixteen petals are enclosed by another garland of sixteen petals, which are now directly addressed as the sixteen *kalas* of the Moon – although they differ from their traditional names. The *shaktis* of these sixteen petals are: Pusha ("nourisher"), Avesha ("anger" or "repulsion"), Shrimanasa ("wealthy mind" or "auspicious thinking"), Rati ("passion"), Priti ("love"), Dhriti ("courage"), Buddhi ("intellect"), Saumya ("gentle one"), Marichi ("ray of light"), Amshu-malini ("garlanded with rays of light"), Shashini ("swift one"), Angira ("self-sacrificing one"), Chhaya ("shadow"), Sampurna-mandala ("full circle or *mandala*"), Tushti ("contentment"), Amrita ("nectar of immortality").

Thus, the original energy of Kameshwari in the form of circle or *bindu* in the middle, gets manifested into the world: firstly through Her five flowery arrows, secondly it spreads to eight directions of the world, and finally it gets filtered through sixteen *swaras* and sixteen *kalas* before it reaches *bhupura* symbolising our earthly plane or borders of material perception.

Swara of Goddess Kameshwari

A, the very first *swara* or vowel of Sanskrit alphabet, is associated with Goddess Kameshwari. Its quality or *kala* is to mask things, like the veil of *maya*, which our world is made of. Kameshwari is a Goddess of illusion and the only one, who can free us from this illusion. Vowel *a* is connected with the life breath itself, as it is the initiator of *pranava*, **aum**, the primordial sound. And, similarly like life force itself, *aṁ*, bij mantra created out of this *swara*, also means "to be quick", which resonates with Kameshwari's impulsive nature, as well as inspires us to control our own life force wisely, without wasting it.

Swara *a* is also connected with the process of negation or separation from something. Similarly like the Moon leaves its perfect unison or perfect octave with the Sun during *Pratipad tithi*, so the power of desire, associated with Devi Kameshwari, temporarily separates us from the wholeness and makes us aware of the feeling of separation or absence of something. Desire, in itself, is nothing else, but realisation, that something is absent or missing – and a longing to have this void filled.

According to *Agni Purana* vowel *a* is also connected to Vishnu and prevention of negative forces.

Nakshatras connected to Goddess Kameshwari

Ashwini nakshatra is connected to *swara* of Goddess Kameshwari, while Her six arms stand for the first six nakshatra *padas* of the zodiac: four *padas* of Ashwini nakshatra and first two *padas* of Bharani nakshatra. With energy of Ashwini nakshatra being so prominent during this *tithi*, no wonder that it is considered as one of the best days for travelling. Ashwini nakshatra is ruled by heavenly physicians, sons of the Sun god, with heads of horses, who are well known because of their speed, as well as giving protection to all travellers and transportation. The *shakti* of this nakshatra is the power to bring quick results. With solar energy being so prominent during *Pratipad tithi*, Goddess Kameshwari also bestows happiness, wealth, mental peace, good health and destroys all diseases. Interestingly, Sun, which is ruling *Pratipad tithi* along with Goddess Kameshwari, is exalted exactly in Ashwini nakshatra, while Mars has his *mulatrikona* sign here. Saturn, on the other hand, the planet of restriction and limits, gets debilitated here.

Ashwini nakshatra is also connected to youthfulness, as well as impulsiveness and many desires. It stands for the creative spark, that creative impulse, which gave birth to the world. The energy of Goddess Kameshwari, born out of the friction of sound separating itself from fullness of unison or perfect octave, can be very fast, impulsive, intense and impatient - like life force itself (also symbolised by Ashwini nakshatra). This sound would be minor second or *rishabha* in *Shukla paksha*, which is connected to fiery Mars, while in *Krishna paksha* it would be major seventh or *nishadha*, the sound of passionate Venus. Being so, fire, passion, love and creativity come together under this *tithi*.

As Ashwini kumars, the twin deities presiding over this nakshatra, were born from Surya dev and Samjna making love in the form of the horses, this nakshatra also stands for our animalistic qualities and uncontrolled desires, which need to be purified. And, similarly, like Ashwini nakshatra natives are naturally curious about the world, talkative, youthful, impulsive, creative, innocent and easily excited, so very similar qualities are shared by *Pratipad tithi* natives. Yet, due to this very quality of excitemenet they also suffer more than others, when they are disappointed and when their expectations are not met. The more they expect, the less fulfilled they feel. That is the side effect of *rajo guna* connected with fire element. Often they also talk without thinking, which sometimes may lead them to saying things, which they might regret later.

It is also quite symbolic, that Ashwini nakshatra is ruled by twin-gods – two gods born of one Sun or one Self. It is the first nakshatra of the zodiac, symbolising not only life force, but some new life, some new beginning being produced due to separation from the Self and entering the world of duality. This is why it is very important for all *Pratipad tithi* natives to rise above dualistic thinking and belief that something or somebody can fulfill them. They need to learn how to find a true fulfillment and true contentment within themselves in the first place. Otherwise, if they will keep leaving the responsibility for their happiness in the hands of other people, they will keep getting disappointed.

This inner fulfillment is symbolised by a pot of nectar in the hand of Goddess Kameshwari. Interestingly enough, Ashwini kumars, even though they were gods, they were initially denied the nectar or the *amrit* – and so they needed to learn how to achieve it with their own efforts. Similarly *Pratipad* natives need to put their own effort into finding fulfillment in life, without over-enthusiastic expectation that things will come to them on their own, as their birth right. Ashwins were also well known of being very fond of honey.

Bharani nakshatra also plays a prominent role in this *tithi*, as its very symbol is *yoni* or vulva (which can be also translated as "origin" or "womb"). Interestingly, it is at the same time the nakshatra ruled by Yamaraj, god of death. It reminds us, that every desire is perishable and that every desire has its price as well. Life energy can be easily wasted through overindulgence in sexual desire or overindulgence in satisfying our desires in any other form. Bharani nakshatra is often connected to purifying our sexual energy and with the need for healthy restriction, as it is a nakshatra ruled by Venus, dwelling in the fiery sign of Aries. It reminds us to focus more on our origin, rather than wasting our precious life force on petty desires.

Bharani nakshatra, being a nakshatra of Venus, is also very creative and sensual, like Goddess Kameshwari Herself. Creativity and a spark of Divine inspiration are some of the most precious blessings from Kameshwari Devi.

There are also three nakshatras, in which *guna* of *rajas* combines with fire element, similarly like on *Pratipad tithi*: Magha, Vishakha and Purva Bhadrapada. All three are very fiery, transformative, bold, fearless, ambitious but also a little bit materialistic sometimes, as well as with a tendency to certain egocentrism. By analysing the nakshatras, which are combining same element and same *guna* as exact *tithi*, we can also learn quite a lot about this lunar day. Same *guna* and same *tattwa* will always bring very similar results.

Tithi, vara and nakshatra resonance

The energy of Goddess Kameshwari is the most incompatible with Wednesday, the day ruled by neutral, calculative and cold Mercury. Whenever a combination of *Pratipad tithi* and Wednesday happens, it is called *samvartaka yoga*, a highly dangerous "combination of dissolution". The energy of Mercury literally dissolves the fertility and creative powers of first lunar day. *Pratipad tithi* also forms *ashubha yoga* or "inauspicious combination", whenever the Moon dwells in Uttarashadha nakshatra – the only nakshatra, which doesn't have an animal counterpart, and thus is considered as the most lonely, cold, sceptical and infertile nakshatra. Uttarashadha nakshatra also becomes *shunya* or fruitless on *Pratipad tithi*.

Creative energies of Goddess Kameshwari find their full expression, whenever *Pratipad tithi* falls on Friday, the day ruled by Venus, as it creates a *siddha yoga* or "combination of accomplishments". If, additionally, this happens, when the Moon dwells in Ashwini, Bharani, Ardra, Punarvasu, Uttara Phalguni, Citra, Swati, Purvashadha, Shatabhisha or Revati nakshatra, it is all the more auspicious.

Sunday, with Sun as its ruler, is also very supportive for the creative energies of Kameshwari Devi. Whenever *Pratipad tithi* happens on Sunday, it forms *amrita yoga* or "combination of nectar". When, additionally, the Moon dwells on such a day in Pushya, Uttara Phalguni, Hasta, Mula, Uttarashadha, Shravana or Uttara Bhadrapada nakshatra, it becomes even more powerful.

Tuesdays, with Mars as their ruler, can be very supportive for the energy of Kameshwari Devi, too, but they can also be very destructive. The final result will depend on the nakshatra. If *Pratipad tithi* occurs on Tuesday and under Ashwini, Margashirsha, Uttara Phalguni, Citra, Anuradha, Mula, Dhanishta or Purva Bhadrapada nakshatra, then it is an excellent combination, *siddha yoga*. If it happens, however, in one of the following nakshatras: Ardra, Punarvasu, Jyeshtha, Purvashadha, Uttarashadha, Shravana, Dhanishta or Shatabhisha, it is *vinasha yoga* or "combination of destruction".

Additionally, if a person is born on *Pratipad tithi* and Tuesday, on any of the days when *siddha yoga* is *not* created, it produces a *tithi dosha* for the person. The personality of such a person will be overly dominated by fire element. If such a person is additionally born on any of the fiery nakshatras (Bharani, Krittika, Pushya, Magha, Purva Phalguni, Vishakha) this *dosha* will be more severe and such a person will need to consciously work on balancing his/her fire element - both in physical body and on psychological level. Such a person can be very short-tempered, impatient and impulsive.

YOGAS FORMED WITH PRATIPAD TITHI

	1	2	3	4	5	6	7
1	amrita		**siddha**	samvartaka		**siddha**	
2	amrita			samvartaka		**siddha**	
3	amrita			samvartaka		siddha	
4	amrita			samvartaka		siddha	
5	amrita		**siddha**	samvartaka		siddha	
6	amrita		vinasha	samvartaka		**siddha**	
7	amrita		vinasha	samvartaka		**siddha**	
8	**amrita / siddha**			samvartaka		siddha	
9	amrita			samvartaka		siddha	
10	amrita			samvartaka		siddha	
11	amrita			samvartaka		siddha	
12	**amrita / siddha**		**siddha**	samvartaka		**siddha / suta**	
13	**amrita / siddha**			samvartaka		**siddha**	
14	amrita		**siddha**	samvartaka		siddha	
15	amrita			samvartaka		**siddha / suta**	
16	amrita			samvartaka		siddha	
17	amrita		**siddha**	samvartaka		siddha	
18	amrita		vinasha	samvartaka		siddha	
19	**amrita / siddha**		**siddha**	samvartaka		**siddha**	
20	amrita		vinasha	samvartaka		siddha	
21	**amrita / siddha /** shunya	shunya	shunya / vinasha	shunya / samvartaka	shunya	**siddha /** shunya	shunya
22	**amrita / siddha**		vinasha	samvartaka		siddha	
23	amrita		siddha / vinasha	samvartaka		siddha	
24	amrita		vinasha	samvartaka		**siddha / suta**	
25	amrita		**siddha**	samvartaka		siddha	
26	**amrita / siddha**			samvartaka		siddha	
27	amrita			samvartaka		siddha	

Kameshwari Devi always resonates well with nakshatras Ashwini, Bharani, Margashirsha, Uttara Phalguni, Hasta, Citra, Swati, Anuradha and Mula. It produces mixed results with nakshatras Ardra, Punarvasu, Purvashadha, Uttarashadha, Shravana, Dhanishta and Shatabhisha, and it has usually bad resonance with Jyeshtha – the most intense nakshatra of Mercury. This indicates that *Pratipad tithi* tends to resonate better with nakshatras of fire and air element, while it doesn't resonate so well with nakshatras of earth and water.

In Vedic month called Pushya (in the end of which Full Moon falls in Pushya nakshatra) *Pratipad tithi* is considered *shunya* and is avoided for any auspicious activities. In Pushya month *Pratipad tithi* often occurs in Uttarashadha nakshatra (in *Shukla paksha*), which is considered *shunya* for *Pratipad tithi*, and Ardra or Punarvasu nakshatra (in *Krishna paksha*), which can additionally intensify some of the negative qualities of this lunar day.

Important *rashis* for *Pratipad tithi* natives

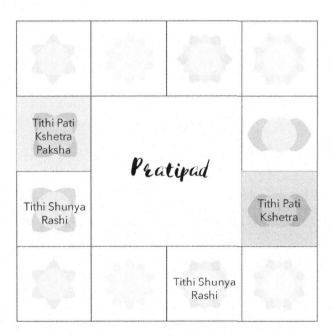

Each *tithi* has a special connection with a number of *rashis*. Understanding those connections can help us not only in understanding our own birth chart on a much deeper level, but in better understanding of the nature of the *tithi* itself.

Two *rashis*, which are of greatest importance for all *Pratipad tithi* natives are Leo and Aquarius. Leo is the *mulatrikona* sign of planetary lord of this lunar day (Sun, *tithi pati kshetra*), while Aquarius is the sign opposite to it (*tithi pati kshetra paksha*), which is the sign revealing, where are we heading in life. It reveals highly sociable nature of all *Pratipad tithi* natives. Social interaction is very important for all people born on the first lunar day in both *pakshas* – with the only difference that *Shukla paksha* natives will be naturally more extravert, talkative and won't mind seeking social interactions in a big groups of people, while *Krishna paksha* natives will be much more introvert and will enjoy their social interactions in more private settings. For all *Pratipad tithi* natives, however, good social interactions are very important and they feel very lonely whenever they need to live in too isolated places. Additionally, sign of Leo being their *tithi pati kshetra*, reveals their deeply creative nature.

Sign of Aquarius, becoming *tithi pati kshetra paksha* for *Pratipad* natives also reveals the biggest challenge in their life: controlling their own desires. In Vedic Astrology we call Aquarius *kumbha rashi*, "sign of the pot", as it represents our inner pot or cosmic receptacle, into which we collect our blessings – similarly like the pot filled with nectar in the hand of Goddess Kameshwari. For some people this pot will be always half empty, while for others it will be always half full. With *Pratipad tithi* the first scenario is usually more common – which is why they need to consciously work on being more grateful for everything they receive in life. The less grateful they will feel in life, the less willing to share they will become, which will stop a natural flow of "nectar" or "sweetness" in their lives and eventually will lead to dissatisfaction.

Signs Leo and Aquarius have also a deeper spiritual meaning for *Pratipad tithi* natives, connected to the movement of energy through the chakras on those lunar days – and reflected in the chakras of the zodiac connected to those *rashis*. In *Shukla paksha* the flow of energy will be more intense in Aquarius (which is another reason why *Shukla paksha* natives are generally more sociable and extravert), while in *Krishna Pratipad* it will be more intense in the sign of Leo (which blesses *Krishna Pratipad* natives with more creativity). As *tithi pati kshetra* and *tithi pati kshetra paksha* are in the case of first lunar day the same as the signs of natural flow of energy in the zodiacal chakras on those days, it also blesses *Pratipad tithi* natives with natural confidence and straightforwardness (unless the Moon or Sun are afflicted).

Tithi shunya rashis or the signs, which are made "fruitless" by *Pratipad tithi*, are Libra (along with its lord, Venus) and Capricorn (along with its lord, Saturn). Interestingly, Libra is the sign of debilitation of the Sun, while Capricorn is the sign, in which Sun is also naturally quite weak. This is why both of these signs are naturally quite vulnerable for all people born on *Pratipad tithi*.

Unless these signs are occupied by Rahu or Ketu, or unless its lords (Venus or Saturn) are placed in 3rd, 6th, 8th or 12th house from ascendant or Moon, or are retrograde, or in conjuction with malefic planet, or, lastly, in nakshatras of Rahu or Ketu, these two signs and houses ruled by those planets won't bring good results for the native. In such a case these signs must be strengthened (by strengthening their lords) to bring good results. *Shunya* planets do produce good results, however, when they transit 3rd, 6th, 8th or 12th house from from ascendant or Moon.

Sadhana for Goddess Kameshwari

Goddess Kameshwari is pleased with red flowers, the light of oil lamps, honey and *kumkum* (red powder). To connect with Her on a deeper level, you can either do a meditation of sitting on Her lap, as given by my Gurudev (described in Chapter 24), or colour Her *yantra* and meditate on it, facing East. For your *sadhana* you can use one of the two mantras below or one of the affirmations. There are couple of more advanced mantras for worship of Goddess Kameshwari in *Tantraraja*, but they are not supposed to be recited without a guidance of a Guru.

Also, as Goddess Kameshwari is connected to *mulagni*, the fire in our *muladhara chakra*, as well as with the Sun, you can also meditate on the Sun in your *muladhara chakra* to connect with Her on a deeper level. Just imagine Sun dwelling in your *muladhara chakra*. It is deeply grounding and purifying for the root *chakra*, as well as calms down the mind and its desires, while energising the body at the same time.

Ultimately, as Goddess Kameshwari, in Her highest form represents the Divine Love, you can also meditate on the Sun dwelling in your heart chakra or the *yantra* of Goddess Kameshwari shining in your heart chakra.

Now, if you think about these two meditations from the perspective of Vedic astrology, they are actually really interesting. In Vedic astrology Sun is associated with *ajna chakra* or third eye chakra (as explained by Sri Yukteshwar – this topic was covered in greater detail in my previous book, *Discovering Youniverse*). *Muladhara chakra* is, on the other hand, governed by Saturn (the ruler of one of the *shunya rashis* of *Pratipad*, Capricorn), Sun's arch-enemy, while heart chakra is governed by Venus, another enemy of the Sun and the ruler of another *shunya rashi* of *Pratipad*, Libra) - which is the sign of Sun's debilitation. Yet, even in the prayer *Aditya Hridayam*, which is considered to be one of the most powerful remedies for the Sun, we are supposed to meditate on the Sun in the heart while chanting it. Perhaps by bringing the light of the Sun down from its "throne" in *ajna chakra* into our heart chakra or root chakra, we purify our consciousness from the ego and pride, so its light can truly enlighten us and get additionally filtered by the prism of Love. There are many such deep secrets hidden behind the exaltation and debilitation place of any planet.

Also, according to *Agni Purana* first lunar days of months *Krittika* (November-December), *Ashwayuja* (October-November) and *Caitra* (April-May) are also sacred to Lord Brahma and chanting Gayatri mantra on any of those days is said to fulfill all our wishes. *Agni Purana* also advices the worship of fire element (the element predominant on this lunar day) during the night of first lunar day of month *Margashirsha* (December-January) with the mantra: *oṁ agnaye namaḥ*. It is advised in *Agni Purana* to fast one day (fifteenth lunar day) before proceeding to any of those *sadhanas*.

Mantras:

oṁ aīṁ hrīṁ śrīṁ aṁ kameśvaryai namaḥ
oṁ aīṁ hrīṁ śrīṁ aṁ amṛtayai namaḥ

Affirmations:

I follow the desire of my Soul.
I allow my true wishes to emerge.
I allow myself to be compassionate.

Questions for self-analysis

Every lunar day is an opportunity to learn something new about ourselves. Nitya Devis and their wisdom can become our guides on this sacred journey. Questions below can help you in recognising certain "shadow" tendencies in yourself, which may arise on *Pratipad tithi*. If you were born on this lunar day, these questions might be of big importance for you in life and allow you to face your weaknesses.

- What are my true desires?
- How can I fulfill them?
- Do I overburden others with my desires and wishes?
- Do I expect too much from myself or others?
- Do I act too impulsively?
- Am I too impatient?
- Do I hear the needs of other people?
- Do I respect the feelings of others?
- Am I too possesive or controlling?
- Do I behave, sometimes, as if I am the center of the world?
- Do I seek too much attention?
- Do I reflect upon my words before uttering them?
- Am I overly concerned with my own comfort?
- Do I spend too much money on fulfillment of my desires?
- How can I find more satisfaction and more joy in my life, without seeking it constantly in something outside of myself?
- How can I dwell more in the present moment and less in the future?
- How can I take more responsibility for my happiness, right here, right now?

Yantra of Goddess Kameshwari

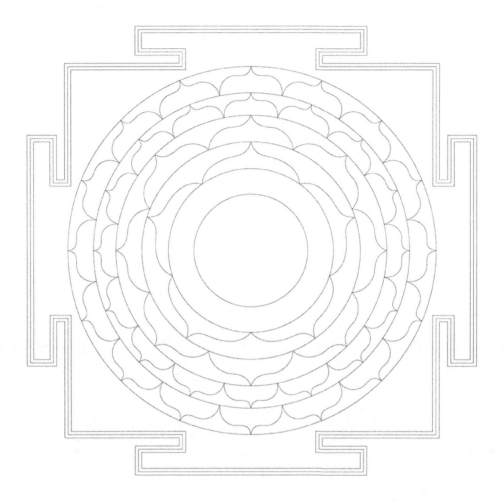

CHAPTER 9

BHAGAMALINI – GARLANDED WITH LUCK
DVITIYA – SECOND LUNAR DAY

bhānu-mandala-madhyasthā bhairavī bhaga-mālinī
padmāsanā bhagavatī padma-nābha-sahōdarī

"Dwelling in the center of the mandala of the Sun, Goddess Bhairavi, Bhagamalini, garlanded with luck, sits in the lotus position, sister of Vishnu."

- Lalita Sahasranama

Kala	Element	Planet	Guna	Yogini	Vowel
manada (pride)	earth	Moon	rajas	North	ā

Stage of consciousness	Divine quality	Deity (Muhurta Cintamani)	Deity (Varahamihira)	Nakshatra connection	Form of Shiva
dreaming (waking)	dhairya (patience)	Brahma	Hari	Ashwini Bharani Krittika	Kalyana

Shukla Paksha

Krishna Paksha

Nadi: ida
Chakra: muladhara
Interval: minor second
Deity (Narada Purana): Agni
House from the Sun: 1 or 2

Nadi: pingala
Chakra: ajna
Interval: major/minor seventh
Deity (Narada Purana): Yama
House from the Sun: 7 or 8

Bhagamalini means "garlanded with luck", "garlanded with fame" or "garlanded with the sun". She brings auspiciousness and victory. As during *Pratipad tithi* Goddess Kameshwari along with the Sun gives us the light to recognise our desires and the truth about ourselves, as well as awakens a creative spark inside of us, so on *Dvitiya tithi*, second lunar day, Goddess Bhagamalini (along with the Moon) makes this spark grow, spread and shine. She becomes more grounded.

Manada or pride is the mood of the Goddess on second lunar day. She becomes more confident in Herself, as this lunar day is now governed by earth element and *guna* of *rajas*. Second lunar day in *Shukla paksha* is also known as *Chandra darshan*, as this is the very first day after the New Moon, when we can actually see it. On *Shukla Pratipad* Moon is usually still to close to the Sun to be visible on te sky – but on *Shukla Dvitiya* we will always see its light for the first time after it disappeared.

As Goddess Kameshwari gives us inspiration on the first lunar day, so Goddess Bhagamalini allows this inspiration to fully blossom and spread its sweet fragrance in all directions. This is why, Vishwadevas, the deities of the directions, Vayu, the god of wind and Brahma, the creator, among others, are the presiding deities of *Dvitiya tithi* with Her. They help to carry the message of the Supreme Goddess in all directions, and thus spread Her fame and Her creativity into the world. Goddess

Bhagamalini gives us luck and helps us to spread our message or inspiration into the world, so it can benefit not only us, but also others. That is why the quality of this lunar day is *mangala*, bringing auspiciousness.

In some tantric scriptures Goddess Bhagamalini is considered a manifestation of Saraswati, *shakti* of Brahma, Goddess of sacred speech, art, learning and intuitive wisdom. Sometimes Her name, Bhagamalini, is translated as "the omniscient one". Even the name of the *yogini* associated with Her is Buddhya-karshini ("the one attracting all intellect") and the syllable of Sri Vidya mantra connected to Her is *e*, *bij* mantra of illusion. Her element is earth. Therefore She helps our inspiration, received from Goddess Kameshwari and Her creative spark, to assume its form, stability and identity in the world. She gives us the power to use our intellect wisely. This is why *Dvitiya* natives are naturally very curious and can often ask many questions. But as the Moon itself, *karaka* of the mind, is co-ruler of this lunar day, they also need to learn how to control the hunger of their mind and intellect and to seek their answers rather in meditation, in the depth of one's own heart.

Some of Her names are: Sarva-vashankari ("all-attracting one"), Bhagini ("auspicious one"), Bhaga-yoni ("having auspicious womb"), Bhaga-rupa ("embodiment of luck"), Sarva-bhaga-vashankari ("the one, who attracts all luck"). She represents the dreaming state of consciousness within waking state. Therefore, She helps our dreams to gain their substance and identity.

As Kameshwari the Goddess is in the fiery, passionate mood of expressing Her desires. As Bhagamalini, She cools down a bit, and proceeds further on Her journey of self-discovery with confidence and grounding, feeling the support of the earth element beneath Her feet. She yearns to spread the fragrance of Her inspiration to all directions of the world. Her desires are getting concretised. She gives us the power of creative self-expression and attracts recognition. Like the Moon, which is co-ruling this *tithi* with Her, She makes everything grow and flourish with Her creative powers. She attracts all prosperity and all abundance – not only on material level, but also on spiritual level. After all, Moon represents the crowd, as well. *Tantraraja* states that whoever worships Bhagamalini Devi, he receives the power to attract the whole world. Goddess Bhagamalini is most often approached for the power to attract others, strength to win over enemies, protection of pregnant women, safe delivery, fertility and preventing abortion or premature birth. If the Moon is afflicted in the chart of a woman born on this lunar day, some issues with fertility or pregnancy might be manifested – which is also a metaphor of issues with giving birth to our ideas in the material world, expressed on the body level.

Bhavanopanishad associates Goddess Bhagamalini with *ahamkara*, ego. Indeed, Her weakness is *manada* or pride. Victorious by nature, She doesn't accept defeat easily. Similarly, people born on *Dvitiya tithi* often have fear of being defeated, and their weakness is their pride. This quality is somehow similar to the victorious energy of Uttarashadha nakshatra, which is also ruled by Vishwadevas. Yet, a strong side of people born on this lunar day is their confidence. In *Shukla paksha* Goddess Bhagamalini blesses everybody with the confidence to express themselves, while in *Krishna paksha* Bhagamalini Devi blesses us with confidence and faith on our spiritual path. She also allows us to see the goodness in ourselves and focus more on our positive side, instead of constantly feeling guilty.

Matsya Purana gives an interesting story about Bhagamalini Devi. She was supposed to be one of the mind-born forms of Divine Mother, created for the purpose of drinking the blood of Andhakas. Andhakasura, "the demon of darkness", had a boon, that whenever a drop of his blood will fall on the ground, his replica will be born. Thus, when the Divine Mother was fighting with him, She was soon surrounded by many Andhakas. Goddess Bhagamalini was invoked then to drink all the blood and prevent Andhakasura from replicating himself further. Perhaps this is why in some tantric scriptures offering a special, herbal wine to Goddess Bhagamalini is advised, to commemorate Her victory over Andhakasura. It also represents a shadow side of Goddess Bhagamalini, "drinking the blood of Her enemies", or becoming a bit heartless on Her journey towards victory. Sometimes addictions can also emerge from *Dvitiya tithi*.

Interestingly, it is said that Andhakasura or "the demon of darkness" was born, when Parvati once playfully covered the eyes of Shiva with her own hands. We can read about it in *Shiva Purana*. It is said that in that moment whole universe was covered in darkness. The sweat that oozed out of Parvati's hands due to touching the body of the Lord fell to the ground and gave birth to a blind boy with characteristics of a demon. It is quite interesting, that Goddess Bhagamalini is considered the one, who actually contributed to defeating this "demon of darkness", as exactly on *Shukla Dvitiya* our night sky, similarly, is for the first time illumined with the cooling rays of the Moon after *Amavasya*. Similarly, Goddess Bhagamalini has the power to dispel the darkness of ignorance and remove it from our mind.

Story from Bhavishya Purana

In *Bhavishya Purana* there is one more story, which is strongly connected to *Dvitiya tithi*: story about Chyavan *rishi* and his wife.

Chyavan *rishi* was quite old. He asked a king to give his daughter to him and the the princess was married off to Chyavan *rishi*. She was deeply devoted to him. When he would sit in his *sadhana* and meditation, she would look after all his needs.

Once, when Chyavan *rishi* was sitting in deep meditation, immersed in *samadhi*, she went to take a bath in a river. Ashwini kumars, the ever-young twin sons of Surya dev (Sun-god) saw her there and wanted her to marry either of them. She refused and told them that she is already married to Chyavan *rishi* – but she said, if they are happy with her, she would like to ask them for granting a boon of youth to her husband. They agreed to give her husband a form like their own, but on one condition: after his body would be transformed, she would have to find her real husband among three of them. Whomsoever she would locate would need to become her husband. She said that she cannot take such a decision without a consent of her husband. Ashwini kumars agreed to it. She went to her husband and discussed the matter with him. Chyavan *rishi* agreed to it, confident in his wife's devotion.

And so, Ashwini kumars took her husband along with them and went inside the river. When they came out, all three of them were glowing and had exactly the same youthful form. It became very difficult for the princess to recognise, who was her real husband. Then she realized that two of these three men standing in front of her were not blinking their eyes and were standing a little bit above the ground, while the third, being a human, was blinking his eyes and standing firmly on the ground. Thus she was able to locate her husband to his contentment.

Chyavan *rishi* felt indebted to Ashwini kumars and asked them what good can he do in return for their favour. They requested him to make them part takers of fire sacrifice. To this request he agreed and asked the king to arrange a *yajna* (fire ceremony) for them. During the ceremony Chyavan *rishi* invited all the divine beings along with Indra, king of heavens, to come to take their part in *yajna* offerings. When Indra saw Ashwini kumars being given a part of the offerings, he became furious and raised his *vajra* weapon to strike and spoil the *yajna*. At that moment Chyavan *rishi* due to the power of his *sadhana* froze Indra in that very hand-raised position. Then, after the discussion with other sages, a compromise was made. Indra was restored to his early form and Ashwini kumars were allowed to take part of *yajna* offerings in the future. And since the entire incident happened on *Dvitiya tithi*, this lunar day also became sacred for Ashwini kumars.

As in every other Vedic story, there is a secret meaning hidden behind this one, as well. One of the shadow sides of *Dvitiya tithi* (and all other lunar days governed by earth element) is too big attachment to outer appearance, which is clearly visible in this story. And, as the wife of Chyavan rishi needed to discern between the truth and the illusion, so the people born on *Dvitiya tithi* often need to learn how to make such discernment in their lives – and they often need to depend more on their own Divine intelligence rather than listen to others. As *Dvitiya* is one of the two lunar days governed by Moon, the danger to mix our own imagination and expectations with the actual voice of our intuition, can be sometimes very high. And, as Ashwini kumars are also the presiding deities of this lunar day, it also reflects its youthful, invigorating and restoring nature.

Meditation with Goddess Bhagamalini

Hue: beautiful and red
Number of heads: 1
Number of eyes: 3
Number of hands: 6
Right hands: pink lotus flower, *ankusha*, 5 flowery arrows
Left hands: blue lotus flower, *pasha*, sugarcane bow
Garments: green

Tantraraja describes Goddess Bhagamalini as beautifully red and dressed in green garments. Green color is associated with North direction, as well as the intellectual energy of Mercury and fertile energy of the Moon. All plants are green in nature, due to the presence of chlorophile, which allows them to do the process of photosyntesis: transforming the sunlight into vital energy. Similar is the energy of Bhagamalini Devi – She allows us to absorb the life-giving and inspiring light of the Sun (symbolised by Kameshwari Devi) and to transform it into life force: to make things grow, to make things blossom.

Similarly like Kameshwari, Goddess Bhagamalini carries in four of Her hands *pasha* (noose), *ankusha* (goad), *ikshu danda* (sugarcane bow) and *pancha bana* (flowery arrows) – the attributes of highest Goddess, Lalita Tripurasundari, which are described along with their meanings in previous chapter. Additionally, in right upper hand She carries a pink lotus flower, while in left upper hand She carries a blue lotus flower.

The difference between pink lotus and blue lotus is not just in their color – pink lotus blossoms during the day, while blue lotus blossoms during the night. Similarly, the all-growing energy of Bhagamalini Devi can help us to blossom in material world, as well as on our spiritual path. With these two lotus flowers the Goddess also reminds us that for everybody in this world there is a right time to blossom. There is a time for the Sun to rise and there is a time for the Sun to set. There is a time for the Moon to rise and there is a time for the Moon to set. For everything and everybody in nature there is a time to rise and time to set – and there is a place in Nature for both rising and setting, success and failure. Goddess Bhagamalini is very much connected to this duality present in nature and all the natural changes. She teaches us to be patient instead of trying to speed up the Nature Herself. For the flower to blossom the right time is needed. If we try to go against Nature's rhythm, and open the flower up with our own hands, before its destined time, we will end up destroying it. This is why the quality of Bhagavan Krishna, which is associated with Bhagamalini Devi is *dhairya*: patience.

Dakshinamurti Samhita describes Goddess Bhagamalini as "garlanded with forest" – or seated in the middle of flowering forest. Nature's creative powers of making everything grow just due to light and water are similar to the vital powers of Goddess Bhagamalini, adorned with green clothes – the One, who makes everything grow and prosper. She is the one, who makes all ideas, desires and inspirations really *alive* and gives them birth into the material world. Through Her womb all is born. If you ever wish to experience the beauty of the evergreen energy of Goddess Bhagamalini, go on a silent walk in the forest on *Dvitiya tithi* and simply observe Her acting through Nature. Bhagamalini Devi also reminds us, that there is no higher wealth on this planet than natural resources and inspires us to respect Mother Nature in any form She takes.

Goddess Bhagamalini is associated with flowering *yoni* or womb, due to a very special shape of Her *yantra*, which has five flower petals within a *yoni* or down-facing triangle. It represents Her creative powers and ability to "bring birth" to many different ideas and desires; to make them manifest in the world.

She also inspires us to get confidence in making our decisions. Interestingly, the very day, when I was writing this chapter, on *Shukla Dvitiya*, 19 November 2017, my Gurudev, Paramahamsa Vishwananda, has written this profound message, which is so much in tune with what Bhagamalini Devi teaches us:

"When we have a larger goal in life, then everything becomes a stepping stone to us for this achievement. Both Hell and Heaven work for us, once we are clear what we long for and when this longing starts burning inside our hearts. Then the whole cosmos will stand for us to support us.

Seeking the Lord fans and kindles this small flame of longing. One is terrified, too, and sees that one's inner structure is shaking, but what's the point of standing on the crossroads? You have to take a decision to go and pass the point of no return. You will have to do it one day anyway, so why delay?"

Kameshwari Devi awakens the desire within us, but it is Bhagamalini Devi that makes it grow and blossom, and allows it to get fully manifested. Yet, for this to happen, we need to have confidence in our path, and clarity about what our soul truly desires. After the first friction of desire separating itself from perfect union, unison of Shiva and Shakti during New Moon, or the perfect octave of Full Moon, Goddess Bhagamalini is slowly bringing us towards more stability and calmer music intervals. Yet, it is still minor second or *rishabha* (ruled by Mars) in *Shukla paksha*, and major seventh or *nishadha* (ruled by Venus) in *Krishna paksha*. It inspires us to leave these inharmonious intervals, and move further, with full confidence and faith, consciously manifesting our truth, creativity and inspiration into the world; shining our own light without any shame, but not falling a prey to our pride.

Like Marianne Williamson (*Dvitiya* native, of course) has beautiful written:

"Our deepest fear is not that we are inadequate. Our deepest fear is that we are powerful beyond measure. It is our light, not our darkness that most frightens us. We ask ourselves, Who am I to be brilliant, gorgeous, talented, fabulous? Actually, who are you not to be? You are a child of God. Your playing small does not serve the world. There is nothing enlightened about shrinking so that other people won't feel insecure around you. We are all meant to shine, as children do. We were born to make manifest the glory of God that is within us. It's not just in some of us; it's in everyone. And as we let our own light shine, we unconsciously give other people permission to do the same. As we are liberated from our own fear, our presence automatically liberates others."

Numerology: 2

Dvitiya tithi is the second lunar day and so it is connected to number 2. As number 1 stands for the Self, so number 2 stands for duality. There are two eyes, two ears, two nostrils, two hands and two legs, through which we perceive the world and react with it. In Vedic tradition Ashwini kumars, the Divine twins, stand for all that is naturally dual. For the Divine play to manifest, the duality is needed. You and me, *yan* and *ying*, masculine and feminine, Sun and Moon, day and night, inhale and exhale, or two different lotus flowers in Devi Bhagamalini's hands. *Shukla paksha* and *Krishna paksha*. Waxing Moon and waning Moon.

Third eye chakra in our energy body has also two petals, which symbolises two opposite energy channels, *ida* and *pingala*, connecting there and merging into one, so the higher, unified state of consciousness may awaken and so we may perceive one eternal Light acting behind the opposites of the external world.

Agni Purana associates number 2 with two *pakshas* or two wings of a bird, which need to act in balance in order to take us to higher realms. But when these "two wings", symbolising the opposites in our mind, are not moving in harmony, then not we are not be capable to rise and grow, as our progress and development is stopped by our own inner conflicts. *Dvitiya* natives can often have some inner conflicts and their mind may sometimes be stuck in duality, thorn between the extremes, symbolised by Moon itself. As long as they will try to resolve these inner issues from the level of the mind, they will stay confused – but when they decide to look at everything with equal eyes, as Lord Krishna says in *Bhagavad Gita*, by stilling their mind in meditation, this is when they will regain their clarity, focus, confidence and peace. This is why second chapter of *Bhagavad Gita*, in which Sri Krishna is encouraging Arjuna to see beyond what physical eyes can perceive, beyon the duality of the world, is very therapeuthic for *Dvitiya* natives. It is there, in second chapter of the *Gita*, that Sri Krishna says:

"The nonpermanent appearance of happiness and distress, and their disappearance in due course, are like the appearance and disappearance of winter and summer seasons. They arise from sense perception and one must learn to tolerate them without being disturbed. The person who is not disturbed by happiness and distress and is steady in both is certainly eligible for liberation."

Second house in Vedic astrology also stands for our assets, values and beliefs that we follow, which is reflected in the qualities of Goddess Bhagamalini. This is why *Dvitiya* natives can be also often a bit stubborn or too radical in their beliefs, too, as they have this tendency to easily run to extremes and classify things as "good" and "bad", "black" and "white".

Even the form of Shiva connected to *Dvitiya tithi* is Kalyana or Vivaha. In this form Lord Shiva is getting married to His natural opposite, Shakti, and He is completed by Her. This is a symbol of balancing the opposites within ourselves and regaining our integrity. There are also Vishnu, Lakshmi and Brahma accompanying the holy couple in this form, which reveals a highly auspicious nature of this lunar day, which naturally attracts good luck.

Yogini in *Kalachakra*: North

On *Dvitiya tithi* the danger comes from the North. It is said that we should avoid travelling into that direction during the second lunar day in any of the two *pakshas*. It also reveals the biggest weakness, which may awaken in us during *Dvitiya tithi*: pride and attachement to worldly splendour. North direction is connected with the Moon in *Kalachakra*, and being so, it makes everything grow and prosper. It also gives, however, attachment to our intellectual achievements, wealth and fame, as it is the direction of Kubera, god of wealth, who is sometimes said to use other humans as his vehicle. Goddess Bhagamalini warns us on this day: "Do not go into that direction. Aim for something higher than self-gratification - and I will provide you all you need on your path. Be patient, and I will make you blossom, like I make all the flowers bloom in their right time. Choose your goals wisely."

North direction is very much connected with our ability to make right decisions and choose right goals in life. After all, it is said to be the direction of *Polaris*, or *Dhruva* star, beyond which Vaikuntha, or the supreme abode of Narayana (and supreme goal of every soul) is placed.

Shaktis of Goddess Bhagamalini

Different *shaktis* or powers of Goddess Bhagamalini dwell in the different places of Her *yantra*. *Tantraraja* doesn't give however a very clear description as to which *shakti* is dwelling in which exact place of Her *yantra*. Their names are: Madana ("desire"), Mohini ("enchanter"), Lola ("playing"), Jambhini ("citron tree"), Udyama ("elevating one" or "the one making effort"), Shubha ("auspicious one"), Hladini ("giving pleasure"), Dravini ("melted one" or "ecstatic one"), Priti ("love"), Rati ("passion"), Rakta ("blood-red"), Manorama ("enchanting the mind"), Sarvonmada ("maddening all"), Sarva-sukha ("giving happiness to all"), Ananga ("bodiless one" – the name of the Cupid), Amitodyama ("rising beyond measure or boundaries"), Analpa ("having many forms"), Vyakta-vibhava ("having confident power"), Vividhavigraha ("having several forms"), Kshobha-vigraha ("having agitating form").

Yantra of Goddess Bhagamalini, indeed, resembles a flowering *yoni*. Eight petals enclosing an empty circle (which most probably symbolise eight directions of the world) dwell in the downward facing triangle, which is the *yoni* or the womb of the yantra. This *yoni* itself is enclosed by 5 petals (most probably representing five causes of desire or five senses). There is, indeed, something deeply ecstatic in this *yantra* and just looking at it has the power to awaken the creative powers within us, as well as to give us the confidence to follow our heart with trust.

Swara of Goddess Bhagamalini

Ā, the second *swara* or vowel of Sanskrit alphabet, is associated with Goddess Bhagamalini. Its quality or *kala* is to hide things. It creates a feeling of nearness: being near to something or coming nearer to something. Similarly like short *a* stands for separation and rejection, so long *ā* stays for agreeing to something and coming closer to something. That is also the major difference between Kameshwari Devi and Bhagamalini Devi. Kameshwari Devi feels: "I am missing something. I am incomplete." Bhagamalini Devi says: "I am moving closer to my fulfillment. Soon I am going to be complete." The basic assumption and the energy is the same, but the focus is different. Kameshwari Devi focuses more on what She doesn't have yet, while Bhagamalini Devi focuses on what She is going to achieve soon. The difference is in the way, how the mind, influenced by these two different goddesses, perceives its goal. Bhagamalini Devi, with Her confidence, goes one step further than Goddess Kameshwari.

Chanting *swara ā* is also said to enhance our power of speech, as confirmed by *Agni Purana*. According to *Agni Purana* vowel *ā* also represents our ancestors (*Pitris*), as well as our boundaries. It reminds us to stay humble regardless of our achievements.

Nakshatras connected to Goddess Bhagamalini

Ashwini nakshatra is connected to *swara* of Goddess Bhagamalini, while Her six arms stand for two last *padas* of Bharani nakshatra and all four *padas* of Krittika nakshatra.

Ashwini, as one of the nakshatras connected with *Dvitiya tithi* or second lunar day, reveals that the nature of this day is still too unstable to make any important decisions – even though it is already much more grounded than impulsive *Pratipad*. It is still the energy, which yearns to fulfill its desires, which is very youthful, impulsive, impatient and even a little bit naive by its nature - but now it also yearns to give birth to them in material world. No wonder that two last *padas* of Bharani nakshatra, Vedic constellation, which has *yoni* as its symbol, are also connected to

Dvitiya tithi and Goddess Bhagamalini. As they would fall in Libra and Scorpio in Navamsha (D9 divisional chart), they reveal more sensual and passionate side of Bharani. Even the word *bhaga* can be translated as the womb.

All four *padas* of Krittika are also connected to this lunar day, which is why Bhagamalini Devi is so confident and ready to bless everybody with luck and victory. After all, Moon gets exalted in Krittika nakshatra, and it is the asterism of the confident Sun. Yet, similarly like Goddess Bhagamalini can also make us too proud or afraid of defeat, so Krittika nakshatra shares similar qualities. Krittika nakshatra and Goddess Bhagamalini can both also bless a person with talent for languages or beautiful manner of writing or speaking.

There are also two nakshatras, in which *guna* of *rajas* combines with earth element, similarly like on *Dvitiya tithi*: Rohini and Shravana, two nakshatras of the Moon, which are not only very sensitive and empathic, but also have a capacity to easily attract others. While Rohini is the nakshatra, which "grows" everything, according to its power, *rohana shakti*, so Shravana has the power to connect everything and to reach with any idea to a much bigger audience. Similarly *Dvitiya tithi* is a true lunar day of our influence in the world – and being the *tithi* governed by Moon itself, it also makes its native very sensitive.

Tithi, *vara* and nakshatra resonance

Goddess Bhagamalini has an abundance of different *yogas* formed with Her lunar day. Due to that She doesn't have any "black" or "white" relationship with any days of the weeks or nakshatras. The quality of duality is greatly visible in all the different relations She forms with other cycles of time.

Generally, the energy of Goddess Bhagamalini resonates the best with Monday, the day ruled by the Moon, who is also the co-ruler of *Dvitiya tithi*. It is all the more powerful, if the Moon dwells on Monday in one of the following nakshatras: Rohini, Margashirsha, Punarvasu, Shravana, Dhanishta, Shatabhisha or Purva Bhadrapada. *Dvitiya tithi*, which falls on Monday, becomes inauspicious only, when the Moon is dwelling in Citra nakshatra, as it forms then *visha yoga* or "poisonous combination".

Another *visha yoga* is said to be created whenever *Dvitiya tithi* falls on Wednesday - yet, at the same time it is also a *siddha yoga* or "combination of accomplishments". Perhaps it reveals, that whenever *Dvitiya tithi* occurs on Wednesday, we may have a tendency to be so much focused on our goals, success and victory, that we might use impure or "poisonous" means for achieving them. If *Dvitiya tithi* falls on Wednesday and Moon dwells in one of the following nakshatras: Rohini, Margashirsha, Ardra, Uttara Phalguni, Anuradha or Uttarashadha, it additionally produces more powerful *siddha yoga*. If, however, Moon would dwell on Wednesday in Ashwini, Bharani, Pushya, Ashlesha, Magha, Mula, Dhanishta or Purva Bhadrapada, it creates *vinasha yoga*.

On *Dvitiya tithi* three different *vinasha yogas* (or "destructive combinations") may occur:

- *Dvitiya tithi* + Tuesday + Ardra, Punarvasu, Jyeshta, Purvashadha, Uttarashadha, Shravana, Dhanishta or Shatabhisha
- *Dvitiya tithi* + Wednesday + Ashwini, Bharani, Pushya, Ashlesha, Magha, Mula, Dhanishta or Purva Bhadrapada
- *Dvitiya tithi* + Friday + Rohini, Punarvasu, Magha, Vishakha, Anuradha, Jyeshta, Shravana or Dhanishta

There are also four different *siddha yogas*, which may occur on *Dvitiya tithi*:

- *Dvitiya tithi* + Monday + Rohini, Margashirsha, Punarvasu, Citra, Shravana, Dhanishta, Shatabhisha, Purva Bhadrapada
- *Dvitiya tithi* + Wednesday + Rohini, Margashirsha, Ardra, Uttara Phalguni, Anuradha or Uttarashadha
- *Dvitiya tithi* + Friday + Ashwini, Bharani, Ardra, Punarvasu, Uttara Phalguni, Citra, Svati, Purvashadha or Revati
- *Dvitiya tithi* + Saturday + Rohini, Swati, Vishakha, Anuradha, Dhanishta or Shatabhisha

In *Agni Purana* it is also stated that whenever *Dvitiya tithi* happens on Tuesday along with Moon dwelling in Magha nakshatra, it will bring gains. Anuradha nakshatra, on the other hand, becomes *shunya* or "fruitless" on *Dvitiya tithi* – yet, if there is another positive *yoga* overriding it, it can still bring good results.

Being so, Bhagamalini Devi and *Dvitiya tithi* always resonate well with Margashirsha, Uttara Phalguni, Svati and Revati nakshatras, which are mostly the nakshatras of air element (excerpt Revati). It doesn't resonate well with Pushya, Ashlesha, Jyeshtha and Mula nakshatras, while it brings different results with Ashwini, Bharani, Rohini, Ardra, Punarvasu, Magha, Citra, Vishakha, Anuradha, Purvashadha, Uttarashadha, Shravana, Dhanishta, Shatabhisha and Purva Bhadrapada nakshatras.

In *Agni Purana* it is also said that sowing seeds on *Dvitiya tithi* and Krittika, Rohini, Uttara Phalguni, Hasta, Anuradha, Jyeshtha or Revati nakshatra is going to attract great prosperity.

On some *Dvitiya tithis* there occurs also an interesting phenomenon known as *dwipushkar* or *tripushkar yoga*. Whenever *dwipushkar yoga* occurs, it is said that all the activities performed on that day will repeat themselves two times in the future. Whenever *tripushkar yoga* occurs, repetition will happen three times. This phenomenon occurs only on *Bhadra tithis* or lunar days of the element of earth – which is why it is said, that we should be very mindful about our thoughts, words and actions on second, seventh and twelfth lunar day. These *yogas* can occur only on Sunday, Tuesday or Saturday.

YOGAS FORMED WITH *DVITIYA TITHI*

	1	2	3	4	5	6	7
1		amrita		vinasha		**siddha**	
2	**tripushkar**	amrita	**tripushkar**	vinasha		**siddha**	tripushkar
3		amrita		visha / siddha			
4		**siddha**		**siddha**		vinasha	siddha / suta
5	**dvipushkar**	**siddha**	**dvipushkar**	**siddha**			dvipushkar
6		amrita	vinasha	**siddha**		**siddha**	
7	**tripushkar**	**siddha**	vinasha / tripushkar	visha / siddha		siddha / vinasha	tripushkar
8		amrita		vinasha			
9		amrita		vinasha			
10		amrita	**gains**	vinasha		vinasha	
11	**tripushkar**	amrita	**tripushkar**	visha / siddha			tripushkar
12		amrita		**siddha**		siddha	
13		amrita		visha / siddha			
14	**dvipushkar**	visha	**dvipushkar**	visha / siddha		**siddha**	dvipushkar
15		amrita		visha / siddha		**siddha**	siddha / suta
16	**tripushkar**	amrita	**tripushkar**	visha / siddha		vinasha	siddha / tripushkar
17	shunya	amrita / shunya	shunya	**siddha** / shunya	shunya	vinasha / shunya	siddha / shunya
18		amrita	vinasha	visha / siddha		vinasha	
19		amrita		vinasha			
20	**tripushkar**	amrita	vinasha / tripushkar	visha / siddha		**siddha**	tripushkar
21		amrita	vinasha	**siddha**			
22		**siddha**	vinasha	visha / siddha		vinasha	
23	**dvipushkar**	**siddha**	vinasha / dvipushkar	vinasha		vinasha	siddha/suta /dvipushkar
24		**siddha**	vinasha	visha / siddha			siddha
25	**tripushkar**	**siddha**	**tripushkar**	vinasha			tripushkar
26		amrita		visha / siddha			
27		amrita		visha / siddha		**siddha**	

Whenever any of the *Bhadra tithis* (2, 7 or 12 lunar day) occur on Sunday, Tuesday or Saturday, and the Moon is dwelling in Margashirsha, Citra or Dhanishta nakshatra (the stars of Mars), *dwipushkar yoga* is occuring, as our energy to take action and make an impact in the world becomes magnified by this *vara*, *tithi* and nakshatra resonance. Whenever this combination happens, however, in the nakshatras of Venus (Bharani, Purva Phalguni or Purvashadha) or Jupiter (Punarvasu, Vishakha or Purva Bhadrapada), which are the natural magnifiers, *tripushkar yoga* will occur.

There is one more *yoga*, which is created on *Bhadra tithis* (*Dvitiya*, *Saptami* and *Dvadashi*), which is not auspicious. It is called *visha kanya yoga*. It is not included in the table above, as it doesn't affect the *muhurta* or the present moment so much – but it has a tremendous effect on the entire life of a person born on any of those days. *Visha kanya* literally means a "poisonous maiden" – yet, regardless of its name, this *yoga* affects both males and females, to the same extent. Only difference is that women, due to their naturally deeper emotional nature, will experience it on a way deeper level than men.

Whenever *visha kanya yoga* occurs in a person's natal chart it reveals that a person will need to deal with some sort of emotional poison in this lifetime. Such a person will either form too deep emotional attachments or... wil abuse other people's attachments and play with their emotions. The person may have a strong tendency to abuse others or... oneself. Sometimes the person will inflict the poison and pain on others, and sometimes one will inflict it on oneself. The final result of how this emotional poison will manifest will depend entirely on person's other planetary placements.

Visha kanya yoga is formed whenever a person is born on *Dvitiya*, *Saptami* or *Dvadashi tithi*, on Krittika, Ashlesha or Shatabhisha nakshatra and Sunday, Tuesday or Saturday. It is a very specific combination. People born on *Bhadra tithis*, which are governed by earth element, can be sometimes very superficial, when it comes to emotions – but they tend to be very attached to the pleasures of the outer world and external appearance of things. When Moon possesing those qualities conjoins Krittika nakshatra, governed by lustful fire-god (Agni), Ashlesha nakshatra, governed by poisonous, sensual and cunning serpents (*nagas*) or Shatabhisha nakshatra, governed by Varuna, god of overflowing cosmic waters and unstoppable passion, it is already a combination, which requires our attention – even if the weekday is different from those listed above. *Bhadra tithi* Moon conjoined with any of those three nakshatras greatly disturbs the emotional behaviour of the person and person's second chakra, which can lead to certain emotional poisons created in the mind of such a person and often to sexually abusive behaviour – both in men and women. Such a person might have very little respect when it comes to emotions of other people (or the opposite thing: no respect towards one's own self) and this is something they need to consciously work on – to control their inner "poisons" and not let them take over their entire psyche.

Additionally, when this combination happens on Sunday, Tuesday or Saturday, it is a strong indicator that other people are going to suffer due to such a person. It doesn't always mean, that the person will willingly inflict pain on others (although often it might be the case), but it can also mean that one will inflict so much pain to oneself, that it will be also very hard to bear for the person's family or partner. For people with *visha kanya yoga* in their natal chart it is of highest importance to control their mind and emotions with the help of spiritual knowledge and meditation. They need to ground their emotions more and work on transforming them on the level of heart chakra. Even such simple meditation like focusing on their heart chakra and visualising a light there (or the form of Goddess presiding their birth *tithi*) would be of great help for them, as it will make them naturally more mindful in all their actions, as well as will develop within them a quality of self-control.

Also, if a person is born on *Dvitiya tithi* and Wednesday, on any of the days when *siddha yoga* is *not* created, it produces *tithi dosha* for the person. The personality of such a person will be overly dominated by earth element. If such a person is additionally born on any of the earthly nakshatras (Rohini, Anuradha, Jyeshtha, Uttarashadha, Abhijit, Shravana or Dhanishta) this *dosha* will be more severe and such person will need to consciously work on balancing earth element, both in physical body and on a psychological level.

In Vedic month called Margashirsha (in the end of which Full Moon falls in Mrigashira nakshatra) *Dvitiya tithi* is considered *shunya* and is avoided for any auspicious activities. In Margashirsha month *Dvitiya tithi* often occurs in Mula nakshatra (in *Shukla paksha*) and Rohini or Mrigashira nakshatra (in *Krishna paksha*) - all three of them being extremely sensitive nakshatras and connected to the Goddess, which additionally exaggerate already sensitive nature of this lunar day.

Important *rashis* for *Dvitiya tithi* natives

Each *tithi* has a special connection with a number of *rashis*. Understanding those connection can help us not only in understanding our own birth chart on a much deeper level, but in better understanding of the nature of the *tithi* itself.

Two *rashis*, which are of great importance for all *Dvitiya tithi* natives are Taurus and Scorpio. Taurus is the *mulatrikona* sign of planetary lord of this lunar day (Moon, *tithi pati kshetra*), while Scorpio is the sign opposite to it (*tithi pati kshetra paksha*), which is the sign revealing, where are we heading in life. As *Dvitiya tithi* is strongly connected to all dualities in life, no wonder that the sign of its direction is fixed – but at the same time being one of the most transformative zodiac signs. *Dvitiya tithi* natives will experience many major transformations in their life. Any planets placed in Scorpio or in angles to Scorpio will furtherly reveal, what will be the nature of those transformations. This is why they will always, above all, seek more stability in life. It is not that easy to get them out of their comfort zone.

Additionally, in *Shukla paksha* Aquarius sign becomes more energised on *Dvitiya tithi* (which reveals more sociable nature of *Shukla Dvitiya* natives, who may sometimes have big friend circles), while in *Krishna paksha* Leo becomes more energised (which is why *Krishna Dvitiya* natives will be more introverted and self-centered).

Tithi Shunya Rashi		Tithi Pati Kshetra	
	Dvitiya		
Tithi Shunya Rashi	Tithi Pati Kshetra Paksha		

Tithi shunya rashis or the signs, which are made "fruitless" by *Dvitiya tithi*, are two dual *rashis*, Sagittarius and Pisces, along with their lord Jupiter. Both of these signs are naturally quite vulnerable for all people born on *Pratipad tithi*, reflecting the mythological conflict between Moon (the planetary lord of *Dvitiya tithi*) and Jupiter (lord of *shunya rashis* for this *tithi*). It is a silent indication for all *Dvitiya tithi* natives that they need to consciously work on being more patient in life, as well as they need to overcome being too focused on the outside and on outer appearance of things, as sometimes they may tend to be a bit shortsighted. It is of highest importance for *Dvitiya tithi* natives to enrich their life with reading the scriptures, studying spiritual knowledge and daily meditation, as their biggest challenge in this lifetime is to overcome their dualistic perception of things and see the Divine unity in everything. This is why it is also very much advised for all *Dvitiya tithi* natives to take a guidance of a self-realised Guru in this lifetime, as it will naturally strengthen their weakened *rashis* of Jupiter.

Unless these signs are occupied by Rahu or Ketu, or unless their planetary lord (Jupiter) is placed 3rd, 6th, 8th or 12th house from ascendant or Moon, or is retrograde, or in conjuction with malefic planet, or, lastly, in nakshatras of Rahu or

Ketu, these two signs and houses ruled by Jupiter won't bring good results for the native. In such a case these signs must be strengthened (by strengthening their lord) to bring good results. *Shunya* planets do produce good results, however, when they transit 3rd, 6th, 8th or 12th house from from ascendant or Moon.

Sadhana for Goddess Bhagamalini

Goddess Bhagamalini is pleased with lotus flowers or forest flowers. We can feel Her energy more by walking barefoot in nature. *Tantraraja* also describes a very ancient mode of Her worship with herbal wines, prepared by exact recipes provided in the scripture, which is a reminiscence of Her victory over Andhakas. To connect with Her on a deeper level, you can either do a meditation of sitting on Her lap, as given by my Gurudev (described in Chapter 24) or colour Her yantra and meditate on it, facing North. For your *sadhana* you can use one of the two mantras below or one of the affirmations. There are couple of more advanced mantras for worship of Goddess Bhagamalini in *Tantraraja*, but they are not supposed to be recited without a guidance of a Guru.

According to *Agni Purana* worshipping *Dvitiya tithi* Moon is the most powerful in *Krishna paksha* of month *Shravana* (August-September). It is said, that whoever worships the Moon and offers him a water oblation on that night, while meditating on the Moon as a younger brother of Lakshmi, (Goddess of Divine Love and wealth), will always enjoy a loving relationship with his wife/her husband.

Mantras:

oṁ aīṁ hrīṁ śrīṁ āṁ bhagamālinīyai namaḥ
oṁ aīṁ hrīṁ śrīṁ āṁ mānadayai namaḥ

Affirmations:

I allow myself to blossom.
I allow myself to shine.
I allow myself to be patient.
I allow myself to be grounded.
I allow myself to notice the goodness in me.
I allow myself to confidently move towards my goals.

Questions for self-analysis

Every lunar day is an opportunity to learn something new about ourselves. Nitya Devis and their wisdom can become our guides on this sacred journey. Questions below can help you in recognising certain "shadow" tendencies in yourself, which may arise on *Dvitiya tithi*. If you were born on this lunar day, these questions might be of big importance for you in life and allow you to face your weaknesses.

- Do I allow myself to shine and blossom?
- Do I allow myself to see goodness in me?
- Do I allow myself to step confidently in life?
- Am I overly confident sometimes?
- Do I remember to stay grounded?
- Am I a bit too impatient?
- Can I allow myself to act without fear of failure?
- Do I remember to respect others while I move towards my goals?
- Do I remember to stay humble, regardless of my achievements?
- Am I seeking too much affection sometimes?
- Am I a bit too attached to the pleasures of the world?
- Am I too attached to my outer appearance or image?
- How is my connection with Nature?
- Do I respect other people's emotions?
- Can I allow myself to go simply go with the flow?

Yantra of Goddess Bhagamalini

CHAPTER 10

NITYAKLINNA – ETERNALLY WET GODDESS
TRITIYA – THIRD LUNAR DAY

nityaklinna nirupama nirvāṇa sukhadayini
nityaśodha śikārupa śrīkāntārdha śarīrini

"Nityaklinna, peerless Goddess always wet with compassion, who appears in the form of sixteen Nitya Devis, and who has a body constituing the half of Shiva, confers the bliss of nirvana."

- Lalita Sahasranama

Kala	Element	Planet	Guna	Yogini	Vowel
pusha (nourisher)	ether	Mars	rajas	Southeast	i

Stage of consciousness	Divine quality	Deity (Muhurta Cintamani)	Deity (Varahamihira)	Nakshatra connection	Form of Shiva
deep sleep (waking)	kshama (forgiveness)	Gauri	Vishnu	Bharani Rohini	Umaskanda

Shukla Paksha

Nadi: ida
Chakra: svadhishthana
Interval: minor/major second
Deity (Narada Purana): Brahma
House from the Sun: 2 or 3

Krishna Paksha

Nadi: pingala
Chakra: vishuddha
Interval: minor seventh / major sixth
Deity (Narada Purana): Shiva
House from the Sun: 8 or 9

Nityaklinna means "eternally wet". Goddess in this form is always moist, which represents Her fertility, as well as compassion. Some interpret Her moisture as reproductive fluid and some interpret it as drops of sweat - as Mangal (Mars) is co-ruling third lunar day along with Her and he was born out of drop of Shiva's sweat, which fallen on the surface of earth. But, above all, Goddess Nityaklinna is always wet with compassion – similarly like Mother Lakshmi, often addressed as *Ardre* ("moist one") in Sri Suktam, which invokes the moisture of Her mercy. After all, the *kala* of the Moon on *Tritiya tithi* is *pusha* – the quality of nourishing.

With ether as Her element, the energy of Goddess Nityaklinna is sweet and gentle like the rain descending from the skies to nourish the earth. Goddess Kameshwari gave us inspiration on *Pratipad tithi*; Bhagamalini Devi gave us confidence to manifest and give birth to it in the world; and Goddess Nityaklinna is the one, who is now nourishing it and making it grow. She blesses us with the power of sustenance – similarly like Lord Vishnu, who is presiding deity of this lunar day according to *Brihat Samhita*.

The energy of Devi Nityaklinna is sweet like the energy of the mother. This is why this lunar day is most often associated with Shiva and Gauri - Goddess in Her motherly form, and Shiva in His form of Divine Father – both bringing nourishment to our home and family. It is said in *Agni Purana* that Shiva and Parvati got married on *Tritiya tithi*. Form of Shiva connected to this lunar day is Umaskanda, which is Lord Shiva seated on a throne with His wife in Her motherly form of Uma ("the giver of light") and Skanda or Kartikeya, their Divine son and commander of gods (often associated with Mars) seated between them as their child. *Tritiya tithi* is, indeed, the best day to take care of our family, home and household. However, as Mars is co-ruler of this lunar day, Goddess also reminds us, that similarly like building home or giving birth to children requires lots of effort and sweat, so nourishing and sustaining our relationships requires lots of conscious effort from our side. On Her day, Goddess Nityaklinna inspires us to make this conscious effort and awaken inside of ourselves the qualities of nourishment, regardless of potential obstacles or nervousness that can appear between us and the other person in the relationship – which is symbolised by Kartikeya seated between Shiva and Uma.

Kartikeya represents the potential of friction or fight that may appear between the partners or friends on *Tritiya tithi*, but he also stands for the power to fight for the relationship, as well as the ability to be more diplomatic, understanding and compromising, when it's needed. After all, it is Kartikeya, who as a child manifested six heads to pacify six Krittikas, his step mothers, who were fighting over which one of them is the best mother. Similarly, sometimes, in order to maintain the relationship, an impossible solution must be found and an additional effort must be made.

As my Gurudev explained, Goddess Nityaklinna is often approached to protect the relationship of people who love each other. She helps us to be more affectionate in thoughts, words and deeds, as well as She gives us the feeling of unity. She helps to harmonise the relationship, awakens mutual understanding and respect between parents and children. The quality of Sri Krishna associated with this phase of the Moon is *kshama* (forgiveness), the most transforming power in any relationship. And to be able to forgive, we need not only the moisture of sweetness and nourishment, but also great courage and strength. Goddess Nityaklinna reminds us that true forgiveness is not the sign of weakness, but the sign of inner power – as it restores our inner power and confidence. She is also the Goddess of restoration, which is why Her lunar day is very auspicious for all renovating works.

Goddess Nityaklinna also has a lot to do with our sensitivity – both in its positive and negative meaning. Interestingly, on 6 December 2017, *Krishna Tritiya*, when I was reviewing this chapter once again, my Gurudev wrote this message:

"There are two types of sensitivity: one is of awareness and the other is of being unaware. The first one is connected with life, with being sensible and sane. The second one is connected with ego (body-mind identification) and with sensations.

Sensitivity is the ability to respond, however, mostly people are sensitive only when it comes to their ego or material gain, and insensitive when it comes to life and responsibility. When the ego is pleased with sensations, one feels good, but when the ego is hurt by somebody else's ego, then one feels bad. It is wrong to think that the ego responds. In reality, the ego never responds. The ego reacts. It reacts because body-mind identification is basically unconsciousness, and accordingly, there is a lack of sensitivity.

More life, more sensitivity; less life, less sensitivity. And what suppresses the inner inherited sensitivity in man? Egoism and a mind filled with selfishness, greed, and arrogance. Such is the state of someone due to lack of sensitivity. One like this needs sensations, meaning stimulus, in order to feel alive, to feel life. But through stimulus of any kind, one can become only more dull and more dead, since stimulus is the way to spend the life energy, vitality, life force.

What is the solution? Meditation, becoming meditative, opening the heart, and serving and contributing to life. Through meditation, one regains one's own sensitivity and sensitivity grows as the meditation deepens. Through opening the heart, one moves from selfishness and logic towards inclusiveness and intelligence. Through serving and contributing, one moves from egoism and selfishness towards unity. All this increases the sensitivity, because, finally, sensitivity is the degree of awareness, as the definition says. That is why becoming more aware means increasing the sensitivity. Ultimately, sensitivity is union with the whole life."

Interestingly, the syllable of Sri Vidya mantra connected to Goddess Nityaklinna is *i*, the syllable of Divine sustainer, Vishnu. The very same syllable is also the *swara* of third lunar day. The *yogini* connected to Her is Ahamkara-karshini, "the one attracting all ego". Goddess Nityaklinna helps us to rise above our ego and to choose to sustain through nourishment and forgiveness, rather than to destroy. Similarly, our sensitivity sometimes can sustain, either through nourishing or protection (bright side of Mars' energy) or destroy (shadow side of Mars).

In our energy body, *svadhishthana chakra* or sacral chakra is mostly influenced during *Shukla Tritiya*, while throat chakra or *vishuddha* is influenced on *Krishna Tritiya*. *Svadhishthana chakra* is the element of water, which resonates with the name and qualities of Nityaklinna Devi, while *vishuddha chakra* is conneced to element of ether, which is the same as the element of this lunar day.

Svadhishthana chakra is also our most personal chakra. *Svadhishthana* literally means "one's own private place" or "one's personal power". As Goddess Nityaklinna is mostly connected with the moisture of our emotions and element of water, similarly like *svadhishthana chakra*, the biggest weakness of people born on *Tritiya tithi* (as well as a weakness, which can emerge on the surface of our consciousness during that day) is taking things too personally and getting a bit too emotional about the external drama of life. One of the most important things that all the people born on *Tritiya tithi* need to consciously work on, is how to take things less personally and overcome their emotional insecurity.

Meditation with Goddess Nityaklinna

> **Hue:** red
> **Number of heads:** 1
> **Number of eyes:** 3
> **Number of hands:** 4
> **Right hands:** *ankusha, abhaya mudra*
> **Left hands:** *pasha,* drinking cup
> **Garments:** red
> **Ornaments:** smeared with red sandalwood paste, beads of sweat on her forehead shining like pearls, crown adorned with half-moon

Tantraraja describes Goddess Nityaklinna as beautifully red, adorned with red clothes and smeared with red sandalwood paste. Beads of sweat on Her forehead shine like pearls and Her crown is adorned with half-moon. Being so, She reflects the intense qualities of Mars (red color and drops of sweat) and the Moon (pearls and half-moon) at the same time, reminding us that motherly energy does not require only the nourishing energy of the Moon, but also the strength of Mars. This is why the quality of this lunar day is *bala,* strength – and why *Tritiya tithi* natives are usually never afraid to make effort in life. After all, if we have a look at the world of Nature, mothers are always the ones that need to be the strongest of all in order to protect their children. This is why, according to *Brihat Parashara Hora Shashtra,* both Moon and Mars can become *karakas* for one's mother in a birth chart. This is also the reason why overprotective behaviour can be a shadow side of people born on this lunar day.

Goddess Nityaklinna has four hands. Two of Her hands are holding *pasha* (noose) and *ankusha* (goad), symbolising control over our likes and dislikes - *raga* (passion) and *dwesha* (repulsion). Lower right hand is showing the gesture of *abhaya mudra* (fearlessness), while lower left hand is holding a drinking cup, symbolising the Divine nectar, *soma.* Again, just with these two hands, She reminds us that on the path of Love and compassion, we need to abandon our likes and dislikes, as well as be fearless (*abhaya mudra*) and sweet (drinking cup) at the same time. Courage and inner gentleness are equally important, and combine together in Her image.

Nityaklinna is also the Goddess of all liquids, as well as intoxication. For a material person a cup in Her hand can stand for intoxicating liquids, while for a *yogi* it represents the nectar of spiritual ecstasy experienced in deep meditation, when the Self is melting in Divine Love. She represents growing above our ego and all the frictions of our lower self. This is why in *Shukla paksha* the music interval She would form with the Sun would be already major second, and minor seventh in *Krishna paksha* – two music intervals, which are already much more harmonious than those represented by Kameshwari Devi or Bhagamalini. Mother Nityaklinna, with Her sweet, nourishing energy, heals all the frictions and opens us for transforming power of forgiveness, to bring more harmony and Love into our lives.

Wedding of Shiva and Parvati

In *Agni Purana* it is said that Shiva and Parvati got married on *Tritiya tithi*. Their marriage was an extraordinary one, as, in reality, it was a symbolic marriage between heaven and earth, human and Divine.

Highest Goddess had incarnated on Earth as a human being, daughter of Himavan, king of the mountains. Her name was Parvati. Since very young age She was attracted to Shiva, which was not very pleasing to Her parents. Shiva, although being the Lord of all, was well known to be an ascetic, covered with ashes from cremation grounds, with matted locks, always detached from the world and immersed in meditation – not the type of groom you would imagine for you daughter. But Parvati didn't give up. She went deep into Himalayas and had performed Her penance there to achieve Shiva as Her husband. And Shiva accepted Her.

During their wedding, however, not everything went exactly as planned. Lord Shiva, being always innocent and very simple, came to the wedding in His normal outfit as a *yogi* – with matted locks, covered with ashes and a garland of skulls. When Parvati's mother saw Shiva in such a terrible outfit, she fainted. Only after efforts from Parvati's side she managed to convince her mother that outer form is not what attracts her in her future husband, but rather the purity of his soul. Parvati also managed to convince Shiva to appear in a beautiful form, suitable for a bridegroom, just for Her wedding, for the sake of her family.

There is a beautiful message hidden behind this story, revealing that for the sake of uplifting our relationships, always some efforts must be taken and some compromises must be accepted – as even God Himself needed to make some effort and compromise in order to establish a relationship. This is why Shiva and Parvati are said to be the ideal couple, and with their two children, Ganesha and Kartikeya, they an example of ideal family, as well. Although each of them is completely different, there is always mutual love, respect and peace between all of them. Although Shiva is a *yogi* and God, while Parvati incarnated as human, Shiva respected Parvati's humanity and Parvati respected Shiva's divinity. Although Shiva is riding on a bull, while Parvati in Her form as Durga Devi rides on a lion, both animals live together in peace on Kailash, Shiva's abode. Similarly, although Kartikeya, Shiva and Parvati's son rides on a peacock, who is a natural enemy of snakes, it doesn't harm snake wrapped around Shiva's neck - and the very same snake never harmed a mouse, who is a *vahana* of Ganesha. That is a true message of Goddess Nityaklinna: respect all, love all and live in peace with all, regardless of the external differences. See the unity in everything. Goddess Nityaklinna strongly inspires us towards unifying things, rather than dividing them.

Numerology: 3

Tritiya tithi is the third lunar day and so it is connected to number 3. There are three *gunas: rajas, tamas* and *sattwa*. Three modes of nature and three modes of action: creation, sustenance and destruction, represented by *trimurti* of Brahma (the creator, *rajas guna*), Vishnu (the sustainer, *sattwa guna*) and Shiva (the destroyer, *tamas guna*). As number three is so closely connected to the way we are taking our action in the outer world, so it is also connected to our third house in Vedic astrology: house of our efforts, relations and speech. Even in the third chapter of *Bhagavad Gita* Lord Krishna is praising *karma yoga* or the *yoga* of performing one's prescribed duty as a sacrifice for the Divine, with full detachment from the fruits of our actions, with these words:

"Everyone is forced to act helplessly according to the qualities he has acquired from the modes of material nature; therefore no one can refrain from doing something, not even for a moment."

Our action itself is Shakti. This is why we have three *shaktis: iccha shakti* (the power of will), *jnana shakti* (the power of wisdom) and *kriya shakti* (the power of action). Interestingly enough, even the weapon of Kartikeya, who is so connected to Mars (co-ruler of *Tritiya tithi*, as well as the planet naturally connected to number 3 and third house in Vedic astrology) is called *shakti*.

3 is also a very mystical number, symbolising unity. As much as number 1 stands for "I", number 2 stands for "you" and "me", number 3 represents the unity of "I", "you" and "we". The possibility of "we" appears for the first time here, bringing a possibility of seeing the underlying unity of the universe. This is also why Lord Shiva as well as many forms of Goddess have three eyes, symbolising their awakened state of consciousness. In *kriya yoga* tradition we say, that with two eyes man can see only the duality, but when the third eye (the energy center between the eyebrows) awakens, we start to perceive unity. This is why number 3 is also associated with Agni in Vedic tradition. Left eye of Shiva is said to be the Moon, His right eye the Sun, and third eye is Agni or Divine fire.

Yogini in *Kalachakra*: Southeast

On *Tritiya tithi* the danger comes from the Southeast. It is said that we should avoid travelling into that direction during the third lunar day in any of the two *pakshas*. It also reveals the biggest weakness, which may awaken in us during *Tritiya tithi*: short temper and anger, which is the most destructive force, obstructing the nourishing qualities of Nityaklinna Devi.

Southeast direction is connected to fire element in Vastu – and fire can be both nourishing and destructive. Be it fire of passion, fire of warmth or fire of transformation, it is always essential in sustaining a relationship. This is why

Southeast is the most important direction in Vastu, when it comes to relationships. Whenever this direction is misbalanced in our home, it will bring troubles and fights in our relations. This is also why in *Kalachakra* (the cycle of destruction) Southeast direction is ruled by Mars, while in *Digchakra* (the cycle of creation) Southeast is ruled by Venus. It reveals to us, that in order to overcome the destructive, fiery qualities of Mars in our relationships, we need to be more centered in the heart (Venus). Goddess Nityaklinna is reminding us the very same thing on *Tritiya tithi* and inspires us to give some extra nourishment and attention to our relationships on that day.

Interestingly, Southeast corner in Vastu, is also connected to Parashurama incarnation of Lord Vishnu (as Parashurama is also connected to Venus). Parashurama was also born on *Tritiya tithi*, which is very symbolic.

Parashurama was a very "short-tempered" incarnation of the Lord, who manifested mostly to purify the earth from the negative influence of egoistic *kshatriyas* (warrior caste). He bathed the entire earth in blood (quite literally), by killing 21 generations of *kshatriyas*, whose corrupted behaviour was causing misbalance in the world. At the end of life, however, he retired back to Himalayas, to spend the rest of his life on *tapasya* or penance – as well as to "atone" for the "sin" of killing so many people. He "realised" that violence is never the way. It is very touching to see that even God Himself needed to "atone" for his "sins" (even if done for a righteous cause) to show the proper way of conduct to all the people. At the end of his life, Parashurama understood, that forgiveness and compassion is the only true way to balance any evil in the world – as no matter how much blood you shed, it won't change the consciousness of people. Similarly, all people born on *Tritiya tithi* must reach this level of realisation and enrich their short-tempered nature with compassionate and forgiving qualities of Goddess Nityaklinna, as this will greatly improve all their relationships. It is of highest importance for them to control their anger and abstain from violence in any form, so their "softer" qualities may awake.

Shaktis of Goddess Nityaklinna

Different *shaktis* or powers of Goddess Nityaklinna dwell in the different places of Her *yantra*, which consists only of *yoni* (down-ward facing triangle), 8 petals and *bhupura*, or border of material perception, enclosing each and every *yantra*.

Each corner of the triangle is occupied by *shaktis*: Kshobini ("agitator"), Mohini ("enchantress") and Lila ("Divine play"), while 8 petals, standing for eight directions of the world, are occupied by *shaktis*: Nitya ("eternal one"), Niranjana ("spotless one"), Klinna ("wet one"), Madantura ("governor of desire"), Madadrava ("intoxicating ecstasy"), Dravini ("ecstatic one" or "melted one"), Vidhana ("wealthy one") and Kledini ("sweating one").

The inner space of the square is also occupied by *shaktis* with the names: Madavila ("amorous play"), Mangala ("auspicious one"), Manmathartha ("wealth of Cupid"), Manasvini ("intelligent one"), Moha ("delusion"), Amoda ("perfume" or "delight"), Manamayi ("made of mind"), Maya ("illusion"), Manda ("slow one") and Manovati ("mindful one").

Swara of Goddess Nityaklinna

I, the third *swara* or vowel of Sanskrit alphabet, is associated with Goddess Nityaklinna. Its quality or *kala* is to cool, which goes very much in tune with cooling energy of Nityaklinna Devi. The repetition of this Sanskrit vowel creates a feeling of compassion or... passion. It cools down anger and allows the quality of Love to manifest itself. It is all about sustaining, nourishing, as well as being open to learn and receive. According to *Agni Purana* vowel *i* is a direct manifestation of Kamadeva or Cupid.

Nakshatras connected to Goddess Nityaklinna

Bharani nakshatra is connected to *swara* of Goddess Nityaklinna, while Her four arms represent four *padas* of Rohini nakshatra – the most favourite mansion of the Moon, where he has his *mulatrikona* position. Even by analysing the qualities of these two nakshatras, we can easily see how passionate nature, as well as the power to make an effort, represented by Bharani nakshatra (nakshatra of Venus in fiery sign of Mars) are interconnected with motherly nourishment and feminine gentleness represented by Rohini nakshatra (nakshatra of Moon in the earthly sign of Venus). The *shakti* of Bharani nakshatra is the power to let go and forgive – to let go with the flow, and allow the waters to cleanse all the impurities and attachments. The *shakti* of Rohini nakshatra, on the other hand, is *rohana shakti*, the power to make things grow. Rohini was also the favourite wife of Moon-god. With the energy of these two nakshatras combined together on *Tritiya tithi*, the feminine, fertile energy is very strong.

It is the most feminine and nourishing lunar day, which makes everything grow. No wonder that one of the most celebrated lunar days in Hindu calendar is *Akshaya Tritiya* – a very special day in a year: *Tritiya tithi* combined with Sun and Moon at their exaltation points. It is said that during such a day, whatever we do or whatever we will invest our life energy into, it will always keep growing and will never diminish in the future. It will be always sustained and supported. This is why often in India people are buying gold on that day. The very same day is also birthday of Lord Parashuram.

Tithi, vara and nakshatra resonance

Goddess Nityaklinna and Her lunar day do not have any "black and white" relationships. It is quite interesting that this form of the Goddess, which is inspiring us towards having more harmonious relationships, doesn't have any 100% clear relationship with any day of the week and any nakshatra. Each relationship changes according to circumstances.

It is said that the energy of Goddess Nityaklinna is the most incompatible with Wednesday, the day ruled by neutral, calculative and cold Mercury, as well as with nakshatras Uttara Phalguni, Uttarashadha and Uttara Bhadrapada – all three of them often being quite cold. Usually, when *Tritiya tithi* falls on any of those three nakshatras, it is *ashubha yoga* ("inauspicious combination"). *Tritiya tithi* also makes these three nakshatras *shunya* or "fruitless".

Whenever *Tritiya tithi* falls on Wednesday, it is called *dagdha yoga* or "burnt combination" - when nourishing energies of this lunar day are a bit "burnt". Interestingly enough, the very same combination is said to produce *amrita yoga* or "combination of nectar", as well. It is furtherly specificied, that whenever *Tritiya tithi* falls on Wednesday and under nakshatras Rohini, Margashirsha, Ardra, Uttara Phalguni, Anuradha or Uttarashadha, *siddha yoga* or "combination of accomplishments" occurs. However, when the same *tithi* occurs on Wednesday and one of the following nakshatras: Ashwini, Bharani, Pushya, Ashlesha, Magha, Mula, Dhanishta or Purva Bhadrapada, *vinasha yoga* or "combination of destruction" is the result.

Interestingly, along with *Ashtami*, another *tithi* of ether element, *Tritiya tithi* forms the biggest amount of *vinasha yogas* or "combinations of destruction". They are as follows:

* *Tritiya tithi* + Wednesday + Ashwini, Bharani, Pushya, Ashlesha, Magha, Mula, Dhanishta or Purva Bhadrapada
* *Tritiya tithi* + Friday + Rohini, Punarvasu, Magha, Vishakha, Anuradha, Jyeshta, Shravana or Dhanishta
* *Tritiya tithi* + Saturday + Bharani, Punarvasu, Pushya, Purva Phalguni, Uttara Phalguni, Hasta, Purvashadha, Uttara Ashadha or Shravana
* *Tritiya tithi* + Sunday + Bharani, Margashirsha, Ashlesha, Vishakha, Anuradha, Jyeshta or Dhanishta

Tritiya tithi is, however, always auspicious, when it falls on Tuesday, day ruled by Mars – those two energies combined together form *siddha yoga*. Additionally, when this *siddha yoga* happens, when the Moon is in Ashwini, Margashirsha, Uttara Phalguni, Citra, Anuradha, Mula, Dhanishta or Purva Bhadrapada, it is even more powerful.

YOGAS FORMED WITH *TRITIYA TITHI*

	1	2	3	4	5	6	7
1			**siddha**	vinasha			
2	vinasha		siddha	vinasha			vinasha
3			siddha	amrita /dagdha			
4			siddha	**siddha**		vinasha	
5	vinasha		**siddha**	**siddha**			
6			siddha	**siddha**			
7			siddha	amrita /dagdha		vinasha	vinasha
8			siddha	vinasha			vinasha
9	vinasha		siddha	vinasha			
10			siddha	vinasha		vinasha	
11			siddha	amrita /dagdha	**gains**		vinasha
12	shunya	shunya	**siddha**	**siddha** / shunya	shunya	shunya	vinasha
13			siddha	amrita /dagdha			vinasha
14			**siddha**	amrita /dagdha			
15			siddha	amrita /dagdha			
16	vinasha		siddha	amrita /dagdha		vinasha	
17	vinasha		**siddha**	siddha		vinasha	
18	vinasha		siddha	amrita /dagdha		vinasha	
19			**siddha**	vinasha			
20			siddha	amrita /dagdha			vinasha
21	shunya	shunya	siddha / shunya	**siddha /** shunya	shunya	shunya	vinasha / shunya
22			siddha	amrita /dagdha		vinasha	vinasha
23	vinasha		**siddha**	vinasha		vinasha	
24			siddha	amrita /dagdha			
25			**siddha**	vinasha			
26	shunya	shunya	siddha / shunya	amrita /dagdha / shunya	shunya	shunya	shunya
27			siddha	amrita /dagdha			

Being so, the only nakshatra, which really resonates with *Tritiya tithi* regardless of all the other circumstances is, interestingly, Ardra – "the moist one"; Vedic constellation, which resembles even the name of Goddess Nityaklinna and is the first nakshatra in the zodiac connected to water element. Ashwini, Rohini, Margashirsha, Purva Phalguni, Uttara Phalguni, Citra, Anuradha, Mula, Uttarashadha, Dhanishta bring different results under *Tritiya tithi*, while Bharani, Punarvasu, Pushya, Ashlesha, Magha, Hasta, Vishakha, Jyeshtha, Purvashadha, Shravana, Purva Bhadrapada and Uttara Bhadrapada bring usually bad results.

In *Agni Purana* it is also stated that whenever *Tritiya tithi* happens on Thursday along with Moon dwelling in Purva Phalguni nakshatra, it will bring gains. The same scripture reveals that sowing seeds on *Tritiya tithi* and Krittika, Rohini, Uttara Phalguni, Hasta, Anuradha, Jyeshtha or Revati nakshatra is going to attract great prosperity.

Additionally, if a person is born on *Tritiya tithi* and Thursday, it produces a *tithi dosha* for the person. The personality of such a person will be overly dominated by ether element. Such a person will need to consciously work on balancing exeggerated ether element - both in physical body and on a psychological level.

Tritiya tithi doesn't become *shunya* or "fruitless" in any of the Vedic months, which is a unique quality of this lunar day.

Important *rashis* for *Tritiya tithi* natives

Each *tithi* has a special connection with a number of *rashis*. Understanding those connections can help us not only in understanding our own birth chart on a much deeper level, but in better understanding of the nature of the *tithi* itself.

Two *rashis*, which are of great importance for all *Tritiya tithi* natives are Aries and Libra. Aries is the *mulatrikona* sign of planetary lord of this lunar day (Mars, *tithi pati kshetra*), while Libra is the sign opposite to it (*tithi pati kshetra paksha*), which is the sign revealing, where are we heading in life. As *Tritiya tithi* is so strongly connected with all relationships in our life, no wonder that it is reflected in the sign of Libra: the sign of finding the right balance, freedom, love and respect in all our relationships. Any planets present in Libra or in angles to it will additionally reveal the way we will seek and form our relationships in life.

Additionally, in *Shukla paksha* sign of Pisces becomes more energised on *Tritiya tithi* (which reveals more peaceful nature of *Shukla Tritiya* natives, whose main objective is simply having peaceful and loving relationships), while in *Krishna paksha* sign of Virgo becomes more energised - which is why *Krishna Tritiya* natives will be a little bit more calculative sometimes in their relations, due to what they need to work a little bit more consciously on uplifting their relationships and bringing into them more "moisture" of sensitivity.

	Tithi Pati Kshetra		
Tithi Shunya Rashi	*Tritiya*		Tithi Shunya Rashi
	Tithi Pati Kshetra Paksha		

Tithi shunya rashis or the signs, which are made "fruitless" by *Tritiya tithi*, are Capricorn (ruled by cold Saturn) and Leo (ruled by burning Sun), signifying two extremes, which are detrimental for any relationship: either being to cold-hearted or too hot-headed. Unless these signs are occupied by Rahu or Ketu, or unless its lords (Sun or Saturn) are placed 3rd, 6th, 8th or 12th house from ascendant or Moon, or are retrograde, or in conjuction with malefic planet, or, lastly, in nakshatras of Rahu or Ketu, these two signs and houses ruled by those planets won't bring good results for the native. In such a case these signs must be strengthened (by strengthening their lords) to bring good results. *Shunya* planets do produce good results, however, when they transit 3rd, 6th, 8th or 12th house from from ascendant or Moon.

Sadhana for Goddess Nityaklinna

Goddess Nityaklinna is pleased with red sandalwood paste and water, as well as avoiding salt on Her lunar day (especially during the month *Phalguna*, March-April). Meditating close to a water body is very much recommended on that day. To connect with Her on a deeper level, you can either do a meditation of sitting on Her lap, as given by my Gurudev (described in Chapter 24), or colour Her yantra and meditate on it, facing Southeast. For your *sadhana* you can use one of the two mantras below or one of the affirmations. There are couple of more advanced mantras for worship of Goddess Nityaklinna in *Tantraraja*, but they are not supposed to be recited without a guidance of a Guru.

Agni Purana also advises to worship Supreme Goddess Lalita on third lunar day and reveals that Tritiya tithi in Shukla paksha in the month of Caitra (April-May) is the dearest to Her. Tritiya tithi is also very auspicious in the month of Margashirsha (December-January). It is called Atma-tritiya or "tritiya of the soul". Whoever worships Divine Mother on that day is going to be blessed by Her with material and spiritual wealth.

Mantras:

oṁ aīṁ hrīṁ śrīṁ iṁ nityaklinnayai namaḥ
oṁ aīṁ hrīṁ śrīṁ iṁ puṣayai namaḥ

Affirmations:

I allow myself to be nourished.
I allow myself to grow.
I allow myself to forgive.

Questions for self-analysis

Every lunar day is an opportunity to learn something new about ourselves. Nitya Devis and their wisdom can become our guides on this sacred journey. Questions below can help you in recognising certain "shadow" tendencies in yourself, which may arise on Tritiya tithi. If you were born on this lunar day, these questions might be of big importance for you in life and allow you to face your weaknesses.

- Am I compassionate and sensitive enough?
- Am I overly sensitive?
- Am I strong enough to forgive?
- Do I make enough effort to sustain my relationships with Love?
- Do I allow myself to be nourished?
- Can I control my anger when needed?
- Am I a little bit overprotective sometimes?
- Do I give enough time to my loved ones?
- Do I take a good care of my home?
- How do I manage my emotions?
- Am I sometimes a bit too lazy?
- Am I brave enough to make a step beyond my comfort zone?
- Do I take things a bit too personally?
- Which relations could be restored or improved in my life?
- In which spheres of life could I see more unity?

Yantra of Goddess Nityaklinna

CHAPTER 11

BHERUNDA – TERRIBLE GODDESS
CHATURTI – FOURTH LUNAR DAY

sarva-maṅgala-rūpādyā satcitananda vigrahā
aṣṭādaśa-supīthasthā bheruṇḍā bhairavī parā

"Praised be the Highest Goddess, Bherunda, Bhairavi, the embodiment of all auspiciousness, the very form of conscious bliss, dwelling in the eighteen pithas (pilgrimage places)."

- Sri Chamundeshwari Ashtottara Shatanama Stotram

Kala	Element	Planet	Guna	Yogini	Vowel
tushti (contentment)	water	Mercury	rajas	Southwest	ī

Stage of consciousness	Divine quality	Deity (Muhurta Cintamani)	Deity (Varahamihira)	Nakshatra connection	Form of Shiva
turiya (waking)	nyaya (justice)	Ganesha	Yama	Bharani Margashirsha Ardra	Vrisharudha

Shukla Paksha

Nadi: pingala
Chakra: svadhishthana
Interval: major second
Deity (Narada Purana): Vishnu
House from the Sun: 2 or 3

Krishna Paksha

Nadi: ida
Chakra: vishuddha
Interval: major / minor sixth
Deity (Narada Purana): Vishnu
House from the Sun: 8 or 9

Bherunda is a very unusual Goddess. Her very name means "terrible one", "ugly one" or "formidable one". The nature of her lunar day is *khala* or cruel. But Bherunda can also mean a pregnant women or the one having a big or clumsy body. First three goddesses were showing us our potential and the beauty hidden within ourselves. Bherunda Devi, on the other hand, shows us all the things we turn our gaze away from; all the things we do not like to see or accept within ourselves.

I have noticed several times, that people born on the lunar day of Bherunda Devi, very often grow up in the "mud" of the world (in rare cases literally in dirty or ugly places), so they can rise above it and focus only on the *atma* or inner beauty. In a way, Divine Mother purposely takes all the beauty of the world away from them initially, so they are forced to seek higher beauty within themselves, and so they can train their inner vision and non-judgement from early years. Bherunda's message for Her children is very clear: "Do not focus on the surface of things. Focus on what is inside." It is Mercury's (who is the planetary co-ruler of this lunar day) shadow quality to focus too much on the surface of things.

Bherunda Devi is the first "strict" form of the Divine Mother and She rules the first *Rikta tithi* or "empty" lunar day, which is connected to element of water and the purifying energy of *moksha*. *Rikta tithis* are considered auspicious only for activities related to purification, detox, demolition, destruction, cleaning and removal. Yet, even though they do not support us in any other activites on material level, they do help us a lot in our spiritual development and purification of our mind.

As Bherunda Devi rules *Chaturti tithi* along with Mercury, She represents our intellect being very active and "pregnant" with many ideas. When a woman is pregnant or when her body is simply big, she would move much slower. Similarly, when intellect is at its peak, very often the body naturally becomes slower or even more lazy and *tamasic*. Shadow side of goddess Bherunda is *tamas*, inertia and stagnation on physical level. This is why very often people born on *Chaturti tithi* have very powerful and speedy intellect, but very weak or slow body. Some sort of *tamasic* energy dwells in their body, even if their mind is very bright and *sattwic*. They also tend to be overly sensitive to many things, especially sounds or dirt. Due to the hightened sensitivity they usually run away from crowded places and their inner energy is truly regenerated only when they are alone. Sometimes they tend to be, however, also overly focused on themselves, which might lead them to loneliness. However, people born on *Rikta tithis* usually don't have a problem with leading a solitary life. They find it more challenging to adjust to their environment.

Ganesha Himself was born on *Chaturti tithi*, and, indeed, his form resembles the qualities of this lunar phase. With His huge head and big body, Ganesha is well known to be rather slow, when it comes to taking physical action, but His intellect is at its peak. With His intelligence He helps His devotees to overcome all the obstacles. But He is at the same time the one, who places obstacles on the way of His devotees, to inspire them to think out of the box and use their own intelligence; to practise their mental strength.

Interestingly, it is said that Lord Ganesha was born from the dirt of Mother Parvati, after She took Her bath and was cleansing Her skin. Mercury, the co-ruler of this lunar day, is a significator of skin, as well. Skin is our sensitivity, as well as our outer border, which can get polluted most easily. Skin also represents, symbolically, the surface of all things or the boundary between ourselves and the external world. Skin of the Divine Mother represents Her intellect and Her *maya*, illusion.

There is a deep symbolism behind this story. If we get stuck on the level of intellect, on the surface, the energy accumulated there can easily become "dirty" and polluted. How symbolic is the fact, that Ganesha was initially beheaded by Shiva Himself. Similarly, on spiritual path, we need to "behead" our intellect at some point, as it is also a part of illusion. It can help us to overcome certain obstacles in the beginning of our journey, but it cannot take us further than that. Lord Ganesha, after all, is a gatekeeper of Mother Parvati, who is Shakti Herself. And the purpose of a gatekeeper is to stay in front of the gate, not to accompany us inside. Similarly Goddess Bherunda reminds us what is the true purpose of our intellect and warns us not to use it to get entangled in worldy "dirt".

On *Chaturti tithi*, Bherunda Devi is inspiring us to bring more attention to all those spheres of our life, where energy is clogged and starts to spoil; where obstacles are dwelling or where the energy became "dirty". The element connected with this lunar day is water, while the element of Mercury, co-ruling this *tithi* along with Goddess Bherunda, is earth. When earth and water come together, the earth becomes very damp and can start to spoil easily, turning into poison, instead of being fertile. Similarly, when our energy is clogged somewhere, and, especially, if we carry lot of negative emotions within, like resentment, bitterness or disgust, and when we don't do anything to actually *purify* them, they soon start to spoil and poison our inner space. Bherunda Devi is the Goddess, who controls all the poisons – those which contaminate the body, and those that contaminate the mind. She inspires us to let go of all of them and allow them to emerge on the surface of our consciousness, so She can help us in removing them.

I still remember very well the process of painting Bherunda Devi's *yantra*. I took upon myself an uneasy task of completing fifteen *yantras* of Nitya Devis in fifteen days, ruled respectively by each one of them. The process itself was a very intense experience. The most interesting experience, however, I had with the *yantra* of Goddess Bherunda. Meditating with Her already before, I was expecting that something unusual may happen during the process of painting Her *yantra*. And, indeed, somehow everything went wrong. I chose the wrong colour in some places, another colour turned to look completely different on the paper, and in result the *yantra* of Bherunda Devi was really the least beautiful one of all of them – at least in my eyes. Thus, even through the process of painting Her *yantra* Goddess Bherunda gave me a lesson of focusing more on what is inside, rather than focusing on external beauty.

On spiritual path, we all know with our mind and with our intelligence that we should focus more on the inner qualities of all things, rather than on the outer reality. We should look for true, inner beauty, rather than judging people, situations or reality itself just by their outer appearance. Majority of people would agree with that statement – in theory. But when it comes to practice, and really *seeing* beyond the external judgements of the mind, we often fail to do so. Just one obstacle on our way, just one situation unpleasant for the ego, is often enough to make us forget about it. Whether we like it or not, subconsciously we always run away from ugliness, poverty, pain and suffering. We refuse to embrace them with love, as it requires immense inner strength to do so. Such mental strength is displayed by Bherunda Devi and symbolised by all the weapons in Her hands. Goddess Bherunda inspires us to have courage and look at all that, which our mind judges as "obstacle", "ugliness", "dirt", "*tamas*" or "weakness" with a gaze of love and acceptance. Not without a reason the *kala* of the Moon connected to Her lunar day is *tushti* – "contentment". Goddess Bherunda teaches us, how to be content with whatever we receive from the world: be it sweetness of pleasant experiences or bitterness of the difficult ones. She stands for transcending the judgement of the mind. She is embodiment of one of the most profound messages from the Gita:

"He who does not hate illumination, attachment and delusion when they are present, nor longs for them when they disappear; who is seated like one unconcerned, being situated beyond these material reactions of the modes of nature, who remains firm, knowing that the *gunas* alone are active; who regards alike pleasure and pain, and looks on a clod, a stone and a piece of gold with an equal eye; who is wise and holds praise and blame to be the same; who is unchanged in honor and dishonor, who treats friend and foe alike, who has abandoned all fruitive undertakings - such a man is said to have transcended the modes of nature (*gunas*)."

Interestingly, the quality of Sri Krishna connected to Goddess Bherunda is *nyaya* or justice. Often we think, that negative things, which are happening in our life are unfair. Whenever something positive happens, however, we take it for granted. But in reality everything always happens according to the Cosmic Law of balance and everything happens for a reason. This Divine justice is what Goddess Bherunda stands for. Yet, when Her qualities join the ego of the person, who is born under *Chaturti tithi*, it can also produce overly judgemental mind, which refuses to accept the Divine justice and wants to do "justice" according to its own whim and temporary feeling. Overly judgemental nature and too much criticism are two biggest weaknesses of all natives born on this lunar day, which come from combination of element of water and *guna* of *rajas*, which are naturally making the judging mind and intellect more active. Combination of element of water and *rajas guna* can also make us overly focused on ourselves and our vulnerability, which may lead to ignoring other people's needs and emotions. *Rajas guna* conjoined with the qualities of water element turns our mind into a stormy ocean, in which some deep purification or "churning" process is happening.

Bherunda Devi warns us also not to go into another extreme: being just "contented" with everything – as some New Age philosophies sometimes tell us to be. Too much of such a "contentment" can have a shadow side as well. Exaggerated *tushti* can lead to inertia, laziness, *tamas* and stagnation, as it won't be inspiring for taking any action in the world. As much as people born on *Krishna Chaturti* sometimes tend to be overly judgemental, so people born on *Shukla Chaturti* often tend to be too inert and too "contented" with everything. Goddess Bherunda teaches us: "Be grateful for whatever God is giving you – but don't let it make you lazy. Express your gratitude through your actions, not just through mere feeling. Use your discernment wisely and avoid habitual judgement or unnecessary criticism. Allow hightened energy of your intellect to make you more mindful and ready to learn, rather than making you too critical."

Meditation with Goddess Bherunda

Hue: molten gold
Number of heads: 1
Number of eyes: 3
Number of hands: 8
Right hands: *ankusha*, spear, *vajra*, sword
Left hands: *pasha*, bow, *gada*, shield
Ornaments: ornaments of celestial beauty, earrings, necklace, armlets, waist-chain, rings on hands and feet

Despite Her name, *Tantraraja* gives a very beautiful description of Goddess Bherunda. Her body has a hue of molten gold and She is adorned with various celestial ornaments, such as earrings, necklace, armlets, waist-chain or rings on hands and feet. Her presence is very powerful with Her eight hands, each carrying a weapon. In Her right hands She is holding *ankusha* (goad, symbolising control over repulsion), spear (symbolising *shakti* or power), *vajra* (lightening-weapon, symbolising Her mental strength) and sword (symbolising Her ability to cut away all the negativities). In Her left hands She is holding *pasha* (noose, symbolising control over attachments), bow (symbolising focus), *gada* (mace, symbolising destruction of the ego) and shield (symbolising protection). Goddess Bherunda is the first Nitya Devi, who is so well equipped with weapons. As Mercury, the planet of intellect, is co-ruling *Chaturti tithi*, so Goddess Bherunda represents our mental strength and ability to cope with obstacles with the power of discernment.

Interestingly, the scriptures don't tell anything about the colour of Her garments, which is why sometimes She is considered to be the only Nitya Devi, who is naked. Goddess Bherunda, indeed, represents our vulnerability itself. As Her name means "ugly one", She represents everything within ourselves, which we consider ugly or are ashamed of. People born on *Chaturti tithi* are especially afraid of being judged by others and they often feel very uncomfortable while receiving any sort of feedback. Bherunda Devi inspires us to look with courage at our weaknesses, and acknowledge their existence, without running away from them. She teaches us, how to overcome one of the biggest obstacles on the path of spiritual development: the feeling of shame - and She gives us all the weapons to do so. She reminds us about the power of our intellect and teaches us to control our emotions and weaknesses, instead of falling prey to them. She inspires us to have courage to see ourselves in the mirror completely "naked", stripped of all illusions of the ego. Through challenges, which She places on our way, She shows us the truth about ourselves and inspires us to be stronger. As Goddess Kamehwari was teaching us love, Goddess Bhagamalini was teaching us confidence and Goddess Nityaklinna was teaching us forgiveness, so Goddess Bherunda teaches us mental strength. And how can we practise our inner strength, if not through confrontation with obstacles?

This is why on Her day, *Chaturti tithi*, Goddess Bherunda is always teaching us through challenges. She is the Mother in the form of a Teacher and She is the one, who takes on Herself an uneasy task of making us stronger and teaching us mental discipline. Her blessings are not like Kameshwari's rays of light, Bhagamalini's power to blossom or Nityaklinna's humidity of compassion. Her blessings come in the form of adversities – in the form of everything, which our mind doesn't like.

My Gurudev published this beautiful message on *Krishna Chaturti*, 7 December 2017, when I was reviewing this chapter, and it felt to me like Goddess Bheruda Herself speaking through these words:

"Love and respect yourself how God made you, as all is a spark of His Love. When life is testing you, make your effort in going beyond it, knowing that He is with you. Don't be like a tortoise: each time there is an obstacle it puts its head inside its shell. Learn to know yourself and become who you are meant to be."

One of the names of Bherunda Devi is *Vishahara* – the destroyer of poisons. She is often approached for protection from poisons and healing from poisoning. She assures good health, prevents death and protects body and mind from contaminated food. Food for the mind is our own thoughts. Goddess Bherunda helps us to remove all the negativities, all the poisons from our mind, so it can be pure, "naked", dwelling in truth, unashamed of itself. Yet, very often, in order to counteract the effect of some poison, another poison needs to be used. Similarly, Goddess Bheruda is the one, who gives the bitter medicine to our mind, so we can be cured of all our inner poisons. The power of intellect often becomes such a bitter medicine, too.

In the great process of churning of the ocean of milk, *Samudra manthan*, which symbolises the process of "churning" our consciousness, the first "blessing" that came out of the ocean was *halahala*, a deadly poison. Similarly, Goddess Bherunda helps in the process of "squeezing" all the poisons out of us in the process of churning our consciousness, so our mind can become pure and "naked" like Her – so our consciousness can be ready for receiving the blessings of next Nitya Devis. If we fail on that step, our mind won't be ready to receive much from other Goddesses, as it will keep "spoiling" in the waters of negative thoughts and emotions, and won't be capable of receiving anything more. Water full of dirt and spoiled matter can never reflect the light.

Bherunda is the only Goddess, who actually takes upon Herself an uneasy task of going right into the mud of our mind's negativities and cleaning it of its impurities. (Interestingly, people born on *Chaturti tithi* often do not like cleaning or dealing with dirty things.) Herself, She is of color of molten gold, reminding us, that if we want to shine like Her, we firsty need to go through the heat of purification, like gold is purified in the fire. Like my Gurudev once beautifully said:

"This Divine Love, which is seated deep inside your heart, is like gold. And when gold is found in nature, it is covered with all the dust. Both gold and diamonds in nature are full of impurities. To get a beautiful jewel, a beautiful stone from a rough diamond, what do you do? You polish it. The same with gold: to get pure gold, you have to purify it, to remove all the impurities from it. It is the same with man. As long as you are stuck in the mind and don't purify the mind, this Love will never shine. You will never realise this Love. Even if you think you know it, because you have read about it or somebody has told you about it, but as long as you don't purify your mind, as long as you don´t purify yourself, it will be difficult to realise this Love."

Interestingly, within the range of ratios connected to *Chaturti tithi* in *Krishna paksha* we find a very interesting one: 360:222.5, which is nothing else but a golden angle, closely connected to golden ratio. It gives yet another profound meaning to Bherunda Devi's golden hue. Even one of Her tantric names in *64 Yogini Namavali* is Tattva Uttama or "the highest *tattva*, the greatest of the elements". Goddess Bherunda reminds us thus, that everything in the universe is always perfect, happening exactly, how it has to be. As my Gurudev beautifully said, "nothing is wrong with the world – apart from the mind of man". It is our mind, that judges things as right or wrong, beautiful or ugly – but if we would have "the eyes to see", like Christ said, we would see that everything in the universe is always in perfect harmony. If we would see our own life from a higher perspective, we would see a deeper meaning behind every single difficulty we ever experienced in life – and a higher beauty hidden in it. If the Divine Mother made all the natural world, starting from the plants and finishing with human, so beautifully designed and crafted with golden angles and ratios, who are we to think that our life itself is any less perfect? How can a man not stand in amazement while observing all the natural patterns, such as Fibonacci spirals present in the natural world? And if even the tiniest details of Nature are so skillfully crafted by Divine Architect, didn't it ever came to your mind that the very same perfection must be manifested through your life, as well? This is one of the most beautiful lessons that I personally learned from Vedic astrology: whatever happens, it does happen for a reason – and this reason has a higher beauty and higher wisdom hidden in it. Sometimes, due to our shortsightedness and limited vision, we might miss the bigger picture and thus start judging our own life or even its Creator – but in reality there is never a single thing that happens without a reason. That is one of the most profound lessons from Bherunda Devi: "Do not look at things superficially. Seek the higher beauty and harmony hidden in everything – because it is there, even if currently you do not have the capacity to see it."

My Gurudev said once, "It is much more beautiful to see with the inner eyes. The light that shines through all these things around you and in you – this is the Truth. Each particle reflects the light of God – this is the Truth. And this Truth is accessible for everybody."

Interestingly enough, within the range of ratios during *Chaturti tithi*, the Moon is at one moment also at 42 degrees distance from the Sun during *Shukla paksha*. It is another very special number, as it is the angular radius of rainbow: 42 degrees counted from the shadow of your head in the opposite direction of the Sun. It is impossible for an observer to see a rainbow from water droplets at any angle other than 42 degrees from the direction opposite the light source. When the first rays of Sun appear after the rain, a rainbow appears, reminding us to accept all the colours of life; reminding us, that there is some beauty hidden in each tear and each difficulty we might be going through. Something beautiful is awaiting after every storm and rain. This is one of the most beautiful messages of Goddess Bherunda for all Her children.

Within waking state of consciousness, *Chaturti tithi* stands for *turiya* or spiritually awakened state of bliss, when we can consciously perceive the inner light. It is also the *tithi* during which our mental activity is at its peak. Swami Sivananda explained, that this is why we worship Ganesha on *Chaturti*, as He removes all the obstacles that may appear on our spiritual path – and majority of those obstacles are created by nothing else but our mind itself.

Interestingly, a syllable of Sri Vidya mantra connected to Goddess Bherunda is *la*, a syllable denoting bliss – while *yogini* connected to Her is Shabdha-karshini, "the one attracting all sounds". Chanting the mantras is one of the best ways to get in tune with Goddess Bherunda and purify ourselves of all the "poisons" of the mind.

In *Shukla paksha* the chakra activated on *Chaturti tithi* is *svadhishthana*, chakra of our emotions, while in *Krishna paksha* throat chakra gets activated with its intense intellectual energy and need for purification. Due to *svadhishthana chakra* and water element being so active during *Chaturti tithi*, similarly like on *Tritiya*, there is a need for us to become a bit more conscious about our emotions and not to give in to the drama of life. Similarly like on *Tritiya*, we may have a tendency to take things too personally on *Chaturti tithi* and get offended easily, which may lead to many bitter feelings. We might have an increased need for our personal space and privacy during this lunar day.

In *Shukla paksha* the sound that is created by Sun and the Moon is much more harmonious than during previous *tithis*: it is major second or *rishabha*, connected to Mars and taking action. In *Krishna paksha*, on the other hand, musical interval between Sun and the Moon is already very harmonious: its range encompasses major sixth and minor sixth or *dhaivata* in Indian *raga*, the sound ruled by Jupiter. *Dhaivata* literally means "the Divine one", as it is the overtone of *gandhara* (or third), which can be perceived, while third is played. It again reveals the most important message of Goddess Bherunda: "Do not look to the outside. Do not hear just the outside. See what is hidden. Hear what is hidden." This is why Goddess Bherunda is also connected to all hidden knowledge and occult sciences.

Connection between esoteric secrets of the world and *Chaturti tithi* can be also explained through one story from *Bhavishya Purana*. Once upon a time Kartikeya, another son of Shiva and Parvati, was writing a great scripture, which explained the physical characteristics of men and how to make predictions based on that. He completed the part about men and he was just about to write a part about women, when Ganesha arrived there and Kartikeya was forced to stop his writing. Due to this he got enraged and broke one tusk of Ganesha – his own brother. When Shiva came to know of all this, he tried to pacify both of them and asked Kartikeya to return the broken tusk to Ganesha.

After that incident, Shiva jokingly asked Kartikeya to tell from his scripture, what can he predict about Him. Kartikeya replied that in future times, Shiva would be called Kapali ("bearing a beggar's pot"). When Shiva heard that, He got furious and threw the scripture into the ocean. Ocean god came out and asked Lord Shiva, what to do with the scripture put into his waters. Shiva asked him to finish it and write a missing part about women. Ocean god replied that he will finish it only, if the whole scripture will be called by his name. Shiva agreed on that and the scripture is known until today as *Samudrika Shastra* ("scripture emerged from the ocean"). The entire incident happened on *Chaturti tithi*.

This story is deeply symbolic. It reveals a shadow side of *Chaturti tithi* natives, who may sometimes be a bit too preoccupied with the outer appearance of things (including their own appearance), but it also reveals their special talent and intuition, when it comes to reading omens, body language or even decoding the messages from the stars. They can naturally connect the different symbols with easiness and interpret the hidden messages of the universe – as Mercury blesses them with Divine translation skills. They are also great in reading other people and their body language – even if there are many other things, which they can usually improve in their emotional intelligence. And, similarly like lord Ganesha, they have a great intellect and memory.

People born on *Chaturti tithi* tend to be also a little bit "moody" or very particular about their surroundings. Places they live in have huge influence on their peace of mind – even though very often they struggle a lot in life before they find a true home. They like to see order and beauty in the space around them, even though they might not be very keen to do the cleaning or "make their hands dirty" themselves - especially when they are born in *Krishna paksha*. This quality and the natural vulnerability of of *Chaturti* natives make their mind resemble a lot the qualities of Moon in the fourth house.

Ganda Bherunda – a mythical bird and a form of Narasimha

When I was researching a bit about Goddess Bherunda, I also came across the story about one mythical creature with a very similar name: Gandha Bherunda, a two-headed bird, which was believed to have an immense magical strength.

Goddess Bherunda is also often connected to occult powers and magic, as well as freeing ourselves from their illusion. Two-headed bird may also symbolise the duplicity of the mind and the duality of the external world, which must be transcended on spiritual path. Goddess Bherunda, in Her naked form, reminds us that on spiritual path there can be no space for duplicity or hypocrisy. Duplicity or hypocrisy are the biggest flaws of the intellect.

One of the forms of Narasimha Deva, an incarnation of Vishnu in the fierce form of half-man and half-lion is also called Ganda Bherunda. It is said that the Lord assumed an eight-headed form, in the moment when He was killing Hiranyakashipu. Interestingly Narasimha took an incarnation on earth during *Chaturdashi tithi* or fourteenth lunar day, which is also *Rikta tithi*, ruled by the element of water – but in the *guna* of *sattwa*, which is the "higher octave" of *Chaturti tithi*.

The story itself, beautifully narrated in *Srimad Bhagavatam*, carries within itself lots of lessons about overcoming the duality of the mind.

Hiranyakashipu was a demon, whose name literally means "golden cushion", symbolising his attachment to his comfort zone and *tamasic* qualities, which is the shadow side of Devi Bherunda. His brother, Hiranyaksha, was killed by Lord Vishnu. However, in reality, it was not just an ordinary killing, but liberation. Hiranyakashipu and Hiranyaksha were in their previous birth celestial gatekeepers (do notice the repetition of the motive of a gatekeeper) of Vaikuntha, the abode of Vishnu. Yet, due to their pride, they were cursed by the saints to be reborn on earth as demons and to become the enemies of their beloved Lord. Lord Vishnu, however, took pity on them and promised them, that whenever they will come on earth, He will appear along with them and liberate them from the bondage of their gross, material bodies. Already in the beginning of this story we can notice one of the most profound messages of Goddess Bherunda: "Do not judge things just by looking at them from the outside. Everything happens for a very good reason and everything is just the *lila* of God. There is a higher meaning behind everything that happens in your life. Don't get so attached to this physical reality and physical body. Intellect is sometimes too limited to understand things properly. See with the heart."

Hiranyakashipu, however, was blind to this truth. When Lord Vishnu liberated his brother, Hiranyaksha, Hiranyakashipu was enraged. He did an intense *tapasya* for thousands of years to please Lord Brahma and ask him for the boon of immortality – to take revenge on Lord Vishnu. After many years, finally, Brahma Dev appeared in front of him. He said, however, very clearly, that he doesn't have a power to grant immortality to Hiranyakashipu, but that he is free to choose any other boon. Hiranyakshipu was thinking for a while, and his intellect was working intensely. Then he asked:

"May no animal, no human and no god be capable of killing me. May it be impossible to kill me during the day or during the night. May it be impossible to kill me on earth or in heaven. May it be impossible to kill me inside a building or outside a building. May it be impossible for any weapon to kill me. May nothing alive or not alive kill me."

Brahma granted Hiranyakashipu his wish. And Hiranyakashipu was happy – for he thought, that with the power of his intellect, he tricked God himself.

After some time, Hiranyakashipu's youngest son was born. But he was very different from any other son of the great demon. In fact, he was a devotee of Vishnu, which was unthinkable to Hiranyakashipu. He tried several times to "brainwash" his child, but to no result. When he saw, that it doesn't work, then Hiranyakashipu tried to torture and even ordered other demons to kill his son several times. But the devotion of a little boy was unbreakable, and the Lord saved him from suffering every single time. His name was Prahlad – "the one giving true pleasure".

Finally, Hiranyakashipu decided to kill his son himself. He called Prahlad to his court and tried one last time to change the mind of his stubborn son. Sarcastically he asked Prahlad: "So, where is your Vishnu? Will he come and protect you now?" Prahlad responded with gentle calmness: "But, father Lord Vishnu is everywhere." Hiranyakashipu asked then, pointing his finger to the nearby pillar: "Oh, really? Everywhere? Is He present in that pillar then?" Prahlad responded calmly: "Of course, father." Hiranyakashipu then rose from his throne in anger and said angrily: "Then look! I am going to destroy this pillar now. I am going to destroy your Vishnu!" Hiranyakashipu took his mace and was just about to hit the pillar. But then the pillar broke suddenly.

A strange, terrifying being appeared from the pillar. He was not a human, not an animal, and not a god. He was half-man, half-lion – Narasimha Deva. Lord Vishnu in the terrifying form of Narasimha appeared to protect the faith of His devotee. His roar was so terrifying that all the worlds were shaking, trembling in fear. He came to liberate Hiranyakashipu from his earthly form and from the poison of his own thoughts – after all, in previous lifetimes, Hiranyakashipu was His devotee, too. Lord in His magnificent incarnation quickly defeated the great demon and took him on the doorstep. When this happened, it was neither day, nor night – it was sunset. Doorstep wasn't inside any building, neither outside, but right on the border. Lord in the form of Narasimha put Hiranyakashipu on His lap, which was neither earth or heaven, and attacked the demon without any weapon – with nothing alive or not alive: He did it with His own nails. And so, Brahma's boon was honoured by the Lord – and yet, He managed to defeat the great demon and protect His devotee.

Initially I didn't plan to include this story in this book. But then, when I saw, that my Gurudev has placed on His twitter account the picture of Narasimha in the form of Ganda Bherunda, with eight heads, exactly when I was writing this chapter,

122

I thought it to be the sign. After meditating on this story, about this terrifying incarnation of the Divine, I understood how closely this story is connected with what Goddess Bherunda is trying to teach us on Her lunar day. Similarly like God in this form needed to transcend all the duality of the world, so Goddess Bherunda inspires us to transcend the duality of our mind. And, similarly like Lord Vishnu in this incarnation needed to find an impossible solution to defeat Hiranyakashipu, so Devi Bherunda inspires us to think out of the box, to overcome the obstacles She may send us. Ultimately, the Highest Goddess is not sending us obstacles to make us feel weak or small. On the contrary, She is just testing our mental strength and inner power, purifying our mind of all the negativities. But to understand, why She is sending us some exact lesson on Her lunar day, we need to learn how to look impartially on the reality around us - beyond good and bad.

Numerology: 4

Chaturti tithi is the fourth lunar day and so it is connected to number 4. There are 4 Vedas or 4 types of knowledge in Vedic culture. No wonder that in original fourth house, the sign of Cancer, Jupiter, who is the *karaka* of wisdom gets exalted. There are also 4 *purusharthas* or goals of human life: *dharma* (sacred duty), *artha* (accumulation), *kama* (gratification) and *moksha* (liberation). Number 4 also stands for four *yugas* or four major cycles of time: *satya* (golden age), *treta* (silver age), *dwapara* (bronze age) and *kali yuga* (current age of ignorance).

Number 4 also symbolises four legs of the bull of *dharma* or righteousness, as described in *Srimad Bhagavatam*. It is said that in *satya yuga* the bull of *dharma* stands firmly on all four legs. In *treta yuga* it stands on three legs. In *dwapara yuga* it stands on two legs only. And in *kali yuga* only one leg is left. These four legs stand for the qualities of austerity, cleanliness, mercy and truthfulness. It is said that the pillar of truthfulness is the only one, which can survive in *kali yuga* – and even for this single quality of righteousness it is hard to do so in the age of ignorance. This is why truthfulness is considered as the most important quality in our age.

Interestingly, even the form of Shiva connected to fourth lunar day is Vrisharudha, the one mounted on the bull Nandi, symbolising Lord Shiva's protection for the principles of *dharma*. This is why people born on *Chaturti tithi* may often follow very high principles – but may also get a bit too fixed about their rules or opinions, as well as too judgemental towards those, who follow different principles.

Number 4 is also associated with four Sanat Kumaras or mind-born sons of Lord Brahma, who remained forever in the forms of little children and are always naked. Interesting enough, if we take into consideration that Cancer, fourth sign of zodiac, is the sign of childhood and our inner, vulnerable self – as well as our feeling of comfort, contentment, and peace of mind. Fourth house is also the house of our comfort zone. This seems to be deeply reflected in the qualities of Goddess

Bherunda, who is sometimes portrayed as naked, as well, and who always seeks purity, comfort, contentment and wisdom.

These four children-sages were always immersed in the state of supreme bliss and rememberance of the Divine, which is why they were never concerned, whether they are wearing any clothes or not. Their consciousness was completely pure and childlike, as their ego was completely burned down in the fire of their realisation and supreme wisdom. Similar childlike innocence is sometimes manifested through *Chaturti tithi* natives, which is why sometimes people born on fourth lunar day may find it hard to "fit" into the society and all its norms. In fact, adjusting themselves to outer norms and limitations is often quite painful process for them. Similarly like Sanat Kumaras, *Chaturti tithi* natives need to learn how to live in the world, but stay detached from the world.

Interestingly enough, these were Sanat Kumars, who cursed two gatekeepers of Lord Vishnu to be born three times on earth as demons, when they were disrespected. *Chaturti tithi* natives also can have a bit "sharp" tongue sometimes, and they can act quite impulsively or even be a bit stingy, when they are disrespected.

There are also four petals in *muladhara chakra*, the energy center at the base of our spine. *Muladhara chakra* is strongly connected to Ganesha, similarly like *Chaturti tithi*. Even the syllable of Sri Vidya mantra (*la*) connected to *Chaturti* is the same like *bij* mantra for root chakra (*lam*). In fact, even the bones of our physical body in the region of *muladhara chakra* region resemble the elephant head of Ganesha a little, with hip bone as his ears and spine as his trunk. People born on *Chaturti tithi* often need to work a little on their inner qualities connected to *muladhara chakra* and element of earth - especially humility, grounding, patience and acceptance. They should never be afraid of "getting dirty" by worldly vibrations. They need to rather consciously work on maintaining the purity of the mind regardless of the outer circumstances.

Lord Brahma, who is also considered to be a presiding deity of *muladhara chakra* has four heads as well – each of them turned towards different direction of the world. This is a silent indicator for all people born on *Chaturti tithi* that there is also a need for them to be more openminded and make their effort to understand different topics of life from different perspectives and not get fixated in their own personal point of view.

Yogini in *Kalachakra*: Southwest

On *Chaturti tithi* the danger comes from the Southwest. It is said that we should avoid travelling in that direction during the fourth lunar day in any of the two *pakshas*. In fact, it is not recommended to travel on *Chaturti tithi* at all, due to its slow energies.

In Vastu, Southwest direction is connected to the heaviest of all elements, earth, and with Rahu, a shadow-planet or lunar node, causing eclipses. In *Kalachakra*, planet Mercury is connected to Southwest direction and his qualities become the most dangerous on that day. Exaggerated and immature intellect, which tries to put a label on everything, is not capable of finding any creative solution. When we habitually categorise everything as good or bad, we are not able to see the reality, and therefore we fail to find the solutions for the obstacles, which Goddess may send on our way. This is where Rahu's energy and Ganesha's support can help us on the day ruled by Bherunda Devi – to stop judging for a moment, and start looking for solutions. It is quite fascinating if you think that both Ganesha and Rahu were beheaded – which is why they are helping us in finding solutions, which reach beyond intellect, beyond the "head".

Shaktis of Goddess Bherunda

Different *shaktis* or powers of Goddess Bherunda dwell in the different places of Her *yantra*. Interestingly, the *yantra* of Bherunda Devi is the first one, which contains also an image of *shatkona* or six-pointed star, which is the basis of golden ratio, as well as symbolises unity between feminine principle and masculine principle; negative particle and positive particle. It is also the first *yantra*, which contains *ashtakona* or eight-angled shape. The shapes within the entire *yantra*, along with their angles, are much sharper than the ones we can find in previous *yantras* - which is already a powerful indication that we are dealing with much sharper and more intense energy here. This also a clear indication, that the very nature of Goddess Bherunda is much more strict than the nature of former Nitya Devis.

In the *yantra* of Bherunda Devi *yoni* or down-facing triangle is enclosed in *shatkona*, six-pointed star, which is enclosed in *ashtakona*, eight-pointed star, furtherly enclosed by eight petals and *bhupura* surrounding the entire structure. Three *shaktis* of three corners of the inner triangle are: Iccha (willpower), Jnana (knowledge) and Kriya (action). Each of the six arms of the six-pointed star is occupied by six *shaktis* of the chakras: Dakini (*vishuddha chakra*), Rakini (*anahata chakra*), Lakini (*manipura chakra*), Kakini (*svadhishthana chakra*), Shakini (*muladhara chakra*) and Hakini (*ajna chakra*). Being so, inner triangle and six-pointed star are symbolising our three innermost powers manifested through our six chakras.

8 corners of *ashtakona*, eight-pointed figure, symbolising 8 directions of the world, are occupied by *shaktis*: Kamala ("lotus flower" or "rose coloured"), Kamini ("lover"), Kirata ("procuress"), Kirti ("glorious one"), Kuttani ("with body made of angles"), Kulasundari ("beauty of the household"), Kalyani ("auspicious one") and Kalakola ("having beautiful breasts"). And on eight petals of the lotus enclosing *ashtakona* dwell following *shaktis*: Vijaya ("victorious one"), Vimala ("purest one"), Shubha ("auspicious one"), Vishwa ("the world"), Vibhuti ("splendour"), Vinata

("humble one"), Vividha ("manifold one") and Virata ("heroic one"). Additionally, Her eight weapons are placed in the space outside the figure of 8 angles.

Swara of Goddess Bherunda

Ī, the fourth *swara* or vowel of Sanskrit alphabet, is associated with Goddess Bherunda. Its *kala* is "controller", which resonates well with Bherunda Devi's nature. Its sound may produce feelings of dejection, sorrow or pain, but it can also give us better perception of things and allow our consciousness to penetrate the veil of *maya*, worldly illusion and see the reality better. Sometimes confrontation with the reality might be painful – but it always leads to purification.

Interestingly enough, according to *Agni Purana* vowel *ī* is connected to Lakshmi ("the one, who knows Her goal") and Rati (Goddess of passion).

Nakshatras connected to Goddess Bherunda

Bharani nakshatra is connected to *swara* of Goddess Bherunda, while Her eight arms stand for all four *padas* of Margashirsha and Ardra.

All four Nitya Devis, Kameshwari, Bhagamalini, Nityaklinna and Bherunda are connected to Bharani nakshatra in this way or the other, as well as with waking state of consciousness or *jagrat*. All four of them are connected to sacred womb of the Goddess, from which everything takes birth into the world. Additionally, two of them, which are connected to Bharani nakshatra by *swara*, Nityaklinna and Bherunda, are all about our comfort zone, wetness, nourishment, stability, vulnerability and sensitivity. Nityaklinna, connected to short vowel *i* is a positive aspect of nourishment and sensitivity, which inspires us towards better relationships and growth, while Bherunda, a prolonged *ī*, represents its negative aspect: oversensitivity or its opposite, energy that became too inert and needs some good stirring.

Margashirsha and Ardra are probably two of the most intellectual nakshatras of the zodiac. While Margashirsha is connected to research and collecting information from many different sources, Ardra stands for focus on our goal and clarity. Both of them have also a very wild nature. Natural beauty of loosen hair and feeling of freedom is for them far more attractive than artificial beauty and pretending to be somebody else, than we truly are. They don't feel the need to make themselves more beautiful just to please someone or somebody, as they usually feel confident enough in their own skin. One of the most beautiful blessings of Goddess Bherunda is this confidence to be our true selves and a healthy detachment from our outer look, which is not a very common thing anymore in today's world. Yet, if this quality gets exaggerated, which tends to happen especially under Ardra nakshatra, it can result in native being born under this asterism or during *Chaturti tithi* a bit too messy and chaotic, as *tamasic* qualities of Bherunda Devi are taking over in such a case.

There is also one nakshatra, in which *guna* of *rajas* combines with water element, similarly like on *Chaturti tithi*: Mula, the nakshatra ruled by chaotic Goddess Nirriti. Interestingly, this nakshatra is right opposite Ardra, the nakshatra of Rudra. This is why Mula nakshatra is ruled by Kali, as well, who looks very similar to Nirriti. Nirriti is a Goddess of chaos. She is said to embody all the negative qualities of a woman: she is said to be ugly, fat, lazy, always detached, independent and bringing bad luck, wherever She goes. She is a negative form of Lakshmi. Some of these qualities may be seen in *Chaturti* natives, as well, especially when it comes to some laziness, slowliness or *tamasic* energy, which they sometimes manifest on external level – even if their inner beauty is often unparallaled.

Planetary ruler of Mula nakshatra is Ketu, which is particularly interesting, as Ketu is also connected to Ganesha. It is also hard to miss the connection between Mula nakshatra and *muladhara chakra* – after, all not only the name is similar, but Mula nakshatra is literally a supermassive black hole in the center of our galaxy, which was symbolic for ancient *rishis* to the irresistible gravitational pull of our root chakra, which keeps us always focused in the outer world, entangled in materialism. Interestingly, both *muladhara chakra* and Mula nakshatra are also presided by Prajapati or Brahma, especially in older scriptures (we can find this connection in the Vedas, *Nakshatra suktam*, more specifically).

Mula nakshatra, being a galactic center, a black hole, also resembles in some way the *Rikta* ("empty") nature of *Chaturti tithi* and some sort of existential emptiness or loneliness, which they may experience from time to time – which often comes simply from them being too focused on themselves. Shadow side of *Chaturti tithi* natives is that sometimes they really think that the world revolves just around them, which is also a shadow side of Mula nakshatra natives. However, similarly like Mula nakshatra natives, *Chaturti tithi* natives often have an unparallaled capacity to absorb spiritual knowledge (or any kind of knowledge, in fact), as well as to unroot lots of hidden knowledge, make some unusual connections and discover new things in their field. They simply have this capacity to go to the very root of every topic or issue.

The ultimate lesson from Mula nakshatra for all *Chaturti* natives is to rise above good and bad, pure and impure, black and white. After all, in black hole everything merges together. This is why ancients were perceiving our magnificent galactic center as Mother Kali Herself, who consumes everything. Her dark skin reminds us that in reality nothing is pure and nothing is impure. She accepts everything, as black colour is the only colour, into which all other colours are eventually merging. Rising above the duality of the mind is the highest life lesson for all *Chaturti* natives. This is why sometimes they might feel attracted to the path of *advaita* or non-duality.

Tithi, vara and nakshatra resonance

The energy of Goddess Bherunda is the most incompatible with Sunday, the day of the burning Sun – as Devi Bherunda is the great enemy of the ego and Her element is water, too. Whenever *Chaturti tithi* falls on Sunday, *visha yoga* ("poisonous combination") occurs, which can awaken some "poisons" in our mind or body. Additionally, if this *visha yoga* happens on one of those transformative nakshatras: Bharani, Margashirsha, Ashlesha, Vishakha, Anuradha, Jyeshtha or Dhanishta, it is called *vinasha yoga* or "combination of destruction". *Chaturti tithi*, which occurs on Sunday, brings positive effects only, when Moon dwells in Pushya, Uttara Phalguni, Hasta, Mula, Uttarashadha, Shravana or Uttara Bhadrapada nakshatra, as their energy is well grounded – this combination is called *siddha yoga* or "combination of accomplishments".

Whenever *Chaturti tithi* occurs on Thursday or Saturday, the days of the great teachers Brihaspati (Jupiter) and Shani (Saturn) it forms respectively *amrita yoga* ("combination of nectar" – Thursday) and *siddha yoga* ("combination of achievement" - Saturday). These *yogas* get even more empowered, if on Thursday, the *Chaturti* Moon dwells in Ashwini, Punarvasu, Pushya, Magha, Swati, Purva Ashadha, Purva Bhadrapada or Revati nakshatra, while on Saturday in Rohini, Swati, Vishakha, Anuradha, Dhanishta or Shatabhisha.

Thus, the blessings of Goddess Bherunda, are the most beneficial on Thursdays and Saturdays, while they are the least beneficial on Sundays, as they can hurt our ego the most on the day ruled by the Sun. It is also quite logical as water element (*Rikta tithi*) can never go really well with fire (fiery weekday).

To summarise, *Chaturti tithi* Moon resonates well with Ashwini, Rohini, Punarvasu, Pushya, Magha, Uttara Phalguni, Hasta, Swati, Mula, Purvashadha, Uttarashadha, Shravana, Shatabhisha, Uttara Bhadrapada and Revati nakshatras. It doesn't resonate well with Bharani, Margashirsha, Ashlesha and Jyeshtha, while it brings mixed results with Vishakha, Anuradha, Dhanishta and Purva Bhadrapada. Unique thing about *Chaturti tithi* is that it doesn't cause *shunya dosha* to any nakshatra.

In *Agni Purana* it is also stated that whenever *Chaturti tithi* happens on Friday along with Moon dwelling in Purva Bhadrapada nakshatra, it can bring death.

Additionally, *Bhavishya Purana* says, that whenever *Chaturti tithi* in *Shukla paksha* falls on Tuesday it is a very auspicious day, called *sukha* ("happiness"). Whoever fasts on that day and worships Lord Ganesha with red flowers and red sandalwood paste, such a person is going to be blessed with good fortune and bodily organs of such person are going to be protected. It brings strength, protection, vitality and health to the body.

YOGAS FORMED WITH *CHATURTHI TITHI*

	1	2	3	4	5	6	7
1	visha		sukha		**siddha**		siddha
2	vinasha		sukha		amrita		siddha
3	visha		sukha		amrita		siddha
4	visha		sukha		amrita		**siddha**
5	vinasha		sukha		amrita		siddha
6	visha		sukha		amrita		siddha
7	visha		sukha		siddha		siddha
8	siddha / visha		sukha		siddha		siddha
9	vinasha		sukha		amrita		siddha
10	visha		sukha		siddha		siddha
11	siddha / visha		sukha		amrita		siddha
12	visha		sukha		amrita		siddha
13	siddha / visha		sukha		amrita		siddha
14	visha		sukha		amrita		siddha
15	visha		sukha		siddha		**siddha**
16	vinasha		sukha		amrita		**siddha**
17	vinasha		sukha		amrita		**siddha**
18	vinasha		sukha		amrita		siddha
19	siddha / visha		sukha		amrita		siddha
20	visha		sukha		siddha		siddha
21	siddha / visha		sukha		amrita		siddha
22	siddha / visha		sukha		amrita		siddha
23	vinasha		sukha		amrita		**siddha**
24	visha		sukha		amrita		**siddha**
25	visha		sukha		siddha	deadly	siddha
26	siddha / visha		sukha		amrita		siddha
27	visha		sukha		**siddha**		siddha

Also, if a person is born on *Chaturti tithi* and Monday or Friday, it produces a *tithi dosha* for the person. The personality of such a person will be overly dominated by water element, which will lead too very turbulent emotional life. If such a person is additionally born on any of the watery nakshatras (Ardra, Ashlesha, Mula, Purvashadha, Shatabhisha, Uttara Bhadrapada, Revati) this *dosha* will be more severe and such a person will need to consciously work on balancing exeggerated water element, both in physical body and on a psychological level. Issues with too much phlegm in the body might be very prominent, when such a combination occurs. According to *Agni Purana* it is best in such case to simply have much more physical movement.

In Vedic month called Magha (in the end of which Full Moon falls in Magha nakshatra) *Chaturti tithi* is considered *shunya* and is avoided for any auspicious activities. In Magha month *Chaturti tithi* often occurs in Shatabhisha nakshatra (in *Shukla paksha*), which is also the middle of its *shunya rashi*, and Magha nakshatra (in *Krishna paksha*) - two nakshatras progress, which can additionally make *Chaturti tithi* a bit more cold, detached and lonely.

Important *rashis* for *Chaturthi tithi* natives

Tithi Pati Kshetra Paksha		Tithi Shunya Rashi	
Tithi Shunya Rashi		*Caturti*	
			Tithi Pati Kshetra

Each *tithi* has a special connection with a number of *rashis*. Understanding those connections can help us not only in understanding our own birth chart on a much deeper level, but in better understanding of the nature of the *tithi* itself.

Two *rashis*, which are of greatest importance for all *Chaturti tithi* natives are Pisces and Virgo. Virgo is the *mulatrikona* sign of planetary lord of this lunar day (Mercury, *tithi pati kshetra*), while Pisces is the sign opposite to it (*tithi pati kshetra paksha*), which is the sign revealing, where are we heading in life. It reveals deeply spiritual, as well as knowledgable nature of all *Chaturti tithi* natives, as well as certain slowliness of their physical body. Higher knowledge, philosophy, spiritual journeys and deeper understanding of things is very important for all people born on fourth lunar day. People born in *Shukla paksha* will be looking more for philosophical and spiritual type of wisdom, while *Krishna Chaturti* natives will have more practical approach, dominated by logic and power of research. All of them will have, however, a deep longing and yearning for knowledge and wisdom. They will also undergo many significant transformations in their emotional life and may experience certain heartbreaks, as well, because this specific Virgo/Pisces axis is connected with exaltation and debilitation place of Venus, and will keep bringing some profound lessons about love to all *Chaturti tithi* natives.

Signs Virgo and Pisces have also a deeper spiritual meaning for *Chaturti tithi* natives, connected to the movement of energy through the chakras on those lunar days – and reflected in the chakras of the zodiac connected to *rashis*. In *Shukla paksha* the flow of energy will be more intense in Pisces (which is another reason why *Shukla Chaturti* natives are generally more easy-going, but also less ungrounded in a way), while in *Krishna paksha* it will be more intense in the sign of Virgo (which blesses *Krishna Chaturti* natives with more grounding, logic, memory, intellect and organisational skills). As *tithi pati kshetra* and *tithi pati kshetra paksha* are in the case of fourth lunar day the same as the signs of natural flow of energy in the zodiacal chakras on those days (similarly like on *Pratipad tithi*), it also blesses *Chaturti tithi* natives with certain inner confidence – yet, also gives them a solitary nature.

Tithi shunya rashis or the signs, which are made "fruitless" by *Chaturti tithi*, are Taurus (along with its lord, Venus) and Aquarius (along with its lord, Saturn) – which are, perhaps, two of the most materialistic zodiac signs, as well as the most connected with our environment and social circles – which is something that *Chaturti tithi* natives are sometimes naturally blind to. Both of these signs are naturally quite vulnerable for all people born on *Chaturti tithi*. It is also important to notice that Taurus and Aquarius are natural 2nd and 11th house, two houses in Vedic Astrology most responsible for our wealth and prosperity. As *Chaturti tithi* is a *rikta* or "empty" *tithi*, those natives may also often have a humble start in life and might need to work a lot to build their prosperity in life.

Unless these signs are occupied by Rahu or Ketu, or unless its lords (Venus or Saturn) are placed 3rd, 6th, 8th or 12th house from ascendant or Moon, or are retrograde, or in conjuction with malefic planet, or, lastly, in nakshatras of Rahu or Ketu, these two signs and houses ruled by those planets won't bring good results for the native. In such a case these signs must be strengthened (by strengthening their lords) to bring good results. *Shunya* planets do produce good results, however, when they transit 3rd, 6th, 8th or 12th house from from ascendant or Moon.

Sadhana for Goddess Bherunda

Goddess Bheruda is mostly pleased with our honesty, as well as chanting of the mantras. She cannot be pleased by any offering lower than that, as She has no tolerance for duplicity of the mind. To connect with Her on a deeper level, you can either do a meditation of sitting on Her lap, as given by my Gurudev (described in Chapter 24), or colour Her yantra and meditate on it, facing Southwest. For your *sadhana* you can use one of the two mantras below or one of the affirmations. There are couple of more advanced mantras for worship of Goddess Bherunda in *Tantraraja*, but they are not supposed to be recited without a guidance of a Guru.

Mantras:

oṁ aīṁ hrīṁ śrīṁ īṁ bheruṇḍāyai namaḥ
oṁ aīṁ hrīṁ śrīṁ īṁ tuṣṭiyai namaḥ

Affirmations:

I allow myself to be strong.
I allow myself to be vulnerable.
I allow myself to overcome all obstacles.
I allow myself to leave my comfort zone.
I allow myself to notice solutions out of the box.
I allow myself to let go of all that is not serving me anymore.
I allow myself to see higher beauty in everything.
I am honouring justice.
I am accepting the dark part of myself.

Questions for self-analysis

Every lunar day is an opportunity to learn something new about ourselves. Nitya Devis and their wisdom can become our guides on this sacred journey. Questions below can help you in recognising certain "shadow" tendencies in yourself, which may arise on *Chaturti tithi*. If you were born on this lunar day, these questions might be of big importance for you in life and allow you to face your weaknesses.

- Am I trying to be too perfect?
- Do I accept my weaknesses?
- Am I brave enough to face my negativities?
- Can I admit that I made a mistake?
- Am I too afraid of criticism?
- Do I spend too much time in my head?
- Is my intellectual energy too strong?
- Do I neglect my body and its needs, sometimes?
- What can I do in order to bring more awareness into my body?
- Am I too lazy sometimes?
- Am I strong enough to overcome my mental habits?
- Can I allow myself to go out of the comfort zone?
- Can I allow myself to be vulnerable?
- Can I embrace with love also the dark parts of myself?
- Can I accept, that both the dark side, and the bright side are needed equally in the world?
- Can I make a conscious effort to see the higher beauty in everything around me?
- How am I honouring justice?
- Am I not a little bit too critical sometimes?
- Can I make a conscious effort to reach for the solutions beyond the intellectual frame?
- Am I not a little bit too calculative sometimes?
- Am I sometimes a little bit afraid to get my hands "dirty" and do the work?
- Do I take things a bit too personally?
- Am I honouring other people's boundaries?
- Am I too closed in my own world and missing something important?

Yantra of Goddess Bherunda

CHAPTER 12

VAHNIVASINI – FIRE-DWELLER
PANCHAMI – FIFTH LUNAR DAY

oḍḍiyāna-pītha-nilayā lalitā viṣṇu-sodarī
daṃṣṭrā-karāla-vadanā vajreśi vahnivāsinī

"Praised be Goddess Vahnivasini, Indweller of the fire and sister of Vishnu, playful Lalita, powerful Vajreśi with terrifying teeth, who dwells in Oddiyana pitha (pilgrimage place)."

- Sri Chamundeshwari Ashtottara Shatanama Stotram

Kala	Element	Planet	Guna	Yogini	Vowel
pushti (strength)	air	Jupiter	rajas	South	u

Stage of consciousness	Divine quality	Deity (Muhurta Cintamani)	Deity (Varahamihira)	Nakshatra connection	Form of Shiva
waking (dreaming)	nirapeksha (impartiality)	Nagas	Chandra	Krittika Punarvasu Pushya	Tripurantaka

Shukla Paksha

Nadi: pingala
Chakra: svadhishthana / manipura
Interval: minor third
Deity (Narada Purana): Gauri
House from the Sun: 2. 3 or 4

Krishna Paksha

Nadi: ida
Chakra: vishuddha / anahata
Interval: perfect fifth
Deity (Narada Purana): Hari
House from the Sun: 8. 9 or 10

Vahnivasini means "the one, dwelling in fire". She is the creative fire within us. Passionate nature of *rajas guna* connects on *Panchami tithi* with sensitivity and lightness of air element. Being connected with the element of air and planet Jupiter, Vahnivasini is much different from the intense heat of Kameshwari and Her passionate nature. Vahnivasini Devi has much more light, creative and inspired energy. Her tantric name in *64 Yogini Namavali* is Shashini – "the swift one". Like the fire of Goddess Kameshwari increases passion and *guna* of *rajas* within us, so the fire of Goddess Vahnivasini is more of a light-giver. It is said in *Lalita Mahamatmya* that when Goddess Lalita was fighting along with all Nitya Devis the demon Bhanduka, and when the demonic forces casted the darkness on the battlefield, it was Goddess Vahnivasini (along with Jwalamalini, Goddess of the fourteenth lunar day, *Caturdashi*) who dispelled the darkness of the battlefield with Her luminous radiance. She made everything visible again. This is why her lunar day is co-ruled by Jupiter, guru among gods – as the very word *guru* means "the one, who dispells the darkness" of our ignorance.

Fire is the element, which always brings light, warmness and transformation. Interestingly enough, if we use the model from Chapter 3, superimposing the *tithis* and the chakras that they are connected to in *Rashi chakra*, zodiacal wheel of Time, we will see that in *Shukla paksha*, *Panchami tithi* would be embracing the zone containing the transformative *gandanta* zone between Pisces and Aries (zodiacal *svadhishthana chakra* and zodiacal *manipura chakra* – a journey from water to fire), while in *Krishna paksha*, *Panchami tithi* would be embracing the zone containing Citra nakshatra (Vedic constellation right between zodiacal *vishuddha chakra* and zodiacal *anahata chakra*), which represents heavenly forces defeating the forces of darkness. Although the name of Citra nakshatra means "shining" or "colorful", denoting its creative nature and artistic skill, Citra is actually the most *tamasic* of all the nakshatras, where the energy of ignorance can be experienced the most – and transformed the most. It reveals Citra's alchemic ability to transform something dark, negative and formless into something bright, positive and having a beautiful form. This is why it is the nakshatra of Divine Architect, Vishwakarma, connected with his artistic skills. Goddess Vahnivasini blesses Her children with very similar qualities.

Exeggerated creative powers and sensitivity can also lead, however, to some indecisiveness. Combination of fire, ether and air makes creative powers of this lunar day sometimes a bit too "airy", to the extent of losing focus on the goal. This is why people born on *Panchami tithi* can often be a bit of day-dreamers, with strong romantic nature. Sometimes they can be a bit too passive, as well, or overly optimistic. Once they focus on something, however, this is when their creative powers truly flourish. Overcoming the distracting energies of this lunar day and awakening withim themselves focus and concentration (qualities of healthy fire element) on the goal will help them greatly.

Interestingly, the quality of this lunar day is called *lakshmi* or ability to bring prosperity, luck and...focus on the goal. The word *lakshmi* itself is derived from *lakshya*, "the goal". Mother Lakshmi is therefore not only the Goddess of prosperity, but, above all, Goddess of *guna* of *sattwa* and complete focus on the highest goal. Because when She came out of the ocean of milk and was thus brought into the world for the first time in Her external form, She immediately approached Lord Vishnu and put a flower garland around His neck, making Him Her Divine husband. That is why She was called Lakshmi - the one, who immediately after birth knew Her highest goal. She knew immediately whom to choose as her husband. This is why prayers to Mother Lakshmi are also very beneficial for every *Panchami tithi* native.

Not without a reason *Panchami tithi* is co-ruled by *nagas* or Divine serpents. Although those serpents are considered to be in Vedic astrology the keepers of all secrets, hidden assets (and hidden talents), as well as full of creative skill, one of the most prominent quality of all snakes is that they don't have limbs and they are extremely flexible. They don't have a definite shape, like other animals have. Similarly people born on *Panchami tithi* often need some time to find their life's purpose and to assume their true "shape". As *Panchami* is also a *gandanta tithi*, they may often experience some sort of confusion about their life's path in the beginning of their life's journey, as well as may tend to be overly flexible, overly optimistic and... overly dependent on others. Even though they value their freedom a lot and have very clear boundaries, in the beginning of life they sometimes have a tendency to depend more on other's people's help than on their own strength.

Vahnivasini is the first Goddess connected to the dreaming state of consciousness. Her yearning is to dream and to create, to reflect the light of Divine inspiration into the world and to shine. She wishes to create Her future with Her ability to dream. Some of Her names are Siddhi-prada ("the one, who blesses with mystical powers or achievements"), Vishwa-vigraha ("the one, who is the form of the world") and Vishwa-ghasmara ("the one, who consumes the world"). Syllable of Sri Vidya mantra connected to Her is *hrim*, the seed mantra of transformation and heart chakra (sometimes called *vahnibija* or "seed of the fire"), while *yogini* connected to Her is Sparsha-karshini ("the one attracting all touch"). This reveals not only a passionate and romantic side of Vahnivasini, but also Her deep inner yearning to make things more tangible, defined, having a form – as Her own energy, full of ether and air element, is completely formless, and therefore it is seeking its form and expression in the outer world. Interestingly, it is also deeply connected with creative powers of Citra nakshatra, as Tvashtar (or Vishwakarma), the Cosmic Architect, is its presiding deity.

The quality of Sri Krishna connected to *Panchami tithi* is *nirapeksha* or impartiality, which is a positive trait of any person born on this lunar day. The shadow side of it, however, can manifest, again, as indecisiveness or lack of ability to choose between different things. Perhaps this is why Vahnivasini Devi has such a variety of different items in Her hands.

A question may arise, how is impartiality different from justice, the quality of the former phase of the Moon presided by Goddess Bherunda? Impartiality carries within itself a detached energy and it has a desire to treat everybody equally, in an impartial way. Justice, on the other hand, is very different from equanimity, as it always looks towards giving everybody, what they deserve – which is very different from giving the same thing to everybody. This is also why Goddess Vahnivasini is much more benevolent than Goddess Bherunda.

Kala of the Moon connected to *Panchami tithi* and Goddess Vahnivasini, is very similar to the one of Nityaklinna Devi: *pushti* – the power to nourish things, make them grow and prosper, as well as the power to give comfort. *Pushti* is also the power to bring wealth and opulence. Indeed, after intensely transformative fourth lunar day, ruled by Bherunda Devi, Goddess Vahnivasini brings us on Her day more comfort, relief and nourishment. Interestingly, two most nourishing Goddesses, Nityaklinna and Vahnivasini, dwell exactly right before Bherunda Devi and right after Bherunda Devi, who is the Goddess bringing us the most difficult energies to deal with.

Meditation with Goddess Vahnivasini

Hue: burning gold
Number of heads: 1
Number of eyes: 3
Number of hands: 8
Right hands: white tiger lily, flowery arrows, citron, golden horn
Left hands: conch, sugarcane bow, red lotus, full moon
Garments: yellow silk
Ornaments: ruby ornaments, diadem with rubies, anklets, waist-chain of gems, pearls and other ornaments

Tantraraja describes Goddess Vahnivasini as a girl in the stage of Her early youth with a burning gold hue. It reveals a very innocent, and sometimes a bit immature and naive part of Vahnivasini Devi. Her golden complexion stands for Her purity – because gold is purified in the fire. Goddess Vahnivasini is known to bestow radiance to the body and give unparalleled beauty. She is dressed in yellow silk, which reveals Her optimistic nature. She is adorned with many ornaments with rubies. *Tantraraja* says that "the strength of the rubies in Her diadem make ruddy the whole surrounding", while Her natural radiance is enhanced by Her anklets, waist-chain of gems, pearls and other ornaments, which appear like a cluster of jewels. This yearning to shine and to express Her light into the world is a very prominent quality of Vahnivasini Devi.

Goddess Vahnivasini has 8 hands. Interestingly, She is the first Nitya Devi, who doesn't hold *pasha* (noose, symbolising control over passions), neither *ankusha* (goad, symbolising control over repulsion), as well as the first Goddess, who is holding such a variety of items in Her hands – and none of them being an actual weapon. In Her right hands She carries a white tiger lily, five flowery arrows (symbolising five senses or five results of desire), a citron and a golden horn. In Her left hands She carries a conch, sugarcane bow (symbolising the mind), red lotus flower and full Moon. Lack of *pasha* and *ankusha* in Her hands actually reveals that for all *Panchami tithi* natives their likes and dislikes are very important – and they don't let go of them too easily. Even though they are naturally very tolerant to other people's likes and dislikes, they don't let go of their own likes and dislikes easily. They tend to be very particular about things.

Vahnivasini is the first Goddess holding a citron fruit in one of Her hands. Interestingly, a citron tree is sometimes called *vahnibija*, "seed of the fire", similarly like mantra *hrim* itself - the mantra purifying the heart chakra. Citron fruit is also used in ayurveda as cardiac tonic, helping the heart. It is also said to help exeggerated *pitta dosha* or fiery constitution. The sour taste of lemon and citron fruit also helps in cooling down fiery *kundalini shakti*, when Her energy becomes too exaggerated. Similarly, Goddess Vahnivasini, sometimes sends us some bitter experiences in life, so our heart can be purified in the fire of transformation. She teaches us to accept both sweet and bitter experiences in life.

A conch in Her left hand symbolises Her creative potential. According to Vedic thought, the universe was created by the power of sound or vibration. This is also why people born under *Panchami tithi* are often very fond of music and art. And, indeed, in *Shukla paksha* the distance between the Sun and the Moon creates the first really harmonious sound: *minor third* or *gandhara* ("the sweet sounding one", ruled by Sun), while in *Krishna paksha* the distance between Sun and the Moon creates the most harmonious of all intervals: perfect fifth or *panchama* ("the fifth one", ruled by Saturn), which is often used in music for finetuning the instruments. Similarly the main motivation of Goddess Vahnivasini is to bring more harmony, light and beauty into the world around Her – to finetune all vibrations.

Interestingly, *tithis* forming the most harmonious intervals often will turn to be not so supportive, when it comes to taking action in material world. They might often bring us lots of contentment or peace of mind, as well as provide us a harmonious environment for our spiritual practice, or romantic mood, but their energy won't be very conductive for taking action. Those intervals, which will produce the highest musical "frictions" will also be the most fiery ones, motivating us towards taking action and heading towards harmony or fulfillment. Those intervals, which are very harmonious, on the other hand, are already contented, satiated and satisfied – they do not have a specific motivation to leave this pleasant space. Vahnivasini Devi, ruling over the first *Purna tithi* ("full" lunar day), holding a Full Moon in Her hand and forming the most harmonious chord in *Krishna paksha*, as well as the first harmonious chord in *Shukla paksha*, is the first "full" Goddess, who feels completely satisfied with Herself and has the only desire to shine Her light into the outer world. Being the first goddess connected to dreaming state, Vahnivasini Devi won't necessarily inspire us to take action – but more to dream, to express ourselves, to be romantic and creative, as well as to simply feel contented and grateful.

Vahnivasini Devi also helps us in the process of learning and education – especially, when it comes to spiritual teachings. She inspires us to become more pure and receptive, so we can be ready to receive spiritual knowledge. This is why *Panchami tithi* is also sacred to *nagas* or mystical snakes, who are not only keepers of secrets, but also symbolise our sensitivity, intuition, as well as *kundalini shakti* Herself and spiritual transformation. Interestingly, on that very day, *Panchami tithi*, *nagas* were saved from a horrible snake sacrifice, where all the snakes were supposed to be killed by offering them in the sacred fire. This is why this day is also very supportive for preserving the sacred knowledge and passing it further with the power of sacred speech and the *mantras*.

Vahni is also one of the names of Goddess Saraswati, Mother of all wisdom, all knowledge and all creative endeavours. All the knowledge is like the fire or *vahni*: it can either show us light or burn us. This danger is represented by the *nagas*, the sacred snakes, as well. These ancient keepers of sacred knowledge were considered to be specifically short-tempered. Exactly when I was writing the chapter of this book on *Panchami tithi*, 23 November 2017, my Gurudev wrote this beautiful message:

"Knowledge is like a samurai's sword. Either it is a deadly weapon or the very soul of the samurai. It is not enough to have knowledge. Even more important is to know, how to handle it – otherwise one can hurt oneself, either through abuse or misuse of it."

Fifth lunar day is also connected to fifth form of Lord Shiva called Tripurantaka or, sometimes, Tripurasundara - similarly like the name of highest Goddess, Lalita Tripurasundari, who is also presiding over *Panchami tithi*. Tripurantaka means "the one, who destroyed the three cities". *Matsya Purana* and *Shiva Purana* describe the story of three imperishable cities build by Mayasura or the architect of the demons (notice the motive of Divine Architect repeating itself), in order to protect them. These were not just ordinary cities. They were floating in the air and each of them was made, respectively, of iron, silver and gold. Each was rotating in its own rhythm. It was said that nothing and nobody can destroy them, unless they are perfectly aligned, which was happening only for a fraction of time, when Moon was going right through Pushya nakshatra (you might like to remember this star) – as the demons received the boon that these cities cannot be destroyed, unless a single arrow pierces all of them at the same time. Shiva in His form of Tripurantaka, with Mount Meru (symbolising our central energy channel, *sushumna*) assuming the form of His bow, Divine snake Ananta Shesha (representing *kundalini shakti*) assuming the form of His bow-string, Vishnu (symbolising devotion) becoming His arrow and Agni (symbolising focus) becoming a tip of His arrow, destroyed the three cities of the demons, when their demonic acts started to get out of control and when they were harrassing the three worlds.

All these stories always have a deeper internal meaning. Three cities of Tripura or three worlds can as well stand for our three bodies: physical body, astral body and casual body. The city of Tripura represents lack of integrity or harmony between these three bodies, which gives birth to *tamasic* energies. A single arrow of Shiva, which destroyed the three cities stands for the quality of focus. Similarly, *Panchami tithi* natives need to find this inner alignment and focus to overcome *tamasic* forces of indecisivenesss or laziness. Focus is one of the most important qualities for them to develop.

Numerology: 5

Number 5 is strictly connected in Vedic literature to five flowery arrows in the hands of the Divine Mother or Cupid. It is connected to five results of the desire and five Kamadevas, which indicates a deeply passionate nature of *Panchami tithi*. This is why it is the best day for a romantic relationship or to conceive a child, as it is also connected to fifth house in Vedic astrology. Number 5 is also associated with 5 elements, out of which the entire universe is born and made, as well as five senses (*jnanendriyas*) and five senses of action (*karmendriyas*), through which we perceive the entire creation and through which our desires are born or satisfied. This is why fifth house in Vedic astrology is also closely connected to romance, fulfillment of desires, children, joy of life and our heart's desire. It is in 5th Chapter of Bhagavad Gita that Lord Krishna says:

"If one is able to tolerate the urges of the senses and control the force of desire and anger, he will be truly happy in this world."

Number five has also a special place in sacred geometry. Five-pointed star, which has golden ratio encoded into it, is in Vedic astrology a symbol of Venus, as it resembles the dance of Venus during its synodic cycle, which looks a little bit like a flower with five petals. Perhaps it has connection to five flowery arrows in the hands of Goddess, as Venus is the ultimate planet of love, romanticism and desire.

When we talk about fifth lunar day and Goddess Vahnivasini, who is "fire-dweller", it is also hard not to mention a very ancient process of purification called *panchagni* or "five fires", which was practised by Mother Parvati Herself to attain Shiva as Her husband. In the process of *panchagni*, the *yogi* seats in the midst of four fires lit on cardinal directions (East, South, West, North), while the fifth fire in the form of the Sun is shining above his head. It is practised during *uttarayana* or northern movement of the Sun. It is said that this sacred process purifies our own destructive "fires" raging within us: *kama* (passion), *krodha* (anger), *lobha* (greed), *moha* (attachment) and *matsarya* (jealousy).

Yogini in *Kalachakra*: South

On *Panchami tithi* the danger comes from the South. It is said that we should avoid travelling into that direction during the fifth lunar day in any of the two *pakshas*. South direction in Vastu is connected with our ability to take action – which is the biggest weakness of all people born on *Panchami tithi*. In *Kalachakra* South is ruled by Jupiter, the most "happy go lucky" type of planet, while in *Digchakra* it is ruled by Mars, which is a clear indication that to avoid this overly optimistic and a bit lazy side of *Panchami tithi* (indicated by Jupiter), we need to increase our ability to take action or increase our inner fire. Jupiter sometimes tends to be a bit selfish, as well, which is sometimes a weakness of people born on *Panchami tithi*. One of their biggest lessons in life is to learn how to make better choices and how to increase their ability to take a righteous action, when it is needed.

Shaktis of Goddess Vahnivasini

Different *shaktis* or powers of Goddess Vahnivasini dwell in the different places of Her *yantra*. Her *yantra* consists of *navayoni* or "nine wombs" (which is the innermost structure of Sri Yantra and a creatrix of the universe), enclosed in twelve petals, which are connected to zodiac signs. Their *shaktis* are named after zodiac signs as well: Mesha (Aries), Vrishabha (Taurus), Mithuna (Gemini), Karka (Cancer), Simha (Leo), Kanya (Virgo), Tula (Libra), Vrishchika (Scorpio), Dhanush (Sagittarius), Makara (Capricorn), Kumbha (Aquarius) and Meena (Pisces). The *shaktis* of the 8 outer triangles of the *navayoni* are called Visphulingini ("sparkling one"), Mangala ("auspicious one"), Sumanohara ("enchantress of the mind"), Kanaka ("golden one"), Ankita ("marked one" or "calculated one"), Vishwa ("the world") and Vividha ("variegated one" or "having numerous forms"). The *shaktis* of the innermost triangle are not mentioned.

The *yantra* of Goddess Vahnivasini is the first one containing *navayoni* figure, which also resembles Her intensely creative nature. Meditating on Her *yantra* allows us to focus our creative energy more, "to give form to the formless" and make it shine and manifest in the world.

Swara of Goddess Vahnivasini

U, the fifth *swara* or vowel of Sanskrit alphabet, is associated with Goddess Vahnivasini. Its quality or *kala* is to seduce, command or accept. It reveals also a passionate side of Goddess Vahnivasini. After all, *Panchami tithi* is often considered as one of the best days for any romantic activities, as it is sacred to Goddess Lalita. The creative and romantic nature of Goddess Vahnivasini, as well as a bit of a quality of indecisiveness, makes *Panchami tithi* resemble a lot the qualities of the fifth house in Vedic astrology – especially Moon in the fifth house.

Agni Purana also states that vowel **u** represents Shiva Himself, as well as His transformative powers.

Nakshatras connected to Goddess Vahnivasini

Krittika nakshatra is connected to *swara* of Goddess Vahnivasini, while Her eight arms stand for four nakshatra *padas* of Punarvasu and Pushya nakshatras. Krittika nakshatra, with Agni or fire-god as its presiding deity, is indeed, closely connected to Goddess Vahnivasini and Her transformative and purifying nature – as well as with Her passionate and creative side. Krittika nakshatra is connected with all the *agni parikshas*, or tests we need to go through in life. On the most mundane level it will represents school exams, while in life it will represent all the life's trials. Goddess Vahnivasini, similarly like Krittika nakshatra, is putting our wisdom, gained by the association with Bherunda Devi, into test. Bherunda Devi, who is co-ruling *Chaturti tithi* along with Mercury, is more about collecting information and seeing the reality the way it is, while Goddess Vahnivasini, co-ruling *Panchami tithi* along with Jupiter, inspires us to turn this knowledge into actual skill and wisdom. The main difference between the two of them is that Bherunda Devi is testing us in much stricter way, while Vahnivasini Devi is more like a kind, nourishing mother, who simply wishes to gently refine our knowledge in the warmness of the fire. Bherunda Devi is this force, which is intensely purifying and melting the gold of our Self by removing its impurities through intense heat of life's trials, while Goddess Vahnivasini is a much more gentle fire needed to give a form to already melted gold.

Punarvasu and Pushya nakshatras connection reveals much calmer nature of this lunar day, when compared to *Pratipad tithi*. It reveals more creative, subtle and nourishing form of Agni, which doesn't want to burn – it wants to support. Krittika, Punarvasu and Pushya are three very pure, brahminic and innocent nakshatras. The *shakti* of Krittika is the power to burn and its deity is Agni, fire-god himself, the giver of light. Punarvasu literally means "the return of light" and it is the nakshatra, in which the Sun would normally change its course from *Uttarayana* to *Dakshinayana*. The *shakti* of Pushya nakshatra, on the other hand, is the power to reflect the Divine qualities or to reflect the light. Similarly, people born on *Panchami tithi* are often very innocent and pure in heart. They have this capacity to reflect the light of Divine inspiration, and due to that they can often be very artistic, or creative in some other way. Yet, similarly like it is with the natives born under Krittika, Punarvasu or Pushya nakshatra, they can get easily distracted due to too much of this creative energy flowing through them, and often tend to be a bit indecisive, or way too passive – or doing too many things at the same time. They light up quickly, but they also burn out quickly. And, similarly like those three nakshatras, *Panchami tithi* natives can sometimes become a bit too naïve, as well.

Pushya nakshatra is also a Vedic constellation, in which Jupiter, Cosmic Guru and co-ruler of *Panchami tithi*, gets exalted. It is also the nakshatra under which Shiva in the form of Tripurantaka destroyed Tripura, the city of the demons. This is why *Panchami tithi* is also connected with Vedic initiations and all our teachers and Gurus, who dispell the darkness of our ignorance.

Connection between *Panchami tithi* and Punarvasu nakshatra is particularly beautiful one. Punarvasu means "return of light" and it is the nakshatra of all repetitive phenomenons and patterns in nature, such as fractals or *déjà vu* experiences. It is connected with all the *yantras*, sacred geometry, patterns and morphogenesis itself. Fascinating thing is that similarly like rainbow's angular radius is 42 degrees from the shadow of your head in the opposite direction of the Sun, so angular radius of *double rainbow*, a rare and beautiful phenomenon is between 50-53 degrees. In *Shukla paksha*, during *Panchami tithi*, Moon will form this 50-53 degrees relationship with the Sun. How great is, really, the depth of Vedic thought?

Interestingly enough, similarly like *Panchami tithi* is associated in Vedic astrology with *nagas* or Divine serpents, so is the phenomenon of rainbow itself. In *Brihat Samhita* we can read that "the rainbow is formed of the expired breath of certain serpents of the Divine order". After all, according to Vedic thought, these are the Divine serpents of the atmosphere that cause rain or restrain it.

There are also three nakshatras, in which *guna* of *rajas* combines with air element, similarly like on *Panchami tithi*: Ashwini, Punarvasu and Hasta – all three are quite dual nakshatras, with fair amount of sense of humour, hyper-optimism, impulsiveness and... indecisiveness. All qualities strongly connected to *Panchami tithi* and Goddess Vahnivasini. In this way, by analysing the nakshatras, which are combining same element and same *guna* as exact *tithi*, we can also learn quite a lot about this lunar day. Same *guna* and same *tattwa* will always bring very similar results.

Tithi, vara and nakshatra resonance

Goddess Vahnivasini has a very good resonance with many days of the week and many nakshatras. In fact, *Panchami tithi* forms the smallest amount of negative *yogas*, which reveals its highly auspicious nature. It creates *visha yoga* or "poisonous combination" only on Sunday *and* when the Moon dwells in Krittika nakshatra, which happens really rarely. The combination of fiery nakshatra connected to Goddess Vahnivasini, fiery day of the Sun and fiery *Panchami tithi* produces some sort of emotional "poison" in the mind and stinginess as the result.

Generally *Panchami tithi* also doesn't go well with Magha nakshatra (unless it is Thursday), as the *shakti* of Magha nakshatra is "the power to leave the body", which additionally exaggerates "formless" energy of this *tithi. Ashubha yoga* is formed with the combination of *Panchami tithi* and Magha, as well as *Panchami* makes Magha nakshatras *shunya* or "fruitless".

Traditionally it is also said that *dagdha yoga* or "burnt combination" happens, whenever *Panchami tithi* falls on Tuesday, day ruled by fiery Mars. Yet, if it happens, when the Moon dwells in Ashwini, Rohini, Uttara Phalguni, Shravana, Purva Bhadrapada or Uttara Bhadrapada nakshatra, this combination transforms into *suta yoga*, one of the very auspicious combinations, which helps us to "extract" *soma* or juice of life through our activities and experience inner joy.

There are four different *suta yogas*, which can be formed on *Panchami tithi*:

- *Panchami tithi* + Sunday + Pushya, Hasta or Mula
- *Panchami tithi* + Monday + Margashirsha, Swati or Shravana
- *Panchami tithi* + Tuesday + Ashwini, Rohini, Uttara Phalguni, Shravana, Purva Bhadrapada or Uttara Bhadrapada
- *Panchami tithi* + Wednesday + Ashwini, Purva Phalguni, Purvashadha or Purva Bhadrapada

YOGAS FORMED WITH PANCHAMI TITHI

	1	2	3	4	5	6	7
1			dagdha / suta	**suta**	**siddha**		amrita
2			dagdha		siddha		amrita
3	**visha**		dagdha		siddha		amrita
4			dagdha / suta		siddha		amrita
5		**suta**	dagdha		siddha		amrita
6			dagdha		siddha		amrita
7			dagdha		**siddha**		amrita
8	**suta**		dagdha		**siddha**		amrita
9			dagdha		siddha		amrita
10	shunya	shunya	shunya/dagdha	shunya	**siddha /** shunya	shunya	amrita / shunya
11			dagdha	**suta**	siddha		amrita
12			dagdha / suta		siddha		amrita
13	**suta**		dagdha		siddha		amrita
14			dagdha		siddha		amrita
15		**suta**	dagdha		**siddha**		amrita
16			dagdha		siddha		amrita
17			dagdha		siddha		amrita
18			dagdha		siddha		amrita
19	**suta**		dagdha		siddha		amrita
20			dagdha	**suta**	siddha	**gains**	amrita
21			dagdha		siddha		amrita
22		**suta**	dagdha / suta		siddha		amrita
23			dagdha		siddha		amrita
24			dagdha		siddha		amrita
25			dagdha / suta	**suta**	**siddha**		amrita
26			dagdha / suta		siddha		amrita
27			dagdha		**siddha**		amrita

Similarly like in the case of *Chaturti*, *Panchami tithi* always brings excellent results and many blessings on Thursdays (*siddha yoga*) and Saturdays (*amrita yoga*), the days of two great cosmic teachers, Jupiter and Saturn. Additionally, when *Panchami tithi* falls on Thursday and one of the following nakshatras: Ashwini, Punarvasu, Pushya, Magha, Swati, Purvashadha, Purva Bhadrapada or Revati, a more powerful *siddha yoga* or "combination of accomplishments" occurs.

Agni Purana also says that combination of *Panchami tithi*, Purvashadha nakshatra and Friday attracts prosperity.

Being so, *Panchami tithi* doesn't resonate well only with Krittika nakshatra – interestingly, the nakshatra presided by Agni, fire god. *Panchami tithi* even becomes *shunya* in Vedic month Kritika, which ends in Full Moon occuring in Krittika nakshatra. It gives different results with Magha (the most detached nakshatra) and has a good resonance with Ashwini, Rohini, Margashirsha, Punarvasu, Pushya, Purva Phalguni, Uttara Phalguni, Hasta, Swati, Purvashadha, Shravana, Purva Bhadrapada, Uttara Bhadrapada and Revati.

In *Agni Purana* it is also said that sowing seeds on *Panchami tithi* and Krittika, Rohini, Uttara Phalguni, Hasta, Anuradha, Jyeshtha or Revati nakshatra is going to attract great prosperity.

Important *rashis* for *Panchami tithi* natives

Each *tithi* has a special connection with a number of *rashis*. Understanding those connections can help us not only in understanding our own birth chart on a much deeper level, but in better understanding of the nature of the *tithi* itself.

You can already see on a picture above that there is something very specific about *Panchami tithi*, which makes it much different from all other lunar days. This is also what makes *Panchami tithi* the most harmonious in *muhurta*, but at the same time the most indecisive when it becomes your birth *tithi*.

First unusual thing, which you can notice is that the flow of energy in zodiacal chakras on *Panchami tithi* encompasses two chakras in *Shukla paksha* and *Krishna paksha*. In fact, *Panchami tithi* stands for transition point between *svadhishthana chakra* and *manipura chakra* in *Shukla paksha* (Pisces/Aries transformative *gandanta* zone in the zodiac), while in *Krishna paksha* it stands for transition point between *vishuddha chakra* and *anahata chakra* (transformative Citra nakshatra). Just by observing this phenomenon, you can easily understand, why *Panchami tithi* natives tend to be a bit indecisive.

If you look even further, you can quite clearly see that all dual signs (Gemini, Virgo, Sagittarius, Pisces) are playing some important role on *Panchami tithi*, which additionally emphasises the dual, transformative and indecisive nature of this lunar day. Similarly like dual signs are connected to finding the right balance between extremes, so *Panchami tithi* natives need to find such balance in their own life, as well as learn how to choose between different things, without doing thousand things at the same time.

There is, however, one more extremely important thing, when it comes to *Panchami tithi*, which additionally exaggerates the quality of indecisiveness in all *Panchami* natives. You can quite clearly notice that *tithi pati kshetra paksha* sign (the sign opposite to the *mulatrikona* sign of the planetary lord of this lunar day, Jupiter) is exactly the same like one of the *tithi shunya rashis*: Gemini. When we understand that *tithi pati kshetra paksha* sign is the sign showing the *Panchami* native the direction in life, while at the same time this sign is made "fruitless" (*shunya*) by this *tithi* itself, then we have a serious problem. Of course, if Gemini is occupied by Rahu or Ketu, or unless its lord (Mercury) is placed 3rd, 6th, 8th or 12th house from ascendant or Moon, or are retrograde, or in conjuction with malefic planet, or, lastly, in nakshatras of Rahu or Ketu, this influence will be naturally nullified. Otherwise it may greatly expand the quality of indecisiveness in *Panchami tithi* native, which may become a great issue in such person's life. If additionally it happens that Moon is dwelling exactly in this sign, Gemini, the person will stay confused about his true path for majority of life, and will have huge problems with making important choices.

Jupiterian, expanding energy naturally dilutes our power to make a choice and sometimes can make us very ungrounded. This quality is especially pronounced in all *Panchami tithi* natives. This is why they must consciously work on becoming more grounded, as well as it is of great importance for them to strengthen their Mercury, who is the lord of two of their *shunya rashis*: Gemini and Virgo. It is of highest importance for them to transform their intellect in such a way, that instead of producing doubts and collecting infinite amount of information, it starts to be more selective and intuitive. Their inner conflict between Jupiter (intuition and wisdom) and Mercury (intellect and information) must be resolved, and both planets must be brought back to balance.

Sadhana for Goddess Vahnivasini

Goddess Vahnivasini is pleased with flowers, citron fruits and singing or chanting the mantras. To connect with Her on a deeper level, you can either do a meditation of sitting on Her lap, as given by my Gurudev (described in Chapter 24) or colour Her yantra and meditate on it, facing South. For your *sadhana* you can use one of the two mantras below or one of the affirmations. There are couple of more advanced mantras for worship of Goddess Vahnivasini in *Tantraraja*, but they are not supposed to be recited without a guidance of a Guru.

Mantras:

oṁ aīṁ hrīṁ śrīṁ uṁ vahnivāsinīyai namaḥ
oṁ aīṁ hrīṁ śrīṁ uṁ puṣṭiyai namaḥ

Affirmations:

I allow myself to shine.
I allow myself to be creative.
I allow myself to learn.
I allow myself to be impartial.
I allow myself to be sensitive.
I allow myself to be focused.

Questions for self-analysis

Every lunar day is an opportunity to learn something new about ourselves. Nitya Devis and their wisdom can become our guides on this sacred journey. Questions below can help you in recognising certain "shadow" tendencies in yourself, which may arise on *Panchami tithi*. If you were born on this lunar day, these questions might be of big importance for you in life and allow you to face your weaknesses.

- What can I learn from universe today?
- How can I bring more harmony into my environment or relations?
- Do I allow my creativity to express itself?
- Do I allow my heart to open up?
- Do I allow myself to shine?
- Can I allow myself to be more independent?
- Do I allow myself to be sensitive?
- Can I be impartial, if needed?
- Am I a bit hyper-optimistic sometimes?
- Do I see the reality clearly or do I prefer to see only what I want to see?
- Do I keep my focus on the right thing?
- Do I allow my intuition to speak up and do I listen to it, when it speaks?
- Am I a bit indecisive due to my own doubts?
- Can I allow myself to make a choice and follow it?
- Can I allow myself to leave my comfort zone?
- Am I trying to do too many things at the same time?

Yantra of Goddess Vahnivasini

CHAPTER 13

VAJRESHWARI – ADAMANT GODDESS
SHASHTI – SIXTH LUNAR DAY

vajreśvari vamadevi vayovastha-vivarjita
siddheśvari siddha-vidya siddha-mata yaśasvini

"Praised be Goddess Vajreśvari, endowed with fame, who is devoid of all old age, and who is the consort of Shiva. She is the Supreme Goddess of siddhas, perfected souls, and the Mother ever ready to help spiritual adepts."

- Lalita Sahasranama

Kala	Element	Planet	Guna	Yogini	Vowel
rati (passion)	fire	Venus	tamas	West	ū

Stage of consciousness	Divine quality	Deity (Muhurta Cintamani)	Deity (Varahamihira)	Nakshatra connection	Form of Shiva
dreaming (dreaming)	niraskata (detachment)	Kartikeya	Agni	Krittika Ashlesha	Nirrita (Nataraja)

Shukla Paksha

Nadi: pingala
Chakra: manipura
Interval: minor/major third
Deity (Narada Purana): Ganesha
House from the Sun: 3 or 4

Krishna Paksha

Nadi: ida
Chakra: anahata
Interval: diminished fifth
Deity (Narada Purana): Surya
House from the Sun: 9 or 10

Vajra means "hard, adamant, cemented, impenetrable" or "a diamond". Similarly, Goddess Vajreshwari is making all things stable, hard, strong, tangible and "cemented". After *Panchami tithi*, when Goddess Vahnivasini gave us Divine inspiration and creativity, on *Shashti*, Goddess in the form of Vajreshwari gives us strength and power to realise all our ideas on material level and to find within ourselves the power to do so. *Panchami tithi* stands for conception and all the love and creativity behind conceiving anything, while *Shashti tithi* stands for birth and making something real and tangible. This is why *Shashti tithi* is considered to be a very auspicious day, when it comes to dealing with real estate or building. Even the syllable of Sri Vidya mantra connected to Goddess Vajreshwari is *ha*, denoting space or breath, while *yogini* associated with Her is Rupa-karshini – "the one attracting all forms". Similarly Goddess Vajreshwari blesses us with the power to give a form to our dreams and manifest the reality. *Bhavanopanishad* indentifies Her with *mahat tattwa* – manifested form of the Divine and Goddess presiding over totality of material energy. That is the main difference between creativity of *Panchami tithi* and creativity of *Shashti tithi*: *Panchami tithi* and Goddess Vahnivasini focus more on the idea itself, while *Shashti tithi* and Goddess Vajreshwari focus on giving actual form to something. But this is also why *Shashti tithi* natives might be sometimes a bit overly focused on the surface of things or on reality which can be perceived just by the senses.

Goddess Vajreshwari is the first of the five goddesses connected to *guna* of *tamas*, while Her element is fire and planetary lord Venus. She represents the fullness of *svapna* or dreaming state of consciousness, giving us capacity not only to dream, but also to *build* our dreams, to give them a stable form in material world; to stop for a moment ever-moving energy of *rajas* and build something, which will stay strong and unmovable for a long time: like a house. Not without a reason She is also a Goddess, who supports us in the sciences of Jyotish and Vastu shastra. Also the quality of this lunar day is to bring *yasha*, "glory" or "fame".

Goddess Vajreshwari gives us strength, confidence and determination to follow our dreams and manifest them in the outer world. Confidence is one of Her biggest blessings. On the day ruled by Her, 24 November 2017, my Gurudev wrote these beautiful words: "Confidence is better than perfection, because perfection means doing our best – but confidence means knowing, how to handle the worst."

People born on Goddess Vajreshwari's day, *Shashti tithi*, can often be very stubborn – in a positive or negative way. They might be a bit inflexible, too. Yet, their adamantness always leads them towards fulfillment of their dreams. They have an enormous capacity to realise their ideas in the world, and they won't let go of them easily, no matter how many times they will fail or how many sacrifices they will need to make in order to achieve their goal.

Interestingly, *vajra* is also the name of the weapon of Indra, which was created from the bones of *rishi* Dadhici. In the past, *rishi* Dadhici had received a boon from Shiva, that his bones will be strong as a diamond (*vajra*). Later on, when Indra needed to face Vrtrasura, a terrible demon harrassing heaven, He asked *rishi* Dadhici, if he could sacrifice his body for the betterment of the world – so Indra could create a weapon out of his bones. *Rishi* Dadhici, being always detached from worldly matters and immersed in the state of Shiva consciousness, gladly agreed. From the bones of the body sacrificed by *rishi* Dadhici, Vishwakarma, the Divine architect, created a powerful weapon striking lightenings: *vajra*. Eventually Indra killed Vrtrasura with this weapon. *Vajra* can also mean "thunderbolt" or "forked", "zigzag", "pillar of light". *Vajra*, the weapon of Indra, is connected to lightenings, storms and electromagnetic force in natural world.

Interestingly, even the nakshatras are called "bones of the zodiac" in Vedas. *Krishna Yajurveda* says: "nakshatras are the form, bones are the stars" – as they give the form to exact planetary influences, similarly like Vishwakarma, the Divine Architect, gives form to the limitless mass of material energy. This might be one of the reasons why Goddess Vajreshwari is also said to bless all on the path of Vedic Astrology, as well as all students of Vastu Shastra.

Devi Vajreshwari, as all other goddesses connected to element of fire, dwells in the corner of the mystical triangle, which resonates with Her sharp, fiery nature. Kartikeya, the warrior son of Shiva and Shakti, and the commander of gods, is often considered to be the presiding deity of *Shashti tithi*, as well. Goddess Vajreshwari is strongly connected with defeating the forces of darkness and our ability to fight, even though Her appearance looks very innocent. She removes all negative forces, entities, ghosts, fears, troubles and protects us from black magic.

Above all, Goddess Vajreshwari helps us to overcome all the negativities within ourselves. She is addressed in *Tantraraja* as *Kantara-sagara-krura-duhkha-sanghata-tarini* or "Destructress of the cruel evils dense like boundless forests or wide ocean". The "cruel evil" is furtherly described as *aviveka* or lack of discrimination – because from lack of discrimination or ignorance all other evils arise. It is said that a person, who worships Vajreshwari Devi is going to be free from *aviveka*.

Interestingly, even though the energy of *Shashti tithi* and Goddess Vajreshwari is so fiery and martian (Mars is literally considered the deity of *Shashti tithi* in some scriptures), the planet, which is co-ruling this lunar day is Venus. It, again, reveals the deep connection between Venus and Mars through *Kalachakra* (Southeast corner) – fire of passion, symbolised by Venus and fire of action, symbolised by Mars. Even the *kala* of the Moon connected to Goddess Vajreshwari is *rati* or passion. Also in our energy body, in *Shukla paksha* the energy of Goddess Vajreshwari is the most powerful in *manipura chakra* (energy centre connected to Mars), while in *Krishna paksha* in *anahata chakra* (energy centre connected to Venus).

The quality of Sri Krishna connected to sixth lunar day and Goddess Vajreshwari is *niraskata* or detachment – as for any idea to get manifested in the world or for anything to be born, some sort of separation and crystalisation of the form must happen. All people born on *Shashti tithi* often have this healthy dose of detachment within themselves. Sometimes, however, due to their adamantness, they also tend to be a bit insensitive or "stone-hearted". This is the shadow side of Goddess Vajreshwari.

Meditation with Goddess Vajreshwari

Hue: red
Number of heads: 1
Number of eyes: 3
Number of hands: 4
Right hands: *ankusha*, pomegranate fruit
Left hands: *pasha*, sugarcane bow
Garments: red
Ornaments: garlanded with red flowers, diadem with rubies

Tantraraja describes Goddess Vajreshwari as a red-hued Goddess dressed in red garments, garlanded with red flowers and adorned with diadem with lustrous rubies. She is surrounded by red ointment. Even Her tantric name in *64 Yogini Namavali* is Rakta Devi or "blood-red Goddess". In Her four hands She carries *pasha* (symbolising control over passion), *ankusha* (symbolising control over repulsion), sugarcane bow (symbolising the mind) and pomegranate fruit (symbolising Her fertile and creative powers). She is seated on the throne of Her *yantra* in a golden boat, which is swaying gently in an ocean of blood. Despite these dreadful surroundings, She looks at Her *sadhaka* with a cooling gaze of mercy and a benign smile.

Ocean of blood symbolises Goddess Vajreshwari's victory over the forces of darkness, as well as Her protection of our vital powers. Ocean of blood represents not only passion and fertility, but our vital powers and life itself. Along with our blood, our life itself flows through our veins. Goddess Vajreshwari, being completely red and adorned with red flowers, ointments and ornaments, represents the intensity of the life force and giving life to all our ideas. Blood and Her intensely red colour also remind us, that whenever we want to realise any of our ideas in the world, we need not only our passion to fuel it, but also an enormous effort and literally "blood sacrifice" – sacrificing our own life force, time and efforts, to make something real and tangible. For no great idea can be realised without some sacrifice from our side. Goddess Vajreshwari teaches us, that everything has its price in the universe. The price for realising something in the world is part of our life itself. This is why in ancient times when in left hand tantric tradition there was still a cruel custom of animal sacrifice, Goddess Vajreshwari was invoked into the sword, which was about to slay the poor animal.

You might wonder, how come that such "blood-thirsty" Goddess is ruling the lunar day connected to Venus? Goddess Vajreshwari is also representing a shadow side of Venus, which is attachment and possesiveness. Strong attachment leads to the need of control, and need of control easily leads to aggression and violence. Have you ever wondered, how come that when a person says "Oh, I love this flower!", the next second the person is cutting the flower to bring it to his or her own home and give his/her eyes a bit of temporary pleasure? Have you ever wondered, what is the cost of all the beauty products, which are so often tested on poor animals? Have you ever wondered how easily the need of possession is appearing in our mind each time we see some cute animal on social media – and how quickly we forget about this animal once we "get it"? That is the shadow side of Venus, which puts self-gratification and possessiveness above compassion. Goddess Vajreshwari inspires us to become more aware of our environment and to realise that every drop of blood, be it of human or of animal, is equally precious, as it is the representant of sacred life force itself – and spilling it without need is not going to attract anything positive into our lives. In ancient Vedic times person needed to ask for forgiveness even when cutting a tree or building a house – as even building of a house was considered a form of violence towards nature and element of ether (space, *antariksha*). No wonder that Goddess Vajreshwari is presiding over the lunar day, which is considered to be the best for starting building process, as well as any other "violent" acts.

Ocean of blood symbolises the womb of the mother, as well. Womb of Cosmic Mother is the universal creatrix of the universe, from which everything emerges and everything takes its form. The intensity and the amount of energy needed during the child delivery is enormous. No wonder that Vedic god of Vastu Shastra and architecture, Tvashtar, is also the god of the womb. That's the law of the universe: whenever something is taking its form and manifests into the world, it requires an enormous amount of energy.

Interestingly enough, the *shakti* of Skanda or Kartikeya, son of Shiva and Shakti, heavenly commander, who co-rules this lunar day is called... Shashti Devi. Shashti Devi is said to be the protector of child birth, pregnancy, as well as benefactor and protector of children. She is the nurturer of pregnant women and young children. Even today in East India we may observe how on sixth day from the moment of child's birth there is a ritual performed for Shashti Devi, so She may protect it from diseases, black magic and misfortunes. Shashti Devi is often depicted with a child on Her lap, which is why sometimes She is considered the same as Goddess Skandamata – sixth form of the Divine Mother (*Mula Prakriti*), worshipped on sixth day of Navaratri (nine nights of the Divine Mother in Vedic tradition). It is said that whoever prays to Her with devotion will beget a child. Such are the creative powers of *Shashti tithi*.

Form of Shiva connected to Shashti *tithi*: Nataraja

The sixth form of Shiva connected to sixth lunar day is probably His most popular form: Shiva as Cosmic Dancer or Nataraja, "king of the dance". In *Mayamatam* this form of Shiva is sometimes addressed as Nirritha or "the Destroyer". Nirritha literally means "the one, who destroys all that is non-moving". Shiva in this form is completely immersed in His cosmic dance, known as *tandava*. *Mayamatam* describes this wonderful form of Shiva:

"Now the dance of Shiva playing with the serpent is described, which is also called twilight dance. Shiva holds the *damaru* drum in His right hand and the fire in the left one. In His right hands He is to have the trident, axe, sword and arrow; in the left He holds the shield and the bow, makes the *danda* (punishment) gesture and carries the noose. His feet are made radiantly beautiful by the delicate movement of the steps of the dance. His right leg is bent and His left foot lifted to the height of His right knee."

The cosmic dance of Lord Shiva symbolises the dance of the atoms and the never-ending *lila* of creation, preservation and destruction. It is said that Lord Shiva in this form is protecting us from all negativities and *Mayamatam* even says that worhsipping this form of the Lord brings the death of the enemy. Knowing that all the true enemies are residing, in reality, within ourselves, in the form of all our negative tendencies, Shiva in this form helps us to overcome all the negative forces within us – similarly like Goddess Vajreshwari.

Numerology: 6

There are six seasons in Vedic calendar. This is why number six is connected to our habits, daily rituals and daily routine – even the sixth house in Vedic astrology is connected to our routine and the way we react to changing seasons in the microcosm of our own life. Healthy routine and healthy habits, as well as personal discipline (symbolised by Saturn) are also very important for all *Shashti tithi* natives, so they can control the excessive qualities of Venus within them. Interestingly, sixth house in Vedic astrology is also connected to environmental concern and the way we treat animals – a very similar lesson that Goddess Vajreshwari is teaching us.

In tantra number six is connected to six *shaktis* of our six chakras, which are placed in the main channel of our energy body. Number six is also connected to six Krittikas or foster mothers of Kartikeya, as well as six heads of Kartikeya manifested to pacify them and compromise with them. And, as Kartikeya is the god of war, number six also stands for our ability to deal with adversities of life and our inner and outer enemies – which is not always just about fighting them, but sometimes about compromising with them. That is, again, the lesson that we learn through sixth house in Vedic astrology.

There are also six petals in *svadhishthana chakra*, the energy center in the sacral region of our spine, which literally means "one's private place" or "one's place of power". These six petals are said to be associated with six impurities of the mind. Sacral chakra is closely connected to water element and all the fluids in our body, including reproductive fluids. *Shukra* (Venus), the planet co-ruling this lunar day is also connected to reproductive fluids in our physical body. In fact Lord Kartikeya himself was born from Shiva's reproductive fluid, which fallen on the ground (which, in itself is quite an interesting story, narrated slightly differently in each *Purana*). Being so, Kartikeya was born out of the womb and without motherly energy being involved in his birth. Kartikeya is also said to represent the ego of Shiva, which also reveals a shadow side of the people born on this lunar day. They may sometimes act in a bit egoistic way, as well as may have a tendency to be a bit impulsive at times.

Yogini in *Kalachakra*: West

On *Shashti tithi* the danger comes from the West. It is said that we should avoid travelling into that direction during the sixth lunar day in any of the two *pakshas*. West, in Vastu and in *Digchakra*, is connected to Saturn and longevity: making things stable, long-lasting, grounded, time-resistant. Its natural opposite force is Venus in *Kalachakra*, which is the co-ruler of *Shashti tithi*. The biggest weakness of Venus is wasting life force on unnecessary actions or desires. Over-indulgence in sexual activities or any other form of desire, slowly destroys our power of discipline, determination, vitality, longevity and health itself.

Venus is said to represent vital fluids in our body, as the name Shukra itself means "sperm". Paramahansa Yogananda once said that to produce one drop of sperm, fourty drops of blood are wasted. Therefore overindulgence in sexual activities naturally decreases our vital powers with time. This is why preservation of our vital fluids or virility, *virya*, is considered so important on spiritual path. Healthy control of our desires (and not only those of sexual nature) simply promotes a better health and gives us more inner power.

Interestingly, Shukracharya, who is planet Venus personified, was the guru of the demons. He was well known for spending lots of his spiritual merit on satisfying his desires. Ultimately, however, he received from Lord Shiva *mrit sanjivini vidya*, or the power to revive the dead, to restore the wasted vital forces. Similarly every person born on *Shashti tithi* must learn in this lifetime how to preserve and regenerate their vital forces, without wasting them on unnecessary things. The right amount of self-discipline, symbolised by Saturn, is crucial for them.

It is also quite interesting that in many variations of folk stories about Shashti Devi, the goddess co-ruling the sixth lunar day, there is always some character, who displays greed or gluttony, and then becomes punished by the Goddess in the form of Shashti. As the element of fire is strongly connected with purification and refining our desires, all three *Nanda tithis* connected to element of fire (*Pratipad*, *Shashti* and *Ekadashi*) seem to be very strongly connected with transformation of our desires and the way we deal with them. On *Pratipad*, when fire element is connected with *guna* of *rajas*, our desires get awakened and we become more aware of them. On *Shashti*, when fire is connected to *guna* of *tamas*, our desires yearn to get a real form, but they can sometimes also make us too lazy or overindulgent, as the energy of *tamas* naturally seeks more stability or inertia. On *Ekadashi tithi*, on the other hand, when the element of fire is connected with *sattwa guna*, a natural need to control our desires and bring more discipline into our lives awakens. *Shashti tithi* and *Ekadashi tithi* are also the only two lunar days, which have their separate entity in the forms of Shashti Devi and Ekadashi Devi.

Shaktis of Goddess Vajreshwari

Different *shaktis* of Goddess Vajreshwari dwell in different places of Her *yantra*. After Goddess Bherunda, Vajreshwari is the first Nitya Devi, whose *yantra* contains a hexagon or *shatkona*, six-pointed star, symbolising the union of feminine and masculine principle. In Her *yantra* six-pointed star encloses *yoni* (downward facing triangle) and is enclosed in 12 petals, and 16 petals, dwelling in *bhupura*.

The *shaktis* of the innermost triangle and *shatkona* stay the same like in the *yantra* of Goddess Bherunda. Three *shaktis* of three corners of the inner triangle are: Iccha (willpower), Jnana (knowledge) and Kriya (action). Each of the six arms of the six-pointed star is occupied by six *shaktis* of the chakras: Dakini (*vishuddha chakra*), Rakini (*anahata chakra*), Lakini (*manipura chakra*), Kakini (*svadhishthana chakra*), Shakini (*muladhara chakra*) and Hakini (*ajna chakra*). Being so, inner triangle and six-pointed star are symbolising our three innermost powers manifested through our six chakras.

Twelve petals enclosing the *shatkona* are occupied by the *shaktis*: Hrillekha ("heart impression"), Kledini ("moisture"), Klinna ("wet one"), Kshobhini ("agitator"), Madantura ("governor of desire"), Niranjana ("pure one"), Ragavati ("full of passion"), Madanavati ("desirous one"), Mekhala ("girdle"), Dravini ("ecstatic one"), Vegavati ("full of emotion") – the name of the last *shakti* is absent in the scripture. In the sixteen petals enclosing them are dwelling sixteen *shaktis*: Kamala ("lotus one"), Kamini ("lover"), Kalpa ("idea"), Kala ("sweet one"), Kalita ("separated one"), Kautuka ("curious one"), Kirata ("procuress"), Kala ("time"), Kadana ("destruction"), Kaushika ("passionate one"), Kambuvahini ("riding on elephant"), Katara ("agitated one"), Kapala ("skull"), Kirti ("glorious one"), Kumari ("young one"), Kumkuma ("red like *kumkum*"). Additionally within the *bhupura* structure are dwelling following *shaktis*: Jambhika ("citron"), Vegini ("emotional one"), Namni ("versed one"), Chapala ("unconstant one"), Peshala ("tender one"), Sati ("perfect wife"), Rati ("passionate one"), Shraddha ("faithful one"), Bhogalobha ("desireous of food"), Mada ("desireous one"), Unmatta ("intoxicated one") and Manasvini ("mindful one" or "wise one").

Swara of Goddess Vajreshwari

Ū, the sixth *swara* or vowel of Sanskrit alphabet, is associated with Goddess Vajreshwari. Its quality or *kala* is to protect or to call. It also awakens compassion, which is in tune with highest nature of the co-ruler of *Shashti tithi*: Venus. According to *Agni Purana* vowel **ū** acts as a guard and protector. It can be quite a violent sound, when used with some other sounds, which reflects the power of Goddess Vajreshwari, the destroyer of all negativities, ignorance and dark forces.

Nakshatras connected to Goddess Vajreshwari

Krittika nakshatra is connected to *swara* of Goddess Vajreshwari, while Her four arms stand for four nakshatra *padas* of Ashlesha nakshatra. Interestingly, Krittika nakshatra has the same presiding deity as *Shashti tithi*, as per some scriptures: Agni, god of fire. Krittika nakshatra is also often associated with Kartikeya, son of Shiva and Shakti, and commander of gods, for whom *Shashti tithi* is sacred, as he was not only nurtured by six mothers (interestingly, six Krittikas), but he also had six heads. Interestingly enough, Kartikeya is an enemy of snakes – who are the presiding deities of another nakshatra connected with *Shashti tithi*, Ashlesha.

The connection between Goddess Vajreshwari and Ashlesha nakshatra, Vedic constellation of sacred snakes, *nagas*, is a very interesting one. Ashlesha nakshatra is considered to be a birth nakshatra of Ketu, South node of the Moon, which is closely connected to snakes. Snakes are sometimes called *vajranga* in Sanskrit, "the ones having a strong body". *Vajrangi* on the other hand, or sometimes even *vajra* is the Sanskrit name for vetiver or kush grass, which is sacred to Ketu. Kush grass or *durva*, has many special qualities. It is a well known symbol of longevity, fertility and strong vital force. Pluck a blade of *durva* grass and it will sprout back - this attribute makes it a powerful symbol of regeneration, renewal, rebirth, fertility, and prosperity. Snakes themselves are often associated with fertility and passion, as well as they are well known from their ability to regenerate and "renew" themselves through shedding their skin.

Snakes (and Ketu Himself) are also strongly connected with magnetic force of earth. Crawling with their bodies closely touching the earth, they sense all changes in environment in advance and hence are the symbols of intuition. They are strongly connected with all earthly energies. In *Bhagavad Gita* Lord Krishna Himself advises everybody to always meditate while sitted on kush grass mat, as it protects the *sadhaka* from all the negative radiations from the Earth and blocks too strong influences of earthly energies, so they do not disturb us in our meditation. Interestingly enough, this is revealed by Lord Krishna in 6th Chapter of Bhagavad Gita.

Ashlesha nakshatra and *Shashti tithi* natives share also a similar weakness, connected to the qualities of the snakes: sometimes they tend to be a bit too cold-hearted and callous, especially if they feel vulnerable. They are also very creative - like *nagas*, the heavenly serpents.

Blades of the razor-sharp *durva* grass have been also converted by ancient *rishis* into potent missiles to kill demons or errant kings. Ashlesha nakshatra itself is connected with the power to destroy the poison and alchemic transformation of negative forces into positive energy. This resonates with Goddess Vajreshwari's ability to defeat the forces of darkness.

Interestingly enough, Shashti Devi, who is considered to be the *shakti* of Kartikeya has a black cat as Her *vahana* (representing Her power to control the negative forces), while male cat is also an animal of Ashlesha nakshatra. Another interesting thing is that one of the names of Shashti devi in *Shashti suktam* is "Manasa", which is a cobra-headed Goddess – the Goddess of mind, Goddess of wisdom, as well as Goddess of fertility and healing. Even until today in Bengal Shashti Devi is associated with Goddess Manasa.

There are also three nakshatras, in which *guna* of *tamas* combines with fire element, similarly like on *Shashti tithi*: Bharani, Pushya and Purva Phalguni – three passionate and very creative nakshatras, but with much more stable and grounded energy than the ones connected to *guna* of *rajas*. Similarly, the energy of *Shashti tithi* is much more stable and grounded than the energy of *rajasic Pratipad*. In this way, by analysing the nakshatras, which are combining same element and same *guna* as exact *tithi*, we can also learn quite a lot about this lunar day. Same *guna* and same *tattwa* will always bring very similar results.

Tithi, vara and nakshatra resonance

Goddess Vajreshwari resonates the best with the energies of passionate Friday, enlightening Sunday and energetic Tuesday. With Sunday and Tuesday it creates "combination of nectar" or *amrita yoga*. Additionally, if *Shashti tithi* falls on Sunday and one of the following nakshatras: Pushya, Uttara Phalguni, Hasta, Mula, Uttarashadha, Shravana or Uttara Bhadrapada, it forms a powerful *siddha yoga* or "combination of accomplishments". Similarly, *siddha yoga* is also formed, if *Shashti tithi* falls on Tuesday and one of the following nakshatras: Ashwini, Margashirsha, Uttara Phalguni, Citra, Anuradha, Mula, Dhanishta or Purva Bhadrapada – or on Friday and one of the following nakshatras: Ashwini, Bharani, Ardra, Punarvasu, Uttara Phalguni, Citra, Svati, Purvashadha or Revati. Additionally, if it is Friday, *Shashti tithi* and Moon dwells in Uttara Phalguni, Swati or Shatabhisha nakshatra it is powerful *suta yoga*.

Shashti tithi can, however, bring negative effects on Friday, as well, if the Moon dwells in one of the following nakshatras: Rohini, Punarvasu, Pushya, Purva Phalguni, Uttara Phalguni, Hasta, Purvashadha, Uttarashadha or Shravana – as then it forms a highly destructive *vinasha yoga*, "combination of destruction". When *Shashti tithi* falls on Friday and in Shravana nakshatra it is considered the most severe, as it additionally forms then *visha yoga*, "poisonous combination" – a day, when our inner poisons emerge on the surface of our consciousness.

There are three possible *vinasha yogas*, which can be formed on *Shashti tithi*:

- *Shashti tithi* + Monday + Bharani, Krittika, Magha, Anuradha, Purvashadha, Uttarashadha or Uttara Bhadrapada
- *Shashti tithi* + Thursday + Krittika, Rohini, Margashirsha, Ardra, Uttara Phalguni, Vishakha, Anuradha or Shatabhisha
- *Shashti tithi* + Friday + Rohini, Punarvasu, Pushya, Purva Phalguni, Uttara Phalguni, Hasta, Purvashadha, Uttarashadha or Shravana

Shashti tithi also makes Rohini nakshatra *shunya* or "fruitless". The *shakti* of Rohini nakshatra is the power of growth and it is frequently associated with pregnancy. It is quite interesting, as Goddess Shashti herself is said to be the protector of pregnancy and growth of the child in mother's womb – while *Shashti tithi* itself, especially if it becomes birth *tithi* or *santana tithi* for a woman (or even a man), sometimes may bring some issues with pregnancy or even fertility.

YOGAS FORMED WITH *SHASHTI TITHI*

	1	2	3	4	5	6	7
1	amrita	visha / hutashana	**siddha**		dagdha	**siddha**	krakacha
2	amrita	vinasha	amrita		dagdha	**siddha**	krakacha
3	amrita	vinasha	amrita		vinasha	siddha	krakacha
4	amrita / shunya	visha / hutashana / shunya	amrita / shunya		vinasha / shunya	vinasha / shunya	krakacha / shunya
5	amrita	visha / hutashana	**siddha**		vinasha	siddha	krakacha
6	amrita	visha / hutashana	amrita		vinasha	**siddha**	krakacha
7	amrita	visha / hutashana	amrita		dagdha	**siddha**	krakacha
8	**siddha**	visha / hutashana	amrita		dagdha	vinasha	krakacha
9	amrita	visha / hutashana	amrita		dagdha	siddha	krakacha
10	amrita	vinasha	amrita / affliction		dagdha	siddha	krakacha
11	amrita	visha / hutashana	amrita		dagdha	vinasha	krakacha
12	**siddha**	visha / hutashana	**siddha**		vinasha	siddha / suta / vinasha	krakacha
13	**siddha**	visha / hutashana	amrita		dagdha	siddha / vinasha	krakacha
14	amrita	visha / hutashana	**siddha**		dagdha	**suta / siddha**	krakacha
15	amrita	visha / hutashana	amrita		dagdha	siddha	krakacha
16	amrita	visha / hutashana	amrita		vinasha	siddha	krakacha
17	amrita	vinasha	**siddha**		vinasha	siddha	krakacha
18	amrita	visha / hutashana	amrita		dagdha	siddha	krakacha
19	**siddha**	visha / hutashana	**siddha**		dagdha	siddha	krakacha
20	amrita	vinasha	amrita		dagdha	siddha / vinasha	krakacha
21	**siddha**	vinasha	amrita		dagdha	vinasha	krakacha
22	**siddha**	visha / hutashana	amrita		dagdha	visha / vinasha	krakacha
23	amrita	visha / hutashana	**siddha**		dagdha	siddha	krakacha

24	amrita	visha / hutashana	amrita		vinasha	**suta / siddha**	krakacha
25	amrita	visha / hutashana	**siddha**		dagdha	siddha	krakacha
26	**siddha**	vinasha	amrita		dagdha	siddha	krakacha
27	amrita	visha / hutashana	amrita		dagdha	**siddha**	krakacha

The energies of Monday, Thursday or Saturday generally do not resonate well with *Shashti tithi* and Goddess Vajreshwari. *Shashti tithi* combined with Saturday, which enhances the adamant energies of this lunar day is called *krakacha yoga* or "combination of a saw", which cuts everything. In combination with the expanding energies of Thursday, *Shashti tithi* forms *dagdha yoga* or "burnt combination". Goddess Vajreshwari assumes, however, the most severe form on Mondays, with which *Shashti tithi* forms both *visha yoga* ("poisonous combination") and *hutashana yoga* ("the combination of oblation consumed by the fire"). Our life force can become significantly weak during such days.

Agni Purana additionally says that combination of sixth lunar day, Magha nakshatra and Tuesday brings affliction.

Being so, *Shashti tithi* resonates well with nakshatras Ashwini, Citra, Swati, Mula, Purva Bhadrapada and Revati, while it doesn't resonate well with Krittika, Rohini, Magha or Purva Phalguni. It has mixed relationships with nakshatras Bharani, Margashirsha, Punarvasu, Pushya, Uttara Phalguni, Hasta, Anuradha, Purvashadha, Uttarashadha, Shravana, Shatabhisha and Uttara Bhadrapada.

In Vedic month called Ashadha (in the end of which Full Moon falls in Uttarashadha nakshatra, also known as Guru Purnima) *Shashti tithi* is considered *shunya* and is avoided for any auspicious activities. In Ashadha month *Shashti tithi* often occurs in Uttara Phalguni or Hasta nakshatra (in *Shukla paksha*), with which it doesn't have good resonance, and Purva Bhadrapada nakshatra (in *Krishna paksha*).

Important *rashis* for *Shashti tithi* natives

Each *tithi* has a special connection with a number of *rashis*. Understanding those connections can help us not only in understanding our own birth chart on a much deeper level, but in better understanding of the nature of the *tithi* itself.

Two *rashis*, which are of greatest importance for all *Shashti tithi* natives are Aries and Libra. Libra is the *mulatrikona* sign of planetary lord of this lunar day (Venus, *tithi pati kshetra*), while Aries is the sign opposite to it (*tithi pati kshetra paksha*), which is the sign revealing, where are we heading in life. Also from spiritual perspective the flow of energy in *Shukla paksha* will be more intense in Aries (which is why *Shukla Shashti* will be more individualistic, dynamic and independent), while in *Krishna Shashti* it will be more intense in the sign of Libra (which is why *Krishna paksha* natives will be more sociable, hardworking and humble). As *tithi pati kshetra* and *tithi pati kshetra paksha* are in the case of sixth lunar day the same as the signs of natural flow of energy in the zodiacal chakras on those days, it also blesses *Shashti tithi* natives with natural confidence and straightforwardness – even though, again, as in the case of *Panchami tithi*, *tithi pati kshetra paksha*, Aries, is also a *tithi shunya* sign. It is true, *Shashti tithi* natives can be a little bit indecisive sometimes, as well – but once they focus on something, they never let go of that idea. The energy of this lunar day is already much more stable and confident than energy of *Panchami tithi*. Yet, combination of *tithi pati kshetra paksha* and *tithi shunya* in Aries for *Shashti tithi* natives, can also make them sometimes a bit selfish or even aggressive in some way, if *tithi shunya* is not nullified.

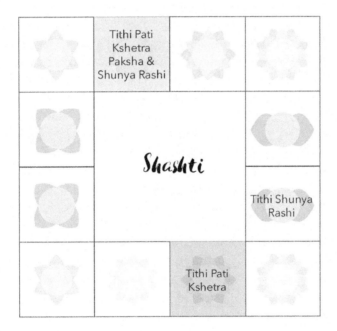

Tithi shunya rashis or the signs, which are made "fruitless" by *Shashti tithi*, are Aries (along with its lord, Mars) and Leo (along with its lord, Sun) – two fiery and independent signs, the first one being exaltation place of Sun and *mulatrikona* of Mars, while the former being the *mulatrikona* sign of the Sun. Both of these signs are naturally quite vulnerable for all people born on *Shashti tithi*. This is a strong indicator for all *Shashti tithi* natives that they need to be a bit more watchful when it comes to their ego and they need to avoid being overly focused on themselves.

Unless these signs are occupied by Rahu or Ketu, or unless its lords (Mars or Sun) are placed 3rd, 6th, 8th or 12th house from ascendant or Moon, or are retrograde, or in conjuction with malefic planet, or, lastly, in nakshatras of Rahu or Ketu, these two signs and houses ruled by those planets won't bring good results for the native. In such a case these signs must be strengthened (by strengthening their lords) to bring good results. *Shunya* planets do produce good results, however, when they transit 3rd, 6th, 8th or 12th house from from ascendant or Moon.

Sadhana for Goddess Vajreshwari

Goddess Vajreshwari is pleased with red flowers and *kumkum* (red powder) offering. To connect with Her on a deeper level, you can either do a meditation of sitting on Her lap, as given by my Gurudev (described in Chapter 24), or colour Her yantra and meditate on it, facing West. For your *sadhana* you can use one of the two mantras below or one of the affirmations. There are couple of more advanced mantras for worship of Goddess Vajreshwari in *Tantraraja*, but they are not supposed to be recited without a guidance of a Guru.

Mantras:

oṁ aiṁ hriṁ śriṁ ūṁ vajreśvariyai namaḥ
oṁ aiṁ hriṁ śriṁ ūṁ ratiyai namaḥ

Affirmations:

I allow myself to be confident.
I allow myself to be strong.
I allow myself to realise things.

Questions for self-analysis

Every lunar day is an opportunity to learn something new about ourselves. Nitya Devis and their wisdom can become our guides on this sacred journey. Questions below can help you in recognising certain "shadow" tendencies in yourself, which may arise on *Shashti tithi*. If you were born on this lunar day, these questions might be of big importance for you in life and allow you to face your weaknesses.

- What do I want to build in my life?
- Do I respect life in its every form?
- How mindful I am about the ways I use my personal life force?
- Am I unnecessarily violent?
- Am I ready to make a sacrifice for the higher purpose?
- Am I sacrificing too much in order to achieve my goals?
- Do I remember to respect others on the way to my goals?
- Am I bit too cold-hearted sometimes?
- Is my possesiveness becoming stronger than my compassion?
- Do I act a bit too egoistically sometimes?
- Am I a bit too stubborn?
- What is my relationship with Nature and my environment?
- Is there something I should change about my habits?
- How do I react to changes in life?
- Can I allow myself to be a bit more flexible, when needed?

Yantra of Goddess Vajreshwari

CHAPTER 14

SHIVADUTI – MESSENGER OF SHIVA
SAPTAMI – SEVENTH LUNAR DAY

bhaktaharda-tamobheda-bhanumat-bhanu-santati
śivaduti śivaradhya śivamurti śivankari

"Praised be Goddess Shivaduti, the messenger of Shiva and the one who is Shiva's very form. She is worshipped by Shiva and She dispenses happiness. She dispels the darkness of ignorance in the minds of Her devotees like the Sun's rays dispel the darkness of the world."

- Lalita Sahasranama

Kala	Element	Planet	Guna	Yogini	Vowel
dhriti (courage)	earth	Saturn	tamas	Northwest	r

Stage of consciousness	Divine quality	Deity (Muhurta Cintamani)	Deity (Varahamihira)	Nakshatra connection	Form of Shiva
deep sleep (dreaming)	tapasya (penance)	Surya	Indra	Rohini Magha Purva Phalguni	Candrashekhara

Shukla Paksha

Nadi: ida
Chakra: manipura
Interval: major third
Deity (Narada Purana): Yama
House from the Sun: 3 or 4

Krishna Paksha

Nadi: pingala
Chakra: anahata
Interval: augmented fourth
Deity (Narada Purana): Kamadeva
House from the Sun: 9 or 10

Shivaduti means "the messenger of Shiva". *Kala* of the Moon connected with this form of the Goddess is *dhriti* – "self-command", "steadiness" or "courage". Shivaduti is sometimes considered also a commander of Shiva's army or the army of the Supreme Goddess. Her tantric name in *64 Yogini Namavali* is Adi Shakti – "the primordial Goddess" or "the primordial power". Indeed, in Her eight arms She is carrying various weapons, which represent Her inner power.

The planet co-ruling *Saptami tithi* with Her is merciless Shani, whose only motivation is to bring everybody on the right track and remind us about our duties, as well as pending debts. Similar is the nature of Goddess Shivaduti. Even the quality of Sri Krishna connected to *Saptami tithi* is *tapasya* or penance. Her syllable in Sri Vidya mantra is *sa*, standing for time, eternity or totality. The form of Shiva connected to Her is Chandrashekhara, "the One wearing the Moon as His ornament" and the only form of Shiva who stays in a perfectly upright position – resembling straightforward and disciplined energy of this lunar day. Shiva is said to be Chandrashekhara, because He is symbolically wearing the Moon in His hair as the symbol of self-control – the control over the unsteady mind.

It is said that the only planet, which can truly control the fickle Moon is Saturn: Shani dev. Shani is said to be *Ishwaramsha* or particle of Shiva Himself. No wonder that the Goddess ruling the *tithi* co-ruled by him is called Shivaduti, or Shiva's messenger. In the same way, like Shani makes us more aware about the influence of Time, so Goddess Shivaduti reminds us about the same on the lunar day governed by Her. On *Saptami tithi* we may often be reminded by others about our pending debts or we might receive a surprising message, guest or business invitation. The role of Goddess Shivaduti is to deliver to us the message of God and to give us justice impartially, according to our actions.

Shivaduti is the steady Goddess. She doesn't wander off Her path. She knows exactly what Her duty is and She is fulfilling it faithfully, while inspiring us to do the same. She is the Divine Mother in the form of the servant of the Lord. Even Lord Shiva Himself took the form of the servant of the Lord, when He incarnated as Hanuman, to show to the world how glorious and how sweet is such selfless service. But to become a true servant of the Lord, a true channel of God's grace, surrender is the first quality, which is needed – and obedience the second one. Goddess Shivaduti teaches us the value of surrender and humility. She often arranges such situations in our life, which immediately polish our ego, making it more surrendered and mature.

When I was writing this chapter, on 25 November 2017, which was also *Saptami tithi*, my Gurudev wrote this beautiful message, so much in tune with the lessons from Goddess Shivaduti:

"In the Gita, Bhagavan said 'for the destruction of the evil-doers', for the destruction of the evil qualities in good people, and 'for the enshrining of the right, I am born from age to age.' Some people may say, 'Oh my goodness! This is a terrible, punishing God.' No, He's not punishing anyone. The 'evil-doers' are the evil qualities, which are present in you as *samskaras*. Nonetheless, through many lives, you have also accumulated a lot of good merit. Due to your good merits, He comes in the form of the Guru, in the form of the Master, to destroy all these inner 'evil-doers', these wicked qualities, to remove them and free you.

God is compassionate. He doesn't punish anyone. He loves everyone equally. And due to that Love, He knows your soul, He knows where to put you. So, when the Lord manifests Himself in different aspects to release you from your negativity, you have to learn how to surrender."

Goddess Shivaduti helps us to be free from all the "evil" *samskaras* and She inspires us to have a closer look at all our habits – as they are, in fact, creating our reality. Shivaduti Devi represents the deep sleep state within dreaming state of consciousness, which represents all our unconscious, mechanic actions, mental and physical habits, which are determining the shape of our reality to a very big extent. As Carl Jung had said, "until you make the unconscious conscious, it will direct your life and you will call it fate." She inspires us to be like Her, "self-commanded", self-controlled and independent, rather than falling a prey to our unconscious habits and repetetive patterns. She gives us the courage, *dhriti*, to break from the chains of habitual actions, fight against the bad habits and regain our inborn freedom. She inspires us to abandon the victim-like mentality and take full responsibility for our lives, by taking it in our hands and by becoming its conscious co-creators.

Goddess Shivaduti is often approached to protect against injustice and unrighteousness, as well as for fulfillment of righteous desires. She always helps those, whose desires are righteous and who do good to others. She destroys all our inner evils, makes our character pleasant to all, as well as blesses Her *sadhaka* with material and spiritual wealth. In *Tantraraja* She is called the Destroyer of all wickedness, who is at the same time ever ready to bestow such objects of desire, which are pleasing to all.

During *Shukla paksha* Her energy is the most intense in *manipura chakra* (connected to warrior planet Mars), while during *Krishna paksha* Her energy is a bit more gentle, as it accumulates more in *anahata chakra* (heart centre). On *Saptami tithi* in *Shukla paksha* the Moon is forming a major third music interval (*gandhara* connected to the Sun) with the Sun, while in *Krishna paksha* it is augmented fourth (*madhyama* connected to the Moon).

It is believed that Sun god, the first planet and first "messenger of God" among the *grahas* was born on *Saptami tithi*. Interestingly Sun-god is also the father of Shani (Saturn), the planetary ruler of this lunar day. There is a very interesting story connected to them in *Bhavishya Purana*.

Story about Sun, Saturn and Shadow

It is said that on *Saptami tithi* Sun-god had appeared in the form of an egg and then developed further in it alone. This is why he was called Martanda – "mortal egg". When Surya dev grew up he received Samjna ("consciousness") as his companion. In some versions of this myth Samjna was a daughter of Daksha Prajapati, while in other versions she was a daughter of Vishwakarma, the Divine architect. Vishwakarma also made a body of Surya dev extremely effulgent.

Before that, when Surya dev was still in his egg, two children were manifested out of him. They were Yama (god of death and righteousness) and Yamuna (remover of all sins) - both created to inspire mortals to follow the path of righteousness and cultivate purity of the mind, intentions and habits, as well as to remind them that they will not live forever, and the consequences of their actions will meet them sooner or later.

Samjna, the wife of Surya dev, was very beautiful, but also very delicate and sensitive. She could not stand the heat of her husband's body. Being so, she decided to leave him for some time, so she can perform her *tapasya*, in order to become able to bear the heat of her husband in the future. As she didn't want to trouble Surya with her problem, for the period of her absence she created another female, which was her exact replica. She was called Chaya – the shadow. Chaya was ordered to replace Samjna for the period of her *tapasya* and act as the wife of Surya dev and mother of his children. When Samjna was performing her *tapasya*, she turned into a mare and roamed in the jungles, so nobody could spot her and trouble her during her spiritual practice.

Chaya played her role perfectly in the absence of Samjna, and Surya dev could not find out the truth. She gave birth to three children, as well: Manu (the first human), Shani (Saturn) and Tapati (penance). As Chaya liked her children more than Yama and Yamuna, conflicts in the family started to arise. Firstly Yamuna and Tapati had an argument and cursed each other to become rivers on earth – but then Surya dev blessed them, that whoever will take bath in their holy waters, will get cured of his sins.

Another incident happened, when Chaya has rebuked Yama without a reason and didn't allow him to sit on her lap, while Manu was there. Yama, god of justice, raised his foot in anger and tried to hit her. Chaya cursed him then, that if he ever put his foot on earth again it will be eaten by insects. After this incident Yama went to his father and explained to him the whole matter and claimed that she is not his mother – for true mother can never curse her own children. When Surya dev found out about the truth, he soothed his son by saying that the moment he will put his foot down on earth, moths will take some flesh and blood and his foot will be cured of the curse. After that Yama was made a god of death. After finding out the truth about Chaya and his wife's absence, Sun-god has also declared that from now on everyone will have a *chaya*, shadow stuck to their bodies and it will never disassociate from it. Thus humans got shadows, which always followed them.

There is a deep symbolism in this story. Similarly like it happened to Sun god, who is a natural *Atma karaka* or significator of the soul in a Vedic birth chart, whenever our consciousness (Samjna) leaves our soul, our shadow qualities (Chaya) start to awaken and our ego starts to take over, along with all its likes and dislikes.

It is said that Sun-god got very angry with Chaya and in the heat of his anger Chaya got burnt. This caused Manu and Shani, her two sons, turn against their father.

Surya dev went looking for Samjna to her father's house, where he told him, that Samjna has left, because she was not able to bear the heat of the Sun. Her whole body was burning. To make herself able to stand this intense heat, she went into the mountains to do her penance. Sun-god found her there in a form of a mare, and assuming the same form, he mated with her. Out of their union twins Ashwini kumars were born, the heavenly physicians with heads of horses. They were named Dasya and Nastya. After that, Surya dev went to Vishwakarma and asked for his effulgence to be reduced, so Samjna can stay with him comfortably. It is said that Sun-god has found Samjna in the forest on *Saptami tithi* and on *Saptami tithi* Ashwini kumars were born to him – and hence it became his most favourite lunar day.

This is one of the reasons why one of the most important life lesson's for each *Saptami tithi* native is how to find a healthy balance in any relationship – as, after all, it is seventh lunar day, and it will resemble a little qualities of Moon in 7th house. Sometimes *Saptami* natives, similarly like the Sun, can "burn" others too much with their own light in relationships, while at other times (more often) they might allow others to overshadowed them too much. Learning how to create a healthy flow of energy in any relationship, even if it sometimes means putting your ego down and being a little bit humble, while at the same time not sacrificing your own integrity, as well as learning how to cooperate with others, are the important life lessons from Goddess Shivaduti, which She is sending us always on Her lunar day. This is why the quality of *Saptami tithi* is called *mitra* or "friendly", as this *tithi* helps us to find true friendship in any relationship. Mitra is also one of the names of Sun-god himself, in His form as Divine Friend of the world, who performed a penance (*tapasya*) on the bank of river Chandrabhaga to bring healing to the world. This is why we can also find powerful healers and Divine messengers born on this lunar day.

Meditation with Goddess Shivaduti

Hue: bright like midday sun in summer
Number of heads: 1
Number of eyes: 3
Number of hands: 8
Right hands: *ankusha*, sword, axe, lotus flower
Left hands: *pasha*, shield, mace, cup made of gems
Garments: red
Ornaments: various ornaments, *navaratna* (nine gems) in Her diadem

Tantraraja describes Goddess Shivaduti as being bright like midday sun in summer. The splendour of the midday sun in summer is the most magnificent – yet, it is also the most burning. Goddess Shivaduti often makes us experience Her presence in the form of this heat, which is burning all our karma and "evil" habits. Her garments are red, which, in Her case, symbolises preparation for the righteous battle. She is adorned with various ornaments, which enhance Her beauty, and nine gems symbolising nine planets in Her diadem. She is, indeed, the Goddess of Time, and the nine planets are the governors of Time. Goddess in this form is reminding us that each action has its reaction and, sooner or later, everything needs to be paid for. She is the Great Regulator of Karmic Debts. She rewards the good deeds and punishes the evil ones, to bring us back on the right path. She smiles gently, surrounded by sages, who are singing Her praises – and by that She reminds us to respect all our elders, *gurus* and teachers.

174

In Her left hands Goddess Shivaduti holds *pasha* (noose to control the desires), shield (to protect from negative influences), mace (to destroy the ego) and cup made of gems, reminding us, that if we decide to take the righteous action, we will be rewarded as well. In Her right hands, Mother Shivaduti is holding *ankusha* (goad to control the repulsion), sword (to cut the negativities), axe (to control our habits with its double edge, balancing the opposites) and lotus flower, symbolising the inner purity of the soul. Lotus flowers grow in the mud, but eventually they rise above it to blossom as the most beautiful of all flowers. Similarly our soul is born in the mud of the world and heavy earthly vibrations, with all their dirt. Goddess Shivaduti helps us to rise above the negativities of the world and above the muddy waters of our mind, so our soul can truly blossom like a lotus flower, revealing its unparalleled beauty and Divine fragrance. Lotus flower is also the attribute of Sun-god, especially when he is represented as Mitra, Divine Friend. Through this subtle symbol Goddess is reminding us about the necessity to develop gentleness in each of our relationships, instead of overshadowing others with our ego and personality like "burning midday sun in summer".

Goddess Shivaduti, ruling *Bhadra tithi* or lunar day connected to element of earth, is very closely connected to earthly vibrations, earth's stability and firmness. She inspires us to be as grounded, humble, reliable and confident, as the ground beneath our feet is. Being connected to Shani, She also teaches us the value of loyalty and responsibility in all our relations. As *Saptami tithi* is almost on the half way of Moon's journey from darkness to fullness (or from fullness to reunion), She reminds us that it is stability, confidence, courage and responsibility that makes us grow and prevents us from going astray.

One of Her names is also Shivakari or "the one who does goodness to all". Goddess Shivaduti reminds us not only about the necessity of loyalty and responsibility in our relations, but also the quality of kindness, a general attitude of wishing well to others, regardless of the circumstances – a quality, which can be born only in a very mature soul. Although armed with so many weapons, ultimately, Goddess Shivaduti is not fighting against anything, but simply protecting the purity of our soul, which is symbolised by the lotus flower in Her hand. Goddess Shivaduti is so compassionate, that even if She would need to inflict pain on Her child, to protect it from pollution, negativity or bigger pain, She would gladly do that. As the representant of Shiva, Time Itself, She always has a long-term plan for the evolution of our soul.

People born on *Saptami tithi* are often reflecting some of the positive qualities of Goddess Shivaduti. Reliability, loyalty, self-discipline, maintaing good habits, courage, long-term planning, kindness or capability to face any obstacles may be some of their qualities. They often become good messengers or they can be good in business. Their destiny is always to be of some service to others. Yet, sometimes it may take them some time in life to truly start manifesting the highest, Divine qualities of Goddess Shivaduti. And they will always learn how to do develop the positive qualities of Goddess through confrontation with their own shadow self.

Numerology: 7

There are seven main *rishis* or sages in Vedic tradition, representing the maturity of the soul and service to human kind. It is said that these seven *rishis* chose to stay forever on Earth, as immortal souls, so their prayers can constantly uplift the souls, which are still stuck in the mud of material life.

There are also seven musical notes and seven colours – seven basic expressions of light and seven basic expressions of sound. Number seven is associated with seventh house in Vedic astrology, as well, which stands for all sorts of relationships. It is here, in original seventh house (Libra), that Saturn, the planet of humility and service (and lord of seventh *tithi*) gets exalted, while Sun (who is born on this *tithi*), the planet of the individual self, gets debilitated. Similarly people born on *Saptami tithi* always want to serve others, like *saptarishis*, whose entire existence is dedicated to the upliftment of collective consciousness – but they may sometimes forget too much about themselves on the way.

The shadow side of *Saptami tithi* natives, however, may sometimes be their lust or looking too much for affection or sense gratification, as number 7 is also connected to seven tongues of Agni dev, fire-god, who was well known to be lustful after food, women and… the wives of *saptarishis*. This is why connection of *Saptami tithi*, Krittika nakshatra, star of Agni dev and seven Krittikas (wives of *saptarishis*), is considered to be particularly fatal, as it increases person's lust enormously and makes a person blinded by that. Lust manifested in people born on *Saptami tithi* doesn't need to be, however, always of sexual nature. It can be also lust for food or other pleasures in life – as well as greed for power. The *nakshatra devata* is going to reveal in such a combination, what is the true desire of *Saptami tithi* native. This is why the quality of self-control is so important to develop for all *Saptami tithi* natives.

Yogini in *Kalachakra*: Northwest

On *Saptami tithi* the danger comes from the Northwest. It is said that we should avoid travelling into that direction during the seventh lunar day in any of the two *pakshas*. In Vastu, Northwest direction is connected with air element, fast exchange of energies, business, friendships and relations. It reflects the transformative energies of Shani, the planet co-ruling *Saptami tithi*, along with Goddess Shivaduti, as well as the planet presiding over Northwest direction in *Kalachakra*. Shani inspires us to find more grounding and stability in our relations, but it can make our relations a bit dry as well. Too much of strictness or discipline, or taking things in life a bit too seriously, is one of the shadow sides of Goddess Shivaduti, which we can experience during *Saptami tithi*. With Her energy yearning for justice and finding balance between opposites, self-righteous behaviour can easily appear in us on *Saptami tithi*. To counteract this powerful influence, cooling and compassionate energies of the Moon (who presides over Northwest in Digchakra) would be very helpful, as well as conscious work towards more humility, flexibility and patience. Flexibility is very often the quality, which people born on *Saptami tithi* may either lack or have it in excess.

Shaktis of **Goddess Shivaduti**

Different *shaktis* or powers of Goddess Shivaduti dwell in the different places of Her *yantra*. Her *yantra* looks very similar like the *yantra* of Goddess Bherunda, which emphasises the similarities between the two goddesses. Both are very strict and protective forms of Divine Mother, which is revealed by many sharp edges in the *yantra*, as well as many weapons in their hands – specifically a sword for removing the negativity and a shield for protection from negativity. Both Goddesses give us strength, courage and confidence to face the dark side of life and fight the obstacles on our way.

The *yantra* of Goddess Shivaduti is made of eight petals enclosing *ashtakona* (a figure with eight angles), enclosing *shatkona* (sixpointed star), enclosing six petals, which finally enclose the inner *yoni* (downfacing triangle). The *shaktis* of the corners of the inner triangle stay the same, as for many other Goddesses: Iccha (will power), Jnana (wisdom) and Kriya (action). Six petals enclosing the *yoni* are: Shiva ("merciful one"), Vani ("message" or "voice"), Durasiddha ("rare accomplishments"), Tyagivigraha ("emodiment of sacrifice"), Nada ("the sound") and Manomayi ("made of the mind"). And, similarly like in the *yantra* of Goddess Bherunda, each of the six arms of the six-pointed star is occupied by six *shaktis* of the chakras: Dakini (*vishuddha chakra*), Rakini (*anahata chakra*), Lakini (*manipura chakra*), Kakini (*svadhishthana chakra*), Shakini (*muladhara chakra*) and Hakini (*ajna chakra*). Being so, inner triangle and six-pointed star are symbolising our three innermost powers manifested through our six chakras and mingled with the qualities of Devi.

The energy of Goddess Shivaduti then furtherly spreads into eight flower petals through *shaktis*: Vagisha ("controller of speech"), Varada ("giver of boons"), Vishwa ("the world"), Vibhava ("opulent one"), Vighnakarini ("maker of obstacles"), Vira ("heroic one"), Vighnahara ("destroyer of obstacles") and Vidya ("knowledge"). The *shaktis* of *ashtakona* figure enclosing them are: Sumukhi ("the one with a beautiful face"), Sundari ("beautiful one"), Sara ("the essence"), Samara ("battle"), Saraswati ("goddess of the essence or sacred speech"), Samaya ("time"), Sarvaga ("omniscient") and Siddha ("accomplished one"). Additionally, in the *bhupura* square following *shaktis* are dwelling: Vihwala ("agitated one"), Karshani ("attractive one"), Lola ("playful one"), Nitya ("eternal one"), Madana ("desirous one"), Malini ("garlanded one"), Vinoda ("humorous one"), Kautuka ("prosperous one"), Punya ("good merit") and Purana ("ancient one").

Swara of Goddess Shivaduti

Ṛ, the seventh *swara* or vowel of Sanskrit alphabet, is associated with Goddess Shivaduti. It starts the cycle of four mysterious *swaras*, which are not actual vowels – but they are still considered as *swaras* in Sanskrit. Interestingly enough, according to Agni Purana, these four *swaras* are connected to *saptarishis*.

The *kala* or quality of *swara* ṛ is wetness. It creates a feeling of obtaining, reaching or aquiring something, meeting with somebody, calling or invocation, which are also the qualities closely associated with Goddess Shivaduti, Shani and *Saptami tithi*. According to *Agni Purana* vowel ṛ is also connected to Aditi, the mother of gods – and the mother of Sun-god himself.

Nakshatras connected to Goddess Shivaduti

Rohini nakshatra is connected to *swara* of Goddess Shivaduti, while Her eight arms stand for four nakshatra *padas* of Magha and Purva Phalguni nakshatras. Similarly like Goddess Shivaduti reminds us about the necessity to form good habits in our daily life and avoid the negative ones, so Rohini nakshatra, being fixed or *dhruva* in nature, stands for all our habits, daily rituals and routine, as well as all cyclic things. Having a chariot or a cart as its symbol Rohini nakshatra reminds us about the cyclic nature of time and ever changing seasons.

There is one beautiful story from the life of Sri Krishna, which I always connect with Rohini nakshatra – not only because Sri Krishna was born on this nakshatra, but because the story itself happened on Rohini nakshatra, as well, on Krishna's first birthday, during His naming ceremony. When Mother Yashoda was busy with preparations for the yagna, fire ceremony, she left Her baby Krishna close to a cart with *puja* utensils. She didn't know that this cart was a demon in disguise, Shakatasura. When Mother Yashoda disappeared for a moment, the cart moved closer to Sri Krishna and tried to collapse on Him. Yet then, Sri Krishna, with a single kick of His little, blue foot, destroyed the cart completely. Lord Krishna was just one year old at this time.

This cart (which is also a symbol of Rohini nakshatra), Shakatasura, symbolises the demon of our bad habits. When we live our lives automatically, without ever stopping for a moment, we drag with ourselves through life such a heavy cart with all the burden of our habits - even if so many of them we actually don't need in our life at all. Sri Krishna being so small in this story, reminds us, about the necessity to frequently get in touch with this pure, innocent, childlike part of ourselves – to live the life with childlike curiosity of what the present moment may bring us, rather than living it in an automatic way, letting our habits take over. This is why Paramahansa Yogananda said beautifully that the only power within us, which has the capacity to destroy our bad habits is... intuition. Because if we live our life intuitively, truly listening to our inner voice and following our inner guidance, which changes from moment to moment, there is no space for living our life automatically or falling a prey to our habits from the past. Baby Krishna in this story represents this power of intuition within us, which is the quality so natural for small children – and opposiite to mature nature of Saturn. This is a deeper spiritual meaning of the name of Goddess Shivaduti Herself – the true "messenger of Shiva" within us is the voice of our inborn intuition, which helps us to overcome shadow qualities of Saturn, planetary co-ruler of *Saptami tithi*.

Magha nakshatra, which is also connected to Goddess Shivaduti, represents the power of detachment. Its *shakti* is "the power to leave the body", which carries with itself the message of sacrifice, so in tune with Goddess Shivaduti and *Saptami tithi*. Magha nakshatra is also the *mulatrikona* zone of Sun, which symbolises inner strength, derived from detachment, hidden in this lunar mansion.

Purva Phalguni, on the other hand, which is the nakshatra connected to Aryama or Bhaga, gods of forming alliances, business partnerships and sacred relationships, as well as signing the agreements, reveals another side of Goddess Shivaduti, which is honouring all our relations and bringing there more loyalty and responsibility. Both Magha nakshatra and Purva Phalguni have rat as their animal, one of the most sociable animals, which teaches us the value of cooperation, as well as determination in overcoming the obstacles. The message of Goddess Shivaduti is very similar.

There are also two nakshatras, in which *guna* of *tamas* combines with earth element, similarly like on *Saptami tithi*: Anuradha and Dhanishta, two nakshatras closely connected to Shani - Anuradha being the nakshatra co-ruled by Saturn, and Dhanishta dwelling exactly between the two signs of Saturn: Capricorn and Aquarius. Both nakshatras have greatly passionate nature and unparallaled courage and boldness. Both Anuradha and Dhanishta have very earthly energy and both are ready to make really courageous steps to achieve their goals, even if this requires certain self-sacrifice from their side. In Anuradha nakshatra it is usually more visible in sacrifices made for the sake of uplifting a relationship, while in Dhanishta it is more visible in sacrifices made to fulfill one's own ambitions. Similarly *Saptami tithi* natives are often very courageous and ambitious, but also ready for self-sacrifice for some higher purpose.

There is also an interesting story in *Bhavishya Purana* about how Sun-god has attacked Hasta nakshatra on *Saptami tithi*, although no specific details are given. This is why Hasta nakshatra, the nakshatra of finding the right balance between giving and receiving, as well as serving others selflessly, is presided by Sun-god, Savitar, and reflects certain qualities of *Saptami tithi* and Goddess Shivaduti, as well. This is also why it is said that whenever *Saptami tithi*, Hasta nakshatra and Sunday happen to be together, it is an extremely auspicious day, especially dear to Sun-god.

Tithi, vara and nakshatra resonance

As Shivaduti is the Goddess of sacred alliances, so Her lunar day forms the biggest amount of different *muhurta yogas* out of all the *tithis*. She resonates best with the energies of Wednesday, when Mercury's powers of discernment and intellect are at their peak. Additionally, when *Saptami tithi* falls on Wednesday and Ashwini, Purva Phalguni, Purvashadha or Purva Bhadrapada nakshatra, it forms powerful *suta yoga*. When Wednesday and *Saptami tithi* combine with Rohini, Margashirsha, Ardra, Uttara Phalguni, Anuradha or Uttarashadha, on the other hand, it forms *siddha yoga*, "combination of accomplishments". The only inauspicious combination with Wednesday and *Saptami tithi* happens when Moon dwells in Bharani nakshatra, the nakshatra of Yamaraj, god of death – *visha yoga* or "poisonous combination" is formed in such a case. Yamaraj, even though son of Sun-god, was always enmious towards Shani, his brother, and planetary co-ruler of *Saptami tithi.*

There are six different *siddha yogas,* which can be formed with *Saptami tithi:*

- *Saptami tithi* + Sunday + Pushya, Uttara Phalguni, Hasta, Mula, Uttarashadha, Shravana or Uttara Bhadrapada
- *Saptami tithi* + Monday + Rohini, Margashirsha, Punarvasu, Citra, Shravana, Dhanishta, Shatabhisha or Purva Bhadrapada
- *Saptami tithi* + Wednesday + Rohini, Margashirsha, Ardra, Uttara Phalguni, Anuradha or Uttarashadha
- *Saptami tithi* + Thursday + Ashwini, Punarvasu, Pushya, Magha, Swati, Purvashadha, Purva Bhadrapada or Revati
- *Saptami tithi* + Friday + Ashwini, Bharani, Ardra, Punarvasu, Uttara Phalguni, Citra, Svati, Purvashadha or Revati
- *Saptami tithi* + Saturday + Rohini, Swati, Vishakha, Anuradha, Dhanishta or Shatabhisha

There are also five different *suta yogas* (auspicious combination connected to extracting *soma* or "juice of life" from the present moment), which are possible with *Saptami tithi:*

- *Saptami tithi* + Sunday + Pushya, Hasta or Mula
- *Saptami tithi* + Monday + Margashirsha, Swati or Shravana
- *Saptami tithi* + Tuesday + Ashwini, Rohini, Uttara Phalguni, Shravana, Purva Bhadrapada or Uttara Bhadrapada
- *Saptami tithi* + Wednesday + Ashwini, Purva Phalguni, Purvashadha or Purva Bhadrapada
- *Saptami tithi* + Saturday + Rohini, Swati or Dhanishta

If *siddha yoga* or *suta yoga* doesn't occur, then whenever *Saptami tithi* falls on Sunday it is called *samvartaka yoga* or highly destructive combination of "dissolution". Only *Pratipad tithi* and *Saptami tithi* can form this *yoga*. Interestingly, the combination of *Saptami tithi*, Sunday and Hasta nakshatra is called, according to *Bhavishya Purana*, *putrada* or the combination, which gives progeny. Such a day is said to be especially auspicious in *Shukla paksha*, when it is called *jaya* ("victorious day"). Any spiritual practice undertaken on that day is said to remove all sins, fulfill all desires, give male children and wealth.

Similarly, combination of *Saptami tithi*, Sunday and Rohini nakshatra is considered very auspicious in *Bhavishya Purana*. It is called *saumyavar* or "day full of light". It is said that any spiritual practice performed on this day will bring eternal results. If this happens, additionally, in *Shukla paksha*, such a day is called *vijaya* ("greatly victorious"), and any spiritual practice performed on that day is said not only to annihilate all the sins of the person, but also to mutiply his good deeds performed on that day by millions of times.

In the same way, if *siddha yoga* or *suta yoga* doesn't occur, then whenever *Saptami tithi* falls on Saturday, it is *visha yoga* or "poisonous combination". *Visha yoga* is also formed with Tuesday (if *suta yoga* doesn't occur), simultaneously with *hutashana yoga* ("the combination of consumed oblation") and, suprisingly, a very positive *amrita yoga* ("combination of nectar") – all three at the same time. Similarly, *amrita yoga* is occuring on each Friday with *Saptami tithi*, but at the same time it is *krakacha yoga* or "combination of a saw". These dual energies and opposites coming together is a very specific thing to *Saptami tithi* (even though it occurs sometimes on other lunar days, too).

There are also three possible *vinasha yogas* or "combinations of destruction" possible with *Saptami tithi*:

- *Saptami tithi* + Monday + Bharani, Krittika, Magha, Anuradha, Purvashadha, Uttarashadha or Uttara Bhadrapada
- *Saptami tithi* + Tuesday + Ardra, Punarvasu, Jyeshtha, Purvashadha, Uttarashadha, Shravana, Dhanishta or Shatabhisha
- *Saptami tithi* + Saturday + Bharani, Punarvasu, Pushya, Purva Phalguni, Uttara Phalguni, Hasta, Purvashadha, Uttarashadha or Shravana

And, on top of all these combinations, *Saptami tithi*, being a *Bhadra tithi*, lunar day connected to the element of earth and our actions in the outer world, also forms the same *dvipushkar* and *tripushkar yogas* as *Dvitiya tithi* and Goddess Bhagamalini, which are described in detail in Her chapter. *Saptami tithi*, being co-ruled by Saturn, reminds us through that about the importance of taking the right actions in the world and sometimes magnifies the results of our actions (either in positive or negative way), so the Divine Mother can teach us to pay a little bit more attention to everything that we think, speak or do.

YOGAS FORMED WITH SAPTAMI TITHI

	1	2	3	4	5	6	7
1	samvartaka		**suta / amrita**	**suta**	**siddha**	**siddha / amrita**	visha
2	**tripushkar**	vinasha	**tripushkar**	visha		**siddha / amrita**	tripushkar / vinasha
3	samvartaka	vinasha	visha / amrita	siddha		krakacha / amrita	visha
4	**saumyavar**	**siddha**	**suta / amrita**	**siddha**		krakacha / amrita	**suta / siddha**
5	**dvipushkar**	**suta / siddha**	**dvipushkar**	**siddha**		krakacha / amrita	**dvipushkar**
6	samvartaka		visha / amrita / vinasha	siddha / losses		**siddha / amrita**	visha
7	samvartaka / tripushkar	**siddha**	visha / vinasha tripushkar	siddha	**siddha**	**siddha / amrita**	vinasha / tripushkar
8	**suta / siddha**		visha / amrita	siddha	**siddha**	krakacha / amrita	vinasha
9	samvartaka		visha / amrita	siddha		krakacha / amrita	visha
10	samvartaka	vinasha	visha / amrita	siddha	**siddha**	krakacha / amrita	visha
11	**tripushkar**		**tripushkar**	**suta**		krakacha / amrita	tripushkar / vinasha
12	**siddha**		**suta / amrita**	**siddha**		**siddha / amrita**	vinasha
13	**siddha / suta**	shunya	visha / amrita / shunya	siddha / shunya	shunya	krakacha / amrita / shunya	vinasha / shunya
14	**dvipushkar**	**siddha**	**dvipushkar**	siddha		**siddha / amrita**	**dvipushkar**
15	samvartaka	**suta**	visha / amrita	siddha	**siddha**	**siddha / amrita**	**siddha**
16	tripushkar		tripushkar	siddha		krakacha / amrita	**siddha / tripushkar**
17	samvartaka	vinasha	visha / amrita	**siddha**		krakacha / amrita	**siddha**
18	samvartaka		visha / vinasha	siddha		krakacha / amrita	visha
19	**siddha / suta**	shunya	visha / amrita / shunya	siddha / shunya	shunya	krakacha / amrita / shunya	visha / shunya
20	**tripushkar**	vinasha	tripushkar / visha / vinasha	**suta**	**siddha**	**siddha / amrita**	tripushkar / vinasha
21	**siddha**	vinasha	visha / amrita / vinasha	**siddha**		krakacha / amrita	vinasha

22	**siddha**	**siddha**	vinasha / suta	siddha		krakacha / amrita	vinasha
23	**dvipushkar**	**siddha**	dvipushkar / visha / vinasha	siddha		krakacha / amrita	**dvipushkar**
24	samvartaka	**siddha**	visha / amrita / vinasha	siddha		krakacha / amrita	**siddha**
25	tripushkar	**siddha**	**suta / amrita / tripushkar**	**suta**	**siddha**	krakacha / amrita	visha / tripushkar
26	**siddha**	vinasha	**suta / amrita**	siddha		krakacha / amrita	visha
27	samvartaka		visha / amrita	siddha	**siddha**	**siddha / amrita**	visha

Additionally, the same *visha kanya yoga* combinations, which happen on *Dvitiya tithi*, take place on *Saptami tithi*, as well. *Saptami tithi* also makes Mula and Hasta nakshatras *shunya* or "fruitless" - unless there is another beneficial combination overriding this result, which can happen only on Sundays.

Also, accoring to *Agni Purana* seventh lunar day in combination with Wednesday and Ardra nakshatra is bringing losses.

To summarise, *Saptami tithi* and Goddess Shivaduti do not resonate well under any circumstances only with two nakshatras: Krittika or Jyeshtha. This is why in Vedic month called Bhadrapada (in the end of which Full Moon falls in Uttara Bhadrapada nakshatra) *Saptami tithi* is considered *shunya* and is avoided for any auspicious activities – as in this month *Saptami tithi* will occur exactly in one of these two nakshatras.

Saptami tithi resonates well under any circumstances with nakshatras Ashwini, Rohini, Margashirsha, Citra, Swati, Vishakha, Purva Bhadrapada and Revati (which are mostly airy nakshatras), while it brings varied results with nakshatras Bharani, Ardra, Punarvasu, Pushya, Magha, Purva Phalguni, Uttara Phalguni, Hasta, Anuradha, Mula, Purvashadha, Uttarashadha, Shravana, Dhanishta or Uttara Bhadrapada.

In *Agni Purana* it is also said that sowing seeds on *Saptami tithi* and Krittika, Rohini, Uttara Phalguni, Hasta, Anuradha, Jyeshtha or Revati nakshatra is going to attract great prosperity.

Important *rashis* for *Saptami tithi* natives

Each *tithi* has a special connection with a number of *rashis*. Understanding those connections can help us not only in understanding our own birth chart on a much deeper level, but in better understanding of the nature of the *tithi* itself.

Two *rashis*, which are of great importance for all *Saptami tithi* natives are Aquarius and Leo. Aquarius is the *mulatrikona* sign of planetary lord of this lunar day (Saturn, *tithi pati kshetra*), while Leo is the sign opposite to it (*tithi pati kshetra paksha*), which is the sign revealing, where are we heading in life. As *Saptami tithi* is strongly connected with our inner need for independence, power, strength and courage, it is perfectly reflected in the sign of Leo, represented by the king of all animals. It also represents the shadow side of *Saptami tithi*, which sometimes manifests as greed for power and control. As it is a fixed sign, it additionally reveals that *Saptami tithi* natives are seeking, above all, stability. Any planets placed in Leo or in angles to Leo will furthermore reveal, in which way this stability will be sought by *Saptami tithi* natives.

Additionally, in *Shukla paksha* sign of Aries becomes more energised on *Saptami tithi* (which reveals more independent and power-seeking side of *Saptami tithi*), while in *Krishna paksha* Libra becomes more energised (which is why *Krishna Saptami* natives are much more sociable, humble and service oriented). It is a very important axis, as it is on this axis that Sun and Saturn get exalted or debilitated. This might be the reason why ancient *rishis* might have associated this specific lunar day with birthday of Sun-god. This also indicates that *Saptami tithi* natives often may face some struggles with power and authority, or being overpowered by others. Placement of the Sun becomes extremely important in the chart of any *Saptami tithi* native.

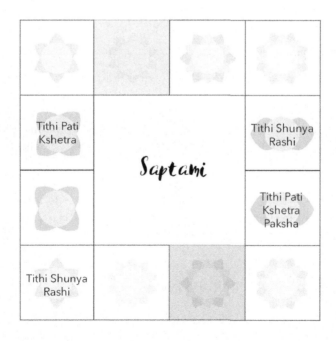

Tithi shunya rashis or the signs, which are made "fruitless" by *Saptami tithi*, are Sagittarius (ruled by Jupiter) and Cancer (ruled by Moon). Both of these signs are naturally quite vulnerable for all people born on *Saptami tithi*. This is the reason why *Saptami tithi* natives often do not find that much comfort in life, and are either often away from their home and country, or another extreme: they are completely stuck in home and their comfort zone.

Unless these signs are occupied by Rahu or Ketu, or unless their planetary lords (Jupiter and Moon) are placed 3rd, 6th, 8th or 12th house from ascendant or Moon, or are retrograde, or in conjuction with malefic planet, or, lastly, in nakshatras of Rahu or Ketu, these two signs and houses won't bring good results for the native. In such a case these signs must be strengthened (by strengthening their lords) to bring good results. *Shunya* planets do produce good results, however, when they transit 3rd, 6th, 8th or 12th house from from ascendant or Moon.

Saptami tithi natives may also face some troubles and obstacles from Rahu, who doesn't resonate well with strict and disciplined energies of *Saptami tithi*. Similarly, people with Rahu very prominent in their chart and personality, won't resonate well neither with *Saptami tithi*, neither with *Saptami tithi* natives.

Sadhana for Goddess Shivaduti

Goddess Shivaduti is pleased, above all, with our righteous actions. To connect with Her on a deeper level, you can either do a meditation of sitting on Her lap, as given by my Gurudev (described in Chapter 24), or colour Her yantra and meditate on it, facing Northwest. For your *sadhana* you can use one of the two mantras below or one of the affirmations. There are couple of more advanced mantras for worship of Goddess Shivaduti in *Tantraraja*, but they are not supposed to be recited without a guidance of a Guru.

Agni Purana also advises worshipping Sun-god on *Saptami tithi* in any month, as it is a birth *tithi* of Sun-god. It is also a natural remedy for all *Saptami tithi* natives, especially if their Sun is afflicted.

Mantras:

oṁ aiṁ hriṁ śriṁ ṛṁ śivadutiyai namaḥ
oṁ aiṁ hriṁ śriṁ ṛṁ dhṛtiyai namaḥ

Affirmations:

I allow myself to be independent.
I allow myself to be courageous.
I allow myself to receive unexpected gifts from the universe.
I allow myself to cooperate.
I am letting go of old habits.
I am honouring the debts from the past.
I see the Divine messenger in every person.

Questions for self-analysis

Every lunar day is an opportunity to learn something new about ourselves. Nitya Devis and their wisdom can become our guides on this sacred journey. Questions below can help you in recognising certain "shadow" tendencies in yourself, which may arise on *Saptami tithi*. If you were born on this lunar day, these questions might be of big importance for you in life and allow you to face your weaknesses.

- Do I allow myself to take bold actions?
- Do I allow myself to leave my comfort zone?
- Am I ready to let go of outdated habits?
- Do I hang too much on the past?
- How is my self-control and self-discipline?
- Could I be more discplined in my daily routine?
- Could I be a bit more humble?
- Am I ready to serve the universe the best way I can?
- Do I allow myself to be independent?
- How am I honouring the debts from the past?
- Do I fulfill my duties faithfully?
- Am I persistent enough in pursuing my goals?
- Do I notice silent messages from the Divine?
- Do I allow the voice of my soul to truly speak up?
- Am I honouring all my relationships?
- Do I see the messenger of the Divine in every person?

Yantra of Goddess Shivaduti

CHAPTER 15

TVARITA – SWIFT GODDESS
ASHTAMI – EIGHTH LUNAR DAY

bhairavī pātu mānnitya bheruṇḍā sarvadāvatu
tvaritā pātu mānnitya mugutārā sadāvatu

"May Goddess Tvarita, Bherunda and Bhairavi always protect me from all sides."

- Kamalatmika Kavacham

Kala	Element	Planet	Guna	Yogini	Vowel
shashini (swift one)	ether	Rahu	tamas	Northeast	ṝ

Stage of consciousness	Divine quality	Deity (Muhurta Cintamani)	Deity (Varahamihira)	Nakshatra connection	Form of Shiva
turiya (dreaming)	aparajita (invincibility)	Shiva	8 Vasus	Rohini Uttara Phalguni	Ardhana-rishvara

Shukla Paksha

Krishna Paksha

Nadi: ida
Chakra: anahata
Interval: perfect fourth
Deity (Narada Purana): Nagas
House from the Sun: 4 or 5

Nadi: pingala
Chakra: manipura
Interval: perfect fourth
Deity (Narada Purana): Shiva
House from the Sun: 10 or 11

There are many versions of the myth of Creation. According to Vedic thought, through the will of Narayana, a golden egg (*hiranyagarbha*) appeared in the waters of creation. This golden egg or *brahmanda* contained a totality of creation within itself – all the worlds and all the elements combined together, ready to give birth to our world. Yet, in almost any of these myths, we can also see some sort of opposing force appearing, as well - a force of chaos, untangling and disintegration, which strives for liberation and release of all the combined energies. One of the oldest myths, narrated in *Tvaritamulasutra*, describes a great battle between forces of chaos and forces of creation, which comes to an end only when Supreme Goddess appears as Tvarita, the one who balances the opposites, and becomes the Protectress of the universe, balancing the forces of chaos.

Tvarita is a very special Goddess amongst all the other Nitya Devis. No other Nitya Devi has such a prominent place in the scriptures. Not only tantric scriptures (which are naturally connected with the worship of Nitya Devis) praise Her, but we can read more about Goddess Tvarita and Her nature also in *Agni Purana*. She even has few ancient scriptures dedicated exclusively to Her, such as *Tvaritamulasutra* or *Tvaritajnanakalpa*.

Goddess Tvarita presides over *Ashtami tithi* or eighth lunar day – exactly on the half way of Moon's journey from darkness to fullness or from fullness to re-union. If we would look at the sky on *Ashtami tithi* we would see exact half of the Moon. Goddess Tvarita is the form of Divine Mother, which balances the forces of darkness and light, chaos and order, creation and destruction. She doesn't favour anybody. She is adorned both with snakes and with peacock feathers (peacocks are natural enemies of snakes). She shows us the way, how to honour both Light and Darkness. Not without a reason it is said that Shani (Saturn), the dispenser of justice, who always looks equally on everybody, was born on *Ashtami tithi*. This is also why the nature of this lunar day is sometimes described as *dvandva* or "conflicting", as inner conflicts may awaken on this lunar day due to opposite forces coming together to confront each ther.

Even the form of Shiva connected to eighth lunar day is Ardhanarishwara – half-Shiva, half-Shakti, representing the natural balance of all opposites existing in the universe. In *Bhavishya Purana* it is said that whenever *Ashtami tithi* falls on Monday in *Shukla paksha*, Shiva and Shakti in the united form of Ardhanarishwara should be worshipped with chandan and kumkum, white and red flowers, as well as 25 oil lamps. Such a day is called *Somashtami* and is considered very auspicious. Due to Shiva in the form of Ardhanarishwara being so connected to this lunar day, the topic of equal rights in our times (especially women's rights) is usually very important and dear to all *Ashtami tithi* natives. They love equality and justice. This is one of the reasons why *yantra* of Goddess Tvarita is just round in shape, surrounded by eight petals – no matter, how you turn it, you will see it the same shape, from every perspective and every angle. Similarly, Moon will looks exactly the same on *Shukla Ashtami* and *Krishna Ashtami*.

As Rahu is the deity co-ruling this *tithi*, while ether is its element, and *guna* is *tamas*, no wonder that this lunar day is connected to the Goddess, who controls the forces of chaos, symbolised by snakes. Whenever the energy of ether, *tamo guna* or Rahu gets exeggerated in our body, we become easily ungrounded and chaotic. Goddess Tvarita helps us to balance all those energies and to destroy (or rather to liberate) all the poisons, which may accumulate within us. She represents the state of *turiya* or state of awakened consciousness within the dreaming state. No wonder that the worship of Goddess Durga, who is Mahamaya, the Great Illusionist, is advised on *Ashtami tithi*. Divine Mother helps us on this day to wake up from the dream of illusion and perceive the reality the way it is. Shiva Himself is the presiding deity of *Ashtami tithi*, too, according to *Muhurta Cintamani*.

In *Shukla Paksha* our bioenergy advances to *anahata chakra* during *Ashtami tithi*, while during *Krishna paksha*, it goes into *manipura chakra*. This *tithi* is quite special during *Shukla paksha*, as it does not only enter the realm of higher chakras, starting from the heart chakra, but also from this lunar day on, the Moon's bright side will cover bigger part of the Moon's visible disc than its dark side. It symbolises advancing from our lower, darker nature into the light and higher harmony. Perhaps this is why one of Tvarita's tantric names in *64 Yogini Namavali* is

Urdvaretada or "the Giver of upward ecstasy". Even Her connection with the snakes and Rahu's energy might come from the fact that during *Ashtami tithi* in *Shukla paksha*, our personal energy will start moving upwards, to the upper chakras, which might trigger our *kundalini shakti* to awaken, as well.

Ashtami is also the only *tithi*, during which the music interval between the Sun and the Moon is exactly the same in both *pakshas*: a perfect fourth, one of the most harmonious intervals associated with *madhyama* ("the middle one" ruled by the Moon) in Indian music. Such perfect intervals, however, are often not conductive for taking any sort of actions in the material world, which is why *tithis* associated with them are often wrongly considered inauspicious. They bring us however a connection with the higher reality and a good stir to our inner energy, which is why they are very supportive for any sort of spiritual practices. This is especially true to *Ashtami*, as during this lunar day, in both *pakshas*, Moon is going to dwell exactly in *kendra* (angles) from the Sun. It is almost as if too big resonance between the Sun and the Moon on *Ashtami* has simply too powerful effect on our mind. Like Tvarita Devi Herself, it yearns to bring everything back to the primordial state of harmony, to liberate all the energies – but initially, this sudden stir in energy can create even bigger chaos on material level. Which is why it is always advised to never take any important decisions or actions on *Ashtami tithi*. It should be a day for contemplation, not for manifestation.

Tvarita, interestingly, is also one of the names of Garuda (celestial eagle in Vedic tradition) as it means "the swift one". Garuda, similarly like Goddess Tvarita Herself, is also considered the enemy of the snakes and chaotic forces, as well as their controller. In some of the Buddhist myths Garuda is even said to emerge as a fully mature being from the primordial egg of creation, which is so connected with Goddess Tvarita's mythology. Garuda's wings beating in unison are in Buddhist tantric tradition a metaphor of unitary nature of duality, revealing the need for all the opposites to exist simultaneously. It also indicates *yogi*'s power to finally transcend this duality with his own efforts and rise above it, like an eagle is rising high to see the full picture and to look at things in a clearer and more detached way.

Goddess Tvarita is often approached for help in the process of learning, education, to protect our health and wealth, to cure the disease and bestow longevity, as well as physical radiance. She also helps to get rid of unnecessary desires. As Her name means "the swift one", *Tantraraja* says, that She is very quick to grant the fruits of worship. Anybody, who prays to Her is not affected by poverty or poison. *Agni Purana* additionally says that a prayer to Goddess Tvarita can even cure from a snake-bite.

Meditation with Goddess Tvarita

Hue: dark blue
Number of heads: 1
Number of eyes: 3
Number of hands: 4
Right hands: *ankusha, abhaya mudra*
Left hands: *pasha, varada mudra*
Garments: green
Ornaments: adorned with fresh leaves, eight fierce serpents, waistchain, anklets, crystal diadem on Her head with crest of peacock feathers, bangles made of peacock feathers (as well as Her umbrella and banner), strings of *gunja* berries decorating Her throat and breasts, which are smeared with red sandalwood paste

Goddess Tvarita is much different from any other Nitya Devi. Being the force of *Prakriti* or Mother Nature Herself, Goddess Tvarita is not adorned with any golden ornaments, but with forest berries, fresh leaves, peacock feathers and snakes, symbolising Her deep connection with the forces of Nature. Scripture compares Her to a tribal woman or huntress. *Tantraraja* describes Goddess Tvarita as a dark-blue maiden in the first flash of youth, dressed in green garments and adorned with fresh leaves, which reveals Her innocence, as well as innocent nature of people born on *Ashtami tithi*.

Eight fierce serpents of the primordial forces of Nature, named Ananta, Kulika, Vasuki, Shankhapala, Takshaka, Mahapadma, Padma and Kartataka are Her ornaments. Interestingly, these eight serpents, along with four other *nagas*, are also the presiding deities of twelve different types of *kala sarpa yoga* identified in Vedic astrology, which are also identified by the position of Rahu, planet co-ruling *Ashtami tithi*. According to *Agni Purana* seven of them also preside over seven days of the week. Serpent Kulika, additionally, is said to preside over all junctions of Time or *gandantas*. Tvarita Devi wears those sacred serpents as Her ornaments, which reveals that She is the Controller of Time itself. In *Shilpa Prakasha* She is called *Kalatmika* or "the Soul of Time". Serpents Ananta and Kulika, both fiery in colour and with 1000 hoods each, are Her earrings. Vasuki and Shankhapala, both yellow in colour and with 700 hoods each, are Her upper arm bangles. Takshaka and Mahapadma, blue in colour and with 500 hoods each, are Her girdle. Padma and Kartataka, white in colour and with 300 hoods each, are Her toe ornaments.

Tvarita Devi, being the destroyer and the controller of poison, is also adorned with peacock feathers. Peacock feathers are present in Her crystal diadem, bangles, umbrella and banner. Interestingly enough, peacocks are natural enemies of the snakes. With these two opposites joined together in the image of Goddess Tvarita, whose dark blue complexion resembles the colour of the primordial waters and the eternal void, into which everything positive and negative eventually merges, Tvarita is truly the Goddess of honouring and balancing the opposites. She reminds us that every force in the universe requires a counterforce, as well. Without the darkness, the light cannot be known. Both are equally important in our spiritual evolution. Ultimately, these were not only *devas* or gods, who were churning the Cosmic Ocean – the efforts of both gods and demons working *together* were necessary. Interestingly, it was Rahu himself, who pointed this fact out to the demigods, when demons were treated unjustly after the process of churning of the Cosmic Ocean – and it was Rahu himself, who paid the highest price for this rebellious act, when his head was separated from his body.

Tvarita is the Mother that doesn't discern. She loves all Her children and all Her creation. While Her upper hands are holding *pasha* (noose for controlling the desires) and *ankusha* (goad for controlling the instinct repulsion), symbolising two primordial instincts or movements of the atoms themselves, Her two lower hands are eternally placed in the position of *abhaya mudra*, granting fearlessness and *varada mudra*, granting boons. Her hands are ever open, blessing all Her children. Indeed, as Her name itself means "the swift one", Goddess Tvarita blesses us with the fruits of our worship very quickly.

Ashtami tithi, due to being the first lunar day presided by Shiva, according to *Muhurta Cintamani*, is also connected to our ability to neutralise all the poisons – in which Goddess Tvarita helps us greatly. Similarly like Shiva, in His innocence and love for His children, both gods and demons, needed to drink the poison to save the world, so sometimes *Ashtami tithi* natives need to "drink the poison" in their life. This symbolic "poison" may take many different forms. Sometimes it is the poison of one's own emotions, sometimes it is the poison of somebody else's negativity. Shiva in His form of Nilakantha, "the one having a blue throat" (as the deadly *halahal* poison coloured His throat in blue), reminds us, that we should always withhold the poison instead of spreading it around through the means of poisonous words (throat chakra), but we should neither swallow it completely and allow it to pollute our inner space. After all, Shiva kept the poison only in His throat and He transformed it there – He didn't allow it to reach His inner space. Similarly people born on *Ashtami tithi* need to learn in life, how to deal with different "poisons" – without spreading them around and without letting them affect their inner space, but rather neutralising them within with the power of introspection

Swiftness of Goddess Tvarita is Her shadow side as well. The *kala* of the Moon associated with Her is *shashini* or "rabbit-like" quality of the Moon, which represents the ever-changing mind; the mind, which is always on the move and never rests. When the mind is not controlled properly it becomes our enemy. It was Krishna Himself, who was born on *Ashtami tithi* and who said that controlled mind is our best friend, while uncontrolled mind becomes our worst enemy. When the disturbing forces of chaos, connected with agitated ether element take over our mind, we easily lose our self-control and sense of direction.

Numerology: 8

There are 8 Vasus, elemental gods, who are the bringers of transformation. This is also why eighth house in Vedic astrology is connected to all sudden changes and transformation, which are brought into our life by the chaotic energy of Rahu. This is why Rahu is also the 8th *graha* among the nine planets in Vedic Astrology. As Rahu is also connected to snakes or *nagas*, so there are eight Divine serpents in Vedic tradition, who are not only bringers of transformation, but they literally make our experience of the influence of Time more tangible. In many cultures snakes are perceived as the symbols of time, due to their longevity and capacity to bring death. Even *ouroboros*, the snake eating its own tail, symbolising the continuity of time, is often represented in the shape of number eight, symbolising the infinity of Time and creation. Such is also the nature of *Ashtami tithi*. It is the most ungrounded of all lunar days and thus allows us to connect to the things beyond time and space. This is also why Goddess Tvarita is adorned with eight snakes. And this is why according to *Narada Purana*, *Ashtami tithi* is ruled by *nagas*, Divine serpents, in *Shukla paksha*, while in *Krishna paksha* it is ruled by Shiva, god of infinite Time.

Number eight is also of highest importance in Vastu Shastra, as well as in some divination methods in India. To capture the exact quality of time and infuse it into space, dividing the space by eight is one of the most sacred mathematical processes in the science of Vastu. 8x8 mandala is the most sacred grid in Vastu science, used for designing temples and other sacred spaces. In *Aintiram*, ancient Vastu scripture, it is written that Time is a pulse of movement in Absolute Space and it consists of eight rhythms.

Number 8 also refers to 8 Matrikas or forms of the Divine Mother, which stand for shadow qualities within us. Story of 8 Matrikas is, once again, connected with demon Andhakasura - "demon of darkness", representing blindness of ignorance and *guna* of *tamas*. In *Bhavishya Purana* it is written, then when Shiva was fighting with Andhakasura, he could not defeat him, as the demon had a boon, that whenever a drop of his blood would fall on the ground, his replica will be born. Then 8 Matrikas (along with other forms of Divine Mother, including Goddess Bhagamalini, according to *Matsya Purana*) manifested from Shiva and other gods to drink the blood of Andhakasura. Their names were: Brahmi (*shakti* of Brahma, the Creator), Kaumari (*shakti* of Kartikeya, son of Shiva and Shakti), Vaishnavi (*shakti* of Vishnu, the Sustainer), Varahi (*shakti* of boar incarnation of Lord Vishnu), Yami (*shakti* of Yamaraj, god of death), Yogeshwari (yogic power), Maheshwari (*shakti* of Shiva) and Mahendri (*shakti* of Indra). As they drank the blood of the demon, also the negative qualities, such as desire, confusion, lust, greed or jealousy were born out of them. As this happened on *Ashtami tithi*, this lunar day became sacred to those 8 forms of the Divine Mother, which also represent 8 shadow qualities within ourselves, that each of us needs to overcome on our spiritual path.

Yogini in *Kalachakra*: Northeast

On *Ashtami tithi* the danger comes from the Northeast. It is said that we should avoid travelling into that direction during the eighth lunar day in any of the two *pakshas*. According to Vastu Shastra Northeast is the most spiritual direction, connected to liberating energies of *moksha*. Similarly *Ashtami tithi* natives are always looking towards liberty and freedom, regardless whether they are searching for it in the outer world or in the deepness of their meditation. Strongly etheric energies of *Ashtami tithi* are always pushing us towards experience of inner freedom and breaking all the boundaries – yet, even the energies of *moksha* can cause some chaos in our life, if we are not grounded enough. Lack of grounding and contact with reality is the biggest issue, which *Ashtami tithi* natives may face, as they often tend to focus only on one side of life, forgetting the other one. This is why even though in *Kalachakra* Northeast is ruled by Rahu, the planetary lord of this lunar day, in *Digchakra* it is ruled by Jupiter – which reveals that following some spiritual authority, scriptures or a living Guru can be of great help for all *Ashtami tithi* natives, as it will help them to become more grounded and respectful towards certain boundaries. Not without a reason it is said that Jupiter is the only planet, which can control Rahu in Vedic astrology. Similarly the energy of Jupiter can be greatly helpful for all *Ashtami tithi* natives, as it will keep their chaotic, circling energy in some healthy boundaries. This will naturally balance the exaggerated qualities of Rahu within them.

Shaktis of Goddess Tvarita

Eight different *shaktis* or powers of Goddess Tvarita, connected to the syllables of Her mantra, dwell in the eight flower petals of Her *yantra*. Their names are: Humkari ("syllable *hum*"), Khechari ("magical power of flying"), Chandi ("fierce one"), Chhedini ("cutting one"), Kshepani ("delaying one"), Strikari ("syllable *strim*"), Humkari ("syllable *hum*") and Kshemakari ("the forgiving one"). Her *yantra* consist only of these eight petals, symbolising the directions of the world, and the void within. It is a metaphor of creation itself, which appeared from the void and manifested in the space as eight directions of the world. Eight is also the number of eternity.

A shape of circle, so prominent in this *yantra*, in Vedic culture is also considered very *tamasic*, as the energy flows in the most chaotic, agitated, unrestrained and unordered way in a circle – as it has no angles to contain it and restrain it. It is also connected to element of *ether* and the most primordial shape of the space. It surely reveals the chaotic side of Rahu, co-ruling this lunar day, as well as the dark side of ether element, which can become very chaotic, if agitated. Even the syllable of Goddess Tvarita in Sri Vidya mantra is *ha* – the syllable of space, breath and Spirit.

Meditation on this *yantra* brings a feeling of lightness, but also certain inner void and even a feeling of pointlessness. It helps to disperse and nullify all the negative energies, but at the same time it can also nullify to certain extent our positive energies, as well. Similarly, people born on *Ashtami tithi*, usually have very light and creative energy; they also tend to be very changeable and fast, but often they may experience at some point in life this feeling of pointlessness, emptiness and inner void. They can be a bit careless, as well. Daily meditation is an absolute must for them to control those intense etheric energies within their minds.

Interestingly, the *yantra* of Goddess Tvarita is one of the very few ones, which looks always the same, regardless of the position you put it in. You can turn it upside down, and it will still look exactly the same. It symbolises the mind running in circle, when too much ether is dwelling in it. It reveals a pointlessness of mind's never-ending story of constantly running towards something new – as, eventually, we will always end up with the very same thing.

This is also why chaotic, unrestrained, intellectual and *tamasic* forces of Rahu, connected to this lunar day, are associated with addictions. Whenever our mind faces this inner void, but doesn't comprehend it through any spiritual insight, its most natural reaction is to try and run away from it. It would run from one pleasure to the other, just to escape this feeling of void and emptiness – quite a pointless running, though, if you take into consideration that 99.99% of the universe as we know it is made of void. This is the state of mind of majority of the people nowadays, especially in the West. We keep running after all the temporary things all the time, believing in the false promise that they will finally bring us fulfillment – while the only true fulfillment lies hidden deep in the inner void itself, beyond the boundaries of our fears. Goddess Tvarita reminds us about the pointlessness of constantly running away from our dislikes and running towards our likes, as it is a never-ending journey, which never brings anything new along with it. Instead, She inspires us to cool the deep waters of our mind, to embrace the opposites and honour both Light and the Darkness, likes and dislikes, by focusing on the Divine and understanding the beauty of Divine romance. This beauty was revealed to the world in the most profound way through life story of Radha and Krishna – the most sublime form of Divine Lovers, who were both born on *Ashtami tithi*.

Radha's and Krishna's eternal Love Story

Whenever I meditate on the Divine Love story of Sri Radha and Sri Krishna, I feel like it is a higher octave of the symbolic romance between Shiva and Shakti. Love story between Shiva and Shakti is beautiful, but love story of Radha and Krishna is *blissful*.

There is no other such a story like story of Radha and Krishna. No other love story has ever moved so many hearts and was treasured so much, for such a long period of time. Not without a reason the Divine Love story of Radha and Krishna is called *nitya lila* or "eternal pastime". To these days their story is played over and over again in the hearts of their devotees and imprinted deeply within them. It is said that the longing of Radha for Krishna was so intense, that it left a permanent blueprint on our planet. Even in our times, in Vrindavan, in the sacred place, where Divine Love story of Radha and Krishna was played by them on Earth, people observe miracles happening every night, which indicate that this sacred Love story is still going on – even if hidden before our physical eyes.

Radha's complexion was golden, Krishna's complexion was dark like a monsoon cloud. Radha was very shy and innocent, while Krishna was very bold and mischievious. Radha's devotion for Her Beloved was single-pointed, while Krishna was giving His Love freely to all the *gopis*. Radha was born on *Shukla Ashtami*, while Krishna was born on *Krishna Ashtami*. They were complete opposites. But Love transformed them into One.

There are many stories about the Divine pastimes of Sri Radha and Sri Krishna. Many of them reveal, how many obstacles and difficulties Radharani needed to go through in order to be just for a moment with Her Beloved. Her devotion was so deep, that She would completely forget about Herself and Her own pain – Her only desire was to serve Krishna and to make Her Beloved Krishna happy. Her Love was so selfless and unconditional, that in our times it is even hard to imagine. She wouldn't mind going barefoot through the dark forest to meet Her Beloved or being beaten up by Her crooked mother-in-law later on. There was nothing that could stand on Her way towards Love. She was like a powerful river overcoming all the obstacles to merge with the ocean.

Many inhabitants of Vrindavan were against their romance, as Radha was officially married to another man. Her mother-in-law would constantly scold Her, while Krishna's grandmother would constantly scold him. All the elder *gopis* of Vrindavan were always doing their very best to prevent Radha and Krishna from meeting each other. Yet, in one of the stories, Krishna Himself has revealed, that in fact, every single person in Vrindavan, every single friend and every single enemy of their Love, was just an expansion of Himself. After all, He was the Supreme God, and Radha was the Supreme Goddess. In secret He revealed to Radha, that even all those *gopis*, who prevent their sacred romance to happen, were His own expansions, which He created to make their Love story... sweeter. For how Love can reveal its greatness, if it is never tested or if there is no obstacle on its way? Nobody remembers love stories, in which everything went smoothly and easily. There is nothing special in Love, which didn't went through the fire of testing. But such a Love, which endured every test and every hardship, and emerged victorious, is the Love that is going to be remembered forever. That was the plan of Lord Krishna – for Radha's love to be remembered forever.

There is a tiny particle of Goddess and tiny particle of Radha within each one of us. Yearning for the Universal Beloved is our soul's true state. But, once this Love starts to awaken, certain obstacles will start to appear on our way, as well. In fact, every single obstacle and difficulty we experience in our lives is just to make the eternal love story between the individual "I" and the universal "You" sweeter – to test, how far are we ready to go for the sake of Love. Krishna Himself has revealed the necessity of counterforce to exist in the universe, and it is also the highest message of Tvarita Devi, which requires certain maturity of the mind to comprehend. All those little tests, all those little difficulties, which often seem so big, are only there to test, how much can we stretch the borders of our Love, how much more we can embrace with it and how much more can we surrender.

Interestingly, the quality of Sri Krishna connected to *Ashtami tithi* is *aparajita* or "being undefeatable" – and it is only the power of Love that makes us truly undefeatable and unstoppable.

My Gurudev, Paramahamsa Vishwananda, has written this beautiful message on *Krishna Ashtami*, 7 February 2018:

"When it comes to loved ones and the spiritual support we can give during a crisis, Love will find the way out. Love will inspire the right words, but also the right silence. Love will give strength to patience and stability. Love will show how important it is to be faithful to Love and, as a result, we will see its power and of what material is the shield of Love.

Everything is attracted to Love. Everything. Light and darkness, good and bad. Openness to life and fearfulness. Foolish and wise. Extroverts and introverts. Beginning and end. Because Love is the source, and everything wants to find itself in the source again, through the source."

It is said, that everything needs to have its limits, boundaries and a healthy balance. But Divine Love is the only quality, which manifests its highest nature, when it is boundless and unrestrained. Divine Love is the only direction, into which the ever-expanding energy of Rahu can be directed completely and left unrestrained, as it will become a source of our spiritual bliss – bliss, which is above joy and sadness. Bliss, which is the way the soul experiences the Infinity. And it is only Divine Love, which can make us rise above the influence of Time.

Swara of Goddess Tvarita

$\bar{R}$, the eighth *swara* or vowel of Sanskrit alphabet, is associated with Goddess Tvarita. It is said to produce the feeling fear, terror or warding something off or exorcising. It invokes the Divine protection and helps us to overcome any negativity on our way, which strongly reflects the qualities of Tvarita Devi. Similarly like the *swara* of previous lunar day, *Saptami*, vowel $\bar{r}$ is also connected with Aditi, the mother of gods, according to *Agni Purana*.

Nakshatras connected to Goddess Tvarita

Rohini nakshatra is connected to *swara* of Goddess Tvarita, while Her eight arms stand for four nakshatra *padas* of Uttara Phalguni. It is very interesting that the two nakshatras connected to Goddess, who controls the forces of chaos, are, indeed, connected to good organisation, having good habits and a healthy routine. Both are of fixed or *dhruva* nature. Specifically Uttara Phalguni nakshatra, ruled by the Sun, represents our ability to control things and take responsibility for our own life energy manifested through different thoughts, words, actions and... choices. Rohini nakshatra is the star of our habits, while Uttara Phalguni is the nakshatra of our choices – both shaping our reality and helping us to bring order into the chaos.

Interestingly, Rohini nakshatra is also connected to controlling the poisons, like Tvarita Devi. Not only the animal of Rohini nakshatra is a male serpent, but even very old depictions of personified Rohini nakshatra (which are available in the collections of one museum in Kolkata) reveal Rohini as a woman standing on the snake and controlling it. When I saw this picture for the first time it reminded me a lot of the image of Mother Mary of Guadalupe.

Rohini nakshatra and Uttara Phalguni have also quite a lot in common. They are both fixed nakshatras, bringing the feeling of stability. The motivation of both of them is *moksha* or liberation – freeing us from all unwanted energies. And the nature of both of them is *manushya* or human, indicating our human weaknesses as well.

Tithi, vara and nakshatra resonance

Ashtami tithi resonates the best with the energy of dynamic Tuesday, when it forms *siddha yoga* ("combination of accomplishments"). This *yoga* is additionally empowered, when it happens with Moon dwelling in Ashwini, Margashirsha, Uttara Phalguni, Citra, Anuradha, Mula, Dhanishta or Purva Bhadrapada nakshatra. Combination of *Ashtami tithi* and Tuesday is inauspicious only, when Moon dwells in Ardra, Punarvasu, Jyeshtha, Purvashadha, Uttarashadha, Shravana, Dhanishta or Shatabhisha nakshatra, as then it forms destructive *vinasha yoga*.

According to *Bhavishya Purana*, *Ashtami tithi* also resonates really well with Mondays. Worship of Shiva and Shakti in the united form of Ardhanarishwara is advised on such days. Whenever *Ashtami* and Monday combine together it is called *somashtami*.

Ashtami tithi also resonates quite well with Wednesday, ruled by grounding energies of Mercury, as it forms with it *amrita yoga* ("combination of nectar") – but at the same time Wednesday and *Ashtami* produce *hutashana yoga* ("combination of consumed fire oblation"), which may in some cases make *amrita yoga* fruitless on this day. *Ashtami tithi*, which falls on Wednesday is called *budhashtami* and it considered a very auspicious day for fasting and spiritual practice, especially if one desires to uplift the energy of one's Mercury in natal chart. Additionally, if *Ashtami tithi* falls on Wednesday and the Moon dwells in one of the following nakshatras: Rohini, Margashirsha, Ardra, Uttara Phalguni, Anuradha or Uttarashadha, it forms a powerful *siddha yoga*. On the other hand, when Moon dwells on *Ashtami tithi* and Wednesday in nakshatras Ashwini, Bharani, Pushya, Ashlesha, Magha, Mula, Dhanishta or Purva Bhadrapada, *vinasha yoga* or "combination of destruction" is produced. Therefore the nakshatra, in which Moon is dwelling on *budhashtami* day must be always carefully analysed.

Ashtami tithi has the worst resonance with Thursday, which is not only the day ruled by Jupiter, but also ether element, which additionally exaggerates the unstable energies of *Ashtami tithi*. On such days *visha yoga* ("poisonous combination") and dangerous *krakacha yoga* ("combination of a saw") are simultaneously formed. Such a combination becomes even more dangerous, if the Moon would dwell in Krittika, Rohini, Margashirsha, Ardra, Uttara Phalguni, Vishakha, Anuradha or Shatabhisha nakshatra, as it would additionally form *vinasha yoga*. *Agni Purana* says that combination of *Ashtami tithi*, Thursday and Dhanishta or Ardra nakshatra can bring death.

Ashtami tithi and Friday bring *dagdha yoga* or "burnt combination", when our life force becomes a bit "burnt down" and exhausted. Additionally, combination of Friday, *Ashtami* and Rohini, Punarvasu, Magha, Vishakha, Anuradha, Jyeshtha, Shravana or Dhanishta nakshatra, bring another *vinasha yoga*.

In total, there are five *vinasha yogas* possible with *Ashtami tithi*:

- *Ashtami tithi* + Sunday + Bharani, Margashirsha, Ashlesha, Vishakha, Anuradha, Jyeshtha or Dhanishta
- *Ashtami tithi* + Tuesday + Ardra, Punarvasu, Jyeshtha, Purvashadha, Uttarashadha, Shravana, Dhanishta or Shatabhisha
- *Ashtami tithi* + Wednesday + Ashwini, Bharani, Pushya, Ashlesha, Magha, Mula, Dhanishta or Purva Bhadrapada
- *Ashtami tithi* + Thursday + Krittika, Rohini, Margashirsha, Ardra, Uttara Phalguni, Vishakha, Anuradha or Shatabhisha
- *Ashtami tithi* + Friday + Rohini, Punarvasu, Magha, Vishakha, Anuradha, Jyeshtha, Shravana or Dhanishta

Goddess Tvarita and *Ashtami* also naturally do not resonate so well with Purva Bhadrapada nakshatra, the impulsive and deeply transformative star of one of the Divine serpents, Aja Ekapada, as it additionally agitates already unstable energy of this lunar day. *Ashtami* and Purva Bhadrapada nashatra are forming *ashubha yoga* or "inauspicious combination". *Ashtami tithi* also makes Purva Bhadrapada nakshatra *shunya* or "fruitless".

YOGAS FORMED WITH *ASHTAMI TITHI*

	1	2	3	4	5	6	7
1		somashtami	**siddha**	vinasha	krakacha	dagdha	
2	vinasha	somashtami	siddha	vinasha	krakacha	dagdha	
3		somashtami	siddha	amrita / hutashana	vinasha	dagdha	
4		somashtami	siddha	**siddha**	vinasha	vinasha	
5	vinasha	somashtami	**siddha**	**siddha**	vinasha	dagdha	
6		somashtami	vinasha	**siddha**	vinasha	dagdha	
7		somashtami	vinasha	amrita / hutashana	krakacha	vinasha	
8		somashtami	siddha	vinasha	krakacha	dagdha	
9	vinasha	somashtami	siddha	vinasha	krakacha	dagdha	
10		somashtami	siddha	vinasha	krakacha	vinasha	
11		somashtami	siddha	amrita / hutashana	krakacha	dagdha	
12		somashtami	**siddha**	**siddha**	vinasha	dagdha	
13		somashtami	siddha	amrita / hutashana	krakacha	dagdha	
14		somashtami	**siddha**	amrita / hutashana	krakacha	dagdha	
15		somashtami	siddha	amrita / hutashana	krakacha	dagdha	
16	vinasha	somashtami	siddha	amrita / hutashana	vinasha	vinasha	
17	vinasha	somashtami	**siddha**	**siddha**	vinasha	vinasha	
18	vinasha	somashtami	vinasha	amrita / hutashana	krakacha	vinasha	
19		somashtami	**siddha**	vinasha	krakacha	dagdha	
20		somashtami	vinasha	amrita / hutashana	krakacha	dagdha	
21		somashtami	vinasha	**siddha**	krakacha	dagdha	
22		somashtami	vinasha	amrita / hutashana	krakacha	vinasha	
23	vinasha	somashtami	siddha/vinasha	vinasha	death	vinasha	
24		somashtami	vinasha	amrita / hutashana	vinasha	dagdha	
25	shunya	somashtami / shunya	**siddha** / shunya	amrita / hutashana shunya /vinasha	krakacha / shunya	dagdha / shunya	shunya

| 26 | | somashtami | siddha | amrita / hutashana | krakacha | dagdha | |
| 27 | | somashtami | siddha | amrita / hutashana | krakacha | dagdha | visha |

It is also said that combination of *Ashtami tithi*, Saturday and Revati nakshatra brings another, more severe, *visha yoga* or "poisonous combination".

To summarise, *Ashtami tithi* and Goddess Tvarita resonate the best only with Citra nakshatra, the most tamasic, but at the same time the most creative star, which has the capacity to give a form to that, what is formless, due to its presiding deity: Tvashtar, the Divine Architect. *Ashtami tithi* doesn't resonate well with Bharani, Krittika, Punarvasu, Pushya, Magha, Vishakha, Jyeshtha, Purvashadha, Shravana and Shatabhisha, and it brings different results with Ashwini, Rohini, Margashirsha, Ardra, Uttara Phalguni, Anuradha, Mula, Uttarashadha, Dhanishta and Purva Bhadrapada.

Additionally, if a person is born on *Ashtami tithi* and Thursday, it produces a *tithi dosha* for the person. The personality of such a person will be overly dominated by ether element. Such a person will need to consciously work on balancing exeggerated ether element, both in their physical body and on a psychological level.

In Vedic month called Chaitra (in the end of which Full Moon falls in Citra nakshatra) *Ashtami tithi* is considered *shunya* and is avoided for any auspicious activities. In Caitra month *Ashtami tithi* often occurs in Ardra nakshatra (in *Shukla paksha*) and Mula nakshatra (in *Krishna paksha*), which is additionally enhancing transformative energies of fierce forms of Shiva (Ardra - Rudra) and Shakti (Mula - Kali) on these lunar days. Ardra and Mula are also often considered as exaltation places of Rahu (Ardra) and Ketu (Mula).

Important *rashis* for *Ashtami tithi* natives

Each *tithi* has a special connection with a number of *rashis*. Understanding those connections can help us not only in understanding our own birth chart on a much deeper level, but in better understanding of the nature of the *tithi* itself.

Two *rashis*, which are of great importance for all *Ashtami tithi* natives are Virgo and Pisces. Virgo is the *mulatrikona* sign of planetary lord of this lunar day (Rahu, *tithi pati kshetra*), while Pisces is the sign opposite to it (*tithi pati kshetra paksha*), which is the sign revealing, where are we heading in life. As *Ashtami tithi* is strongly connected with our inner need for freedom and breaking boundaries, as well as balancing the opposites, and honouring both light and darkness, it is perfectly reflected in spiritual nature of the sign of Pisces. Being a dual sign, it also reveals a dual nature of *Ashtami tithi* natives, as well as their inner urge to find the balance between the opposites – be it within themselves, or in the outer world. Equanimity and equal rights are very important for them. Any planets placed in Pisces or in angles to Pisces will furtherly reveal, in which way this equality will be searched for by *Ashtami tithi* natives, and which sort of transformations they will experience in life. They might often go through different extremes in life before they find a right balance. Due to Pisces being so important sign for them, they also love to travel, especially to spiritual places – and they may emotionally benefit from that a lot.

Both signs of Mercury, Gemini and Virgo (Virgo being a *tithi pati kshetra*, as well) are also *shunya rashis* ("fruitless signs") for all *Ashtami tithi* natives. Both of these signs are naturally quite vulnerable for all people born on *Ashtami tithi*. *Tithi pati kshetra* being at the same time their *shunya rashi* can also make them take some "headless" or illogical decisions in the beginning of life. As Mercury is connected with stability, logic and boundaries of the earth element, this quality becomes naturally afflicted for all *Ashtami tithi* natives, as eighth lunar day, with its speedy, chaotic, restless and freedom-seeking energy naturally destroys those qualities to certain extent. This is why *Ashtami tithi* natives need to be especially careful, when it comes to respecting other people's (or social) boundaries, because if they fail to do so, they may easily invite trouble. They need to find in life a right balance between healthy need to express their freedom, while not obstructing somebody else's freedom on their way. Balance is the keyword for their spiritual development with three dual signs being so important from the perspective of their birth *tithi*.

Unless Gemini and Virgo are occupied by Rahu or Ketu, or unless their planetary lord (Mercury) is placed 3rd, 6th, 8th or 12th house from ascendant or Moon, or is retrograde, or in conjuction with malefic planet, or, lastly, in nakshatras of Rahu or Ketu, these two signs and houses won't bring good results for the native. In such a case these signs must be strengthened (by strengthening their lord) to bring good results. *Shunya* planets do produce good results, however, when they transit 3rd, 6th, 8th or 12th house from from ascendant or Moon.

Additionally, in *Shukla paksha* Taurus sign becomes more energised on *Ashtami tithi* (which reveals more stability-seeking and materialistic side of *Shukla Ashtami* natives), while in *Krishna paksha* Scorpio becomes more energised (which is why *Krishna Ashtami* natives are much more spiritual and often undergo many major transformations in life). It is a very important axis, as it is on this axis that Moon gets exalted and debilitated. Some scholars also say, that Rahu and Ketu get exalted and debiliated on this axis, as well. It clearly reveals a deeply transformative nature of this lunar day and many internal and external transformations, which *Ashtami tithi* natives often need to go through, before they find their true path in life.

Ashtami tithi natives may also face some troubles and obstacles from Jupiter (teachers and education), who doesn't resonate well with chaotic energies of *Ashtami tithi*. Similarly, people with Jupiter very prominent in their chart and personality, won't resonate well neither with *Ashtami tithi*, neither with *Ashtami tithi* natives.

Sadhana for Goddess Tvarita

There is a whole chapter in *Agni Purana* dedicated to Goddess Tvarita, Her mantras and different forms of worship. She is pleased with different kinds of flowers, such as jasmine, *champaca*, *ashoka* or *madhuka*, as well as with sesame seeds. Interestingly, one of the rituals associated with Goddess Tvarita, which is said to pacify the netherworlds (described in Chapter 24) and the waters of primordial chaos, is whirling round water in the pot, while repeating Her name and the syllable *om*. It clearly has a connection with a "hollow" *yantra* of Goddess Tvarita and controlling the forces of chaos.

To connect with Her on a deeper level, you can either do a meditation of sitting on Her lap, as given by my Gurudev (described in one of the previous chapters), or colour Her yantra and meditate on it, facing Northeast. For your *sadhana* you can use one of the two mantras below or one of the affirmations. There are couple of more advanced mantras for worship of Goddess Tvarita in *Tantraraja*, but they are not supposed to be recited without a guidance of a Guru.

Mantras:

oṁ aiṁ hriṁ śriṁ r̄ṁ tvaritāyai namaḥ
oṁ aiṁ hriṁ śriṁ r̄ṁ śaśinyai namaḥ

Affirmations:

I allow myself to find balance.
I allow myself to find order and harmony.
I honour the Light and the Darkness.
I allow myself to be free.

Questions for self-analysis

Every lunar day is an opportunity to learn something new about ourselves. Nitya Devis and their wisdom can become our guides on this sacred journey. Questions below can help you in recognising certain "shadow" tendencies in yourself, which may arise on *Ashtami tithi*. If you were born on this lunar day, these questions might be of big importance for you in life and allow you to face your weaknesses.

- Do I see both sides of things: light and dark?
- Am I acting in too speedy and too hectic way?
- Am I breaking some boundaries, which I shouldn't break?
- Am I too chaotic?
- Do I allow my freedom to express itself in a healthy way?
- Am I honouring both Light and Darkness?
- How can I bring more order into my life?
- Do I notice out of the box solutions?
- Do I respect other people's boundaries?
- Do I waste my creative life force on pointless activities?
- Am I trying to run away from something?
- Am I too obsessed about something?
- Am I too much dwelling in the future?
- Am I too impatient or impulsive?
- How can I calm my mind more?

Yantra of Goddess Tvarita

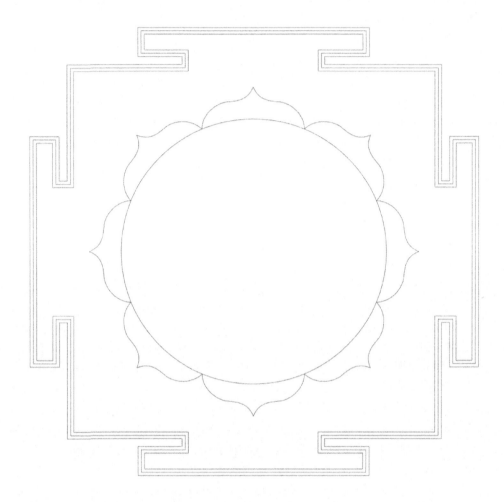

CHAPTER 16

KULASUNDARI – HIDDEN BEAUTY
NAVAMI – NINTH LUNAR DAY

ati-madhura-capa-hastam aparimita-moda-bana saubhagyam
arunam atisaya-karunam abhinava-kulasundarim vande

"I bow to infinitely compassionate Goddess Kulasundari, red like rising sun, the most beautiful One, fresh and youthful, residing in Her abode in muladhara chakra, with celestial sugarcane bow in Her hand and arrows of infinite delight as Her wealth."

- Lalita Trishati

Kala	Element	Planet	Guna	Yogini	Vowel
chandrika (moonlight)	water	Sun	tamas	East	lṛ

Stage of consciousness	Divine quality	Deity (Muhurta Cintamani)	Deity (Varahamihira)	Nakshatra connection	Form of Shiva
waking (deep sleep)	dhanashila (generosity)	Durga	Nagas	Rohini Hasta Citra Swati	Harihara

Shukla Paksha

Nadi: ida
Chakra: anahata
Interval: augmented fourth
Deity (Narada Purana): Chandra
House from the Sun: 4 or 5

Krishna Paksha

Nadi: pingala
Chakra: manipura
Interval: major third
Deity (Narada Purana): Shiva
House from the Sun: 10 or 11

After *Ashtami tithi*, when Goddess in the form of the Moon has crossed the half way between Her and Her goal, a new, fresh cycle is starting. Goddess is getting more and more excited, the closer She gets to Her goal. In *Shukla paksha* She becomes more excited to reach Her fullness, while in *Krishna paksha* She becomes more excited to reunite with Shiva in the form of the Sun on the New Moon day. The primordial desire, which has set Her on this journey, represented by Her form of Goddess Kameshwari, becomes kindled in Her again, when She appears in the form of Goddess Kulasundari on *Navami tithi*, the first day after *Ashtami*. Even one of the names of Goddess Kulasundari is Kameshwari, while Her tantric name in *64 Yogini Namavali* is Kamini "the One, who is the desire itself". Not without a reason *Navami* is also considered a birth *tithi* of planet Venus. This is why Sun is a co-ruler of *Pratipad tithi*, as well as *Navami tithi*. Even the syllable in Sri Vidya mantra is the same for both *tithis*: ka, representing the desire, as well as its creative power. The same burning desire and the same creative power manifests on both of these lunar days. Now, when Goddess crossed the half way between Her and Her goal, Her confidence in achieving it becomes stronger and She feels more powerful. This is why from *Navami tithi* onwards Divine Mother will keep appearing in much more powerful forms, with many more heads and many more hands. This is also why the nature of this *tithi* is addressed as *ugra* or fierce.

Yet, the energy of *Navami tithi* is not so fiery like *Pratipad*, even though they have the same planetary co-ruler. The element for *Navami tithi* is water, which reveals a bit more grounded and much more firm and confident energy than a combination of Sun and fire. While Goddess Kameshwari uses all Her energy to awaken the fire of desire within us, Goddess Kulasundari is more oriented towards action, protection and sustainment, rather than creation.

Kulasundari means "the most beautiful in Her abode" or "the most beautiful in Her family". She is the Mother in the full meaning of this word. On material level Her qualities are reflected in their fullness in all mothers of this world – in all the householders. Similarly like every mother needs to be good in multitasking, juggling with cleaning, cooking, taking care of children and in our times their professional career as well, so Goddess Kulasundari has many hands, revealing many different spheres of life She needs to take care of. She is the most generous one – even the quality of Sri Krishna connected to Her is *dhanashila*, beneficience. Kulasundari Devi teaches us to honour the value of home, mother and homemade things. Lord Rama Himself was born on *Navami tithi* and gave the whole world a lesson, how important is one's home, lineage and family – and how big responsibility comes with that.

On esoteric level, the true abode of the Goddess is our *muladhara chakra*, where fraction of Her energy dwells within us as *kundalini shakti*, ready to awaken. She is our *shakti*, our inborn potential, our *mulagni*, our spiritual power and our consciousness itself. She is the most beautiful one in the microcosm of our energy body. She is Goddess Tripurasundari Herself. Even *yogini* connected to Her is called Citta-karshini – the one attracting all consciousness.

On *Navami tithi* our consciousness enters the level of deep sleep, where no images, no dreams and no actions occur. Within this deep sleep level, Goddess Kulasundari represents waking state. She stands for the sacredness of selfless action. Whenever we serve, truly from the heart, we never notice how time passes by, as our awareness of "I" is absent – we become completely absorbed in the action itself. Such a perfect state of mind creates a true flow and harmony in life.

Goddess Kulasundari is also said to be a manifestation of Saraswati – Goddess of learning, arts, sacred speech and Divine knowledge. Kulasundari Devi is often approached to give us ability to protect ourselves, as well as She helps children and youngsters in learning, giving them strength to study. *Tantraraja* says that Her sadhaka becomes all-knowing. All the Vedas are present in Her.

Yet, combination of water element, *guna* of *tamas*, as well as Sun being the planetary ruler of this lunar day, sometimes makes *Navami tithi* natives also a bit self-centered, vain or proud. They may have a tendency to be overly focused on themselves. After all, warrior Goddess Durga is also a presiding deity of this *tithi*. *Navami tithi* natives love to win, and hate to lose. When they lose, they might easily fall into depression, self-blame and low self-esteem. *Navami tithi* is possibly the most emotionally challenging lunar day, with extremely introverted energy and lots of inner turmoil going on. *Tamasic* energy deeply affects our inner waters on this lunar day, making us either completely inert, or way too "stormy". The energy of this *tithi* does help us, however, in overcoming all the obstacles and facing our inner and outer enemies.

Not without a reason all *Rikta tithis* or "empty" lunar days, are called in that way, as they often make us face some sort of existential emptiness. It does not only indicate a solitary nature of all people born on *Rikta tithis*, but also certain emptiness, which they may feel inside of them. This is also why people born on lunar days governed by water element are not very sociable, as they get too easily exhausted with shallow conversations. They are always looking for some depth in everything, and they rarely find it in any relationship. In fact, *Rikta tithi* natives can get easily emotionally disturbed even in the most loving relationship. Sometimes they simply have a tendency to look too deeply into things.

One of the most important things for all people born on watery lunar days is to understand, that the true depth and true fulfillment is something that they will never find in this world – as they will become truly fulfilled only in the ultimate relationship with God Himself. As long as they are living on this Earth, however, they also need to learn how to respect all other relations, even if sometimes they are "bored" in them. Especially *Navami tithi* natives need to learn, how to focus less on themselves and what "they receive" in a relationship, but rather to express the highest nature of their natal Moon and be generous – focusing more on what they are giving, rather than on what they are receiving. After all, what we are giving and what we are contributing to the world are the only two things, which we can control in any way. What we are receiving is never in our hands.

Similarly like on *Ashtami*, our bioenergy is more active in *anahata chakra* on *Shukla Navami*, while in *Krishna paksha* it is more active in *manipura chakra*. Music interval formed during *Navami tithi* is augmented fourth in *Shukla paksha*, associated with *madhyama* ("the middle one" ruled by the Moon) or more harmonious major third in *Krishna paksha*, associated with *gandhara* ("sweet sounding one" ruled by the Sun) in Indian raga. This is why *Shukla Navami* will be naturally much more active, impulsive and fiery in nature, as it forms less harmonious interval, which creates certain friction in the mind – while *Krishna Navami* natives will be naturally more prone to experiencing some sort of existential emptiness or loneliness, but also naturally more introverted and experiencing more transformations in life.

Ninth form of Shiva connected to *Navami tithi* is Harihara – half-Vishnu (the sustainer) and half-Shiva (the destroyer). Perhaps it is because during *Navami* night we can still see the Moon as half from our earthly perspective. Harihara form of Shiva also symbolises a mystical union between worshipper and object of worship – because not only Shiva is a well-known devotee of Vishnu, but Vishnu is a devotee of Shiva as well. The union between sustaining and destructive powers of the universe and their perfect balance is embodied in this sacred form of Shiva.

Meditation with Goddess Kulasundari

Hue: red
Number of heads: 6
Number of eyes: 3 on each head
Number of hands: 12
Right hands: cup made of gems, rosary of coral beads, lotus, citron, *kamandalu,*
vyakhyana mudra
Left hands: conch, book, lotus, golden pearl, garland of gems, *varada mudra*
Garments: red
Ornaments: red ornaments, crown adorned with priceless gems and rubies, earrings, neck-chains, armlets, waist-chains, anklets, clusters of gems

Tantraraja describes Goddess Kulasundari as being red like rising sun, seated on a red lotus and smeared with blood. She is adorned with various red ornaments, a crown with priceless gems and rubies, earrings, neck-chains, armlets, waist-chains, anklets and clusters of gems on Her breasts, hightening Her own brightness. This image may frighten in the beginning. Yet, blood is here not a symbol of any terrifying activities of the Goddess, but rather the symbol of the lineage we come from and all the blood relations we share. Blood does not only carry within itself a powerful life force given to us by our parents or our genetic information, but also all the knowledge of our lineage and our ancestors. Goddess Kulasundari, being the Goddess of the Sacred Knowledge, reminds us through this symbol that receiving knowledge just from a book isn't sufficient enough. It must be received through the lineage or through the blessing of the fully realised master, a Guru, who can transfer this *shakti* just through his mere sight, word or touch. Some sort of initiation is required for any form of knowledge to become an actual realisation. Goddess Kulasundari, presiding over *Navami tithi*, which has a lot in common with position of the Moon in the ninth house (the house of spiritual lineage, Guru, father and higher learning), is thus a Goddess of initiation.

Different artificats, which Goddess Kulasundari is holding in Her hands, represent different forms of learning and different ways of receiving the teachings. In Her right hands She is holding cup made of gems (representing the nectar of sacred knowledge), rosary of coral beads (representing the need of mantra repetition), lotus flower (representing the purity of the soul, necessary to receive the sacred knowledge), citron (representing all the bitter experiences, through which we learn in life), *kamandalu* (water pot representing ascetic mode of life, as well as receptivity, our ability to receive the teachings), while Her last hand is in the position of *vyakhyana mudra* or giving the instruction – representing the need of obedience. In Her left hands She is holding conch (representing sacred speech and invocation of sacred presence), book (representing book knowledge and scriptures), another lotus flower, golden pearl (representing wisdom refined in the fire of our experience), garland of gems (representing prosperity, which comes with the knowledge), while Her last hand is in the position of *varada mudra* or giving the boons and blessings.

Numerology: 9

Nine is the number strongly connected with *Prakriti*, Mother Nature Herself. There are nine main forms of the Divine Mother, which are nine representations of forces of Nature, worshipped each year on the festival known as *Navaratri*: nine nights of the Divine Mother. Nine interwoven triangles are also creating the most mystical and the highest of all *yantras*, symbolising the complexity of all the cosmic forces in the universe: Sri Yantra – *yantra* of the Highest Goddess, Lalita Tripurasundari. Sri Yantra is often addressed as *navayoni* or "nine sacred wombs" as it is believed that through the sacred geometry of Sri Yantra the entire universe was born and brought into being. There are nine planets in Vedic astrology, as well.

Not without a reason number nine is considered so sacred and so deeply connected with Divine Mother, *Prakriti*. It is not only the highest one-digit number, but whenever you multiply any number by nine, add the resulting digits and reduce them to a single digit, it always becomes nine again. Being so number 9 is not only a number reflecting infinity, but also continuity of Nature. Perhaps this is why in the Vedas number nine is most often connected to nine *prajapatis* (sometimes called as nine *brahmas*) or progenitors of mankind, through whom the entire humanity was born: Bhrigu, Pulastya, Pulahu, Kratu, Angiras, Marici, Daksha, Atri and Vasishta. This is another reason why Goddess Kulasundari and *Navami tithi* are so connected to our lineage and family, which we come from.

Our family lineage, our father, as well as our religion, rules we follow, and even our soul's dharma and path in this lifetime are represented by ninth house in Vedic astrology. This is one of the many reasons why *Navamsha*, ninth divisional chart, is considered to be one of the most sacred charts in Vedic astrology, as it reveals our inner self. Interestingly, Venus, the planet, which is said to be born on *Navami tithi*, becomes one of the most important planets in *Navamsha* chart.

In *nadi* astrology sign of Sagittarius, ninth sign in Vedic astrology, is often considered the sign of one's soul – and therefore is taken as default lagna or ascendant. Even in Vastu tradition number nine stands for individuality. Numbers 8 and 9, as well as their ratio 9:8 are the basis of entire Vastu Shastra. There is this mysterious quote in *Aintiram*:

"As a collective whole, Shiva is one, his eight forms being unified with Him (one with eight). As a distinctly manifest Divine, Shiva is one, surrounded by His eight forms (one added with eight = 9)."

Thus, number nine stands for our spiritual origins, lineage, our inborn nature, as well as our individuality and our soul's unique path in this world. The main message of Goddess Kulasundari is: "Know where are you coming from and where are you heading. Follow your unique path in life and your soul's call, but respect your origins, as well."

Yogini in Kalachakra: East

On *Navami tithi* the danger comes from the East, similarly like on *Pratipad*. It is said that we should avoid travelling into that direction during the ninth lunar day in any of the two *pakshas*. Similarly like in the case of *Pratipad tithi*, pride and need for power are two shadow sides of ninth lunar day. East direction is also connected to our family lineage, ancestors and father – which reveals, that some issues with our family may occur on *Navami* day as well. On ninth lunar day we need to be especially watchful that the qualities of our ego don't overshadow the light of our soul.

Goddess Kulasundari has a lot do with our character and with the way, how do we manifest our individuality in the outer world. After all, *Navami tithi* is also sacred to Durga, as Divine Mother in this powerful form has defeated the demon of ego on *Navami tithi*. Similarly *Navami tithi* natives have naturally a very powerful character, but it is hard for them to accept defeat or failure.

On 8 February 2018, *Krishna Navami*, my Gurudev has written this beautiful message, which is very much in tune with the main life lesson coming to us on this day lunar day:

"Character: usually understood as an expression of morality and strength. That's not wrong but it is not clearly said.

Character is integrity. Integrity of spiritual strength (which means a lot of energy and awareness), of mental clarity, and emotional stability and authenticity. It is not about ego identity, but about spirituality and its expression through an individual. It is not about a superiority complex (a superiority which is ego-based), but about the power of the Truth."

Navami tithi natives sometimes also tend to be a little bit too judgemental and may try to be "too perfect". They might be a bit oversensitive, when it comes to their image, as well. And, as parents often perceive their children as extension of their image, this is another reason why *Navami tithi* natives may sometime experience some issues with the family, which will be almost always connected to too much indentification (Sun's qualities) with other members of our family, as well as too many expectations.

Shaktis of Goddess Kulasundari

Different *shaktis* or powers of Goddess Kulasundari dwell in different places of Her *yantra*. Her *yantra* consists of eight petals (symbolising eight directions or eight *siddhis*) enclosing *navayoni*, "the nine wombs", which is the innermost structure of Sri Yantra. Being so, Her *yantra* is very similar to the *yantra* of Goddess Vahnivasini. Three angles of the innermost triangle are occupied by *shaktis*: Bhasha ("speech"),

Saraswati ("Goddess of sacred speech or essence of knowledge") and Vani ("voice"). Eight triangles around it are occupied by *shaktis*: Sanskrita ("ancient one" or "Sanskrit language"), Prakrita ("primordial one"), Para ("supreme one"), Khadgarupa ("the one in the form of a sword" – symbolising the power of discernment), Vittarupa ("the one in the form of wealth"), Ramya ("beautiful one"), Ananda ("blissful one") and Kautuka ("desirous one"). Eight petals enclosing *navayoni* are occupied *ashta matrikas* or Eight Mothers: Brahmi (*shakti* of Lord Brahma, the creator), Maheshwari (*shakti* of Lord Shiva, the destroyer), Kaumari (*shakti* of Kartikeya, commander of gods), Vaishnavi (*shakti* of Lord Vishnu, the sustainer), Varahi (*shakti* of Lord Varaha, the boar incarnation of Vishnu and the destroyer of ego), Mahendri (*shakti* of Indra, king of gods), Chamunda (a form of Goddess Durga) and Mahalakshmi.

Yantra of Goddess Kulasundari, with the power of voice and speech at its very center, and the *shaktis* of *ashta siddhis* or eight mystical powers around, reminds us about the greatness of the power of word. Through word and through sacred speech, Guru can initiate the disciple into the sacred knowledge; but through word also the curse may be spoken. Words can awaken love or hatred, happiness or sadness, invoke blessings or invoke curses. Goddess Kulasundari reminds us that everything in the universe is a vibration and our voice itself, being the most powerful of all the instruments, carries a particular powerful vibration, which can influence others greatly. It is even scientifically proved that out of all the instruments human voice has the biggest power on our body on celullar level. Mother Kulasundari reminds us to use this power wisely and to never abuse it.

Swara of Goddess Kulasundari

Lṛ, the ninth *swara* or vowel of Sanskrit alphabet, is associated with Goddess Kulasundari. Its quality or *kala* is *yoni* or the womb, which represents not only the creative powers of Goddess Kulasundari and Her ability to give birth to many new things, but, again, also a blood connection and connection with our family – both spiritual and material one. It represents the power of initiation, which is like a second birth. *Swara* **lṛ** also means clinging to, sticking to, adhering to or holding, which denotes all the sacred bondages we form in this lifetime and all the responsibility that comes with that. According to *Agni Purana* vowel **lṛ** is connected to Diti, sister of Aditi and mother of various beings.

Nakshatras connected to Goddess Kulasundari

Rohini nakshatra is connected to *swara* of Goddess Kulasundari, while Her twelve arms stand for all four nakshatra *padas* of Hasta, Citra and Svati. All four nakshatras connected to Goddess Kulasundari are very creative and skillful, as well as deeply connected with protection of home and building or decorating our home. Similarly, people born on *Navami tithi* are often very creative and have some special manual skills, as well as value their living place a lot - and love to have it beautiful. They are often very fond of homemade things, and sometimes they are making some homemade goods themselves.

Interestingly, Hasta nakshatra is often connected with the practice of *mudras* or sacred gestures (popularly known as yoga for the hands). Goddess Kulasundari is the first Nitya Devi, who is showing some sort of mudra, different than traditional *abhaya* and *varada mudras*: *vyakhyayana mudra*, the mudra of giving the instruction. She also represents all the manual skills She blesses all Her children with. Additionally, Hasta nakshatra is the nakshatra, in which Mercury gets exalted, which represents intelligence used for its highest purpose: learning. Indeed, it often happens, that when *Navami* natives don't find depth in their relationships, they are often seeking it in science or sacred wisdom.

A connection between Citra nakshatra and Goddess Kulasundari is also a very interesting one. A symbol of Citra nakshatra is a pearl or a jewel, while Goddess Kulasundari also holds a golden pearl in one of Her hands. Pearl is an ancient symbol of Divine wisdom. It is produced by nature in the most extraordinary way. When a little speck of dust, sand or dirt enters the oyster, and starts to irritate it, oyster doesn't spit it back. It cannot do that. Instead, it is enveloping it in its own saliva to give it more round and more bearable shape. In result, a pearl is produced – one of the most precious objects on our planet. Goddess Kulasundari is reminding us that similarly we should never act impulsively and react immediately, when we encounter a difficult experience. We should never "spit out" our negative energy on others – which would often be a natural reaction of Citra nakshatra natives, as it is not only the most *tamasic* of all the nakshatras, but also one of the most impulsive and expressive ones. The energy of *Navami tithi* is very similar. Instead, we should rather try to internalise such an experience, analyse it and introspect – as with every difficult, bitter experience of life, there is some great life lesson coming. If there would be nothing else for us to learn, we wouldn't invite such an experience at all. But because life itself is a constant process of learning, we should always stay humble and embrace, what life is giving us, like the oyster does, without spitting it out – but rather embracing it with our love and turning something irritating into a pearl of wisdom, which would enrich our inner space. This is one of the most beautiful life lessons that Citra nakshatra and Goddess Kulasundari are sending us.

Citra nakshatra is also quite fascinating, when you add to it the perspective, that Venus is debilitated in Virgo or earthly portion of this nakshatra, while it has its *mulatrikona* place in Libra or airy portion of Citra - while it is said that *Navami tithi* itself is birthday of Venus and its creative energies

Svati, on the other hand, is the nakshatra, in which Sun, the co-ruler of *Navami tithi* is heading towards its deep debilitation. It is a very interesting thing when you realise that Lord Rama was born on *Navami tithi* and when you read through how much injustice and humilitation He needed to go through, before He could truly shine and become a king. Similarly *Navami* natives sometimes need to go through some challenging experiences and make some sacrifices, before they can truly shine in life.

There are also two nakshatras, in which *guna* of *tamas* combines with water element, similarly like on *Navami tithi*: Purvashadha and Uttara Bhadrapada – interestingly, two nakshatras which are watery and fiery at the same time, similarly like *Navami tithi* natives. Both are dwelling at the very heart of two dual signs of Jupiter, Sagittarius and Pisces, and both are reflecting the invigorating, energising and purifying aspect of water element. Similarly like shadow side of Purvashadha and Uttara Bhadrapada nakshatras is some sort of running away from earthly energies and too much focus on oneself, as well as certain impulsiveness, so the very same shadow qualities reflects through *Navami tithi* natives.

Tithi, vara and nakshatra resonance

Goddess Kulasundari has the best resonance with vibrations of Thursday, a day of the celestial Guru, Jupiter. Whenever *Navami tithi* falls on Thursday, it forms *amrita yoga* or "immortal combination" – but at the same time it forms also not so auspicious *hutashana yoga* or "combination of consumed oblation". Therefore the results of *Navami tithi* falling on Thursday would be mixed. Also depending on the nakshatra, in which such combination would happen, the results would be different. If it happens, when Moon dwells in Ashwini, Punarvasu, Pushya, Magha, Swati, Purvashadha, Purva Bhadrapada or Revati, then it is a powerful *siddha yoga*. Yet, when Moon dwells in Krittika, Rohini, Margashirsha, Ardra, Uttara Phalguni, Vishakha, Anuradha or Shatabhisha nakshatra, then it is *vinasha yoga* or "combination of destruction".

Similar situation happens on Saturdays. Whenever *Navami tithi* occurs on Saturday, the day of another great teacher, Shani, *dagdha yoga* ("burnt combination") and *siddha yoga* ("combination of accomplishments") happen simultaneously. If Moon dwells on Saturday in Rohini, Swati, Vishakha, Anuradha, Dhanishta or Shatabhisha nakshatra, *siddha yoga* gets empowered. But when Moon dwells on such a day in Bharani, Punarvasu, Pushya, Purva Phalguni, Uttara Phalguni, Hasta, Purvashadha, Uttarashadha or Shravana, another *vinasha yoga* or "combination of destruction" occurs.

Navami tithi and Goddess Kulasundari do not resonate well with Wednesdays, which are the weekdays ruled by Mercury. Whenever *Navami tithi* falls on Wednesday it forms *krakacha yoga* or "combination of the saw", one of the most inauspicious and dangerous combinations. Additionally, if *Navami tithi* occurs on Wednesday and the Moon dwells in Ashwini, Bharani, Pushya, Ashlesha, Magha, Mula, Dhanishta or Purva Bhadrapada, another *vinasha yoga* occurs. The fourth and the last *vinasha yoga* possible on *Navami tithi* happens, when it is Sunday and the Moon is dwelling in one of the following nakshatras: Bharani, Margashirsha,

Ashlesha, Vishakha, Anuradha, Jyeshta or Dhanishta.

Vibrations of *Navami tithi* also do not resonate well with Fridays (ruled by Venus). Whenever *Navami tithi* falls on Friday, *visha yoga* or poisonous combination is formed, as the water element is ruling both the weekday and the *tithi* in such case, which can agitate our emotions a lot and cause our inner poisons to emerge on the surface of our consciousness.

Navami tithi also causes *shunya dosha* to Krittika nakshatra and a combination o *Navami tithi* and Krittika is also called *ashubha yoga*. Since both *tithi* and nakshatra in this combination are governed by the Sun, and it is also an exaltation nakshatra of the Moon, self-centered energies of *Navami tithi* can turn into egoism in this combination.

In general *Navami tithi* resonates really well only with Swati and Revati nakshatras. It brings mixed results with Ashwini, Rohini, Punarvasu, Pushya, Magha, Vishakha, Anuradha, Purvashadha, Dhanishta, Shatabhisha and Purva Bhadrapada, and negative results with Bharani, Krittika, Margashirsha, Ardra, Purva Phalguni, Uttara Phalguni, Hasta, Jyeshtha, Mula, Uttarashadha or Shravana.

Also, if a person is born on *Navami tithi* and Monday or Friday, it produces *tithi dosha* for the person. The personality of such a person will be overly dominated by water element, which will lead too very turbulent emotional life. If such a person is additionally born on any of the watery nakshatras (Ardra, Ashlesha, Mula, Purvashadha, Shatabhisha, Uttara Bhadrapada, Revati) this *dosha* will be more severe and such person will need to consciously work on balancing exeggerated water element, both in one's physical body and on a psychological level. *Agni Purana* additionally says that a combination of Friday, *Navami tithi* and Purvashadha nakshatra causes deep afflictions, due to too much of water element present in such a combination.

In Vedic month called Ashwayuja (in the end of which Full Moon falls in Ashwini nakshatra) *Navami tithi* is considered *shunya* and is avoided for any auspicious activities. In Ashwayuja month *Navami tithi* often occurs in Shravana nakshatra (in *Shukla paksha*) and Punarvasu nakshatra (in *Krishna paksha*) - two very sensitive nakshatras, connected to our ability to nourish things, as well as listen to others in emphatic way. As *Navami tithi* is already a very sensitive lunar day, the combination with any of these two nakshatras, can additionally exaggerate it, as well as cause some uneasiness to the mind.

YOGAS FORMED WITH *NAVAMI TITHI*

	1	2	3	4	5	6	7
1				krakacha vinasha	**siddha / amrita**	visha	siddha / dagdha
2	vinasha			krakacha vinasha	amrita / hutashana	visha	vinasha
3	shunya	shunya	shunya	krakacha / shunya	shunya / vinasha hutashana	visha / shunya	siddha / dagdha shunya
4				krakacha	vinasha	visha	**siddha**
5	vinasha			krakacha	vinasha	visha	siddha / dagdha
6				krakacha	vinasha	visha	siddha / dagdha
7				krakacha	**siddha / amrita**	visha	vinasha
8				krakacha vinasha	**siddha / amrita**	visha	vinasha
9	vinasha			krakacha vinasha	amrita / hutashana	visha	siddha / dagdha
10				krakacha vinasha	**siddha / amrita**	visha	siddha / dagdha
11				krakacha	amrita / hutashana	visha	vinasha
12				krakacha	vinasha	visha	vinasha
13				krakacha	vinasha	visha	vinasha
14				krakacha	amrita / hutashana	visha	siddha / dagdha
15				krakacha	**siddha / amrita**	visha	**siddha**
16	vinasha			krakacha	vinasha	visha	**siddha**
17	vinasha			krakacha	vinasha	visha	**siddha**
18	vinasha			krakacha	amrita / hutashana	visha	siddha / dagdha
19				krakacha vinasha	amrita / hutashana	visha	siddha / dagdha
20				krakacha	**siddha / amrita**	visha / affliction	vinasha
21				krakacha	amrita / hutashana	visha	vinasha
22				krakacha	amrita / hutashana	visha	vinasha
23	vinasha			krakacha vinasha	amrita / hutashana	visha	**siddha**

24				krakacha	vinasha	visha	**siddha**
25				krakacha vinasha	**siddha / amrita**	visha	siddha / dagdha
26				krakacha	amrita / hutashana	visha	siddha / dagdha
27				krakacha	**siddha / amrita**	visha	siddha / dagdha

Important *rashis* for *Navami tithi* natives

Each *tithi* has a special connection with a number of *rashis*. Understanding those connections can help us not only in understanding our own birth chart on a much deeper level, but in better understanding of the nature of the *tithi* itself.

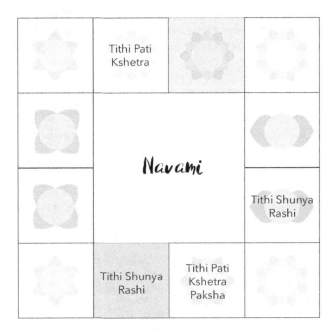

Two *rashis*, which are of great importance for all *Navami tithi* natives are Aries and Libra. Aries is the exaltation sign of planetary lord of this lunar day (Sun, *tithi pati kshetra*), while Libra is the sign opposite to it (*tithi pati kshetra paksha*), which is the sign revealing, where are we heading in life. As *Navami tithi* is strongly connected with finding our individual life path, while honouring those that were here before us, no wonder that the sign connected to the direction in life of *Navami tithi* natives is Libra. Libra is also *mulatrikona* sign of Venus, revealing passionate nature of *Navami tithi* natives, as well as their need to find the right balance between giving and receiving, cooperation and independence. It is also important to notice that *tithi* lord himself, Sun, gets exalted and debilitated on this exact axis.

Additionally, in *Shukla paksha* sign of Taurus becomes more energised on *Navami tithi* (which reveals more sensual and materialistic side of *Shukla Navami* natives), while in *Krishna paksha* Scorpio becomes more energised (which is why *Krishna Navami* natives have much more intense and impulsive personality, as well as are way more often interested in esoteric sciences). It is a very important axis, as it is on this axis that Moon gets exalted and debilitated.

Leo and Scorpio, signs of two fiery planets, Sun and Mars, become *shunya rashis* or "fruitless" for all *Navami tithi* natives. Both of these fixed signs are naturally quite vulnerable for all people born on *Navami tithi*. *Navami tithi* natives need to consciously work on building their healthy self-esteem in this lifetime, as they might have some problems with that, especially in the beginning of life. They might either face issues with low self-esteem or its natural opposite, coming from the mechanism of compensation: false pride, covering up hurted ego. Finding a healthy self-esteem by anchoring themselves in the heart, is one of the most important thing for all *Navami tithi* natives. Meditation with heart chakra and simply visualising a light there could be very helpful for them, similarly like for *Pratipad* natives.

Unless Leo and/or Scorpio are occupied by Rahu or Ketu, or unless their planetary lords (Sun and/or Mars) are placed 3rd, 6th, 8th or 12th house from ascendant or Moon, or are retrograde, or in conjuction with malefic planet, or, lastly, in nakshatras of Rahu or Ketu, these two signs and houses won't bring good results for the native. In such a case these signs must be strengthened (by strengthening their lords) to bring good results. *Shunya* planets do produce good results, however, when they transit 3rd, 6th, 8th or 12th house from from ascendant or Moon.

Navami tithi natives may also face some troubles and obstacles from Mercury (communication or community), who doesn't resonate well with individualistic and independent energies of *Navami tithi*. Indeed, *Navami tithi* natives often meet with obstacles from their community – this happened even to Lord Rama Himself. Similarly, people with Mercury very prominent in their chart and personality, won't resonate well neither with *Navami tithi*, neither with *Navami tithi* natives.

Sadhana for Goddess Kulasundari

Goddess Kulasundari is pleased with white flowers. *Tantraraja* says, that when She is worshipped for the attainment of knowledge, she should be imagined as white, and if for the attainment of wealth, as golden. To connect with Her on a deeper level, you can either do a meditation of sitting on Her lap, as given by my Gurudev (described in Chapter 24), or colour Her yantra and meditate on it, facing

East. For your *sadhana* you can use one of the two mantras below or one of the affirmations. There are couple of more advanced mantras for worship of Goddess Kulasundari in *Tantraraja*, but they are not supposed to be recited without a guidance of a Guru.

Meditation on heart chakra and visualising the light of the Sun in it is also very therapeuthic for *Navami* natives.

Mantras:

oṁ aiṁ hriṁ śriṁ lṛṁ kulasundariyai namaḥ
oṁ aiṁ hriṁ śriṁ lṛṁ candrikayai namaḥ

Affirmations:

I allow myself to learn.
I allow myself to be generous.
I allow myself to be humble.
I bow down to my lineage.

Questions for self-analysis

Every lunar day is an opportunity to learn something new about ourselves. Nitya Devis and their wisdom can become our guides on this sacred journey. Questions below can help you in recognising certain "shadow" tendencies in yourself, which may arise on *Navami tithi*. If you were born on this lunar day, these questions might be of big importance for you in life and allow you to face your weaknesses.

- Do I respect my elders and my lineage?
- Am I humble enough to learn something in life?
- How is my self-esteem?
- Am I too focused on my self?
- Am I trying to get too much attention from others?
- Do I respect boundaries of others?
- Can I allow my heart to open up more?
- Am I indentifying myself too much with my knowledge?
- Am I too concerned about my image?
- Am I imposing my personal ambitions on other members of my family?
- Do I respect individual choices of every person?
- Do I expect too much from myself or other people?
- Am I ready to accept my defeat or mistake?
- Am I trying to impose my point of view on others?

Yantra of Goddess Kulasundari

CHAPTER 17

NITYA – ETERNAL MOTHER
DASHAMI – TENTH LUNAR DAY

nirlepa nirmala nitya nirakara nirakula
nirguna nishkala shanta nishkama nirupaplava

"Hail to Nitya, eternal Goddess, the purest one, free from all impurities, free from all external contacts, free from all afflictions, free from all desires, free from all qualities. She is ever-peaceful, beyond the gunas of rajas, sattwa and tamas, not limited by any form and never agitated."

- Lalita Sahasranama

Kala	Element	Planet	Guna	Yogini	Vowel
kanti (beauty)	air	Moon	tamas	North	Īr

Stage of consciousness	Divine quality	Deity (Muhurta Cintamani)	Deity (Varahamihira)	Nakshatra connection	Form of Shiva
dream (deep sleep)	saundaryamaya (full of beauty)	Yama	Dharma	Rohini Vishakha Anuradha Jyeshtha	Chandesha-anugraha

Shukla Paksha

Nadi: pingala
Chakra: anahata / vishuddha
Interval: diminished fifth
Deity (Narada Purana): Kartikeya
House from the Sun: 4, 5 or 6

Krishna Paksha

Nadi: ida
Chakra: manipura / svadhishthana
Interval: major/minor third
Deity (Narada Purana): Yama
House from the Sun: 10, 11 or 12

Nitya means "eternal" – but devotees call Her Nityamba or "eternal mother". Goddess Nitya represents Divine Mother in Her eternal, ever-unfolding form. Even Her names in the *shloka* from *Lalita Sahasranama* above, consists only of Her names in negative form: She is not this, neither that. She is free from everything and She is above everything. Like the element of air itself, which is connected to Her lunar day, She is not restricted by anything. Freedom is one of Her most important qualities.

By meditating on Her *yantra*, we can understand, that Goddess Nitya represents the whole creation and life itself in their infinite manifestations. She is the Goddess of all the patterns in life, all the fractals and the perfect Divine harmony present in every aspect of creation. The *kala* of the Moon connected with Her is *kanti* or beauty. Even the quality of Sri Krishna associated with Her is *saundaryamaya* – "the one made of beauty" or "the one with illusion of beauty". Being the Goddess of all the patterns, She is also the Goddess of all illusions. She helps us to recognise all the patterns in our own life, to read the signs from the Divine with the power of our intuition and recognise certain repetitive events as silent indicators of greater truths about ourselves.

Goddess Nitya is the storehouse of infinite information and *akashic* records. Her tantric name in *64 Yogini Namavali* is Jnana-swarupini, "the embodiment of wisdom". Yet, Her all-encompassing influence can be a bit overwhelming for the mind, as well, or even cause some confusion. Confusion, however, is just a sign, that some deeper truth is going to be revealed to us soon – it is a sign, that our mental energy is stirred and churned, so the essence can emerge. That is why people born on *Dashami tithi* are often a little bit indecisive, similarly like *Panchami tithi* natives, and tend to be confused about their path in life. They perceive infinite possibilities of the world and they feel overwhelmed by them, not knowing, which path is the best for them. They also often doubt themselves. But once they decide to truly listen to their intuition and inner guidance, as well as notice all the signs on their way, it is when life's infinite possibilities truly unfold before them.

Bhavishya Purana also connects *Dashami tithi* with the story of appearance of the goddesses of ten directions. Being so, for all the people born on this lunar day, it is of highest importance to find the right direction in life – and often it can be for them the biggest challenge, too. They are often very sensitive to different energies, moods and vibrations, which makes them easily lose sense of direction. These "indecisive" energies within them, fueled by self-doubt, are happening also due to specific placement of *Dashami tithi* in super-imposed zodiacal chart presented in Chapter 3. Similarly like *Panchami tithi* and all other *Purna tithis*, it dwells exactly in one of the nakshatras of the Mars (Margashirsha) and in the most intense *gandanta* point between Scorpio and Sagittarius (Jyeshtha and Mula nakshatra), which makes the transformative and "indecisive" energies of this lunar day at their peak. After all, this lunar day is ruled by the Moon, the most changeable and the most fickle of planets, representing our mind itself. Learning how to control their mind and reconnect with their power of intuition is one of the most important life lessons for all people born on *Dashami*– which is why daily meditation is so essential for them. Regular meditation is the only thing, which can give them power to control their mind and stay focused, regardless of the circumstances.

Due to their indecisive nature, people born on *Dashami tithi* also tend to change their jobs or work places a lot. Moon in the mood of *Dashami tithi* behaves thus very similarly like Moon in the tenth house.

As *Dashami tithi* is co-ruled by the Moon, similarly like *Dvitiya*, there are some similarities between those two, as well. Both *tithis* are connected with growth of things, blossoming and spreading. *Dvitiya tithi*, being connected with the earth element brings a bit more grounded growth, while *Dashami*, being connected to element of air, simply grows anything it touches, in all directions. Any thought that will appear in our minds on *Dashami tithi*, will be expanded by the energy of this lunar day. This is why we need to be very careful about our thoughts and intentions on this day, and keep our mental energy under control. One of the names of Goddess Nitya is Sarvatmika or "the soul of all things".

On *Dashami* our bioenergy dwells in our subtle body between heart chakra and throat chakra in *Shukla paksha*, and between *manipura chakra* and *svadhishthana chakra* in *Krishna paksha* - which, once again, reveals a bit indecisive nature of all *Purna tithis* governed by air element. This is why they need to consciously place certain borders in life, and find some grounding and stability. The most important thing for *Dashami tithi* natives is to control their countless thoughts, emotions, dreams and doubts, and to give them the right direction, so this energy can become more constructive.

However, as during *Dashami tithi* Sun and Moon form a bit less harmonious music intervals than during *Panchami*, the nature of *Dashami tithi* is much more active – which is even visible in many heads and hands of Goddess Nitya. In *Shukla paksha* Sun and Moon form diminished fifth interval or *panchama* in Indian raga (ruled by Saturn), which denotes way more active nature of *Shukla Dashami* natives, while in *Krishna paksha* Sun and Moon are forming major third or minor third (depending on their exact distance) or *gandhara* in Indian raga, "sweet sounding one", ruled by the Sun. This is why *Krishna Dashami* natives will be naturally more indecisive.

Dashami natives are also naturally very gentle and sensitive people, often with very light and sweet personality, as the nature of this lunar day is *saumya* or "gentle". These are also the qualities of air element. But the same air element can make easily distract them and make them lose focus frequently, if not balanced by regular practice of meditation.

Syllable of Sri Vidya mantra connected to Goddess Nitya is *la* denoting bliss, while *yogini* associated with Her is Dhairya-karshini – "the one, attracting all gravity, firmness or constancy'. Goddess Nitya, with the airy energies of the Moon being so powerful on Her lunar day, indeed, stands for the blissful vibrations of creation, which are seeking their stability, firmness and constancy in the material world. Very often people born on this lunar day go through constant ups and downs in life and finding their own stability is quite a challenge for them. They need to take a very good care of finding their routine and foundation in life. They are, however, at the same time very good "sustainers". With Moon's energies being so prominent on this lunar day, they simply know how to keep things growing by nourishing them with their energy. Once their creative energies are focused into sustaining something, they find their true contentment and stability.

Meditation with Goddess Nitya

Hue: like the rising sun
Number of heads: 6
Number of eyes: 3 on each head
Number of hands: 12
Right hands: *ankusha*, book, flower arrows, sword, skull, *abhaya mudra*
Left hands: *pasha*, white lotus, sugarcane bow, shield, trident, *varada mudra*
Garments: red
Ornaments: luminous crown on her head, she is adorned with rubies

Tantraraja describes Goddess Nitya as coloured like the rising sun and dressed in red garments. When the Sun is rising, it has a powerful directional strength – and so Goddess Nitya is blessing Her natives with confidence, but sometimes a bit of pride and arrogance, as well. She has six heads, with three eyes on each on Her faces, and twelve hands. In Her right hands Goddess Nitya is holding *ankusha* (for control over repulsion), book (for knowledge), flower arrows (for control over desires), sword (for power of discrimination), skull (for reminding us that everything ends one day) and *abhaya mudra* (for dispelling all fears). In Her left hands She is holding *pasha* (noose for control over passions), white lotus flower (for purity), sugarcane bow (for control over mind), shield (for protection from negativities), trident (for control over three *gunas*) and *varada mudra* (for bestowing blessings).

Even though the description of Her *shaktis* presiding over Her *yantra* is missing in *Tantraraja*, the scripture explains beautifully, how all moving bodies are controlled by Her and by Her all the souls dwell in their respective bodies. She pervades all things and She is the consciousness (*caitanya*) in all. She is Sarvatmika, or "the soul of everything". She is the presiding Goddess of all the *dhatus* (tissues) and *dakinis* (goddesses of the chakras) in human body. Her *shaktis* are countless and form a complete cycle. Being so, Goddess Nitya, "Eternal One", stands for limitless potential of human brain and our very own mind.

Have you ever thought, what would this brain be capable of, if we would be able to access its full capacity and limitless information? Have you ever though, what would this mind, which can be at 10 places at a time, be capable of, if we focus it and simply tune it into the flow of the universe? This is what Goddess Nitya stands for: the limitless capacity of human mind, which, when focused, can do miracles – unfocused, however, can cause only troubles. Like Bhagavan Krishna said in the Gita: "Controlled mind is your best friend. Uncontrolled mind, your worst enemy." Similarly the intense mental energy of Goddess Nitya can either make a person a genius, or cause a mental disorder, by trapping a person in countless thoughts and doubts, which are leading nowhere. This is the biggest danger for *Dashami tithi* natives, which I have personally seen a lot in my personal astrology practice.

Sadhaka of Goddess Nitya is said to become *khechara* ("flying") and blissful. She is often approached to give us strength on our spiritual path and She awakens in us many *siddhis* or mystical powers. Yet, with spiritual energy being so intense on Her lunar day, if people born on *Dashami tithi* do not have any other planetary influences to balance it, they may often become easily ungrounded, too imaginative and "too flying".

All the limitless *shaktis* and infinite potential of the higher octave of Moon itself (which is our very own mind), which *Dashami tithi* stands for, are visible in the *yantra* of Goddess Nitya, with countless garlands of flower petals enclosing each other and going deeper and deeper. Two flower petals (same number like in *ajna chakra*) enclose four flower petals (same number like *muladhara chakra*), which enclose six flower petals (same number like *svadhishthana chakra*), which enclose eight flower petals (in tantric tradition *anahata chakra* is sometimes perceived as having 8 petals instead of 12), which enclose ten flower petals (same number like *manipura chakra*), which enclose sixteen flower petals (same number like in *vishuddha chakra*), which finally enclose *shatkona*, six-pointed star, presided by six *dakinis* or *shaktis* of all the six chakras. Being so, the *yantra* of Goddess Nitya represents all the chakras in our energy body, one enclosing another, forming a never-ending pattern, revealing limitlessness of human spiritual potential. After all, the Divine *nitya lila* or so-called "eternal pastime" is played in the universe through each and every single one of us.

Have you ever wondered, why the same story about the Divine might be sometimes so significantly different in different scriptures? After all, if all the scriptures where revealed through enlightened sages, who have limitless access to all the information in the universe and unbiased truth, how can those stories be so different? This is because of the Divine *nitya lila*, which happens at every moment in time – but in every moment it is slightly different. The pattern stays the same, but the details are different. It is said that every *lila* or the pastime of the Divine, is always repeating itself in various universes – be it other galaxies or the microcosm of our own lives. Studying astrology is, in fact, nothing else, but analysing how the different patterns and different *lilas* of the Divine are manifesting in each person's individual life. Goddess Nitya stands for this *nitya lila* or eternal pastime of the Divine, with all its complexities, patterns, fractals and symbols manifesting themselves through countless inner and outer universes. She is truly the Goddess of Eternity.

Numerology: 10

There are 10 Vishwadevas, Gods of the world, "makers of light", as well as 10 *digpalas* - guardians of ten direction. According to *Varaha Purana*, when Brahma, the Creator, started to think about a base, on which he should build the whole creation, ten powers came out of his ears. They were in the form of ten beautiful young girls and asked for areas to live in, as well as wanted husbands fit for them.

So Brahma gave them the cosmic space in 10 directions of the world for all of them to dwell. Thus they became the ten directions of the cosmos and occupied their respective areas. After that Brahma generated ten Digpalas, protectors of the directions, and married them to these ten *shaktis*. Purva (East) was married to Indra, Paschima (West) to Varuna, Uttara (North) to Kubera, Dakshina (South) to Yama, Ishani (Northeast) to Shiva, Agneyi (Southeast) to Agni, Nairritti (Southwest) to Nirritti, Vayavyi (Northwest) to Vayu, Adho (zenith) to Adi Shesha and Urdhva (nadir) to Lord Brahma Himself.

Even tenth house and tenth divisional chart (D10) in Vedic astrology stand for the direction we choose to take and manifest our *dharma* in the outer world. No wonder, that *Dashami tithi* natives often have problems, with choosing the right direction in their life, as they are too overwhelmed with the qualities of all the different directions influencing them. They love to do ten things at the same time. However, regardless of how hard it is for them to find their own direction in the beginning of life, they can be usually quite good in showing this direction to others – if they only awaken within themselves a healthy discernment between emotion, imagination and true intuition.

The multifarious nature of *Dashami tithi*, with Vishwadevas so connected to this lunar day also gives us energy to spread and manifest our ideas into the world, as well as the energy to attract the right audience. Enhanced energy of the Moon on this lunar day gives our ideas the ability to reach masses and attract the crowds, as well as fame. In this way *Dashami tithi* is also a bit similar to *Dvitiya*, another lunar day, which has Moon as its planetary ruler. This is why both of these lunar days are excellent for going out to the world with any idea and investing your energy in reaching more people. Intensified energy of the Moon will help you on that day to reach the masses and it will attract much larger audience.

Divine avatars of Vishnu are also ten in number and they symbolise the ten stages of evolution of human consciousness and the ever-unfolding and ever-expanding story of humanity itself – along with its cosmic *lila* with the Divine.

There is also a great need for all *Dashami tithi* natives to work more on improving their *manipura chakra*, which has 10 petals, as well. It is connected to element of fire and the capacity to focus and follow with full determination one chosen direction, without going astray. Interestingly, the planet connected to *manipura chakra* is Mars. It is also believed that Mars was born on *Dashami tithi*. This is why different scriptures are, suprisingly, agreeing that Yamaraj (god of death, restriction and self-discipline), whose other name is Dharmaraj (protector of righteousness) is the presiding deity of *Dashami tithi*. Both Yama and Mars are presiding over South direction in Vastu, which is connected with our ability to focus and use our life force in a constructive way.

Interestingly, South direction is right opposite North, from which "danger" is said to be coming on *Dashami tithi* – which reveals that travelling towards South is the most auspicious on this day. On a deeper level it reveals that all *Dashami tithi* natives should work more on disciplining and controlling their minds, as well as bringing more focus and pragmatism into their lives. Yamaraj, being a god of all karmic records and habits also reminds us about the shadow side of Goddess Nitya, Infinite Goddess of Illusion, *Mahamaya*, who is getting us trapped in countless patterns, countless thoughts, countless habitual behaviours or overwhelmed by outer splendour of the material world. Yamaraj reminds us that on spiritual path it is absolutely necessary to put certain discipline on the mind, so it doesn't get trapped into *maya*, which lures us with its infinite forms.

Additionally, tenth form of Shiva connected to tenth lunar day is Chandeshanugraha. Shiva in this form becomes an archer in the posture of "drawer of the bow". Shiva is said to be the master of archery, which represents His complete focus on the goal – a quality so needed for all *Dashami tithi* natives. Praying to Lord Shiva in this form could be therefore greatly helpful for them.

Yogini in *Kalachakra*: North

On *Dashami tithi* the danger comes from the North, similarly like on *Dvitiya*. It is said that we should avoid travelling into that direction during the tenth lunar day in any of the two *pakshas*. In *Kalachakra* North direction is connected to Moon, while in Vastu Shastra it is connected to Mercury – which is why people born on *Dashami tithi* sometimes reflect some of the shadow qualities of these two planets: doubts, too much imagination or simply being too much in the mind. They need more grounding, more dwelling in the present moment and sometimes to simply think more rationally. They also need to overcome the negative qualities of the Moon with the help of positive quality of Mercury: *viveka* or power of discrimination.

North direction is also well known in Vastu as direction, which attracts prosperity and fame – which makes abundance grow in our lives. Similarly, whenever *Dashami tithi* natives use their power of the mind and intellect constructively, with good dose of focus and grounding, they are ready to move the entire world with their ideas and thus attract Divine prosperity. And, as green colour positively enhances North direction in Vastu, so green colour is also very therapeuthic for the restless mind of *Dashami tithi* native. Spending enough time in Nature, like walking in the park or forest, as well as practising *hatha yoga*, is very helpful for *Dashami* natives, as well.

Swara of Goddess Nitya

Ḷr, the tenth *swara* or vowel of Sanskrit alphabet, is associated with Goddess Nitya. Its quality or *kala* is lust or desire. Its vibration makes all things tremble, sway, rock or vibrate. According to *Agni Purana* vowel Ḹr is also connected to Kartikeya, warrior son of Shiva and Shakti – which once more reveals the hidden connection between Mars and *Dashami tithi*. It is also interesting to note that similarly like Goddess Nitya, even Kartikeya has six heads.

Nakshatras connected to Goddess Nitya

Rohini nakshatra is connected to *swara* of Goddess Nitya, while Her twelve arms stand for four nakshatra *padas* of each of the following nakshatras (mostly falling in the sign of Scorpio, ruled by Mars): Vishakha, Anuradha and Jyeshtha. This is a very interesting combination. On one side we have Rohini, which is the most favourite nakshatra of the Moon, while on the other side of zodiac we have Vishakha, Anuradha and Jyeshtha – three least favourite nakshatras of the Moon. While Moon's *mulatrikona* place is in Rohini, its debilitation place is in Vishakha. This unusual connection between the nakshatra of growth (Rohini) and nakshatras of intense transformation (Vishakha, Anuradha and Jyeshtha) is what often results in some sort of feeling of confusion, which all *Dashami tithi* natives may experience. Finding their own routine and stability might be often a challenge for them in early life, and they may often experience sudden ups and downs. Changing "moods" and "seasons" of life have a great influence on their sensitive psychology. They are also greatly influenced by their surroundings and they tend to absorb other people's emotions like a sponge. This is why establishing a healthy daily routine can be greatly therapeuthic for them and allow them to re-center more easily.

It is also interesting to note that Vishakha nakshatra is often considered a birth nakshatra of Kartikeya, who is the *devata* of Mars.

People born on *Dashami tithi* must be very careful about all the things they allow to grow in their minds. They should never use powerful energies of Rohini to grow doubts, fears or negative thoughts in their minds. They should rather use it to consciously focus on something positive. This is why daily meditation practice is quite literally a must for all people born on this lunar day, as it helps them to be more centered and gives some discipline to their minds.

There are also two nakshatras, in which *guna* of *tamas* combines with air element, similarly like on *Dashami tithi*: Margashirsha and Citra, which are, interetingly, two nakshatras of Mars. Like all three nakshatras of Mars, Margashirsha and Citra are dwelling right opposite the transformative *gandanta* zones of the zodiac. Another characteristic of nakshatras co-ruled by Mars is that half of them is always dwelling in earthly sign and another half in airy sign, which reveals some inner conflict between material and spiritual world within the mind of the native, as well as some sort of indecisiveness – which are two qualities very characteristic for *Dashami tithi* natives, too., This is why by analysing the nakshatras, which are combining same element and same *guna* as exact *tithi*, we can also learn quite a lot about this lunar day. Same *guna* and same *tattwa* will always bring very similar results.

Tithi, vara and nakshatra resonance

Goddess Nitya is called Trailokya-vimala in *Kamalatmika Kavacham*: "the purest in the three worlds". This might be one of the reasons why Her lunar day produces the smallest amount of *yogas*, and just a few negative ones.

Dashami tithi resonates the best with the vibrations of Thursdays and Saturdays – two days of the week ruled by Cosmic Teachers, Jupiter, and Saturn. On Thursdays it produces a beneficial *siddha yoga* or "combination of accomplishments", while on Saturdays it produces *amrita yoga* or "combination of nectar". Combination of Saturday and *Dashami tithi* becomes inauspicious only, when it happens with Moon in Ashlesha nakshatra according to *Agni Purana*.

Tuesdays and Fridays are, on the other hand, the most inauspicious in combination with *Dashami tithi*. It produces *hutashana yoga* or "combination of consumed fire oblation" with Fridays, and when the Moon dwells additionally in one of the following nakshatras: Rohini, Punarvasu, Magha, Vishakha, Anuradha, Jyeshtha, Shravana or Dhanishta, it results in destructive *vinasha yoga*. Combination of *Dashami tithi* and Tuesday, on the other hand, produces a very dangerous *krakacha yoga* or "combination of a saw" - and it becomes even more severe with Moon dwelling in Ardra, Punarvasu, Jyeshtha, Purvashadha, Uttarashadha, Shravana, Dhanishta or Shatabhisha.

In *Agni Purana* it is also said that sowing seeds on *Dashami tithi* and Krittika, Rohini, Uttara Phalguni, Hasta, Anuradha, Jyeshtha or Revati nakshatra is going to attract great prosperity.

Being so, *Dashami tithi* resonates relatively well only with Uttara Phalguni, Hasta and Revati nakshatras. It brings different results under Rohini, Anuradha and Jyeshtha, and usually brings bad results with Ardra, Punarvasu, Magha, Vishakha, Purvashadha, Uttarashadha, Shravana, Dhanishta and Shatabhisha. As you can see, it forms quite small amount of *yogas*.

Dashami tithi, similarly like *Chaturti*, doesn't cause *shunya dosha* to any of the nakshatras. And similarly like *Chaturti tithi*, in Vedic month called Magha (in the end of which Full Moon falls in Magha nakshatra) *Dashami tithi* is considered *shunya* and is avoided for any auspicious activities. In Magha month *Dashami tithi* often occurs in Mrigashira nakshatra (in *Shukla paksha*) and Jyeshtha nakshatra (in *Krishna paksha*). As these two nakshatras are strongly connected with our ability to take action in life, as well as powers of research and making choices, *Dashami tithi* occuring on any of these two nakshtras can easily agitate and confuse the powers of those nakshatras, as well as make person too big perfectionist.

YOGAS FORMED WITH *DASHAMI TITHI*

	1	2	3	4	5	6	7
1			krakacha		siddha	hutashana	amrita
2			krakacha		siddha	hutashana	amrita
3			krakacha		siddha	hutashana	amrita
4			krakacha		siddha	hutashana / vinasha	amrita
5			krakacha		siddha	hutashana	amrita
6			krakacha/vinasha		siddha	hutashana	amrita
7			krakacha/vinasha		siddha	hutashana / vinasha	amrita
8			krakacha		siddha	hutashana	amrita
9			krakacha		siddha	hutashana	amrita / affliction
10			krakacha		siddha	hutashana / vinasha	amrita
11			krakacha		siddha	hutashana	amrita
12			krakacha		siddha	hutashana	amrita
13			krakacha		siddha	hutashana	amrita
14			krakacha		siddha	hutashana	amrita
15			krakacha		siddha	hutashana	amrita
16			krakacha		siddha	hutashana / vinasha	amrita
17			krakacha		siddha	hutashana / vinasha	amrita
18			krakacha/vinasha		siddha	hutashana / vinasha	amrita
19			krakacha		siddha	hutashana	amrita
20			krakacha/vinasha		siddha	hutashana	amrita
21			krakacha/vinasha		siddha	hutashana	amrita
22			krakacha / vinasha		siddha	hutashana / vinasha	amrita
23			krakacha / vinasha		siddha	hutashana / vinasha	amrita
24			krakacha/vinasha		siddha	hutashana	amrita
25			krakacha		siddha	hutashana	amrita
26			krakacha		siddha	hutashana	amrita
27			krakacha		siddha	hutashana	amrita

Important *rashis* for *Dashami tithi* natives

Each *tithi* has a special connection with a number of *rashis*. Understanding those connections can help us not only in understanding our own birth chart on a much deeper level, but in better understanding of the nature of the *tithi* itself.

Two *rashis*, which are of great importance for all *Dashami tithi* natives are Cancer and Capricorn. Cancer is the sign ruled by planetary lord of this lunar day (Moon, *tithi pati kshetra*), while Capricorn is the sign opposite to it (*tithi pati kshetra paksha*), which is the sign revealing, where are we heading in life. Interestingly, Cancer is also a debilitation place of Mars (the planet that is said to be born on *Dashami tithi*), while Capricorn is its exaltation place. Indeed, *Dashami* is a very special *tithi*, as it reflects the transition stage between formlessness and chaotic energy of *Ashtami*, and disciplined, focused energy of *Ekadashi*. Similarly, life path of all *Dashami tithi* natives is going out of their comfort zone (Cancer) and transcending their deep emotional nature, to stand out of the crowd and follow their life's true dharma and their soul's true direction, symbolised by sign of Capricorn, original tenth house in Vedic astrology. Even though *Dashami tithi* natives are not afraid of hard work and taking action, sometimes their emotional and ungrounded nature can simply take them away from performing their duties, which is something that they need to learn how to control in this lifetime. This is why Cancer and Capricorn are also exaltation and debilitation place of a planet, which is the counterforce of Mars in *Kalachakra*: Jupiter.

Similarly like on *Panchami*, another *Purna tithi* governed by air element, the transitions between two different chakras become energised both in *Shukla paksha* and *Krishna paksha* during *Dashami tithi*. In *Shukla Dashami* the energy dwells between signs of Taurus and Virgo, embracing Margashirsha nakshatra, which reveals a very researchful, active, but also fickle-minded nature of *Shukla Dashami* natives, while on *Krishna Dashami* the energy dwells in *gandanta zone* between Scorpio and Sagittarius, revealing more intense, transformative, self-doubting and introverted nature of *Krishna Dashami* natives. As both zones are very transformative and intense, perhaps this is why *Dashami tithi* occuring with Moon actually dwelling in those places is considered *shunya* or inauspicious.

Leo and Scorpio, signs of two fiery planets, Sun and Mars, become *shunya rashis* or "fruitless" for all *Dashami tithi* natives – same like for *Navami tithi*. Both of these signs are naturally quite vulnerable for all people born on *Dashami tithi*. *Dashami tithi* natives, similarly like *Navami* natives, need to consciously work on building their healthy self-esteem in this lifetime, as they might have some problems with that, especially in the beginning of life. Differently from *Navami* natives, *Dashami* natives have more tendency to fall into low self-esteem or depression – but they may also try to compensate that with false pride. Ego of *Dashami tithi* natives is generally very vulnerable and one of their most important life lessons is to take things a bit less personally and learn some healthy distance and detachment.

Unless Leo and/or Scorpio are occupied by Rahu or Ketu, or unless their planetary lords (Sun and/or Mars) are placed 3rd, 6th, 8th or 12th house from ascendant or Moon, or are retrograde, or in conjuction with malefic planet, or, lastly, in nakshatras of Rahu or Ketu, these two signs and houses won't bring good results for the native. In such a case these signs must be strengthened (by strengthening their lords) to bring good results. *Shunya* planets do produce good results, however, when they transit 3rd, 6th, 8th or 12th house from from ascendant or Moon.

Dashami tithi natives may also face some troubles and obstacles from Sun, who doesn't resonate well with too imaginative energies of *Dashami tithi*. Similarly, people with Sun very prominent in their chart and personality, won't resonate well neither with *Dashami tithi*, neither with *Dashami tithi* natives.

Sadhana for Goddess Nitya

Goddess Nitya is pleased with white flowers, scent of jasmine and calmness of your meditaition. To connect with Her on a deeper level, you can either do a meditation of sitting on Her lap, as given by my Gurudev (described in Chapter 24), or colour Her yantra and meditate on it, facing North. For your *sadhana* you can use one of the two mantras below or one of the affirmations. There are couple of more advanced mantras for worship of Goddess Nitya in *Tantraraja*, but they are not supposed to be recited without a guidance of a Guru.

Mantras:

oṁ aiṁ hriṁ śriṁ Īṛṁ nityayai namaḥ
oṁ aiṁ hriṁ śriṁ Īṛṁ candrikayai namaḥ

Affirmations:

I allow myself to be creative.
I allow myself to hear the voice of my true intuition.
I allow myself to break all the unhealthy patterns.
I allow myself to find the right direction in life.
I allow myself to stand out of the crowd.

Questions for self-analysis

Every lunar day is an opportunity to learn something new about ourselves. Nitya Devis and their wisdom can become our guides on this sacred journey. Questions below can help you in recognising certain "shadow" tendencies in yourself, which may arise on *Dashami tithi*. If you were born on this lunar day, these questions might be of big importance for you in life and allow you to face your weaknesses.

- Do I control my mind and thoughts or do I allow them to constantly run aimlessly?
- How can I become a bit more organised in my thoughts, goals and acitons?
- Am I falling a prey to some of my doubts or emotions?
- Do I see certain patterns in some of my emotions or behaviors?
- Do I act mechanically or habitually, blocking my own creativity?
- How can I allow my creativity to express itself more?
- Is it the voice of my true intuition, or rather emotions or imagination speaking to me today?
- Can I reach with my ideas a bigger audience?
- Can I allow myself to stand out of the crowd and present my ideas to the world?
- Am I taking things too personally?
- Do I react too emotionally?
- Am I ready to accept a healthy criticism?
- Am I ready to receive an objective feedback from the universe?
- Do I allow the luring energy of illusion to entrap me?
- Do I fall a prey to certain emotional or habitual patterns?
- Do I allow my ego to overshadow the voice of my soul?

Yantra of Goddess Nitya

CHAPTER 18

NILAPATAKA – GODDESS WITH A BLUE FLAG
EKADASHI – ELEVENTH LUNAR DAY

osthe nilapataka vyad adhare ijayavatu
urdhva-dante sada patu devi mam sarvamangala

"May Goddess Nilapataka protect my upper lip. May Goddess Vijaya protect my lower lip. May Goddess Sarvamangala protect my teeth."

- Kamalatmika Kavacham

Kala	Element	Planet	Guna	Yogini	Vowel
jyotsna (aura)	fire	Mars	sattwa	Southeast	e

Stage of consciousness	Divine quality	Deity (Muhurta Cintamani)	Deity (Varahamihira)	Nakshatra connection	Form of Shiva
deep sleep (deep sleep)	nrtyajna (best in dance)	Vishwadeva	Rudra	Margashirsha Mula Purvashadha Uttarashadha	Kamari

Shukla Paksha

Nadi: pingala
Chakra: vishuddha
Interval: perfect fifth
Deity (Narada Purana): Surya
House from the Sun: 5 or 6

Krishna Paksha

Nadi: ida
Chakra: svadhishthana
Interval: minor third
Deity (Narada Purana): Chandra
House from the Sun: 11 or 12

Nilapataka is intense Goddess of eleventh lunar day, which is associated in *Bhavishya Purana* with eleven *rudras*, fierce forms of Shiva – God of ascetics, *yogis*, *moksha*, destruction and transformation. Similarly, the energy of Goddess Nilapataka is very intense and Her presence extremely powerful. *Ekadashi tithi*, co-ruled by Mars and fire element, is a very transformative combination. Its intense heat was since ages harnessed by *yogis* for spiritual purposes: to fast, focus on meditation and purify the mind and the body from all the poisons.

Ekadashi tithi and the deep, blue hue of Goddess Nilapataka, stand for the deep sleep state of consciousness, within all the four lunar days connected to the deep sleep state. On *Ekadashi tithi*, our mind is the most absent and is connected with its deepest nature. This is why its nature is *ananda* or "giving bliss". Now, depending on, all the "monsters" and "poisons" that we are growing in our unconscious mind, all these negativities can emerge on the surface of our consciousness during *Ekadashi*, which is why fasting and conscious purification is so recommended during that day. On the other hand, if we are really sincere with ourselves and our desire to connect with the Supreme is pure, this is also the best day to make such a connection. As Swami Sivananda explained, during *Ekadashi tithi* our mental activity is the lowest. If we additionally lower it by fasting and conscious spiritual practice throughout the day, we can have the chance to catch a glance of the Supreme and touch the higher Reality. Not without a reason *kala* of the Moon associated with this lunar day is *jyotsna* or "Divine halo". Only due to intense spiritual practice and penance our aura gets strengthened and starts to emanate a sort of halo or Divine energy. Goddess Nilapataka helps us on *Ekadashi* to make our own bioenergy field much stronger – and gives us many hints, how to do that.

The music intervals, which are formed by the Sun and the Moon during *Ekadashi tithi* are also very harmonious. In *Shukla paksha* it is a perfect fifth or *madhyama* (ruled by Saturn), while in *Krishna paksha* it is a minor third or *gandhara* (ruled by Sun). This is also why *Ekadashi tithi* is usually much more intense in *Shukla paksha* and even fasting is a bit harder than in *Krishna paksha*. Interestingly enough, *Panchami*, *Ashtami*, *Ekadashi* and *Purnima* or *Amavasya* are the only lunar days, which always produce harmonious music intervals, in both *pakshas*. During *Krishna Ekadashi* Sun and Moon are also at one point at 50-53 degrees distance, which is the distance needed to form a double rainbow.

Ekadashi tithi starts the cycle of last five lunar days governed by *guna* of *sattwa*, and stands for the most *sattwic* or the most refined manifestation of the fire element. It represents turning our inner fire inside and harnessing its intense heat for the purpose of our personal transformation, instead of burning everything around us. *Ekadashi tithi* is the direct manifestation of the fire of *tapasya* or penance.

It is also one of the holliest days for all the Vaishnavas. On each *Ekadashi* they would fast and focus their minds on Lord Vishnu to attract His blessings. And no wonder: *Srimad Bhagavatam* itself says that "among all the Vaishnavas, Shiva Himself is the greatest". *Ekadashi tithi*, being connected to Shiva's own power of *tapasya* or penance, as well as His eleven forms, inspires each devotee to make a good use of their will power, control their senses on that day and focus fully on their Supreme Goal.

Each *Ekdashi tithi* also has its name and story in Vaishnava tradition, which is often connected to the nakshatra, in which it occurs. For example, *Ekadashi tithi* in Margashirsha month, which falls in *Shukla Paksha* (when I was writing this chapter), often coincides with Moon dwelling in Uttara Bhadrapada or Revati nakshatra (always in the liberating sign of Pisces) and hence is called *Mokshada Ekadashi* or "*Ekadashi*, which bestows liberation".

Highly spiritual nature of *Ekadashi tithi* might be also connected to the fact, that according to some scriptures, it is a birth *tithi* of Jupiter, Guru of gods. Apart from spiritual wealth, however, *Ekadashi tithi* is also said to grant material wealth, too, especially to those who do charity and honour spiritual laws.

According to *Varaha Purana*, when Brahma was once thinking about his desire to create, Vayu, wind-god appeared from his mouth. Wind started flowing with great power and raised dust all around and rained. Then Brahma asked it to stop and take a form. It came into a form and appeared as Kubera. Brahma told him to become the guard of all the wealth in the world, as well as North direction (which is also connected to *moksha* in Vastu) – and as it happened on *Ekadashi tithi*, this lunar day was given to Kubera, as well.

Story about Ekadashi Devi

Ekadashi is also the only lunar day (apart from *Shashti*), which has a separate Goddess as its personification. A story about appearance of Ekadashi Devi can be found in *Padma Purana*.

At the beginning of the material creation, when Supreme Lord, Narayana, created the moving and nonmoving living entities, simultaneously, for the purpose of giving a free choice to human beings, he also created the embodiment of all sins called Papa Purusha. The different limbs of this personality were constructed of the various sinful activities. His skin was black, and his eyes were yellow. He is inflicting extreme misery upon sinful persons. Upon seeing this embodiment of sin, God started to think to himself:

"I am the creator of the miseries and happiness of all living beings. Because I have created this personality of sin, who gives distress to all dishonest, deceitful, and sinful persons, now I must also create someone who will control him."

At this time God created the personality known as Yamaraj, god of death, and the different hellish planetary systems. According to scriptures, those living entities, who are very sinful will be sent after death to Yamaraj, who will in turn, according to their sins, send them to a hellish region to atone for their sins and purify them.

After some time, Lord Vishnu went to hellish regions to visit Yamaraj. When Yamaraj saw that Lord Vishnu had arrived, he immediately washed His feet and made an offering unto Him. He then had Him sit upon a golden throne. The Supreme Lord, Vishnu, became seated on the throne, whereupon He heard very loud crying sounds coming from the southern direction (direction of hellish regions in Vedic tradition). He became very surprised and thus enquired from Yamaraj, "From where is this loud crying coming?" Yamaraj replied, "My Lord, the different living entities from earthly plane have fallen into the hellish regions. They are suffering extremely for their misdeeds. The horrible crying is because of suffering from the inflictions of their past bad karma." After hearing this Lord Vishnu went to the hellish region to the south. When the inhabitants saw who had come, they began to cry even louder. The heart of God became filled with compassion. Lord Vishnu thought to Himself, "I have created all this progeny, and it is because of me, that they are suffering."

After the merciful Lord thought over what He had previously considered, He suddenly manifested from His own form the deity of the lunar day *Ekadashi*. Since then the different souls suffering from the results of their bad karma began to follow the vow of *Ekadashi* and were then elevated quickly to the higher, heavenly realms. It is said that the lunar day of *Ekadashi* is the selfsame form of the Lord Vishnu.

Since Ekadashi Devi has appeared, the influence of Papa Purusha started to decrease drastically. Seeing the situation, he approached Lord Vishnu with folded hands, praying: "I am your child, as well - and it is through me that you wanted distress to be given to the living entities who are sinful. But now, due to the influence of Ekadashi, I have became all but destroyed. My Lord, you know very well, that after I die, all of your parts and parcels who have accepted material bodies will become liberated and therefore return to the spiritual realm – and so, your Divine *lila* on earth will be finished very quickly, as there will be no soul left on earthly plane. Please, save me from Ekadashi. No type of pious activity can bind me. But Ekadashi only, being your own manifested form, can impede me. Out of fear of Ekadashi I have fled and taken shelter of men, animals, insects, hills, trees, moving and nonmoving living entities, rivers, oceans, forests, heavenly, earthly, and hellish planetary systems, demigods and other heavenly beings. I cannot find a place where I can be free from fear of Ekadashi. Oh my master! I am a product of your creation, so therefore mercifully direct me to a place where I can reside fearlessly."

Seeing the poor condition of Papa Purusha, God took mercy on him and said: "Do not lament any longer. Just listen, and I will tell you, where you can stay on the auspicious *Ekadashi tithi*. On this day you can take shelter of food in the form of grains. My form as Ekadashi Devi will no longer impede you in this form."

And from then on everybody is avoiding eating grains on *Ekadashi tithi*, as Papa Purusha is taking shelter in grains on this lunar day. In fact, even from scientific point of view, abstaining from grains at least two times a month greatly helps our organism to purify itself and helps our digestive system to rest at least a little bit. As *Ekadashi tithi* represents the fullness of the deep sleep state of consciousness, it is a perfect time for us to slow down a little, abstain from worldly activities, turn inwards, contemplate and connect with the Divine. Consciousness is in a very special state on *Ekadashi tithi* due to mental activity being silenced to a big degree.

There is one more story about Ekadashi Devi and Her appearance, narrated in *Garga Samhita*. There was once a demon called Mura – demon, symbolising our own ego. The demon, whose fortress was in Chandravati ("city of the Moon" – or symbolic "city of the mind"), became so powerful that he overpowered all the demigods and forcibly took their city, Amaravati ("city of immortality"). All the gods, all the *devas* represent in that story our inner powers, which become weakened, when ego takes over.

Demon Mura has rendered all the gods ineffective. They rushed to Lord Vishnu to ask him for help. Vishnu has promised to kill the egoistic demon. The fight between the two was a terrible one. Lord Vishnu used all the possible weapons on the demon, but Mura refused to die. Finally, overcome by pushing blows of the Lord, Mura was defeated and laid unconscious on the blood-stained battlefield. Feeling tired after the battle, Lord Vishnu went away from the battlefield and journeyed to Badarikashrama high in the Himalayas to rest. He entered a beautiful cave called Hemavati ("golden cave") and laid down, entering a deep slumber.

Similarly, whenever we are fighting an uneasy battle with our ego, we often get tired, and we retire back to our comfortable "golden cave" or simply our comfort zone. Whenever we feel tired by inner spiritual battle, and we go back to material consciousness (symbolic golden cave), it is then that our inner soul (Vishnu) falls asleep. That is another meaning behind the deep sleep state of consciousness connected with *Ekadashi tithi*. And this is usually then, when we rest "for a moment", when we lose this awareness and focus on our goal for a moment, that the ego attacks again. The same happened in the story.

When Vishnu was lying down in His deep sleep, demon Mura had collected himself from a battlefield and started to look for his opponent. When he saw Vishnu sleeping peacefully in a golden cave, he found it to be the perfect opportunity to finish Him off. He raised a sword, ready to kill Lord Vishnu and... at the very same moment he was blinded by some extraordinary effulgence. A powerful, warrior form of a Goddess was standing in front of him, manifested from Lord Vishnu's chest. With a quick movement of Her sword, She cut the head of the demon. And then Lord Vishnu woke up.

Seeing the head of the demon next to Him and a wonderful form of Goddess in front of Him, Lord Vishnu has asked: "Who are you, Devi?" Goddess replied: "My Lord, I am born from your very own body, the moment this demon raised his sword to kill you. I have killed Mura." Lord Vishnu looked at Her with astonishment and said: "Devi, I am very pleased with you. Please ask for any benediction you desire." The Goddess replied: "My Lord, if you are pleased with me and wish to give me a boon, then just as you have allowed me to protect you, who protects the entire universe, please give me the power to deliver any person who honors me on this day by eradicating any and all of their greatest sins." Lord Vishnu replied: "So be it, Devi. You are the manifestation of my spiritual energy. Since you have appeared on this day of *Ekadashi tithi*, your name shall be Ekadashi Devi. Anyone who follows the vow of Ekadashi, honoring you, will be relieved from all sinful reactions and attain inexhaustible heavenly and transcendental happiness."

Being so, Goddess Ekadashi represents our spiritual power, which is always alert and always ready to protect us, if we honour Her and if we consciously cultivate our connection with the Divine on a daily basis. She is the power of our own penance or any spiritual practice or sacrifice we have ever performed, who will always rush to help us exactly when we might need it the most.

Meditation with Goddess Nilapataka

Hue: sapphire blue
Number of heads: 5
Number of eyes: 3 on each head
Number of hands: 10
Right hands: *ankusha*, *shakti*, sword, arrows, *abhaya mudra*
Left hands: *pasha*, banner, shield, bow, varada mudra
Garments: red
Ornaments: hands adorned with lustrous gems, decked mostly with pearls, clusters on gems on various parts of her body

Tantraraja describes Nilapataka as sapphire-blue Goddess dressed in red garments and seated on a lotus flower, which symbolises Her purity and rising above the impurities of the world. Her red garments stand for Her determination, power and intense, fiery energy, while Her blue hue reminds us about the necessity of self-control and self-restriction, which are the qualities of sapphire-blue Shani.

Her blue hue also stands for neutralising all the poisons and absorbing all the impurities. When during the churning of the cosmic ocean, *halahala*, deadly, blue poison, emerged from it, it was Shiva Himself, who saved the situation, by drinking the poison. Similarly, during the process of our spiritual transformation, "churning" of our consciousness, which Goddess Nilapataka stands for, many such poisons emerge on the surface. Goddess in this form reminds us not to spread them around and lose the control over our temper on Her lunar day, but rather to withdraw our senses, "swallow" the poison, and withhold its intensity, similarly like Lord Shiva did – as this will make us and our will power stronger. Will power itself and ability of self-control is connected to our *manipura chakra* (the chakra of the element of fire in our subtle body), which, interestingly, opposite to the common belief, is also said to be of sapphire colour in *Yoga Kundalini Upanishad*.

On spiritual path, everything can become poison, if not controlled. On 29 November 2017, *Shukla Dvadashi*, when I was writing this chapter, my Gurudev wrote this beautiful message:

"If one tries to get out of negative entanglements, it is important not to get entangled in another entanglements, as one may get so badly caught into it, that it may prove to be worse than before. Let the knowledge of true Love be one's aim as Love is eternal and nothing can poison it."

Goddess Nilapataka holds in Her ten hands only weapons: *ankusha* (goad for control over repulsion), *shakti* (spear for inner power), sword (for cutting all the negativities with the power of wisdom), arrows (for focus), bow (for self-discipline), shield (for protection), banner (for achievements or *siddhis*) and *pasha* (noose for control over desires). Her two last hands are in the gestures of *abhaya mudra* (fearlessness) and *varada mudra* (granting boons). Being armed with so many weapons Goddess Nilapataka stands for our inner strength, will power, determination, independence and self-discipline. She blesses us with confidence derived from self-restriction, celibacy and fasting, which are excercising our will power.

Nilapataka Devi is known in *64 Yogini Namavali* as Siddhida, giver of mystical powers or achievements, known as *siddhis*. Those *siddhis* are most probably represented as the *ashtakona*, eight-angled figure in Her *yantra*. She is also the only Nitya Devi holding a banner, which reveals Her achievements. Her name itself means "a blue flag". She blesses all the sincere *yogis* with many mystical powers – with the greatest one, "the blue flag", being the achievement of self-control, as all other achievements emerge from this one. It also reveals the deep connection of this lunar day with the energies of Ketu (whose symbol is a banner). Flag indicates going on a war – but blue flag reveals that this war is of inner nature: it is the fight with our own senses and destructive tendencies. It is the inner fight to regain our self-control and will power.

Fire element, which does not only purify us, but also inspires us towards self-control, celibacy, purity, transformation and refinement of our desires, is at its peak on *Ekadashi tithi*. If not channeled properly, however, it can easily awaken in us some sort of anger, irritation or nervousness. *Ekadashi tithi* is also the day, on which our ability to control ourselves is going to be weaker than ever before. All our passions and desires will attack us with double force on that day, like demon Mura attacked Lord Vishnu during His deep sleep - especially if we consciously decide to rise above them. As Mahavatar Babaji Himself said: "It is the duty of the gods to test humanity on their path of attaining the Supreme Being of each one's personal inner Universe" – as without test we would never exercise our strength and will power. *Ekadashi tithi*, among all other lunar days, is such a spiritual "gym", which helps us to train the muscles of our consciousness.

Even the form of Shiva connected to this lunar day is Kamari or "the enemy of Kama, god of the desire". He is holding a bow, ready to shoot an arrow at Kamadev, which represents his focus on the supreme goal and defeating all the passions. This is another reason why fasting, celibacy and general control over one's desires is greatly advised on this day, to honour Shiva in this special form. As much as *Ekadashi tithi* can bring us closer to the Divine, if we control our passions on that day, so it can also bring us more down, if we fall prey to them on that day. Deep sleep within deep sleep state of consciousness can lead us on *Ekadashi tithi* either to deeper contact with the Divine, if we use the slowed mental activity on that day to reach This, what is higher than the mind – but if we don't have any such aspirations, it can also lead us to a *tamasic* mental slumber and weakening of the life force.

Goddess Nilapataka, being armed with so many weapons, as well as with Her hands in the positions *abhaya mudra* and *varada mudra* also stands for our independence and ability to take righteous action. She represents our capacity to take care of ourselves, without any external help. On Her day, She will always reveal us to which extent we are strong and independent – and She will also show us the way, how can we improve it, if we are attentive enough to read Her signs. Divine Mother in the mood of Goddess Nilapataka wants to make Her child strong and independent, so it can take care of itself in the world and so it can be strong on its path.

We need to be careful, however, not to go to another extreme, which is often a trait of *Ekadashi tithi* natives: becoming overly independent, to such an extent that we don't accept anybody else's input and we want to do everything on our own – as this is yet another face of ego and pride. As multifarious and multitalented Vishwadevas, "worldly gods", often associated with ten deities of the directions, are also co-ruling this lunar day, so *Ekadashi* natives also have some of their traits. Similarly like Vishwadevas, they are often multitalented, but differently from *Dashami* natives, they are very focused at the same time. They don't like confusion and they don't resonate well with confusing energies of *Dashami tithi*. Due to that they sometimes may have a trouble with accepting other people's input, as due to their perfectionism they simply don't believe that somebody else can do something as good as they do it themselves. They have a tendency to rather do everything alone. The cause of that lies usually in the fact, that in the beginning of life they might have been let down by others several times, due to what they learned to never depend on anybody else excerpt themselves, and to always work harder than anybody else. It is essential for them, however, to also learn how to accept the help from others, when it is needed – otherwise, they might easily overburden themselves with too much work.

Various gems and jewells, which are beautifying the sapphire body of Goddess Nilapataka, are symbolising the gems of wisdom and spiritual knowledge, as She is decked "mostly with pearls" – the only gems, which are created by nature through the power of friction. Similarly like oyster doesn't spit a grain of sand, but rather accepts it and tries to transform this irritating object into something pleasant, so a true *yogi* always withdraws his senses, and accepts all the negativities without "spitting them out" and poisoning his surroundings – but rather transforming them into something positive. This spiritual maturity and power of self-control is something that Goddess Nilapataka is inspiring us towards.

As during *Shukla Paksha* Moon often dwells in the sixth house from the Sun, while in *Krishna Paksha* Sun is in the third house from the Moon, our "debating" nature can awaken a lot during those days. Goddess Nilapataka reminds us to rather withdraw this power, instead of wasting it and to transform it into something positive. It is essential to control our power of speech on *Ekadashi tithi*, as it is the most powerful weapon and the most powerful poison in the world, which hurts much more than anything else. Unrestricted, negative speech is also the shadow side of Mars, planetary co-ruler of this lunar day.

Goddess Nilapataka is associated with syllable *hrim* in Sri Vidya mantra, which stands for transformation, as well as with *yogini* Smritya-karshini – "the one attracting all memory". Being so, Nilapataka Devi is often approached both to help us in our studies and to strengthen our memory, but also to grant us spiritual wisdom and awaken inside ourselves a spiritual memory: rememberance of our spiritual nature. She is often approached also to give success in exams or job interviews. She guides people to their true dharma in life and She helps those, who are just, in court cases.

Goddess Nilapataka also helps us in harnessing our intellectual energy and organising all the information, which our mind is collecting on its journey through life (symbolised by previous Goddess Nitya), so we can become more focused, instead of become overloaded with too much information or duties.

Numerology: 11

Eleven Rudras or eleven forms of Shiva are connected with number 11 in Vedic tradition. They are sometimes identified with Maruts, or wind-gods – because similarly like Rudras, Maruts are the bringers of transformation. They are "the winds of time", which stand for air element and constant exchange of energy. In Rig Veda they are said to dwell in the atmosphere, between heaven and earth. Being the wind-gods, they also represent the life force itself.

Brihadaranyaka Upanishad indentifies eleven Rudras with ten vital forces or ten *pranas* in our physical body, with eleventh particle being the soul itself - or Shiva. Like Bhagavan Krishna said in the Bhagavad Gita: "Among Rudras (*pranas*) I am Shiva (the soul)". And as ten *pranas* are connected to ten petals of *manipura chakra*, no wonder that in Vedas solar plexus chakra has the same colour like hue of Goddess Nilapataka – dark blue, "like monsoon cloud". This reveals that Goddess Nilapataka truly stands for self-mastery: mastery over our life force and perfect self-control. Perhaps this is why *Ekadashi tithi* is sometimes associated also with Kubera, god of wealth – because for true wealth to manifest in our life, a good dose of self-control, determination and focus is needed. Strong *manipura chakra* and *sattwic* fire element is needed to attract and accumulate wealth in our life.

In Vedic astrology 11th house is also connected to air element and exchange of energy – which in our mundane life happens mostly on the level of our social circles and gains. Original 11th house, Aquarius, is *mulatrikona* sign of Saturn and has Shatabhisha nakshatra at its heart, which might explain, why fasting is so beneficial on *Ekadashi tithi*. Fasting is not only naturally signified by Saturn in Vedic astrology, but even the symbol of Shatabhisha nakshatra is an empty circle, while its *shakti* is the power to heal – perhaps a silent indication for us from the ancient *rishis*, that fasting is one of the most efficient ways to get rid of any disease and detox our body.

Interestingly enough, in Chapter 11 of Bhagavad Gita, Lord Krishna also reveals to Arjuna His Cosmic Form, which has countless hands, countless heads, countless eyes... Because all hands, all heads and all eyes of the world are His. 10 and 11 verse of 11 Chapter of the Gita are saying:

"Arjuna saw in that universal form of the Lord unlimited mouths, unlimited eyes, unlimited wonderful visions. The form was decorated with many celestial ornaments and bore many divine upraised weapons. He wore celestial garlands and garments, and many divine scents were smeared over His body. All was wondrous, brilliant, unlimited, all-expanding."

This is another secret reason for sacredness of *Ekadashi tithi*. If we fast with devotion on this lunar day, we can attain the grace of the Lord and perceive a glimpse of His glory. Reading 11th Chapter of the Bhagavad Gita is very auspicious on *Ekadashi tithi* and very therapeuthic for *Ekadashi tithi* natives – as it allows them to understand on a deeper level that Divine energy is working through everybody, not only through them.

Yogini in *Kalachakra*: Southeast

On *Ekadashi tithi* the danger comes from the Southeast, similarly like on *Tritiya*. It is said that we should avoid travelling into that direction during the eleventh lunar day in any of the two *pakshas*. Except that direction, it is actually a very good day for travelling.

Southeast, being the direction connected with the element of fire at its peak, represents intense transformative energies of *Ekadashi tithi*, as well as warns us not to get burnt by their intense heat. Anger, irritation and nervousness can easily appear on *Ekadashi*, if we do not harness those energies through some sort of spiritual discipline. And, as Southeast is also connected to Venus and all its pleasures, Goddess Nilapataka warns us that on Her day all the pleasures can turn for us into poisons. As an example, if we may have a need to eat some delicious food during that day, our body may feel sick afterwards. Goddess Nilapataka reminds us that every pleasure has its price. With fiery energies being at their peak on *Ekadashi tithi*, no wonder that ancient *yogis* always recommended complete fasting on that day or at least avoiding all *tamasic* and *rajasic* foods.

Swara of Goddess Nilapataka

E, the eleventh *swara* or vowel of Sanskrit alphabet, is associated with Goddess Nilapataka. Its quality or *kala* is to agitate things. Indeed, on *Ekadashi tithi* all the energies are stirred up and our consciousness is intensely churned and transformed, so it can become more refined, and so the true nectar can emerge from it. No wonder that this *swara* is also connected with Margashirsha nakshatra,

Vedic constellation ruled by Soma himself – as extracting *soma* or "nectar of life" always requires some effort and some good stirring from our side.

And, as Margashirsha nakshatra is considered to be a birth star of Parvati, even according to *Agni Purana* vowel **e** is connected to Devi Herself, as well as fire element. It also represents the fire of our mental power and focus.

Nakshatras connected to Goddess Nilapataka

Margashirsha nakshatra is connected to *swara* of Goddess Nilapataka, while Her ten arms stand for four nakshatra *padas* of Mula and Purvashadha, as well as first two *padas* of Uttarashadha. Margashirsha, which is a dynamic nakshatra ruled by Mars, is very much in tune both with the fiery and energetic nature of Goddess Nilapataka, as well as with Her wisdom – after all, Margashirsha is the nakshatra of research, learning and seeking one's path. Its *shakti* is the power to find fulfillment, which is symbolised by the deity o this nakshatra: Soma, personified Moon or inner nectar. Similarly like people born under Margashirsha nakshatra often seek fulfillment and wisdom in many different sources at the same time, but find it only when they start to seek it in spirituality, rather than in the perishable pleasures of material world, so it often happens for all the people born on *Ekadashi tithi*. As long as their energy is distracted, constantly dwelling in ten different directions, constantly running to a new adventure in life, they feel dissatisfied. True satisfaction comes to them, when they find their focus and inner connection with the Divine. Only when their "condense" their consciousness and "churn it" with great focus and spiritual effort, they will get to *soma* or nectar of life. This is why both for Margashirsha natives and *Ekadashi* natives it is so vital to learn how to control their powerful intellect.

Too fiery energy of *Ekadashi tithi* in combination with its connection to Rudras and Margashirsha nakshatra (nakshatra of Soma, nectar of immortality), can also lead *Ekadashi tithi* natives to certain addictions or abuse of intoxicating substances, which is something they need to be especially careful about. They usually run into addictive substances to erase certain feeling of bitterness and lack of satisfaction in life, which is very similar trait to Margashirsha nakshatra natives. Yet, finding such a temporary "nectar of immortality" never solves their problems, as it is the true *soma*, the true nectar of life, satisfaction derived from dwelling in the present moment and contact with the Divine that can truly fulfill them.

The connection between Goddess Nilapataka and *Ekadashi tithi* with the three nakshatras of Sagittarius, Mula, Purvashadha and Uttarashadha, is also revealing us a little bit more about the nature of this lunar day and Goddess Herself. In some of the *nadi* astrology scriptures, sometimes they would address a planet sitting in Sagittarius as the planet "dwelling in the forest" – and not without a reason. Sagittarius is not only the sign of higher education, which Goddess Nilapataka also stands for, but, above all, it is the sign of spiritual purification. In *Shukla paksha* this purification happens on the level of throat chakra (*vishuddha*), while in *Krishna paksha* it happens on the level of sacral chakra (*svadhishthana*). Mula nakshatra reminds us to get back to our roots and to remember our spiritual origin – after all, it is a *mulatrikona* place of Jupiter, Cosmic Teacher. In Purvashadha our true spiritual purification happens in the waters of Apas, the water deity of this nakshatra. Uttarashadha reminds us to focus on our goal. Ultimately, this is why the fiery sign of Sagittarius is called this way: for it is all about our focus and discipline of the mind. In some of the ancient *nadi* scriptures the sign of Sagittarius was also considered a default ascendant and the true sign of the soul.

On the other hand, people with prominent planets in these nakshatras and sign of Sagittarius may often become also a bit too rigid in their mind or even fanatic. That is also the shadow side of Goddess Nilapataka and people born on *Ekadashi tithi*. Especially in *Krishna paksha*, when the bright qualities of this *tithi* set, and when Sun is often dwelling in the third house from the Moon, the debating and "I am right" type of behaviour can easily awaken.

There is also one nakshatra, in which *guna* of *sattwa* combines with fire element, similarly like on *Ekadashi tithi*: Krittika, the very first nakshatra of the zodiac, which is the most sacred for starting a fire ceremony in Vedic tradition. No wonder: it is the nakshatra presided by Agni, fire-god himself. Its power is to burn all impurities and refine all our desires (symbolic story of Agni dev seducing wives of *saptarishis*, also called *krittikas*), so our inner fire can become more focused and disciplined, serving a higher purpose. Such is also the purifying power of *Ekadashi tithi*. And, similarly, like shadow side of Krittika nakshatra is sometimes being overly critical or judgemental, so it is the shadow side of *Ekadashi tithi* natives.

Tithi, *vara* and nakshatra resonance

Goddess Nilapataka resonates best with the vibrations of fiery Sundays and Tuesdays, when it forms *amrita yoga* or "combination of immortality". Additionally, when *Ekadashi tithi* occurs on Tuesday and one of the following nakshatras: Ashwini, Margashirsha, Uttara Phalguni, Citra, Anuradha, Mula, Dhanishta, Purva Bhadrapada, it forms a powerful *siddha yoga*. *Siddha yoga* also occurs whenever *Ekadashi tithi* falls on Friday, and if it happens, when the Moon is dwelling in nakshatras Ashwini, Bharani, Ardra, Punarvasu, Uttara Phalguni, Citra, Svati, Purvashadha, Shatabhisha or Revati, it is all the more powerful. If, however, Moon dwells in nakshatras Rohini, Punarvasu, Magha, Vishakha, Anuradha, Jyeshta, Shravana or Dhanishta during *Ekadashi tithi* on Friday, it forms a dangerous *vinasha yoga* or "combination of destruction".

Ekadashi tithi is, apart from *Shashti*, the only lunar day that really doesn't resonate well with Rohini nakshatra, as it forms with it *ashubha yoga*, or "inauspicious combination" – and similarly like *Shashti tithi*, it causes *shunya dosha* to Rohini. Fiery energies of Goddess Nilapataka do not resonate well with growing energies of Rohini, and similarly like *Shashti* can even obstruct pregnancy or fertility of the native. Similarly, *Ekadashi tithi* forms two inauspicious *yogas*, whenever it occurs on Mondays: *dagdha yoga* ("burnt combination") and *krakacha yoga* ("combination of a saw"), as its intense energy is literally burning and cutting the creative, nourishing and growing potential of the Moon on Monday. Additionally, if *Ekadashi tithi* falls on Monday and Bharani, Krittika, Magha, Anuradha, Purvashadha, Uttarashadha or Uttara Bhadrapada nakshatra, it forms another *vinasha yoga* or "combination of destruction".

Ekadashi tithi also seem to not resonate well with saturnian energies of Saturday, as Goddess Nilapataka's strict nature may become too prominent on those days. Whenever *Ekadashi* falls on Saturday, it is *hutashana yoga* or "combination of consumed oblation". Even fasting becomes a bit harder on Saturdays combined with *Ekadashi tithi*. Additionally, if it happens on Bharani, Punarvasu, Pushya, Purva Phalguni, Uttara Phalguni, Hasta, Purvashadha, Uttarashadha or Shravana nakshatra, it produces *vinasha yoga* or combination of destruction again.

Being so, there are three possible *vinasha yogas*, which can be formed with *Ekadashi tithi*:

- *Ekadashi tithi* + Monday + Bharani, Krittika, Magha, Anuradha, Purvashadha, Uttarashadha or Uttara Bhadrapada
- *Ekadashi tithi* + Friday + Rohini, Punarvasu, Magha, Vishakha, Anuradha, Jyeshta, Shravana or Dhanishta
- *Ekadashi tithi* + Saturday + Bharani, Punarvasu, Pushya, Purva Phalguni, Uttara Phalguni, Hasta, Purvashadha, Uttarashadha or Shravana

Ekadashi tithi generally resonates very well with such dynamic nakshatras like Ashwini, Margashirsha, Ardra, Citra, Swati, Mula, Shatabhisha, Purva Bhadrapada or Revati. It brings mixed results with Bharani, Punarvasu, Uttara Phalguni, Anuradha, Purvashadha or Dhanishta, and usually negative results with Rohini, Krittika, Pushya, Magha, Purva Phalguni, Hasta, Vishakha, Jyeshtha, Uttarashadha, Shravana or Uttara Bhadrapada.

In *Agni Purana* it is also said that sowing seeds on *Ekadashi tithi* and Krittika, Rohini, Uttara Phalguni, Hasta, Anuradha, Jyeshtha or Revati nakshatra is going to attract great prosperity. The same scripture reveals that combination of Tuesday, *Ekadashi tithi* and Ardra nakshatra causes affliction, due to transformative energy of Rudra getting too intense on such a day.

In Vedic month called Chaitra (in the end of which Full Moon falls in Citra nakshatra) *Ekadashi tithi*, similarly like *Ashtami*, is considered *shunya* and is avoided for any auspicious activities. In Chaitra month *Ekadashi tithi* often occurs in Ashlesha or Magha nakshatra (in *Shukla paksha*) and Uttarashadha or Shravana nakshatra (in *Krishna paksha*), with which *Ekadashi tithi* generally doesn't produce beneficial results.

YOGAS FORMED WITH *EKADASHI TITHI*

	1	2	3	4	5	6	7
1	amrita	dagdha / krakacha	**siddha**			**siddha**	hutashana
2	amrita	vinasha / krakacha	amrita			**siddha**	hutashana / vinasha
3	amrita	vinasha / krakacha	amrita				hutashana
4	amrita / shunya	vinasha / krakacha / dagdha / shunya	amrita / shunya	shunya	shunya	shunya / vinasha	hutashana / shunya
5	amrita	dagdha / krakacha	**siddha**				hutashana
6	amrita	dagdha / krakacha	amrita / affliction			**siddha**	hutashana
7	amrita	dagdha / krakacha	amrita			siddha / vinasha	hutashana / vinasha
8	amrita	dagdha / krakacha	amrita				hutashana / vinasha
9	amrita	dagdha / krakacha	amrita				hutashana
10	amrita	vinasha / krakacha	amrita			vinasha	hutashana
11	amrita	dagdha / krakacha	amrita				hutashana / vinasha
12	amrita	dagdha / krakacha	**siddha**			**siddha**	hutashana / vinasha
13	amrita	dagdha / krakacha	amrita				hutashana / vinasha
14	amrita	dagdha / krakacha	**siddha**			**siddha**	hutashana
15	amrita	dagdha / krakacha	amrita			**siddha**	hutashana
16	amrita	dagdha / krakacha	amrita			vinasha	hutashana
17	amrita	vinasha / krakacha	**siddha**			vinasha	hutashana
18	amrita	dagdha / krakacha	amrita			vinasha	hutashana
19	amrita	dagdha / krakacha	**siddha**				hutashana
20	amrita	vinasha / krakacha	amrita			**siddha**	hutashana / vinasha
21	amrita	vinasha / krakacha	amrita				hutashana / vinasha
22	amrita	dagdha / krakacha	amrita			vinasha	hutashana / vinasha
23	amrita	dagdha / krakacha	**siddha**			vinasha	hutashana
24	amrita	dagdha / krakacha	amrita			**siddha**	hutashana

25	amrita	dagdha / krakacha	**siddha**				hutashana
26	amrita	vinasha / krakacha	amrita				hutashana
27	amrita	dagdha / krakacha	amrita			**siddha**	hutashana

Important *rashis* for *Ekadashi tithi* natives

Each *tithi* has a special connection with a number of *rashis*. Understanding those connections can help us not only in understanding our own birth chart on a much deeper level, but in better understanding of the nature of the *tithi* itself.

Tithi Shunya Rashi		Tithi Pati Kshetra Paksha	
	Ekadashi		
Tithi Shunya Rashi	Tithi Pati Kshetra		

Two *rashis*, which are of great importance for all *Ekadashi tithi* natives are Taurus and Scorpio. Scorpio is the sign ruled by planetary lord of this lunar day (Mars, *tithi pati kshetra*), while Taurus is the sign opposite to it (*tithi pati kshetra paksha*), which is the sign revealing, where are we heading in life. Taurus is an exaltation sign of the Moon, while Scorpio is deblitation place of the Moon. Scorpio is also said to be one of the most poisonous signs and sometimes, dark blue colour is also associated with it. Similarly, life's path of *Ekadashi tithi* natives is to learn some healthy self-control and controlling their martian nature, so they can experience more stability and joy in life, symbolised by Taurus. Transforming all their inner poisons and negativites will simply make their life in the outer world much easier. Yet, as *Ekadashi tithi* natives often experience so many transformations in life, they always naturally look more towards stability, accumulation and security. Feeling secure in the material world is extremely important to them. Taurus and Scorpio are both fixed signs, which reveals this deep need for stability and grounding for all *Ekadashi tithi* natives.

Additionally, in *Shukla paksha* sign of Gemini becomes more energised on *Ekadashi tithi* (which reveals more eloquent, debating, scientific and intellectual side of *Shukla Ekadashi* natives), while in *Krishna paksha* Sagittarius becomes more energised (which is why *Krishna Ekadashi* natives usually are much more inclined towards spiritual life and are way more philosophical).

Sagittarius and Pisces, two dual signs of Jupiter, the Cosmic Teacher (who is, interestingly, said to be born on *Ekadashi tithi*), become *shunya rashis* or "fruitless" for all *Ekadashi tithi* natives. Both of these signs are naturally quite vulnerable for all people born on *Ekadashi tithi*. This is also why it is so important for all *Ekadashi* natives to engage in some spiritual discipline in any form in this lifetime, as it will naturally strengthen both of the signs of Jupiter. In our energy body Jupiter stands for *svadhishthana chakra*, which is connected to water element, while intense, fiery energies of *Ekadashi tithi* naturally dry it up. Interestingly, water element often tends to be weak in the body of all spiritually inclined people, due to intensity of inner fire of *tapasya* or transformation. This can lead, however, in long term, also to issues with kidneys or reproductive organs. This is why it is of great importance for all *Ekadashi tithi* natives to always drink a sufficient amount of water, as well as natural juices, which keep body well hydrated – such as aloe vera or coconut water.

Unless Sagittarius and/or Pisces are occupied by Rahu or Ketu, or unless their planetary lord (Jupiter) is placed 3rd, 6th, 8th or 12th house from ascendant or Moon, or is retrograde, or in conjuction with malefic planet, or, lastly, in nakshatras of Rahu or Ketu, these two signs and houses won't bring good results for the native. In such a case these signs must be strengthened (by strengthening their lords) to bring good results. *Shunya* planets do produce good results, however, when they transit 3rd, 6th, 8th or 12th house from from ascendant or Moon.

Ekadashi tithi natives may also face some troubles and obstacles from Mars, who additionally agitates the fiery energies of this lunar day. Indeed, *Ekadashi* natives often need to learn how to control their impulsiveness, as well as may sometimes lose lots of their precious life energy on unnecessary fights and debates. Similarly, people with Mars very prominent in their chart and personality, won't resonate well neither with *Ekadashi tithi*, neither with *Ekadashi tithi* natives.

Sadhana for Goddess Nilapataka

Goddess Nilapataka is pleased with complete fasting or at least avoiding eating any grains, garlic, onion, aubergine and all animal products or other *tamasic* or *rajasic* foods, as well as obstaining from sexual activities during Her lunar day. As our digestive system is getting extremely sensitive on each *Ekadashi tithi*, with its fiery energies becoming very intense, any food can easily turn into poison in our body on this day – which is why ancient *yogis* were always extremely strict with their diet on that day and usually fasted completely. Fasting on *Ekadashi tithi* has the power to uplift our consciousness and fulfill any of our desires. I experienced that personally.

To connect with Goddess Nilapataka on a deeper level, you can either do a meditation of sitting on Her lap, as given by my Gurudev (described in Chapter 24), or colour Her yantra and meditate on it, facing Southeast. For your *sadhana* you can use one of the two mantras below or one of the affirmations. There are couple of more advanced mantras for worship of Goddess Nilapataka in *Tantraraja*, but they are not supposed to be recited without a guidance of a Guru.

Mantras:

om aim hrim śrim em nilapatakayai namah
om aim hrim śrim em jyotsnayai namah

Affirmations:

I am able.
I am strong.
I allow myself to be independent.
I have control over my passions.

Questions for self-analysis

Every lunar day is an opportunity to learn something new about ourselves. Nitya Devis and their wisdom can become our guides on this sacred journey. Questions below can help you in recognising certain "shadow" tendencies in yourself, which may arise on *Ekadashi tithi*. If you were born on this lunar day, these questions might be of big importance for you in life and allow you to face your weaknesses.

- How do I handle all the inner and outer poisons?
- How is my self-control?
- Can I be more disciplined in some sphere of life?
- Do I depend on myself or on others?
- Do I have control over my desires?
- Can I control my tongue a little bit more?
- Can I let go of my resentment and bitterness?
- Can I allow myself to face bravely all the difficulties in life?
- Can I allow myself to be more independent?
- Am I stressing myself too much about something?
- Can I accept the input of other people, instead of doing everything myself?
- Do I look for fulfillment in perishable things?
- How can I find a true fulfillment in life?

Yantra of Goddess Nilapataka

CHAPTER 19

VIJAYA – VICTORIOUS GODDESS
DVADASHI – TWELFTH LUNAR DAY

vijaya vimala vandya vandaru-jana-vatsala
vagvadini vamakeśi vahni-mandala-vasini

"Hail to Vijaya, pure, victorious Goddess with lovely locks, who is adorable Mother loving Her devotees. She is the power of sacred speech and She is dwelling in the circle of fire."

- Lalita Sahasranama

Kala	Element	Planet	Guna	Yogini	Vowel
sri (wealth)	earth	Mercury	sattwa	Southwest	ai

Stage of consciousness	Divine quality	Deity (Muhurta Cintamani)	Deity (Varahamihira)	Nakshatra connection	Form of Shiva
turiya (deep sleep)	sangitajna (best in singing)	Hari	Surya	Ardra Uttarashadha Abhijit Shravana Dhanishta	Kalanasha

Shukla Paksha

Nadi: pingala
Chakra: vishuddha
Interval: minor/major sixth
Deity (Narada Purana): Indra
House from the Sun: 5 or 6

Krishna Paksha

Nadi: ida
Chakra: svadhishthana
Interval: major second
Deity (Narada Purana): Vishnu
House from the Sun: 11 or 12

Vijaya Devi is a victorious Goddess of twelfth lunar day. After the inner battle happening within us on *Ekadashi tithi*, Vijaya Devi brings us victory and success on *Dvadashi*. Whenever we fast or pray intensely with some intention on *Ekadashi tithi*, *Dvadashi tithi* is the day. on which we are going to see the results of our prayers. In *Krishna paksha* the Sun and the Moon would form a golden angle in one moment of *Dvadashi tithi* (360:222.5), as well as they would be 42 degrees apart, which is in nature necessary to form a rainbow – known in mythology as a bridge between heaven and earth.

On *Dvadashi tithi* consciousness experiences *turiya* state within the deep sleep state. This is why a deep feeling of peace can be often experienced on this lunar day. In *Shukla paksha* the Sun and the Moon would form minor sixth or major sixth music interval (*dhaivata* or "the Divine one" ruled by Jupiter in Indian raga), while in *Krishna paksha* they would form major second (*rishabha* ruled by Mars). This is why *Krishna Dvadashi* usually has more active energy.

The *kala* of the Moon connected to *Dvadashi tithi* is *sri* or wealth. Its nature is *yasha* or "giving fame" or "glory". Even tantric name of Goddess Vijaya in *64 Yogini Namavali* is Vasuda or "the giver of wealth". Goddess Vijaya blesses us with many different types of wealth: material wealth, fame, wealth of wisdom or spiritual wealth. *Dvadashi tithi* stands for the most refined or the most *sattwic* manifestation of the element of earth, which results in *artha*, power to accumulate material or spiritual wealth. This is why *Dvadashi* natives are usually naturally fortunate and successful in life, if the Moon or *tithi* lord are not afflicted. Not without a reason *Dvadashi tithi* is also a birthday of Goddess Bhuvaneshwari, "Mother of the Universe", who is said to be the most peaceful, gentle, radiant and generous of all the Mahavidyas (ten manifestations of the Divine Mother). People pray to Mother Bhuvaneshwari frequently to give them wealth, fame and victory, which are very similar blessings to those of Goddess Vijaya.

Dvadashi tithi is also a birth *tithi* of Mercury or Budha. Perhaps this is why it is one of the most pleasant and conflict-free lunar days, due to Budha's neutral nature. Similarly like Budha, however, people born on *Dvadashi* sometimes tend to be overly attached to their appearance and outer look – as Mercury is a *karaka* of skin, and it is a planet directly connected to Goddess Lalita Tripurasundari Herself, "the most beautiful in the three worlds".

This attachment to external appearance itself, can, unfortunately, also bring about their own doom. They may tend to focus too much on the surface of things and external side of things. Even though it is one of the most conflict-free lunar days, still, whenever Mercury, as *tithi* lord or any of his nakshatras (Ashlesha, Jyeshtha or Revati) is heavily afflicted (especially when it corresponds to exact *karana*, *tithyamsha* and *yoga*, time of the day, as well as some *shunya dosha*), it can cause a heavy affliction to the mind of the person – as Mercury is naturally unfriendly towards Moon. This might be one of the reasons why, statistically, biggest amount of serial killers is born on this lunar day. But this happens only when many afflictions, especially the affliction towards *tithi* lord himself, occur together.

As *Dvadashi tithi* is also co-ruled by Mercury, it also gives us a wonderful power of speech, eloquence and debating. Mercury also blesses *Dvadashi* natives with great sense of humour, as well as mimicking skills. It makes our intellect and mind more organised, grounded and practical. Our bioenergy gets stronger in *vishuddha chakra* on *Dvadashi tithi* in *Shukla paksha* (revealing more talkative and sociable nature of *Shukla Dvadashi* natives), while in *Krishna paksha* it gets stronger in *svadhishthana chakra* (revealing that *Krishna Dvadashi* natives are a bit more attached to material pleasures).

Also, due to very proud gods presiding *Dvadashi tithi* (Surya, Indra, Vishnu, Hari), *Dvadashi* natives may sometimes be a little bit too proud and they may have a problem with accepting other people's authority. In general they don't like authorities or politics – even though they can be very patriotic sometimes. They are naturally very confident and often have naturally high self-esteem. Usually they are also very righteous and living in a righteous world is very important for them. They can be, however, a bit self-righteous, as well.

Syllable of Sri Vidya mantra connected to Goddess Vijaya is *sa*, which means "time", "eternity" or "totality", while *yogini* connected with Goddess Vijaya is Nama-karshini – "the one attracting name and fame". This is why *Dvadashi tithi* natives usually attract fame easily. Their image and appearance are very important to them due to that, as well.

Goddess Vijaya stands for success and makes one succeed in everything. She also gives us the power to win any battle in life, internal or external, and good results in whatever we do. She is often approached to win the battle, win in debate or success in trade. She makes everything successful and auspicious. In *Tantraraja* it is said that a person who worships Her and Her *yantra*, becomes happy and successful in every way. This is also one of the reasons, why *Dvadashi* natives generally do not like to lose in life.

Indeed, *Dvadashi* is one of the most auspicious and most flawless *tithis*. There are very few flaws possible with this lunar day due to its highly auspicious energy. Even the form of Shiva connected to *Dvadashi* is called Kalanasha or "destroyer of flaws", "destroyer of impurities". Interestingly, all three forms of Shiva, which are connected to the lunar days, on which our focus is very important (*Dashami*, *Ekadashi* and *Dvadashi*), are holding bows and arrows, symbolising focus and aiming at the right goal.

Meditation with Goddess Vijaya

Hue: lustrous red like rising sun
Number of heads: 5
Number of eyes: 3 on each head
Number of hands: 10
Right hands: *ankusha*, *chakra*, sword, arrows, citron
Left hands: *pasha*, conch, shield, bow, water lily
Garments: yellow
Ornaments: brilliant crown with crescent moon on her forehead, decked with all kinds of ornaments

Tantraraja describes Goddess Vijaya as having a lustrous red hue like a rising Sun. She has five heads and ten arms. In Her right hands She is holding *ankusha* (goad for controlling the instinct of repulsion), *chakra* (discus of cosmic consciousness), sword (to cut all the negativities), arrows (for focus) and citron fruit (for healing), while in Her left hands She holds *pasha* (noose for controlling the passions), conch (for invoking the Divine blessings and sound of victory), shield (for protection), bow (for discipline) and water lily (symbolising beauty). Her clothes are yellow, which reveals Her optimistic nature. She is adorned with all kinds of ornaments and there is a crescent Moon on Her forehead, which reveals Her control over mind. She is full of confidence, optimism and benevolence.

It is said that Goddess Vijaya assumes fierce form during the day, while She is more benevolent during the night, which is Her very special feature. During the day Goddess Vijaya is more oriented on victory and focuses more on external side of things, while during the night time She becomes more benevolent and blesses Her natives with eloquence, as well as power to learn. This also reminds us that whenever we are studying *tithis*, we should always pay attention, whether the person is born during the daytime or during the night-time, as the strength of the Moon will be different in both cases. This seems to be especially important for *Dvadashi tithi*. Perhaps it is because it is co-ruled by Mercury, closest planet to the Sun. Indeed, Mercury, being a neutral planet, can be very benevolent in nature, but quite severe, as well, depending on the conditions he is undergoing in an exact moment in time.

Yantra of Goddess Vijaya is a bit similar to the *yantra* of Tvarita Devi. There are only eight flower petals, enclosed by another garland of sixteen flower petals. The names of the *shaktis* of this *yantra* are unfortunately unknown. It is quite interesting, however, that three the most "flawless" and the most moderate lunar days, which have finding the right balance in life as their primary motivation, *Ashtami*, *Dvadashi* and *Trayodashi*, have very similar "empty" *yantras*, enclosed only by a circle of petals. This reflects very light and swift energy of those lunar days.

Numerology: 12

Number 12 is associated in Vedas with twelve Sun-gods called the Adityas. Each of the 12 Adityas is presiding over one zodiac sign. Whenever Sun is transiting each of those zodiacal houses, it assumes the form of the Aditya associated with it. In Vedas they are depicted as benevolent gods, who bring light, success, wealth, fame and victory. Rig Veda says that they are "bright and pure as streams of water, free from all guile and falsehood, blameless, perfect". They are said to be "true to eternal law" and the "debt-exactors". "Never do they slumber, never close their eyelids, faithful, far-ruling for the righteous mortal." This is also why justice and righteousness is so important for all *Dvadashi tithi* natives. You can read more about 12 Adityas in my other book, *12 Vedic Suns*.

Adityas are "easy to approach and easy to talk to". They are also said to know the secrets in everyone's hearts. They are the ones, who bring the light of wisdom and enlightenment. This is also why twelfth house in Vedic astrology is associated with *moksha* or final goal of human life: liberation. It is also the house of secrets and hidden talents, as well as the house of debts (along with 6th house) and losses. Above all, however, 12th house is the house of final goal and completion. As much as 11th house is connected to all our efforts, wishes, desires, gains and social interactions, 12th house is the house of final satisfaction and rest after achieving our goals.

Twelve is also the number connected human experience and human limitations, as my Gurudev once revealed. This is also why Sri Ram, Divine incarnation of Vishnu, often addressed as Maryada Purushottam ("the one, who stayed within limits of humanity") has 12 Divine qualities manifested through him, instead of 16. Beyond twelve zodiac signs, the supernatural experience begins. There are twelve petals in *anahata chakra*, in which the spark of Supersoul is said to dwell in a human. Three chakras below heart chakra are governed by three elements, which are visible in the world (earth, water and fire) – but from heart chakra up start the elements, which are not visible (air and ether), as well as experiences, which can be only felt, but not explained. The spiritual experiences start from heart chakra.

Yogini in *Kalachakra*: Southwest

On *Dvadashi tithi* the danger comes from the Southwest, similarly like on *Chaturti*. It is said that we should avoid travelling into that direction during the twelfth lunar day in any of the two *pakshas*. Southwest direction in Vastu is connected to grounding energies of earth element and *artha* (accumulation). *Dvadashi tithi* natives naturaly have a tendency to accumulate things and get overly attached to earthly vibrations, which is why this direction won't support them.

Interestingly, as Southwest is connected in Vastu also to eccentric energies of Rahu, so Southwest is also connected to Varaha avatar or boar incarnation of Vishnu (who, according to *Brihat Parashara Hora Shastra*, embodied higher octave of Rahu's energies in the world) – who was also born on *Dvadashi tithi*. Varaha avatar, Lord Vishnu in the form of a boar, has uplifted Mother Earth from the waters of chaos (Rahu's energy), when the demonic forces has submerged her there. As my Gurudev explained, this story symbolically depicts water element overpowering earth element and drowning of our mind into the waters of chaos, *tamas* and materialism. Varaha avatar, who became the husband of Mother Earth, symbolises not only restoring our mind its stability and healthy grounding, but also raising it above the mundane vibrations.

Swara of Goddess Vijaya

Ai, the twelfth *swara* or vowel of Sanskrit alphabet, is associated with Goddess Vijaya. Its quality or *kala* is to give things or grant boons, while its deity is Shiva, "the benevolent One"– similarly like the deity of Ardra nakshatra, which is connected to this *swara*. *Bij* mantra **aim** is also connected to Saraswati, Goddess of learning and higher wisdom. Interestingly, even in English "aim" means a goal, which is the main focus of Ardra nakshatra.

Some legends say, that when Saraswati was offended by Brahma, who was Her father, but became lustful towards Her, She fled away from him in a form of a deer to seek shelter of Lord Shiva. It is said that Lord Shiva cut the fifth head of lustful

Brahma exactly under Ardra nakshatra. As *Dvadashi tithi* is in a sense a higher octave of *Chaturti*, because they are both co-ruled by Mercury, it also carries within itself an important message about understanding the true purpose of our intellect and true purpose of wisdom, without abusing it for the sake of our greed, which is the esoteric meaning of the lust of Brahma. Each of us is a miniature of Brahma, the creator. Whenever we try to abuse Goddess Saraswati or Divine knowledge for our materialistic purposes, it is Shiva Himself, God of destruction, who will bring us back on the right path and crush our ego, so we can understand our mistake.

Nakshatras connected to Goddess Vijaya

Ardra nakshatra is connected to *swara* of Goddess Vijaya, while Her ten arms stand for last two *padas* of Uttarashadha nakshatra and four nakshatra *padas* of Shravana and Dhanishta. Exactly within these nakshatras, in last degrees of Uttarashadha and first degrees of Shravana, dwells the victorious 28th nakshatra, Abhijit, which is closely connected to Lord Krishna. All these nakshatras resonate with victorious and successful nature of Goddess Vijaya. Uttarashadha is also the nakshatra, in which Sun originally changed its course into *Uttarayana* – and from then on our days are becoming brighter and longer, while everything we do becomes more effortless, because during *Uttarayana* we receive more grace and light of wisdom from the Divine. Such is also the energy of Goddess Vijaya and *Dvadashi tithi*.

There is also a very special connection between Shravana nakshatra and *Dvadashi tithi*. Shravana nakshatra is very much connected to the story of Vamana avatar (dwarf incarnation of Lord Vishnu), who was also born on *Dvadashi tithi*. He came on earth in the most humble form of a dwarf brahmin, revealing the most important Divine quality for all *Dvadashi* natives to develop: humility. The Lord in such humble form approached the demon king of that times, Bali, to ask for a charity. He asked only for three footsteps of land. Bali Maharaj, even though he was a demon, was very righteous and generous, and as he recognised the brahmin to be some great personality, he encouraged him to ask for more. But Vamana stood by his choice of three footsteps of land, explaining that a person, who cannot be satisfied with three paces of land, won't be satisfied with anything – and thus giving a powerful lesson about controlling one's greed to the world and especially to all *Dvadashi* natives, who may sometimes manifest this weekness. After Bali Maharaj washed feet of Lord Vamana, the Lord suddenly assumed a gigantic form. In this huge form of His, with the first footstep He covered the entire material plane, and with the second footstep He covered the entire spiritual world. There was no place, where He could place His third footstep, so He asked Bali Maharaj: "Where shall I put my third footstep? Your promised me three footsteps of land." Bali, being humbled by the magnificent form of the Lord, humbly asked: "Please, place your third footsep on my head." The Lord gladly agreed. This story beautifully portrays the most *sattwic*, the most pure and the most beautiful quality of earth element for all *Dvadashi* natives to develop: humility.

Dhanishta, another star connected to *Dvadashi tithi*, is also the nakshatra, in which Mars becomes exalted - which reveals more energetic nature of this *tithi* and strong ability to take action, which it blesses us with. And, similarly like Dhanishta nakshatra natives may sometimes have a hard time respecting somebody's authority, so *Dvadashi* natives may sometimes face similar issue.

There are also two nakshatras, in which *guna* of *sattwa* combines with earth element, similarly like on *Dvadashi tithi*: victorious Uttarashadha and perfectionistic Jyeshtha, two very ambitious nakshatras, which are always looking towards perfection, success and victory – as well as do not deal very well with defeat. Similar is the nature of people born on *Dvadashi tithi*.

Tithi, vara and nakshatra resonance

Goddess Vijaya resonates best with watery vibrations of Mondays and Fridays, when Her lunar day produces beautiful *amrita yoga*, "combination of nectar". If on *Dvadashi* Monday Moon additionally dwells in Rohini, Margashirsha, Punarvasu, Citra, Shravana, Dhanishta, Shatabhisha or Purva Bhadrapada nakshatra, it produces even more powerful *siddha yoga*. Same thing happens on Fridays in nakshatras Ashwini, Bharani, Ardra, Uttara Phalguni, Citra, Swati, Purvashadha or Revati. *Dvadashi tithi* resonates really well also with the weekday of its planetary ruler, Wednesday. If, additionally, *Dvadashi* Moon dwells on Wednesday in nakshatras Rohini, Margashirsha, Ardra, Uttara Phalguni, Anuradha or Uttarashadha, another powerful *siddha yoga* is formed.

In total, there are five *siddha yogas* possible on *Dvadashi tithi*:

- *Dvadashi tithi* + Sunday + Pushya, Uttara Phalguni, Hasta, Mula, Uttarashadha, Shravana or Uttara Bhadrapada
- *Dvadashi tithi* + Monday + Rohini, Margashirsha, Punarvasu, Citra, Shravana, Dhanishta, Shatabhisha or Purva Bhadrapada
- *Dvadashi tithi* + Wednesday + Rohini, Margashirsha, Ardra, Uttara Phalguni, Anuradha or Uttarashadha
- *Dvadashi tithi* + Friday + Ashwini, Bharani, Ardra, Uttara Phalguni, Citra, Swati, Purvashadha or Revati
- *Dvadashi tithi* + Saturday + Rohini, Swati, Vishakha, Anuradha, Dhanishta or Shatabhisha

Combination of *Dvadashi tithi*, Saturday and Rohini, Swati or Dhanishta nakshatra, additionally forms auspicious *suta yoga*.

Dvadashi tithi has the worst resonance with Sunday, the day of the burning Sun, when it forms three inauspicious *yogas* at the same time: *dagdha yoga* ("burnt combination"), *hutashana yoga* ("combination of consumed fire oblation") and the most dangerous *krakacha yoga* ("combination of a saw"). Our ego may become way too inflated and way too destructive on such days.

Dvadashi tithi doesn't resonate well with the vibrations of Ashlesha nakshatra, as well. Mercurian energies of *Dvadashi tithi* become too materialistic or even used for bad purposes under Ashlesha nakshatra. *Dvadashi tithi* also causes *shunya dosha* to Ashlesha nakshatra.

Whenever *Dvadashi tithi* combines with Thursday and Krittika, Rohini, Margashirsha, Ardra, Uttara Phalguni, Vishakha, Anuradha or Shatabhisha nakshatra, it also forms *vinasha yoga* or "combination of destruction".

In addition to all these combinations, *Dvadashi tithi*, being a *Bhadra tithi*, lunar day connected to the element of earth and our actions in the outer world, also forms the same *dvipushkar* and *tripushkar* yogas like *Dvitiya tithi* and *Saptami tithi*, which are described in detail in previous chapters. *Dvadashi tithi*, being co-ruled by Mercury, reminds us to use blessed and successful energies of this lunar day for constructive purposes, rather than just for the satisfaction of our ego, as all the actions undertaken on those days will be repeated in the future.

Additionally, the same *visha kanya yoga* combinations, which happen on *Dvitiya* and *Saptami tithis*, take place on *Dvadashi tithi*, as well. *Visha kanya yoga* combination becomes especially severe, when it happens on *Dvadashi tithi* and Sunday.

Taking all these influences into consideration, *Dvadashi tithi* resonates very well with energies of Ashwini, Bharani, Pushya, Hasta, Swati, Mula, Purvashadha, Uttarashadha, Shravana, Dhanishta, Purva Bhadrapada, Uttara Bhadrapada or Revati nakshatra. It brings mixed results with Rohini, Margashirsha, Ardra, Uttara Phalguni and Anuradha, and has really bad resonance only with two nakshatras of extreme water element (Ashlesha and Shatabhisha) and two nakshatras of extreme fire element (Krittika and Vishakha). As earth element is in its more *sattwic* and stable state on *Dvadashi tithi*, it naturally resonate with things, which are moderate and sustainable, which is why it doesn't resonate at all with any of the extremes. Extreme water element drowns the earth, while extreme fire element burns it.

In Vedic month called Vaishakha (in the end of which Full Moon falls in Vishakha nakshatra, also knows as birthday of Lord Buddha) *Dvadashi tithi* is considered *shunya* and is avoided for any auspicious activities. In Vaishakha month *Dvadashi tithi* often occurs in Uttara Phalguni or Hasta nakshatra (in *Shukla paksha*) and Shatabhisha nakshatra (in *Krishna paksha*), which are the nakshatras, that can easily agitate too calculative or cold side of *Dvadashi tithi*.

YOGAS FORMED WITH DVADASHI TITHI

	1	2	3	4	5	6	7
1	krakacha	amrita		siddha		**siddha**	
2	**tripushkar**	amrita	**tripushkar**	siddha		**siddha**	**tripushkar**
3	krakacha	amrita		siddha		amrita	
4	krakacha	**siddha**		**siddha**		amrita	**siddha/suta**
5	krakacha / dvipushkar	**siddha**	**dvipushkar**	**siddha**		amrita	**dvipushkar**
6	krakacha	amrita		**siddha**		**siddha**	
7	krakacha / tripushkar	**siddha**	**tripushkar**	siddha		amrita	**tripushkar**
8	**siddha**	amrita		siddha		amrita	
9	krakacha / shunya	amrita / shunya	shunya	siddha / shunya	shunya	amrita / shunya	shunya
10	krakacha	amrita		siddha		amrita	
11	krakacha / tripushkar	amrita	**tripushkar**	siddha		amrita	**tripushkar**
12	**siddha**	amrita		**siddha**		**siddha**	
13	**siddha**	amrita		siddha		amrita	
14	krakacha / dvipushkar	**siddha**	**dvipushkar**	siddha		**siddha**	**dvipushkar**
15	krakacha	amrita		siddha		**siddha**	**siddha/suta**
16	krakacha / tripushkar	amrita	**tripushkar**	siddha		amrita	**siddha / tripushkar**
17	krakacha	amrita		**siddha**		amrita	**siddha**
18	krakacha	amrita		siddha		amrita	
19	**siddha**	amrita		siddha		**siddha**	
20	krakacha / tripushkar	amrita	**tripushkar**	siddha		amrita	**tripushkar**
21	**siddha**	amrita		**siddha**		amrita	
22	**siddha**	**siddha**		siddha		amrita	
23	krakacha / dvipushkar	**siddha**	**dvipushkar**	siddha		amrita	**siddha / dvipushkar**
24	krakacha	**siddha**		siddha		amrita	**siddha**
25	krakacha / tripushkar	**siddha**	**tripushkar**	siddha		amrita	**tripushkar**
26	**siddha**	amrita		siddha		amrita	
27	krakacha	amrita		siddha		**siddha**	

Important *rashis* for *Dvadashi tithi* natives

Each *tithi* has a special connection with a number of *rashis*. Understanding those connections can help us not only in understanding our own birth chart on a much deeper level, but in better understanding of the nature of the *tithi* itself.

			Tithi Pati Kshetra
	Dvadashi		
Tithi Shunya Rashi			
Tithi Pati Kshetra Paksha		Tithi Shunya Rashi	

Two *rashis*, which are of greatest importance for all *Dvadashi tithi* natives are Gemini and Sagittarius. Gemini is the sign ruled by planetary lord of this lunar day (Mercury, *tithi pati kshetra*), while Sagittarius is the sign opposite to it (*tithi pati kshetra paksha*), which is the sign revealing, where are we heading in life. Sign of Sagittarius being *tithi pati kshetra paksha* for *Dvadashi* natives, reveals that education and success in life, as well as following *dharma* and righteousness, are very important in their life. Additionally, Gemini and Sagittarius being two dual signs, reveal that *Dvadashi* natives undergo many changes in life, and their appearance (and weight) may change a lot with time. It also reveals their moderate nature, which doesn't resonate well with any extremes and always seeks balance in everything.

Additionally, sign of Gemini gets more energised in *Shukla paksha*, which reveals more eloquent, sociable and dynamic nature of *Shukla Dvadashi* natives, while in *Krishna paksha* Sagittarius gets more energised, which reveals more introverted, moderate and philosophical side of *Krishna Dvadashi* natives – as well as their bigger need for stability and righteousness. As the zodiacal chakras on the same axis as *tithi pati kshetra* and *tithi pati kshetra paksha* are energised on *Dvadashi tithi*, it also reveals a natural self-confidence of *Dvadashi* natives and often blesses them with certain integrity.

Libra (ruled by Venus) and Capricorn (ruled by Saturn) become *shunya rashis* or "fruitless" for all *Dvadashi tithi* natives. Both of these signs are naturally quite vulnerable for all people born on *Dvadashi tithi* – and both of them are closely connected to Saturn. In Libra Saturn gets exalted (while Sun gets debilitated), while Capricorn, the sign of hard work, is ruled Saturn. This reveals that *Dvadashi tithi* natives may sometimes run away from hard work or facing hard truths of life. Their naturally optimistic and confident personality sometimes expects the success to come to them by itself, which is their biggest weakness. They may also sometimes take their wealth, education or position in society for granted – not realising that it is a privilige of the few.

Unless Libra and/or Capricorn are occupied by Rahu or Ketu, or unless their planetary lords (Venus and/or Saturn) are placed 3rd, 6th, 8th or 12th house from ascendant or Moon, or are retrograde, or in conjuction with malefic planet, or, lastly, in nakshatras of Rahu or Ketu, these two signs and houses won't bring good results for the native. In such a case these signs must be strengthened (by strengthening their lords) to bring good results. *Shunya* planets do produce good results, however, when they transit 3rd, 6th, 8th or 12th house from from ascendant or Moon.

Dvadashi tithi natives may also face some troubles and obstacles from Moon, who doesn't resonate so well with grounded, balanced and moderate energies of *Dvadashi tithi* – as Moon always yearns to undergo different emotional changes. Similarly, people with Moon very prominent in their chart and personality, won't resonate well neither with *Dvadashi tithi*, neither with *Dvadashi tithi* natives. For *Dvadashi* natives, who experience certain problems from the Moon, prayer to Goddess in the form of Bhuvaneshwari is an excellent remedy.

Sadhana for Goddess Vijaya

Goddess Vijaya is pleased with giving donations or charity. To connect with Goddess Vijaya on a deeper level, you can either do a meditation of sitting on Her lap, as given by my Gurudev (described in Chapter 24), or colour Her yantra and meditate on it, facing Southwest. It is said in *Tantraraja* that if we invoke Her blessings during a war, She should be visualised seated on a lion, and when we invoke Her for blessings, we should visualise Her comfortably seated in *sukhasana*. For your *sadhana* you can use one of the two mantras below or one of the affirmations. There are couple of more advanced mantras for worship of Goddess Vijaya in *Tantraraja*, but they are not supposed to be recited without a guidance of a Guru.

Mantras:

oṁ aiṁ hriṁ śriṁ aiṁ vijayayai namaḥ
oṁ aiṁ hriṁ śriṁ aiṁ śriyai namaḥ

Affirmations:

I allow myself to be successful.
I allow myself to be confident.
I allow myself to be courageous.

Questions for self-analysis

Every lunar day is an opportunity to learn something new about ourselves. Nitya Devis and their wisdom can become our guides on this sacred journey. Questions below can help you in recognising certain "shadow" tendencies in yourself, which may arise on *Dvadashi tithi*. If you were born on this lunar day, these questions might be of big importance for you in life and allow you to face your weaknesses.

- Do I allow myself to be successful?
- Am I stepping confidently on the path of achieving my goals?
- Do I nourish some unnecessary self-doubt?
- How can I bring different extremes in my life into balance?
- Am I grounded enough?
- Am I too preoccupied with outer appearance of things?
- How can I attract more Divine abundance into my life?
- Which thoughts or beliefs are stopping me from manifesting the fullness of my Divine potential?
- Do I remember to stay grateful and humble?
- Am I overly focused on the surface of things?

Yantra of Goddess Vijaya

CHAPTER 20

SARVAMANGALA – ALL-AUSPICIOUS ONE
TRAYODASHI – THIRTEENTH LUNAR DAY

sarva-śakti-mayi sarva-mangala sadgati-prada

sarveśvari sarva-mayi sarva-mantra-svarupini

"Hail to Sarvamangala, all-auspicious Goddess, who is the power behind everything, who is the Goddess of everything and who is everything. She is the essence of all mantras and she leads on the path to salvation."

- Lalita Sahasranama

Kala	Element	Planet	Guna	Yogini	Vowel
priti (love)	ether	Jupiter	sattwa	South	o

Stage of consciousness	Divine quality	Deity (Muhurta Cintamani)	Deity (Varahamihira)	Nakshatra connection	Form of Shiva
waking (turiya)	nitavati (righeousness)	Kamadeva	Kamadeva	Punarvasu Shatabhisha	Dakshinamurti

Shukla Paksha

Nadi: ida
Chakra: ajna
Interval: major sixth / minor seventh
Deity (Narada Purana): Mahendra
House from the Sun: 6 or 7

Krishna Paksha

Nadi: pingala
Chakra: muladhara
Interval: major/minor second
Deity (Narada Purana): Kamadeva
House from the Sun: 12 or 1

Sarvamangala means all-auspicious one. Goddess in this form presides over thirteenth lunar day, which is sometimes called *Pradosha* or "flawless one", and considered as one of the most auspicious *tithis*. It is "removes all shortcomings and increases all auspiciousness". One of the names of Goddess Sarvamangala is Chandratmika, "the very soul of the Moon". *Trayodashi tithi* is the first of the three lunar days representing *turiya* or spiritually awakened state of consciousness. Swami Sivananda wrote about it beautifully:

"On the thirteenth lunar day Nature assists the worshipper in waking up from his mental deep sleep and in becoming aware of the fourth state, (*turiya*). The yogi who practices his yoga on *Pradosha* ("flawless one", another name of thirteenth lunar day) gets these experiences of Lord Shiva quite readily."

Thirteenth lunar day starts the last three *tithis*, which are connected to the state of *turiya*, the state "beyond this world". According to Vedic thought, all the worldly energies can be classified into twelve different modes, connected to twelve zodiac signs, twelve chakras of classical Indian music or twelve modes of energy (feminine and masculine energy in each of the six chakras) in our subtle body. Thus, number twelve stands for the completion of our human experience. *Trayodashi tithi*, the thirteenth lunar day, represents reaching beyond these twelve modes of Nature; beyond the tangible world. This is why *Trayodashi tithi*, as well as *Chaturdashi* and *Purnima* or *Amavasya* are also connected either with return to root chakra (on *Krishna Paksha*) or ascent to third eye chakra and beyond (in *Shukla Paksha*), transcending the elements of lower chakras.

As *Trayodashi tithi* is co-ruled by Jupiter, Cosmic Teacher, it strengthens our connection with our inner guidance and allows us to see things more clearly. Yet, even though everything that Teacher does is always for the benefit of the student, sometimes he needs to teach through being strict, as well. Similarly, Goddess Sarvamangala, although very benevolent in nature, and always giving blessings, sometimes blesses us also in a harsh way, through bitter experiences in life. This is why some scriptures say, that She is holding a citron, and not a pomegranate fruit in Her hand.

On 1 December, *Trayodashi tithi*, when I was writing this chapter, my Gurudev, Paramahamsa Vishwananda, beautifully explained the difference between Satguru and a teacher:

"When it comes to the transmission of knowledge, the main difference between a teacher and a Satguru is that a teacher teaches us, but a Satguru reminds us.

What is this difference? A teacher needs our heads, our minds and logic, but a Satguru seeks only an open heart. Transmission of knowledge with a teacher happens through a certain process, but with a Satguru it happens instantly. How well we digest the knowledge of the teacher depends on our mental ability. But how well we digest the knowledge of the Satguru depends on our openness and inner intensity."

Similarly, *Trayodashi* puts us in the state of higher receptivity, so we may become more open for inner or outer guidance of our Satguru – and so we can stand the intensity of the teachings and all the challenging experiences that come with that.

The energies of *moksha*, liberation and spiritual and material acceleration are at their peak on *Trayodashi tithi*. It is not only a lunar day co-ruled by Jupiter (whose element is ether), but it is also presided by element of *sattwic* ether. Etheric vibrations of *Trayodashi tithi* speed up and accelarate everything. They have potential to accelarate our progress both in material life and spiritual life. This is why the nature of this lunar day is *jaya* or "giving victory". It can be a very positive thing - yet, energies, which are getting transformed or exchanged too fast, can also become destructive and lead to too intense transformation, or even manifest in some aggressive way. In fact, there was even an exact research done, which had as its goal determining the lunar day, on which the biggest amount of accidents happen. It turned out to be *Trayodashi tithi* in *Shukla paksha* – when its energies are the most active.

This will especially affect people with *vata dosha*, who might feel some irritation or nervousness on thirteenth lunar day. Even from the point of view of music, the interval formed by distance of Sun and Moon during *Trayodashi tithi*, is starting the sequence of the least harmonious intervals: in *Shukla paksha* it ascends from major sixth into minor seventh (*nishadha* in Indian raga, ruled by Venus), while in *Krishna paksha* it descends from major second to minor second (*rishabha* in Indian raga, ruled by Mars). In both *pakshas* there is a musical tension between Sun and Moon, which is yearning to be resolved. Sometimes it will manifest as increased desire or passion, and sometimes as aggression or nervousness.

As element of ether is also connected to fast exchange of energy, while Jupiter himself is connected with our family and partnership, our libido is also empowered on *Trayodashi tithi* - which is why it is also a very good day for love exchange. According to some scriptures *Trayodashi tithi* is presided by Kamadeva, god of human love and desire. Goddess Sarvamangala is also connected to *priti* or love, thirteenth *kala* of the Moon. She inspires us towards more mature, forgiving and compassionate relationships. Sometimes She may also "stir up" energies in our relationships and speed up certain processes to make the transformation of our negative qualities faster.

Story about Star, Moon and Jupiter

Goddess Sarvamangala, being called Chandratmika "the soul of the Moon", as well as having Jupiter and Kamadeva co-ruling Her lunar day, is also very much connected with the story of Brihaspati (Jupiter), Chandra (Moon) and Tara (Star). *Varaha Purana* clearly connects that story with *Trayodashi tithi*.

According to the scriptures, young and handsome Chandra, Moon-god, went to the ashram of Brihaspati (Jupiter) to learn the Divine knowledge. However, being very young and romantic, Moon-god had fallen in love with wife of Brihaspati, Tara. Tara, being often neglected by her husband, who was always engrossed in his rituals and spiritual development, fell in love with Chandra, as well. It is said that this feeling of passion awakened within them on *Trayodashi tithi* in *Krishna paksha*, right before *Amavasya* or New Moon – when feminine and masculine principles are merging. On *Chaturdashi*, they crossed all the boundaries: Chandra abducted Tara and made love with her. On *Shukla Pratipad*, however, Chandra understood his mistake and returned Tara back to Brihaspati.

This story has a very deep, symbolic meaning. Tara symbolises one of the nakshatras, one particle of ourselves, which our Moon "falls in love" with. This is our natal nakshatra, the star occupied by the Moon in our natal chart. Similarly, our mind "falls in love" with some of our internal qualities, thinking: "this is me", "this is mine". Every such "this is me" or "this is mine" is taking our Divine perception (symbolised by Jupiter) and feeling of fullness away from us – because every "this

275

is me", automatically creates some "this is not me". This is how our mind functions. Similarly our natal Moon naturally gets indentified with the qualities of our natal star, nakshatra, and starts to perceive everything, which is connected to that nakshatra, as very personal – which naturally gives rise to likes and dislikes, passion and repulsion. Divine perception, on the other hand, never gets attached to any "star", as it perceives everything as equal, full and equally important. Nothing is more special or less special in the eyes of Divine perception.

In *Varaha Purana* it is said that the entire incident was observed by Dharma, god of righteousness (sometimes associated with Yamaraj), who felt so hurt after seeing this, that he decided to retire to the forest. Similarly, whenever chastity and mutual respect between partners is gone, the *dharma* and the culture of the society starts to deteriorate – because *dharma* always starts in our own home. As soon as Dharma had left to the forest, *adharma*, unrighteousness, started to spread everywhere. People, gods and demons started to kill each other mercilessly. Finally lord Brahma, along with other demigods and with some demons, started to search for Dharma. They found him roaming in the form of a buffalo in the jungle and humbly requested him to return. Finally, Dharma agreed. Since that time *Trayodashi tithi* became sacred to Dharma, as well.

This story is also very symbolic to *Trayodashi* natives. As the form of Goddess presiding over their lunar day is Sarvamangala, "all-auspicious one", who is blessing everybody with all wealth, they often feel either very blessed in life or... very unappreciated. As the energy of Kamadev is very intense on this lunar day, increasing all desires, *Trayodashi* natives may sometimes feel that they never have enough. Never enough knowledge, never enough money, never enough pleasure, never enough love... It can manifest in any sphere of life, depending on the position of the natal Moon. They may often feel that they deserve more than what they have – like Tara did. And whenever they feel that they don't have enough (or they feel that "they are not enough"), they may easily try to compensate it in this way or the other, like Tara compensated lacks in her married life with the romance with Chandra. This is something that *Trayodashi* natives need to be especially careful about. One of the most important qualities for them to develop in life is gratitude and appreciation for everything that they receive from the Divine.

Ultimately, that was also a lesson for Brihaspati (Jupiter) in this story, who is the co-ruler of *Trayodashi tithi*. When Tara returned back to his home she was pregnant – but not with his child. She was pregnant with Chandra's child. When Brihaspati realised that, he got furious, and he cursed the child, that he will be born as a neuter – neither male, nor female. The name of this child was Budha – Mercury. After the child was born, however, Brihaspati regreted acting so impulsively and he accepted Mercury as his own child – who turned to be his most intelligent student ever. Divine perception (Jupiter) accepted intellect (Mercury), the son of mind (Moon), as his own child. Similarly, *Trayodashi tithi* natives need to learn how to accept with gratitude whatever God is giving them – because we never know, which blessings are hidden behind each of our life situations and we should never judge things too quickly by acting too impulsively. Impulsiveness is, indeed, one of the qualities, which *Trayodashi tithi* natives need to learn how to control.

Meditation with Goddess Sarvamangala

Hue: golden
Number of heads: 1
Number of eyes: 3
Number of hands: 4
Right hands: pomegranate fruit
Left hands: golden pot with money
Garments: red

Goddess Sarvamangala is of golden hue and is dressed in red garments, decked with rubies and pearls. She is seated on Her *yantra* resembling lotus flower. Her eyes full of mercy resemble the Sun and the Moon, and She is smiling gently. She is the ruler of the *kalas* of the Moon, the Sun and the Fire, who are also Her *shaktis*. She is surrounded on all sides by her *shaktis*, who are like herself and by others 70 in number who have originated from the solar, lunar, and fiery letters.

Goddess Sarvamangala has two hands – even though in some scriptures she is sometimes portrayed with 4 hands. Some scriptures describe Her as holding pomegranate fruit and golden pot of money, while others describe Her as holding a citron and showing *varada mudra* with another hand. She is always described as a very benevolent Goddess, who fulfills all the wishes of Her devotees. Similarly like Vijaya Devi, She is the bringer of all wealth: material wealth, wealth of knowledge, wealth of love and spiritual wealth. She is often approached to help us progress in material and spiritual life. Her blessings spread in all directions, similarly like the petals of Her *yantra*.

Similarly like the *yantras* of Tvarita and Vijaya Devi, the *yantra* of Goddess Sarvamangala is very simple: just an empty space enclosed by flower petals. It reflects not only the purity and simplicity of this lunar day (as well as certain innocence of people born on *Trayodashi*) but also very speedy energies acting on those lunar days, which are seeking their stabilisation and equilibrium.

Interestingly, in case of all the three *yantras*, no matter how you turn them around, you will always see the *yantra* as the same. Similarly, *Ashtami*, *Dvadashi* and *Trayodashi tithi* natives have the capacity to look at things with equanimity. Unless their Moon is afflicted, they have this natural tendency to wish good to everybody, similarly like Goddess Sarvamangala, regardless of people's faults or their past. They have a lot of understanding for other people and they understand that everybody needs his own time to grow. They are usually peace loving people, who don't like going into any conflicts. Due to Jupiterian energies being so strong in them, they manifest the qualities of a benevolent mother.

Numerology: 13

Number 13 is, interestingly, not associated with anything in Vedas. It is not connected to any group of deities. Perhaps this is why *Trayodashi tithi* is often called *Pradosha* – "stainless one". It is here, in *Trayodashi tithi*, that the stage of consciousness from beyond this world is starting - the stage of spiritual awakening: *turiya*. Similarly, number 13 represents reaching beyond the human experience of 12 zodiac signs and entering the spiritual realm and spiritual perception.

Interestingly, in 13 chapter of *Bhagavad Gita*, Lord Krishna explains to Arjuna how to be the observer in our daily activites and how to always know the difference between *Prakriti* (Nature) and *Purusha* (Spirit), as well as the field (*kshetra*) and knower of the field (*kshetrajna*). And similarly like *Trayodashi tithi* reflects the energies from beyond physical world, so in Chapter 13, verse 13, Bhagavan Krishna says these profound words: "I shall now explain the knowable, knowing which you will taste the eternal. Brahman, the spirit, beginningless and subordinate to Me, lies beyond the cause and effect of this material world."

In one of the first verses of 13 Chapter Lord Krishna explains the qualities of truly knowledgable person:

"Humility (*amānitva*); pridelessness (*adambhitva*); nonviolence (*ahimsā*); tolerance (*kṣānti*); simplicity (*ārjava*); following a Guru (*ācāryopāsana*); purity (*śauca*); steadiness (*sthairya*); self-control (*ātma-vinigraha*); renunciation of objects of senses (*indriyārtheṣu vairāgya*); absence of false ego (*anahaṅkāra*); the perception of the miseries of birth, death, old age and disease (*janma mṛtyu jarā vyādhi duḥkha doṣānudarśana*); detachment (*asakti*); freedom from entanglement with children, wife, home and the rest (*nabhiṣvaṅgaḥ putra-dāra-gṛhādiṣu*); even-mindedness amid pleasant and unpleasant events (*nityaṁ ca sama-cittatvam iṣṭāniṣṭopapattiṣu*); constant and unalloyed devotion to me (*mayi cānanya-yogena bhaktir avyabhicāriṇī*); aspiring to live in a solitary place (*vivikta-deśa-sevitvam*); detachment from the general mass of people (*aratir jana-saṁsadi*); constant knowledge of the Self (*adhyātma-jñāna-nityatvaṁ*); having the knowledge of the Supreme Truth (*tattva-jñānārtha-darśanam*) – all these I declare to be knowledge, and besides this whatever there may be is ignorance."

Yogini in *Kalachakra*: South

On *Trayodashi tithi* the danger comes from the South, similarly like on *Panchami*. It is said that we should avoid travelling into that direction during the thirteenth lunar day in any of the two *pakshas*. The biggest danger of Southern direction (which is connected to Jupiter in *Kalachakra* and to Mars in *Digchakra*), which may manifest during *Trayodashi tithi* is selfishness, impulsiveness and quarrelsomeness, as well as the attitude of "knowing better". Goddess Sarvamangala inspires us to rise above such selfish qualities within us and inspires us to bless everybody (instead of cursing) and everything that comes our way – as everything is a blessing in disguise.

Besides that, *Trayodashi tithi* is actually a perfect day for travelling. Goddess Sarvamangala is often approached to protect people during their journey and She provides protection to all modes of transportation – as She is Herself very swift in nature.

Shaktis of Goddess Sarvamangala

Different *shaktis* or powers of Goddess Sarvamangala dwell in the different places of Her *yantra*, resembling a lotus flower with empty space inside - which represents boundlessness of ether element. As ether element itself is strongly connected with the power of sound and speech, many of Her *shaktis* have names of Goddess Saraswati – Goddess of sacred speech, sacred sound and sacred vibrations.

Eight innermost lotus petals are presided by *shaktis*: Bhadra ("auspicious one" or "protector"), Bhavani ("mother of all life"), Bhavya ("future"), Vishalakshi ("the one, having wide eyes"), Suvismita ("wonderstruck one"), Karuna ("compassionate one"), Kamala ("desirous one" or "the one resembling lotus flower") and Kalpa ("imagination"). Sixteen lotus petals enclosing them are presided by *shaktis*: Kala ("time"), Purini ("ancient one"), Nitya ("eternal one"), Amrita ("immortal one" or "nectarean one"), Jivita ("alive"), Daya ("compassionate"), Ashoka ("the one without sadness"), Amala ("pure one"), Purna ("full one"), Punya ("good merit"), Bhagya ("good luck"), Udyata ("ready one" or "active one"), Viveka ("discrimination"), Vibhava ("prosperity"), Vishwa ("universal one") and Vitata ("wide one"). And 32 lotus petals enclosing these sixteen are presided by *shaktis*: Kamini ("loving one" or "desirous one"), Khechari ("flying one"), Sarva ("soul of everything"), Purana ("ancient one"), Parameshwari ("highest controller"), Gauri ("fair complexioned one"), Shiva ("merciful one"), Ameya ("immeasurable one"), Vimala ("purest one"), Vijaya ("victorious one"), Para ("highest one"), Pavitra ("pure one"), Padmini ("lotus-like one"), Divya ("Divine one"), Vishweshi ("the controller of the universe"), Shiva-vallabha ("beloved of Shiva"), Asheshartipa (meaning is not clear), Ananda ("blissful one"), Ambujakshi ("lotus-eyed one"), Anandita ("full of bliss"), Varada ("giver of boons"), Vakprada ("giver of sweet speech"), Vani ("voice" or "resounding one"), Vividba (meaning is not clear), Veda-vigraha ("personification of Vedas or all knowledge"), Vidya ("wisdom" or "wise one"), Vagishwari ("the controller of speech"), Saridhya (meaning is not clear), Sariyata (meaning is not clear), Sarasvati ("goddess of all *rasas*"), Nirmala ("pure one") and Danartipa (meaning is not clear).

Swara of Goddess Sarvamangala

O, the thirteenth *swara* or vowel of Sanskrit alphabet, is associated with Goddess Sarvamangala. Its quality or *kala* is brightness. According to *Agni Purana* it is connected with the qulities of Brahma, the Creator, who created the entire universe from the primordial all-auspicious vibration **om**. Similarly like the Guru Himself, syllable **o**, which is forming *bij* mantra **om**, dispells all the darkness of our ignorance, connects us to inner guidance and harmonises all dissonances in our energy body. Every mantra starts with mantra **om**. Chanting **om** is invoking the Divine blessings from beyond this world.

Nakshatras connected to Goddess Sarvamangala

Punarvasu nakshatra is connected to *swara* of Goddess Sarvamangala, while Her four arms stand for first two *padas* of Shatabhisha nakshatra. Punarvasu is a nakshatra ruled by Jupiter, Cosmic Guru Himself, similarly like *Trayodashi tithi*. Punarvasu nakshatra is closely connected to both *tithis* co-ruled by Jupiter: *Panchami* and *Trayodashi*. Something very special happens in Punarvasu nakshatra, as well: it is the place, where originally *Dakshinayana* would start and Sun would change its course from northern into the southern. In Punarvasu nakshatra the energies of the Sun reach their peak, or third eye chakra in our energy body, and then they slowly start to descend as grace and teachings during *Dakshinayana*, or southern movement of the Sun. Lord Shiva, who was Himself the first Guru, turned to southern direction while giving His teachings and hence was called Dakshinamurti ("the embodiment of southern direction"). Even in Kalachakra *Trayodashi tithi* is connected to Southern direction. This is also why the best direction to face during *Trayodashi* is North, the opposite direction to the direction of *yogini* – the opposite direction that Shiva is facing, so we can symbolically face Him and learn from Him.

Interestingly enough, the thirteenth form of Shiva connected to *Trayodashi tithi* is Dakshinamurti himself – Shiva in the form of a teacher. He is seated on the throne on the top of a hill with Apasmara, demon of ignorance, under his right foot. His left foot rests on his right tigh. One of his right hands is holding a rosary (for repetition and chanting the mantras), another is in the gesture of teaching. In two of His left hands Shiva is holding the book (for scriptural knowledge) and the flame (for internal knowledge, born through burning down our ignorance).

The connection between Goddess Sarvamangala, *Trayodashi tithi* and Shatabhisha nakshatra is also a special one. In ancient times it was considered to be the star of kings, rulers and wealthy people. It is also the nakshatra of secret knowledge, spiritual healing and power of forgiveness. Similarly like Shatabhisha natives, people born under *Trayodashi tithi* sometimes tend to be a bit harsh or even cruel in speech (although truthful). They often have a need to conquer their enemies, and due to that may suffer much grief in isolation. They are independent in thoughts and actions, but can sometimes act without thinking, impulsively. That is the shadow side of speedy energies of Goddess Sarvamangala.

And, as Shatabhisha nakshatra is also sometimes associated with addictions or mythical "drop of nectar" pursued by Rahu, who is the ruler of this nakshatra, similarly people born on *Trayodashi tithi* may sometimes have some sort of addiction. Interestingly, Nityananda Mahaprabhu, who was born on this lunar day, was often described by his disciples as being "constantly drunk with the Divine name". Repetition of the mantras is one of the most powerful remedies for any person born on *Trayodashi tithi*, especially if they experience its shadow side.

Tithi, vara and nakshatra resonance

Trayodashi tithi, being such an auspicious lunar day doesn't form any negative *yoga* with any day of the week. This is true to all *tithis* connected to *turiya* or awakened state of consciousness, connecting us to the energies from beyond this world. Only two different *vinasha yogas* or "combinations of destruction", as well as one *visha yoga*, "poisonous combination" occur on very specific days of the week, when combined with certain nakshatras. Two *vinasha yogas* possible on *Trayodashi tithi* are:

- *Trayodashi tithi* + Sunday + Bharani, Margashirsha, Ashlesha, Vishakha, Anuradha, Jyeshtha or Dhanishta
- *Trayodashi tithi* + Thursday + Krittika, Rohini, Margashirsha, Ardra, Uttara Phalguni, Vishakha, Anuradha or Shatabhisha

Additionally, *Trayodashi tithi* creates *ashubha yoga* or "inauspicious combination" with two airy nakshatras, Citra or Swati, which are naturally agitating already intense and swift energy of *Trayodashi tithi*. *Trayodashi tithi* also causes *shunya dosha* to these two nakshatras, as sometimes it may give birth to over-indulgence or overly compensative or very dissatisfied nature.

Also, Thursday with *Trayodashi* and Anuradha produces *visha yoga* or "poisonous combination", while Thursday, *Trayodashi* and Ashlesha nakshatra can cause death according to *Agni Purana*. There are some beneficial *yogas* created with *Trayodashi tithi* and Thursday, though. This combination is very beneficial, when Moon is dwelling in Ashwini, Punarvasu, Pushya, Magha, Swati, Purvashadha, Purva Bhadrapada or Revati.

Trayodashi tithi resonates very well with productive and proactive energies of Tuesday, when it forms *siddha yoga* or "combination of accomplishments". Energy of Mars is also a natural remedy for Jupiter, the co-ruler of this lunar day, who becomes of great help, whenever Jupiter's energies become too philosophical and stagnated. Combination of Tuesday and *Trayodashi tithi* becomes even more powerful and auspicious, when the Moon is dwelling in Ashwini, Margashirsha,

Uttara Phalguni, Citra, Anuradha, Mula, Dhanishta or Purva Bhadrapada nakshatra.

Energies of Goddess Sarvamangala and *Trayodashi tithi* resonate really well also with Wednesdays – their combination is producing auspicious *amrita yoga* ("combination of nectar"), which becomes even more powerful if Moon is dwelling in Rohini, Margashirsha, Ardra, Uttara Phalguni, Anuradha or Uttarashadha. It is quite interesting, considering the fact that Mercury, the planetary ruler of Wednesday, was a child of relationship between Tara and Moon.

To summarise, *Trayodashi tithi* has the best resonance with nakshatras Ashwini, Punarvasu, Pushya, Magha, Mula, Purvashadha, Uttarashadha, Purva Bhadrapada and Revati. It brings different results with Rohini, Margashirsha, Ardra, Uttara Phalguni, Citra, Swati, Anuradha and Dhanishta, and usually bad results with Bharani, Krittika, Ashlesha, Vishakha, Jyeshtha and Shatabhisha.

Additionally, if a person is born on *Trayodashi tithi* and Thursday, it produces a *tithi dosha* for the person. The personality of such a person will be overly dominated by ether element. Such person will need to consciously work on balancing exeggerated ether element, both in one's physical body and on a psychological level.

In Vedic month called Jyeshtha (in the end of which Full Moon falls in Jyeshtha nakshatra) *Trayodashi tithi* is considered *shunya* and is avoided for any auspicious activities. In Jyeshtha month *Trayodashi tithi* often occurs in Vishakha nakshatra (in *Shukla paksha*) and Bharani nakshatra (in *Krishna paksha*), which can make overindulgent side of this *tithi* a bit too strong.

YOGAS FORMED WITH *TRAYODASHI TITHI*

	1	2	3	4	5	6	7
1			**siddha**	amrita	**siddha**		
2	vinasha		siddha	amrita			
3			siddha	amrita	vinasha		
4			siddha	**amrita / siddha**	vinasha		
5	vinasha		**siddha**	**amrita / siddha**	vinasha		
6			siddha	**amrita / siddha**	vinasha		
7			siddha	amrita	**siddha / suta**		
8			siddha	amrita	**siddha**		
9	vinasha		siddha	amrita	death		
10			siddha	amrita	**siddha**		
11			siddha	amrita			
12			**siddha**	**amrita / siddha**	vinasha		
13			siddha	amrita			
14	shunya	shunya	**siddha /** shunya	amrita / shunya	shunya	shunya	shunya
15	shunya	shunya	siddha / shunya	amrita / shunya	**siddha /** shunya	shunya	shunya
16	vinasha		siddha	amrita	vinasha		
17	vinasha		**siddha**	**amrita / siddha**	vinasha / visha		
18	vinasha		siddha	amrita			
19			**siddha**	amrita			
20			siddha	amrita	**siddha / suta**		
21			siddha	**amrita / siddha**			
22			siddha	amrita			
23	vinasha		**siddha**	amrita			
24			siddha	amrita	vinasha		
25			**siddha**	amrita	**siddha**		
26			siddha	amrita			
27			siddha	amrita	**siddha / suta**		

Important *rashis* for *Trayodashi tithi* natives

Each *tithi* has a special connection with a number of *rashis*. Understanding those connections can help us not only in understanding our own birth chart on a much deeper level, but in better understanding of the nature of the *tithi* itself.

Two *rashis*, which are of great importance for all *Trayodashi tithi* natives are two dual signs: Pisces and Virgo. Sign of Pisces is ruled by the planetary lord of this lunar day (Jupiter, *tithi pati kshetra*), while Virgo is the sign opposite to it (*tithi pati kshetra paksha*), which is the sign revealing, where are we heading in life. It is also a very important axis, as in those signs Mercury and Venus get exaltated or debilitated. Similarly, people born on *Trayodashi tithi* naturally experience many transformations in life – and one of their most important life lessons is often to learn how to manifest love in its higher nature. Not without a reason *kala* of the Moon connected with *Trayodashi* is *priti* or love. *Trayodashi tithi* natives sometimes tend to be a little bit too idealistic, when it comes to Love – and generally when it comes to many things in life. One of their most important life lessons is to learn how to be a bit more realistic and how to expect less from people and reality – but rather being grateful for everything they receive in life.

Additionally, in *Shukla paksha* sign of Cancer becomes more energised on *Trayodashi tithi* (which reveals more emotional and comfort seeking side *Trayodashi tithi*), while in *Krishna paksha* Capricorn becomes more energised (which reveals more materialistic and grounded nature of *Krishna Trayodashi* natives). Interestingly, on this very axis Jupiter and Mars get exalted or debilitated. This might be one of the many reason why ancient *rishis* might have associated this specific lunar day with Jupiter and Southern direction. Additionally, on *Shukla Trayodashi*, the energy for the first time enters the zodiacal *ajna chakra*, sign of Cancer, thus starting to move to the South (*dakshinayana*). Perhaps this is one of the reason why *Trayodashi tithi* is connected to the energies "out of this world" and Divine qualities, which can awaken within us only with a blessing of the Master, not with just our own effort.

Sometimes, however, *Trayodashi tithi* natives may have a tendency to expect from the world a little bit too much. They might expect that everything will come to them effortlessly, without much work needed from their side. That is the shadow side of Jupiter, which may manifest a bit of a "happy-go-lucky" attitude. This is why this influence must be balanced by the proactive energies of Mars. Otherwise, without enough effort from their side, *Trayodashi tithi* natives may easily face some huge disappointments in life.

Tithi shunya rashis or the signs, which are made "fruitless" by *Trayodashi tithi*, are Taurus (ruled by Venus) and Leo (ruled by Sun). Both of these signs are naturally quite vulnerable for all people born on *Trayodashi tithi*. This is the reason why *Trayodashi tithi* natives often like to really indulge into things, and when they feel that they don't experience enough pleasure in life (due to both pleasurable signs being a little bit defected), they might have a tendency to try to compensate that with something else.

Unless these signs are occupied by Rahu or Ketu, or unless their planetary lords (Venus or Sun) are placed 3rd, 6th, 8th or 12th house from ascendant or Moon, or are retrograde, or in conjuction with malefic planet, or, lastly, in nakshatras of Rahu or Ketu, these two signs and houses won't bring good results for the native. In such a case these signs must be strengthened (by strengthening their lords) to bring good results. *Shunya* planets do produce good results, however, when they transit 3rd, 6th, 8th or 12th house from from ascendant or Moon.

Sadhana for Goddess Sarvamangala

Goddess Sarvamangala is pleased with chanting the mantras. To connect with Goddess Sarvamangala on a deeper level, you can either do a meditation of sitting on Her lap, as given by my Gurudev (described in Chapter 24), or colour Her yantra and meditate on it, facing South. For your *sadhana* you can use one of the two mantras below or one of the affirmations. There are couple of more advanced mantras for worship of Goddess Sarvamangala in *Tantraraja*, but they are not supposed to be recited without a guidance of a Guru.

Mantras:

oṁ aiṁ hriṁ śriṁ oṁ sarvamangalayai namaḥ
oṁ aiṁ hriṁ śriṁ oṁ pritiyai namaḥ

Affirmations:

I wish good to everybody.
I allow auspiciousness and abundance to enter my life.
I accept everything as a blessing from the Divine.
I allow myself to learn and hear my inner guidance.
I allow myself to be grateful.
I allow myself to love.

Questions for self-analysis

Every lunar day is an opportunity to learn something new about ourselves. Nitya Devis and their wisdom can become our guides on this sacred journey. Questions below can help you in recognising certain "shadow" tendencies in yourself, which may arise on *Trayodashi tithi.* If you were born on this lunar day, these questions might be of big importance for you in life and allow you to face your weaknesses.

- Am I grateful enough?
- Do I accept everything as a blessing from the Divine?
- Do I allow the inner voice of my heart to guide me through life?
- Am I acting too impulsively?
- Am I ready to learn on my mistakes?
- Am I trying to compensate something?
- Am I expecting too much from other people?
- Am I idealising some things or people too much?
- Do I put enough effort from my side?

Yantra of Goddess Sarvamangala

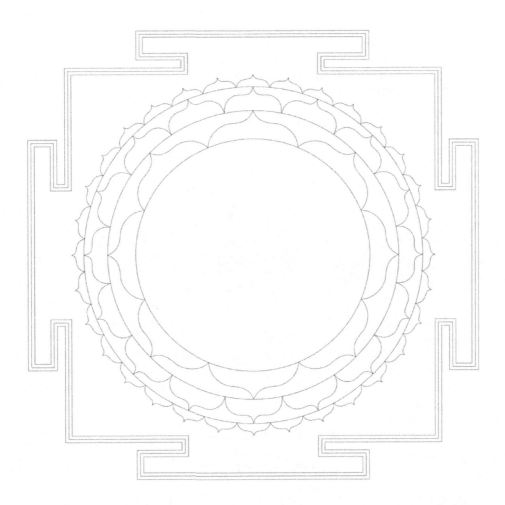

CHAPTER 21

JWALAMALINI – GARLANDED WITH FLAMES
CHATURDASHI – THIRTEENTH LUNAR DAY

kiricakra-ratharudha-dandanatha-puraskrta

jvalamalini-kaksipta-vahni-prakara-madhyaga

"Hail to Goddess Lalita, who is preceded by Dandanatha, the commander of Her army, and who is dwelling in the center of the rampart of fire created by Goddess Jwalamalini."

- Lalita Sahasranama

Kala	Element	Planet	Guna	Yogini	Vowel
angada (self-sacrifice)	water	Venus	sattwa	West	au

Stage of consciousness	Divine quality	Deity (Muhurta Cintamani)	Deity (Varahamihira)	Nakshatra connection	Form of Shiva
dreaming (turiya)	satyavan (truthfulness)	Rudra	Kali	Punarvasu Shatabhisha Purva Bhadrapada Uttara Bhadrapada Revati	Bhikshatana-murti

Shukla Paksha

Krishna Paksha

Nadi: ida
Chakra: ajna
Interval: minor/major seventh
Deity (Narada Purana): Indra
House from the Sun: 6 or 7

Nadi: pingala
Chakra: muladhara
Interval: minor second
Deity (Narada Purana): Shiva
House from the Sun: 12 or 1

Goddess Jwalamalini, "garlanded with flames", presiding over fourteenth lunar day, is the most intense of all Nitya Devis, which is revealed by Her standing position. Ruling the fourteenth lunar day along with Venus, standing in the circle of flames, and being connected to fourteenth *kala* of the Moon, *angada* ("self-sacrifice"), Goddess Jwalamalini represents the last stage of the Goddess before reaching fullness on the Full Moon day or union on the New Moon day: the stage of complete self-sacrifice and burning the ego in the flames of the Supreme Love. Goddess Jwalamalini represents fire of devotion, which is so intense that it burns all the karma. Interestingly, both *tithis* co-ruled by Venus are very strongly connected with our ability to sacrifice ourselves for the higher purpose – as, ultimately, this is exactly what Love is: a sacrifice of our own ego.

The need for self-sacrifice on the path of one's spiritual growth is expressed in the most beautiful and esoteric way already in the Vedas, in the description of preparing *soma* or symbolic nectar of life for the fire sacrifice. Soma, which was sometimes considered as identical with the Moon, the representant of our very own mind, was pressed intensely in the pressing stones and then purified in intense heat, so its essence can be derived and so it can become worthy of God's offering. One of the hymns to Soma in Rig Veda says:

"Wide spread out for thee is the sieve of thy purifying, O Master of the soul; becoming in the creature thou pervadest his members all through. He tastes not that delight who is unripe and whose body has not suffered in the heat of the fire; they alone are able to bear that and enjoy it who have been prepared by the flame."
- *Rig Veda IX.83*

Interestingly enough, *Chaturdashi* is often considered as a birth *tithi* of the Moon or Soma. Similarly our own consciousness must be purified through sieve, through pressing stones, and ultimately, through the heat of the fire itself, in which the mind loses its individual identity, to become completely filled with Divine light. This intense process of transformation and purification is what Goddess Jwalamalini stands for. She represents the most *sattwic* manifestation of the element of water, connected with *moksha* or liberation.

Interestingly enough, according to *Taittiriya Brahmana* there was only one *naga*, serpent *rishi*, who possesed the knowledge of pressing the *soma* and preparing it as holy offering. One of the names of Goddess Jwalamalini in *64 Yogini Namavali* is Nagini or "the serpent lady". Clearly, Goddess Jwalamalini is closely connected with intensity of awakening *kundalini shakti*, spiritual energy at the base of our spine, which is often depicted as a serpentine force.

In *Shukla paksha*, when Sun and Moon are forming major seventh music interval or *nishadha*, seventh *swara* of Indian raga ruled by Venus, the energy of Goddess Jwalamalini is the most intense, reflecting the tension before reaching complete fullness of Her powers. In *Krishna paksha*, on the other hand, when Sun and the Moon form a music interval, which is even smaller than minor second, it reveals the last friction before the union. In both *pakshas* Goddess Jwalamalini stands for this last friction before the final release of energy. This is also why the energy of *Chaturdashi tithi* is the most intense of all lunar days. Its nature is *ugra* – "fierce",This is why on this lunar day we can often feel nervous, irritated, have sudden bursts of anger or even become aggressive or violent. The intensity of water element (connected to *moksha*) and burning flames of Goddess Jwalamalini, as well as the friction of inharmonious music interval produced by Sun and Moon on this lunar day, naturally lead to releasing all the energies stored within us. This is also why some of the world's most prominent dictators, who have greatly abused their power, violated the boundaries of other countries and people, and inflicted great pain on the world, were also born on this lunar day. Generally, due to intense nature of this lunar day, people born on *Chaturdashi tithi* will always seek intense experiences in life.

Goddess Jwalamalini is such a form of Divine Mother, which is going to sacrifice everything in the fire of Love. While other Goddesses are sitting peacefully and smiling gently, Goddess Jwalamalini is standing, ready to drag us towards the higher level of consciousness, if needed – and She refuses any arguments. Does

Love ever ask, if anybody is ready for Her?

On Her lunar day, Goddess Jwalamalini, often sends us many life tests to purify our ego in their intense heat, so our heart can become ready to receive Love and melt into Love. Like my Gurudev beautiful wrote:

"Testing times may arise in the form of troubles. Often one doesn't want to see it and tries to bypass it. But life is like this. Life is a great lesson. If you don't face your problem, if you don't face your negative quality and look at it in the eyes, you'll never become strong. If you always try to go sideways, you will not learn anything."

Goddess Jwalamalini is the One, who makes sure, that you do not run away from your life's tests. She keeps you for entire day on Her burning lap, so your consciousness can transform in the heat of Her Love. Even the *yogini* She is connected to is called Atma-karshini ("the one attracting the soul"), while the syllable of Sri Vidya mantra She is connected to is *la*, the *bij mantra* of bliss. Goddess Jwalamalini burns everything that stands between your individual soul and Supreme soul; between your current level of consciousness and next level of consciousness; between you and your soul's true bliss.

When Highest Goddess, Lalita Tripurasundari, was fighting with demon Bandhaka, to bring burnt Kamadeva (god of love) back to the world, and restore its fertility, and when the demonic forces casted the darkness on the battlefield, it was Goddess Jwalamalini (along with Vahnivasini), who dispelled the darkness with Her intense light and flames. She made everything visible again. It was also Goddess Jwalamalini, who created a protective circle of fire around the army of Lalita, so none of other Nitya Devis can be harmed. Similarly, in the microcosm of our energy body, Goddess Jwalamalini creates such a protective circle of fire around our own chakras, when we do our *kriya yoga* practice, and thus burns all the negativities and karmas stored in them.

The quality of Lord Krishna connected with Goddess Jwalamalini is *satyavan* or being truthful. Jwalamalini Devi burns all our illusions about ourselves or the world, so we can pierce through *maya* and transcend our limitations. "Truth leads to salvation" – Goddess Jwalamalini is embodiment of that saying. She leads us closer to who we truly are by burning all the negativities inside of us and removing all that is standing between our true Self and our current state of consciousness. This is why according to different scriptures Kali, fierce form of Divine mother or Rudra, fierce form of Shiva, are the presiding deities of *Chaturdashi tithi*, as well.

Even form of Shiva connected to that lunar day is Bhikshatanamurti – Lord in the form of a mendicant. He is completely naked, representing a complete sacrifice and surrender of the ego, exposure of the truth and not being concerned with the energies of the outer world. *Chaturdashi tithi* natives carry within themselves a very similar energy. They are rarely concered about what other people think of them.

They always stay sincere and are ready to speak out even the most unpleasant truth. Yet, due to that, they may also sometimes "burn down" some of their relationships. Even though usually they are naturally humble and not too concerned with other people and their opinions, *Chaturdashi* natives may sometimes have a tendency to seek too much attention from their loved ones or close friends. However, their lack of concernment about opinions of other people and being a little bit too self-centered sometimes (like it happens in the case of all *Rikta tithi* natives), may also make people born on this lunar day cross or violate the boundaries of other people too often. They simply do not have this inner sensitivity, which could tell them: "Hey, you should not say that. You should not go that far. You should not talk too much. You should not overwhelm other person with your presence so much" – that is the side effect of water element, which knows no boundaries. Presence and energy of *Chaturdashi* natives is as intense as the presence of Goddess Jwalamalini Herself and they need to learn in life not to overwhelm other people with that. This is why they are often not only very independent in life, but they may also have a tendency to either spend their life alone or in a fairly detached relationship.

As Goddess Jwalamalini represents the last stage and the last step of the Goddess before reaching Her fullness, people born on Her lunar day may sometimes be also kind of "stagnated" on the last stage of relationship, professional project or some level of spirituality. They often have this difficulty with completing things or taking the final step in any sphere of life. If the Moon or *tithi rashi* is in anyway damaged, then they might experience this issue with the quality of self-sacrifice. One of their most important life lessons is embracing the change and understanding that for something to be completed and for something new to be born, something old must die. Perhaps this is why Goddess Jwalamalini is sometimes associated with snakes, who are embodiment of change. Similarly like snakes shed their skin few times a year and embrace their own vulnerability in this sensitive moment, so *Chaturdashi tithi* natives need to embrace the changes, which life is bringing them, endure the vulnerability, which comes with that and welcome something new in their lives – as no human has ever reached the fullness of his potential without making some sacrifices.

Self-immolation of Sati

According to *Varaha Purana*, *Chaturdashi tithi* is connected with self-immolation of Goddess Sati. Sati was the first earthly incarnation of Goddess Shakti, counterpart of Shiva. She married Shiva against the wish of Her parents, which created a lot of disagreements between Her and Her earthly father, Daksha Prajapati – who happened to be a great enemy of Lord Shiva. For the pauper and skull-carrying Shiva, Daksha had nothing but disgust and never forgave his daughter Sati for wedding him.

One day, Daksha Prajapati, organised a huge *yajna*, fire sacrifice. His intention was, however, neither pure, neither spiritual. Through that *yajna* he wanted only to insult Shiva and hurt his own daughter, Sati. To insult them, he invited all the gods to take part in the great fire ceremony, except his daughter and his son-in-law. But Goddess in the form of Sati, being still very young and naive, covered by the same *maya* by which all other beings on earth get delusioned, had a desire to go to the *yajna* anyways, despite not being invited. She expressed Her wish to Lord Shiva and wanted to convince Him to go with Her, as well. Lord Shiva told Her, however, that She should not go there uninvited and He warned Her that something disastrous will happen, if She will decide to go. Disappointed and a little angry with the answer of Her husband, Sati decided to go anyway – with Him or without Him. She had full faith in the love of Her parents, believing that they will welcome Her with all honours.

Unfortunately, that was not the case. The moment Sati entered the fire ceremony, She quickly realised, that She is unwelcome here. She wasn't greeted by anybody and Her presence enraged Daksha Prajapati to such an extent, that He started to insult Shiva in Sati's presence. Poor Sati was completely broken inside. She could not stand even one bad word spoken against Her Beloved in Her presence. And so, She decided that it is better to die than to hear those insults – and She entered the sacrificial fire Herself, immolating Herself completely, and reflecting the fullness of the qualities of Goddess Jwalamalini, "garlanded with flames".

Shiva got furious when He heard what happened. From His hair He manifested a dangerous warrior, Virabhadra, a particle of His own self, and ordered him to go and destroy the *yajna* of Daksha Prajapati, to avenge the death of His wife and His Shakti. Virabhadra created a great chaos in the entire place of fire sacrifice, injured many gods, and decapitated Daksha Prajapati – which was a symbolic death of his arrogance and ego. Head of Daksha Prajapati was burnt by the flames of fire sacrifice.

The entire story reveals the importance of sacrifice as a form of purification in Vedic culture. Only when we sacrifice something, we get truly purified and our ego is getting refined in the flames of spiritual fire. Interestingly, *Chaturdashi tithi* is also said to be the birthday of Goddess Chinnamasta – a form of the Divine Mother, who decapitates Herself, symbolising the supreme form of sacrifice: sacrifice of the "head" or the lower self. This is why the energies of *Chaturdashi tithi* may sometimes seem so disturbing from earthly perspective, as they inspire us to sacrifice something towards we are the most attached: our own ego. Interestingly, Ketu itself, the only *graha* without a head (and therefore strongly connected to Goddess Chinnamasta), gets greatly agitated during fourteenth lunar day, too, and sometimes can act too violently or aggressively in the chart of the native.

Meditation with Goddess Jwalamalini

Hue: moonlike
Number of heads: 6
Number of eyes: 3 on each face
Number of hands: 12
Right hands: ankusha, sword, arrow, mace, flame, abhaya mudra
Left hands: pasha, shield, tortoise, lotus flower, trident, varada mudra
Garments: red

Goddess Jwalamalini is the only Nitya Devi, who is standing, which is revealing Her intense nature, impatient to experience fullness or union. She stands on the lotus flower and is surrounded by flames from all sides, which is symbolising Her purity and the capacity to burn the karma. Yet, even though surrounded by flames, Her hue is cooling and moonlike, revealing Her loving nature. Mother always wants what is best for Her child and whatever She is doing, She does it out of Love.

Goddess Jwalamalini has 12 hands. In Her right hands She is carrying: *ankusha* (goad to control repulsion), sword (to cut the negativities), arrow (to focus on the goal), mace (to destroy the ego), flame (to burn and refine everything) and shows *abhaya mudra*, gesture of granting fearlessness. In Her left hands She is holding: *pasha* (noose to control all the passions), shield (to protect from negative forces), tortoise (symbolising controlling the senses and stability), lotus flower (symbolising purity), trident (to rise above the three *gunas*) and shows *varada mudra*, gesture of granting boons.

Tortoise in one of Her left hands is a unique thing in the image of Goddess Jwalamalini. Its symbolism is closely connected to Saturn, as the avatar of Vishnu, who is connected to Shani, is Kurma avatar, the tortoise incarnation of the Lord, who appeared in such a form to stabilise the process of churning of the ocean of milk (metaphoric process of "churning" of our own consciousness). Interestingly, the energies of Shani are often considered as a natural remedy for Venus, when her energies become overly passionate – and *Chaturdashi tithi* is ruled by Venus, too. Very often we can become too irritated or impatient on *Chaturdashi tithi*, due to passionate energies of Venus being too intense. Goddess Jwalamalini, holding a tortoise in Her hand, reveals us that the way to endure all the tests and intensity She might send us on Her day is patience, introspection, tolerance and withdrawing. "One who is able to withdraw his senses from sense objects, as the tortoise draws his limbs within the shell, is to be understood as truly situated in knowledge", says Lord Krishna in *Bhagavad Gita*. This is why in the past it was often adviced to fast on *Chaturdashi tithi*, especially during *Krishna Paksha*, when its intensity is even higher – as Goddess gets even more impatient to unite with Shiva. Such a night, day before *Amavasya*, is called *Shivaratri* or "night of Shiva" – when the soul is impatient to experience the bliss of union, and when all the energies are directed towards withdrawal.

Numerology: 14

Number 14 is of great importance in Atma Kriya Yoga practice, which is very clear for all the practitioners. This is why Goddess Jwalamalini is very strongly connected with *kriya yoga* practice itself, as She is the fire, which purifies our chakras and burns down all the karma, when we do our *kriyas*. It is also said that out of 16 Divine qualities represented by Nitya Devis and *kalas* of the Moon, only 14 of them can be achieved by our own spiritual effort. The last two can be given to us only through the grace of God and the Master. This is why number 14 stands for our own personal effort on spiritual path. And this is why the 14th quality of the Moon is self-sacrifice – because only when we achieve this last Divine quality of surrender, the grace of God can enter into us and we can be completed, self-realised. Thus number 14 stands for our human effort to uplift our consciousnes. This is why there are 14 most important energy channels in our subtle body.

Number 14 is also associated in Vedic tradition with 14 Manus or protectors of mankind.

Yogini in *Kalachakra*: West

On *Chaturdashi tithi* the danger comes from the West, similarly like on *Shashti*. It is said that we should avoid travelling into that direction during the fourteenth lunar day in any of the two *pakshas*. In *Kalachakra* West direction is ruled by passionate Venus, while in *Digchakra* it is ruled by withdrawed Saturn. Venus represents for longing for union, while Saturn symbolises separation. Combination of those two create an intense longing and craving, which, when turned to any other object than the Supreme, can become pretty destructive, awakening in us too much anger, impatience and irritation. This intensity is healed by dispassionate energies of Saturn, who provides us a healthy distance and allows us to look at things more objectively. This is also why *yantra* of Goddess Jwalamalini is so similar to the *yantras* of Goddesses Nilapataka, Bherunda or Shivaduti – the "sharp" or restriction giving forms of the Divine Mother.

Shaktis of Goddess Jwalamalini

Different *shaktis* or powers of Goddess Jwalamalini dwell in the different places of Her *yantra*. All shapes within the entire *yantra*, along with their angles, are very sharp, similarly like the *yantras* of Goddesses Bherunda, Shivaduti and Nilapataka, who are more fierce and sharp in nature. This is also a clear indication, that the very nature of Goddess Jwalamalini, similarly like other three, is much more strict than other Nitya Devis.

In the *yantra* of Jwalamalini Devi *yoni* or down-facing triangle is enclosed in *shatkona*, six-pointed star, which is enclosed in *ashtakona*, eight-pointed star, furtherly enclosed by eight petals and *bhupura* surrounding the entire structure. Three *shaktis* of three corners of the inner triangle are: Iccha (willpower), Jnana (knowledge) and Kriya (action). Each of the six arms of the six-pointed star is occupied by six *shaktis* of the chakras: Dakini (*vishuddha chakra*), Rakini (*anahata chakra*), Lakini (*manipura chakra*), Kakini (*svadhishthana chakra*), Shakini (*muladhara chakra*) and Hakini (*ajna chakra*). Being so, inner triangle and six-pointed star are symbolising our three innermost powers manifested through our six chakras.

8 corners of *ashtakona*, eight-pointed figure, symbolising 8 directions of the world, are occupied by *shaktis*: Ghasmara ("devourer"), Vishwa-kabala ("the one who swallows the universes"), Lolakshi ("hungry-eyed"), Lola-jihvika ("hungry-tongued"), Sarva-bhaksha ("all-devouring"), Sahasrakshi ("thousand-eyed"), Nisariga ("companionless") and Samharti-priya ("the one, who delights in destruction"). And on eight petals of the lotus enclosing *ashtakona* dwell following *shaktis*: Achintya ("incomprehensible one"), Aprameya ("immeasurable"), Purnampa ("all-comprehending"), Durasadi ("difficult to attain"), Sarvaga ("all-pervading"), Siddhi-rupa ("personification of *siddhi* or attainment"), Pavana ("purifier") and Ekarupini ("the one with singular form").

If we look at the *shaktis* of Devi Jwalamalini, we can easily feel the intensity of this lunar Goddess and Her intensely purifying power, which cleanses a person of all karma. Her form itself and Her *shaktis* resemble a little Vishwa-rupa or Universal Form of the Lord, which Sri Krishna has revealed to Arjuna on a battlefield of Kurukshetra. Upon seeing this glorious, yet terrible to the mind and ego, form of Lord Krishna, He prayed to Him thus:

"O mighty-armed one, all the planets with their demigods are disturbed at seeing Your great form, with its many faces, eyes, arms, thighs, legs and bellies and Your many terrible teeth; and as they are disturbed, so am I. O all-pervading Viṣṇu, seeing You with Your many radiant colors touching the sky, Your gaping mouths, and Your great glowing eyes, my mind is perturbed by fear. I can no longer maintain my steadiness or equilibrium of mind. O Lord of lords, O refuge of the worlds, please be gracious to me. I cannot keep my balance seeing thus Your blazing deathlike faces and awful teeth. In all directions I am bewildered."

Similar is the intensity of presence of Goddess Jwalamalini, who appears fearful to the ego, as She burns it with Her purifying flames and thus cleanses us of all the karma caused by the identification with our thoughts, words or actions.

Swara of Goddess Jwalamalini

Au, the fourteenth *swara* or vowel of Sanskrit alphabet, is associated with Goddess Jwalamalini. Its quality or *kala* is to become like a lover. It awakens the feeling of invoking, adressing, naming or calling somebody – like a lover would call His Beloved. Goddess Jwalamalini, indeed, is the depth of the longing of the lover to reunite with his or her Beloved. Not without a reason mantra **om** or **aum** is often at the beginning of every other mantra. It helps to invoke the presence of our Beloved deity with Love, devotion and yearning for union. It reminds us both about the intimate union between our soul and its Cosmic Beloved, but at the same time emphasises strongly the small distance that is still left before union, and sometimes makes it unbearable. This is why people born on *Chaturdashi tithi*, interestingly, sometimes tend to be quite indecisive in life, especially when it comes to their spiritual path. They tend to stay for too long on this level "just before the union" or even give up on something, just when they are about to reach it. When they are just one step away from success, they sometimes tend to let go of their dream, due to their impatience. This is the shadow side of Goddess Jwalamalini. This is why path of *bhakti* or devotion, which utilises this inner longing and focuses it on Divine alone, can be the most supportive for *Chaturdashi* natives.

According to *Agni Purana* vowel **au** is connected to Maheshwara, Lord Shiva Himself, who purifies us in the fire of our spiritual practice and devotion, so we can transcend our ego and reach the Supreme.

Nakshatras connected to Goddess Jwalamalini

Punarvasu nakshatra is connected to *swara* of Goddess Jwalamalini, while Her twelve arms stand for last two *padas* of Shatabhisha nakshatra, four *padas* of Purva Bhadrapada, four *padas* of Uttara Bhadrapada nakshatra, as well as first two *padas* of Revati. Punarvasu nakshatra, in which the Sun changes its course from *Uttarayana* to *Dakshinayana*, after reaching the peak of its energies in zodiacal third eye chakra (you can read much more about this topic in my previous book, *Discovering Youniverse*), also represents the consciousness reaching the peak of its energy just before the final union with the Divine.

Last four nakshatras of the zodiac, which are connected to Goddess Jwalamalini and fourteenth lunar day as well, also symbolise last stages of consciousness and rising above the mundane vibrations. Shatabhisha nakshatra is connected to Varuna, god of Cosmic Order, who sees everything with his thousand eyes – similarly Goddess Jwalamalini exposes all the lies and make all the deep truths visible before us, like She enlightened the battlefield with Her luminous flames during a war with Bandhakasura in *Lalita Mahatmya*. Varuna is also a god of overflowing water element and never-ending passion.

Purva Bhadrapada, on the other hand, represents the fiery nature of Goddess Jwalamalini, with its intense *shakti* of spiritual elevation. In fact, Purva Bhadrapada nakshatra, ruled by Aja Ekapada or "one-footed serpent", and having a pillar of light as its symbol, symbolises *kundalini shakti* Herself, and all the intensity and purification, which comes with Her awakening. Not without a reason this nakshatra is often associated with the intensity of Lord Narasimha, who manifested himself out of a pillar. Its animal representative is a male lion, as well. Interestingly, Lord

Vishnu manifested Himself as Narasimha avatar exactly on *Chaturdashi tithi*.

Purva Bhadrapada nakshatra sometimes is also associated with "one-footed goat" instead of "one-footed serpent". The connection between goat and Purva Bhadrapada nakshatra is particularly interesting. Goat is not only an animal representing sacrifice (unfortunately these intelligent beings were sacrificied into the fire in the past), but it is also the vehicle or *vahana* of Agni, fire-god. It is also connected to the goat head of Daksha Prajapati. It is said that, when Daksha got decapitated by Lord Shiva (symbolising the death of the ego), after unfortunate event of self-immolation of Goddess Sati, he understood his mistake and he asked Shiva for forgiveness. And Lord Shiva did forgive him – and replaced his head with the head of a goat. Since then, Daksha Prajapati was called Ajamukha: "facing the eternal" or "always looking towards the one, which is unborn".

Significantly, the entire incident happened in the course of a *yajna*, fire sacrifice, the offering up of the lower self to the Supreme Self. Similarly Purva Bhadrapada nakshatra, with goat as its symbol, symbolises self-sacrifice of the ego, so it can start perceiving the eternity or spiritual unity underlying the material existence. Such is also the energy and the motivation of Goddess Jwalamalini: to "decapitate" our ego, so we can perceive the Eternal.

Uttara Bhadrapada nakshatra, ruled by Ahir Budhnya or "the snake who carries the burden of the universe", stands for the need to stabilise this intense energy and is closely connected with the tortoise in the hand of Goddess Jwalamalini, as it is the nakshatra co-ruled by Saturn. It is also connected with the need to sacrifice our ego at the end of our spiritual path, to become more humble and more selfless, like Ahir Budhnya or Ananta Shesha Himself.

Uttara Bhadrapada is also the nakshatra, in which Mercury reaches his maximum debilitation point, as logic must be abandoned on the final stage of soul's path towards union. Interestingly, on *Shukla Chaturdashi*, which was on 2 December 2017, when I was writing this chapter, my Gurudev wrote this beautiful message:

"Logic needs information about something or someone in order to function according its nature of functioning. But Love doesn't need any information about someone to happen. Logic needs certain convictions in order to enter into knowing. Love doesn't need any conviction, Love simply happens.

To know something or someone logically, one uses analysis, which is the action of a sharp knife. And yet, using logic we can only know parts, but not the whole. To know someone or something through Love, only what is needed is openness, acceptance, and inclusiveness. When we fall in love with someone, it happens even without knowing anything about the person. That is why we know that information about that person is not needed. Still, Love is happening, and due to this Love we can feel the person we love, and through Love, we get to know this person, and even more due to Love, we know the best in that person. Due to Love we can understand the worst in a person, but still we can have understanding and Love continues. That is why we say Love is unconditional. And Love creates deep intimacy, whereas logic creates distance.

Logic is a tool for survival, but Love is the way of existence. Love has its own logic, but logic stays for itself and is only that: a mental faculty."

It is quite interesting, that Goddess Jwalamalini is so closely connected with these two *rudras* or snake forms of Shiva presiding over Purva Bhadrapada and Uttara Bhadrapada nakshatras, who are directly connected to *kundalini shakti* and our *muladhara chakra*. One of Jwalamalini's names in *64 Yogini Namavali* is Nagini or "the snake lady", which directly describes Her as *kundalini* force within us. Indeed, Her energy is the most intense in *muladhara* in *Krishna paksha*, and in *ajna chakra* in *Shukla paksha*.

Revati nakshatra, which symbolises reaching final union and the ending stage of our journey through life's intricate pathways, has a particularly deep connection with Goddess Jwalamalini and *Chaturdashi tithi*, as this lunar day is co-ruled by Venus, as well as connected to the energies of Saturn in Digchakra. Revati is the nakshatra, in which Venus, the planet of union, reaches its highest exaltation point, while at the same time it is a birth star of Shani – the planet, who makes sure, we choose the right path in life. Energies of Venus and Saturn are intimately connected in Revati nakshatra and their find their final resolution and final union in this last nakshatra of the zodiac.

Tithi, *vara* and nakshatra resonance

Goddess Jwalamalini resonates the best with grounding energies of Saturday, connected to Saturn. Whenever *Chaturdashi tithi* occurs on Saturday, it is powerful *siddha yoga*, "combination of accomplishments". If additionally, the Moon dwells on such a day in Rohini, Swati, Vishakha, Anuradha, Dhanishta or Shatabhisha nakshatra, it is all the more powerful. *Chaturdashi tithi* also has a good resonance with Thursdays, ruled by another Cosmic Teacher (Jupiter), and when it happens on Thursday and Ashwini, Punarvasu, Pushya, Magha, Swati, Purvashadha, Purva Bhadrapada or Revati it forms another *siddha yoga*.

The energies of *Chaturdashi tithi* and Goddess Jwalamalini become very dangerous only, when it happens on Sunday and in Bharani, Margashirsha, Ashlesha, Vishakha, Anuradha, Jyeshtha or Dhanishta nakshatra, as it forms then *vinasha yoga* or "combination of destruction". Fiery energies of the Sun, combined with fiery energies of Goddess Jwalamalini, as well as any of those intense nakshatras, can lead to some destructive manifestation of Jwalamalini's transformative energies.

YOGAS FORMED WITH CHATURDASHI TITHI

	1	2	3	4	5	6	7
1					**siddha**		siddha
2	vinasha	affliction	affliction	affliction	amrita / affliction	affliction	siddha / affliction
3					amrita		siddha
4					amrita		**siddha**
5	vinasha				amrita		siddha
6					amrita		siddha
7					**siddha**		siddha
8					**siddha**		siddha
9	vinasha				amrita		siddha
10					**siddha**		siddha
11					amrita		siddha
12					amrita		siddha
13					amrita		siddha
14					amrita		siddha
15					**siddha**		**siddha**
16	vinasha				amrita		**siddha**
17	vinasha				amrita		**siddha**
18	vinasha				amrita		siddha
19					amrita		siddha
20					**siddha**		siddha
21					amrita		siddha
22					amrita		siddha
23	vinasha				amrita		**siddha**
24					amrita		**siddha**
25					**siddha**		siddha
26					amrita		siddha
27					**siddha**		siddha

According to *Agni Purana*, combination of *Chaturdashi tithi* and Bharani nakshatra, the star of self-sacrifice, is bringing affliction, as well. As *Chaturdashi tithi* is ruled by liberating (*moksha*) element of water and the *shakti* of fiery Bharani nakshatra, the star of God of Death, is the power to "let go" or "let the water takes away", too intense combination of water and fire element mixing together both on this lunar day and Bharani nakshatra, can produce some aggressive, transformative energies or even lead to violence or actual death.

Also, if a person is born on *Chaturdashi tithi* and Monday or Friday, it produces a *tithi dosha* for the person. The personality of such person will be overly dominated by water element, which will lead too very turbulent emotional life. If such a person is additionally born on any of the watery nakshatras (Ardra, Ashlesha, Mula, Purvashadha, Shatabhisha, Uttara Bhadrapada, Revati) this *dosha* will be more severe and such a person will need to consciously work on balancing exeggerated water element, both in one's physical body and on a psychological level.

In Vedic month called Phalguna (in the end of which Full Moon falls in Purva Phalguni nakshatra) *Chaturdashi tithi* is considered *shunya* and is avoided for any auspicious activities. In Phalguna month *Chaturdashi tithi* often occurs in Magha nakshatra (in *Shukla paksha*) and Shravana nakshatra (in *Krishna paksha*. It doesn't cause, though, *shunya dosha* to any of the nakshatras, similarly like *Chaturti* and *Dashami*.

Important *rashis* for *Chaturdashi tithi* natives

Each *tithi* has a special connection with a number of *rashis*. Understanding those connections can help us not only in understanding our own birth chart on a much deeper level, but in better understanding of the nature of the *tithi* itself.

Two *rashis*, which are of great importance for all *Chaturdashi tithi* natives are two fixed signs: Taurus and Scorpio. Sign of Taurus is ruled by the planetary lord of this lunar day (Venus, *tithi pati kshetra*), while Scorpio is the sign opposite to it (*tithi pati kshetra paksha*), which is the sign revealing, where are we heading in life. It is also a very important axis, as in those signs Moon (who is said to be born on *Chaturdashi tithi*) gets exaltated or debilitated. *Chaturdashi tithi* natives often experience many transformations in life, which is why feeling of stability and their comfort zone are extremely important for them. They can be a bit stingy, if you "invade" their personal bubble – even if they tend to do it themselves quite often, when it comes to others.

They can be also greatly protective about their loved ones. When they love somebody, they love whole-heartedly. Their love and self-sacrifice knows no limits. This is why, unfortunately, sometimes their love may be also abused by others. They tend to attract abusive relationships and it is extremely hard for them to let go of any such a relationship, even if it is destructive for them – as they are forming extremely strong emotional attachments with their loved ones. Due to that, whenever they experience a heartbreak, it is very difficult for them and they can hold within themselves all the resentment and bitterness connected to that for years. They need to consciously work on expanding their heart a little bit more and being a little bit more forgiving (not only for others, but above all, for themselves) and releasing all the negative emotions from the past. Sometimes they tend to hang on the past for way too long – even if it happens just on subconscious level, it still affects them greatly and can sabotage their happiness in the present moment.

Tithi Shunya Rashi		Tithi Pati Kshetra	Tithi Shunya Rashi
		Caturdashi	
Tithi Shunya Rashi	Tithi Pati Kshetra Paksha		Tithi Shunya Rashi

Additionally, in *Shukla paksha* sign of Cancer becomes more energised on *Chaturdashi tithi* (which reveals more protective and emotional side of *Shukla Chaturdashi* natives), while in *Krishna paksha* Capricorn becomes more energised (which reveals more strong and enduring side of people born on *Krishna Chaturdashi*). On this very axis Jupiter and Mars get exalted or debilitated, as well. People born in *Shukla Chaturdashi* will naturally reflect more qualities of exalted Jupiter or debilitated Mars (philosophical nature, but also procrastination, when it comes to taking the final step to the next level in life), while people born in *Krishna Chaturdashi* will naturally reflect more qualities of exalted Mars and debilitated Jupiter (proactive and enduring nature, but may sometimes find problems with full dedication to spiritual path or higher principles, due to certain material attachments).

Tithi shunya rashis or the signs, which are made "fruitless" by *Chaturdashi tithi*, are all dual signs: Gemini, Virgo (both ruled by Mercury), Sagittarius and Pisces (both ruled by Jupiter). All four of these signs are naturally quite vulnerable for all people born on *Chaturdashi tithi*, as all four of them are connected to all the transformations and all the duality, which we are experiencing in life. Intensely transformative energy of *Chaturdashi tithi* additionaly agitates the energy of those signs and may sometimes make them manifest their shadow qualities instead of their blessings.

Unless these signs are occupied by Rahu or Ketu, or unless their planetary lords (Mercury or Jupiter) are placed 3rd, 6th, 8th or 12th house from ascendant or Moon, or are retrograde, or in conjuction with malefic planet, or, lastly, in nakshatras of Rahu or Ketu, these two signs and houses won't bring good results for the native. In such a case these signs must be strengthened (by strengthening their lords) to bring good results. *Shunya* planets do produce good results, however, when they transit 3rd, 6th, 8th or 12th house from from ascendant or Moon.

Chaturdashi tithi natives may also face some troubles and obstacles from Ketu, who adds to the fire of already burning fourteenth lunar day. This is why *Chaturdashi* natives may sometimes find it difficult to stay detached from a situation or to severe some unhealthy emotionally ties in their lives – but at the same time sacrificing this, what must be sacrificed, is their biggest life lesson. Similarly, people with Ketu very prominent in their chart and personality, won't resonate well neither with *Chaturdashi tithi*, neither with *Chaturdashi tithi* natives.

Sadhana for Goddess Jwalamalini

Goddess Jwalamalini is pleased with fasting and any sort of spiritual meditation or *sadhana*. She is also the Goddess who blessess all *kriya yoga* practitioners. She is pleased by fire rituals and the light of oil lamps, as well. But She is the most pleased, whenever She sees our sincerity and truthfulness, as well as patience, humility and ability to sacrifice ourselves for the higher purpose. *Tantraraja* additionally says that by drinking water, into which the presence of Goddess Jwalamalini is invoked (by holding a pot with water and chanting Her mantra or by placing the water over night on Her *yantra*, especially on *Chaturdashi tithi*), the digestive fire is increased in our body.

To connect with Goddess Jwalamalini on a deeper level, you can either do a meditation of sitting on Her lap, as given by my Gurudev (described in Chapter 24), or colour Her yantra and meditate on it, facing West. Sitting on the lap of Goddess Jwalamalini is a particularly powerful meditation, as Her intense fiery energies are not so easy to handle. For your *sadhana* you can use one of the two mantras below or one of the affirmations. There are couple of more advanced mantras for worship of Goddess Jwalamalini in *Tantraraja*, but they are not supposed to be recited without a guidance of a Guru.

Mantras:

oṁ aiṁ hriṁ śriṁ auṁ jvalamaliniyai namaḥ
oṁ aiṁ hriṁ śriṁ auṁ angadayai namaḥ

Affirmations:

I allow myself to embrace all the difficulties.
I allow myself to be patient.
I allow myself to be tolerant.
I surrender to Love.
I am letting go of all the bitterness and resentment from the past.

Questions for self-analysis

Every lunar day is an opportunity to learn something new about ourselves. Nitya Devis and their wisdom can become our guides on this sacred journey. Questions below can help you in recognising certain "shadow" tendencies in yourself, which may arise on *Chaturdashi tithi*. If you were born on this lunar day, these questions might be of big importance for you in life and allow you to face your weaknesses.

- Do I welcome transformation in my life or do I resist it?
- Am I allowing the Divine to purify me?
- Am I ready to surrender my ego to let my soul shine?
- Is "being right" more important to me than Love?
- What stops me from achieving real fullness in life?
- Do I allow myself to be patient and tolerant?
- Do I honor and respect other people's boundaries?
- Do I show understanding for other people's emotions?
- Is my ego burning some of my relationships?
- Am I ready to make some sacrifices in my life for the higher purpose?
- Am I sacrificing too much?
- Do I hang on too much of bitterness and resentment from the past?
- Do I follow some destructive pathway only because I am too scared to let go of some of my attachments?
- Am I too attached to things, which are not serving me anymore?
- Am I ready to move forward in life?
- What stops me from making a final step to the next level?
- What stops me from manifesting the fullness of my potential?

Yantra of Goddess Jwalamalini

CHAPTER 22

CITRA – COLORFUL GODDESS
PURNIMA / AMAVASYA – FIFTEENTH LUNAR DAY

oṁ pūrṇam adaḥ pūrṇam idaṁ pūrṇāt pūrṇam udacyate
pūrṇasya pūrṇam ādāya pūrṇam evāvaśiṣyate

*"Om. This is fullness and that is fullness. Fullness comes forth from the fullness. Take
fullness away from the fullness, and only fullness shall remain."*

- Isha Upanishad

Kala	Element	Planet	Guna	Yogini	Vowel
purna (fullness)	air	Saturn / Rahu	sattwa	Northwest / Northeast	aṁ / aḥ

Stage of consciousness	Divine quality	Deity (Muhurta Cintamani)	Deity (Varahamihira)	Nakshatra connection	Form of Shiva
deep sleep (turiya)	sarvajnata (omniscience)	Chandra / Pitris	Vishwadevas / Pitris	Revati	Kankalamurti

Shukla Paksha

Nadi: ida
Chakra: sahasrara
Interval: perfect octave
Deity (Narada Purana): Nagas
House from the Sun: 6. 7 or 8

Krishna Paksha

Nadi: pingala
Chakra: below muladhara
Interval: unison
Deity (Narada Purana): Pitris
House from the Sun: 12. 1 or 2

Citra means "bright, wonderful, splendid, shining, colourful, variegated, speckled, excellent" or "picture". On Full Moon, fifteenth lunar day, the blessings of all the previous Nitya Devis combine, and send their auspicious rays of many qualities in all directions, shining in their full splendour. The nature of this lunar day is *saumya* or "gentle", "beneficial". As during Full Moon all the energy in our subtle body accumulates in *sahasrara chakra*, which is a multifarious thousand-petalled lotus on the top of our head, representing the seat of the Divine itself, where all the colours are present like a spiritual rainbow, so the energy of Citra Devi during Full Moon is colourful, multifarious, full and complete - like a rainbow. On New Moon, on the other hand, when all *kalas* of the Moon symbolically "die" and reunite with the Supreme to give birth to a new beginning, our energy accumulates even below *muladhara chakra*, in the seat of *kundalini shakti*. Perhaps this is why this lunar day is also associated to *nagas* or Divine serpents, according to *Narada Purana*.

Goddess Citra represents the final stage of the journey of the Goddess: reaching the fullness or return to nothingness; complete light or complete darkness; unison or perfect octave – which are, in their essence, identical. The bright light of the Full Moon symbolises the highest octave of any colour; while the darkness of the New Moon symbolises all colours merged back together into the primordial darkness. The brightest shade of any colour is white. The darkest shade of any colour is black. Similarly, on Full Moon and New Moon day everything unites and dissolves, so something new may be born.

Goddess Citra teaches us, that all the colours of life, all the rays of light, and all the shadows of darkness, in their very essence, are the manifestation of the same omnipresent Divine force, which gives birth to everything, sustains everything and, ultimately, absorbs everything within Itself. In the fullness of Citra Devi or in Her complete darkness, there is a space for everything and everybody; for every feeling, every experience, every mood and every energy. As Goddess Tripurasundari during the Full Moon, She embraces everything with Love and spreads Her light and blessings to all, equally. As Mother Kali during the New Moon, She absorbs everything, cleanses all the impurities and reveals the depth of Her compassion, which embraces and absorbs everything within its darkness. She doesn't discern between pure and impure, because all is Hers.

On Full Moon and on New Moon day the Goddess becomes complete – hence the *kala* of the Moon connected to Her is *purna* or completion. *Yogini* connected to Her is Amrita-karshini, "the one, attracting all nectar" or satisfaction, as all the "drops of nectar" or *kalas* of the Moon unite together to spread their light during the Full Moon – similarly like all of them are collected back to their source during the New Moon. Syllable of Sri Vidya mantra connected to Her is *hrim*, the *bij mantra* of transformation – similarly like for *Panchami tithi*. And similarly like in case of *Panchami* and *Dashami*, previous *Purna tithis* governed by air element, so in case of *Purnima* or *Amavasya* there might be also some quality of indecissiveness very prominent in the personality of the person born on any of these lunar days - especially Full Moon. The shadow side of the *kala* of fullness is lack of motivation to go out of this fullness, this symbolic comfort zone, and realise something in the world. This is why neither Full Moon nor New Moon support us in any material activities – they are supportive only for spiritual practices.

After meditating with Goddess Citra both on Full Moon and New Moon, it is hard to say, which one of them is more beautiful. She is beautiful in Her fullness, and She is beautiful in Her union with Shiva. None of Her faces is more beautiful than the other. Perhaps this is why in the form of the Moon She undergoes constant transformations, to spread the fullness of Her beauty and make us appreciate the depth of this Divine game; wondrous beauty of world's duality.

My Gurudev wrote so beautifully on Full Moon in Rohini nakshatra, 3 December 2017, when I was writing this chapter:

"Freedom is liberation and dependence is attachment. For the soul, there should be no attachment of any type, as it will bring one to the bottomless pit. Let go of everything, which keeps one away from attaining the ultimate reality of the Self.

Cut off connection from those things which one experiences with annoyance. Let go of all differences in your mind. Rise above the duality of the mind, the likes and dislikes. Let all become equal. Have no prescriptions or expectations in your mind and heart. Treat all the same way you are treating Guru and God. Have only the desire of attaining the Grace of Giridhari. When it seems difficult, don't let go, as the soul doesn't do anything. Only wait for the Divine to offer His Love and Grace."

This truth is beautifully reflected in the form of Shiva associated with this lunar day: Kankalamurti or the one who carries a corpse. In the form of Kankalamurti Shiva carries a corpse on his trident to remind us that sooner or later everything perishes and dissolves – the true fullness can be found only in the depth of one's own soul. Shiva in this form reminds us not to get attached to anything external, as all, sooner or later, turns into bones and ashes.

Interestingly enough, according to some scriptures, *Purnima* is a birth *tithi* of Rahu, while *Amavasya* is a birth *tithi* of Ketu. Only on one of these two *tithis* solar and lunar eclipses can happen, which are directly caused by the positions of Rahu and Ketu. Rahu and Ketu are both strongly connected to our subconsciousness and its polarities: extreme passion (Rahu, obssesion) and extreme repulsion (Ketu, complete detachment). Light and shadow; *persona* and shadow self. No wonder that fifteenth lunar day is connected to deep sleep state of consciousness within *turiya* or spiritual awakening. During each Full Moon and each New Moon we have a much deeper connection with our subconsciousness and all its powers, including its unlimitied knowledge. After all, subconsciousness is this part of ourselves, which is always connected to collective consciousness, as well as all the akashic records, and can easily access any information. Perhaps this is why fifteenth Divine quality of Lord Krishna is *sarvajnata* or "omniscience". Similarly, people born on *Purnima* or *Amavasya* like to be "omniscient" or to know everything. They are interested literally in everything and they are usually very open-minded and curious in nature.

Additionally, whenever Full Moon or New Moon occur in close proximity to Rahu and/or Ketu, we experience partial or full eclipses, which is the time during which our connection both to higher spiritual realms (superconsciousness), as well as our lower subconsciousness, with its infinite possibilities, is much deeper. This might be one of the reasons why *Amavasya* or New Moon is sacred to Pitris or ancestors – as they bless us with the power to see, what is beyond this world. This power can be however either constructive or destructive, depending on whether we will connect on those days to lower ghosts or Supreme Spirit. This is why it is said that one should watch one's thoughts on New Moon and Full Moon days, as they have the power to materialise themselves in our lives. My Gurudev said that especially during *Purnima*, which magnifies everything, we should watch our thoughts and focus only on what we truly desire – as these desires will be fulfilled. This is why Full Moon is so auspicious for all sort of spiritual practices.

Meditation with Goddess Citra

Hue: lustrous like the rays of rising sun
Number of heads: 1
Number of eyes: 3
Number of hands: 2
Right hands: *ankusha* (or *abhaya mudra*)
Left hands: *pasha* (or *varada mudra*)
Garments: variegated colour
Ornaments: *navaratna*, nine precious jewels

Goddess Citra is completely full in Her simple form. She doesn't need anymore any additional weapons to overcome obstacles, as She represents the achievement itself. She is full, complete and contented. Her hue is lustrous like the rising sun, revealing Her shining confidence, and Her garments are of variegated color, which reveals Her variegated nature. A pure smile illumines her face. She is all-bliss (Sarvananda-mayi) and ever-existent (Nitya) and she grants all desires. The only thing that She has for us are Her blessings. This is why some tantric scriptures describe Her as having only two hands, showing *abhaya mudra* (granting fearlessnes) and *varada mudra* (granting boons), while other scriptures say that She rather holds in those two hands *pasha* (noose for controlling passions) and *ankusha* (goad for controlling repulsion). (There are also scriptures, which depict Her with four hands; but that would be inconsistency, if we consider that all the arms of all Nitya Devis should add up to 108 in total.)

Her *yantra* itself represents the fullness of all Divine energies. With *navayoni* or mystical "nine wombs" of Sri Yantra in the center, enclosed in eight lotus petals, sixteen lotus petals and 32 lotus petals, the *yantra* of Goddess Citra represents full manifestation of Divine principles and Her creative powers. The names of the *shaktis* presiding over different parts of Her *yantra* are unfortunately unknown.

Numerology: 15

Number 15 is associated with fifteenth lunar day, which corresponds directly to the number of the *tithis* or lunar days in one fortnight (*paksha*) and fifteen Nitya Devis or powers of time. Fifteen is the number of three *gunas* or modes of nature multiplied by the number of five elements – and being so it represents the fullness of fifteen different types of energies present in the entire Creation. Everything that exists can be classified into one of those fifteen qualities or *kalas* – as everything has one of the *gunas* predominant and one of the *tattwas* predominant within itself.

Yogini in Kalachakra: Northwest / Northeast

On *Purnima* the danger comes from the Northwest, while on *Amavasya* it comes from Northeast. It is said that we should avoid travelling into those directions during these times. In Vastu science Northwest is connected with element of air, while fifteenth lunar day represents the most *sattwic* manifestation of air element. This can, indeed, make our mind a bit ungrounded, due to too strong element of air agitated and increasing fast exchange of energy on that day. Northwest is also ruled by the Moon in Vastu. This is why there is always highest mental activity happening in our mind on Full Moon days, as the water element within our body is the most agitated. Agitated water element with agitated air element may cause some people problems with falling asleep on Full Moon days, or even lack of appetite or digestive issues. This is affecting especially people born on watery (*Rikta*) or airy (*Purna*) tithis, as well as people with very sensitive Moon in a birth chart. Some scientific form of meditation, such as Atma Kriya Yoga or *hatha yoga* practice is very helpful and grounding for them on Full Moon days (and around Full Moon).

Purnima can also cause some skin issues for people born on this lunar day, due to exaggerated energies of Saturn on this *tithi*. This is one other beautiful reason, why people born on *Purnima* are advised to pray to Supreme Goddess, Lalita Tripurasundari – as she is said to be the "skin" of Narayana. She is also Mahavidya connected to planet Mercury. Prayers to Divine Mother in this form can be greatly helpful in overcoming all skin issues.

Northeast, on the other hand, is connected to water element in Vastu. On *Amavasya* or New Moon, the "danger" comes from that direction. Indeed, on New Moon day water element is "at its lowest" in our physical body. We may feel naturally more tired and need more rest and hydration on New Moon days. We may also feel psychologically a bit gloomy or irrititated on *Amavasya*, depending on our own mental constitution. People, who are unfamiliar with withdrawn energies of the New Moon, if they are already suffering from depression, will often feel even worse on this day. In fact, it is scientifically proven that biggest number of suicides happens exactly on New Moon.

Amavasya is a symbolic death of the Moon, his own *moksha* – which is also connected to liberating energies of Northeast direction in Vastu. And, similarly, like Northeast is the best place to do your meditation according to Vastu Shastra, so *Amavasya* night is also one of the best times to do meditation. The "danger", which comes from that direction on New Moon day is the danger of "losing the ground beneath our feet", becoming ungrounded and too much in the head or too "flying" – and too lazy to take action in the real world, as a result of that. This is a quality of *Amavasya tithi* natives, which they need to learn, how to balance. They often tend to be too withdrawn from the world, like the Moon himself is withdrawing on New Moon night to recharge others.

Interestingly, due to this withdrawal of the Moon on *Amavasya* night, it is said that this is the best time to collect all the healing herbs. There is a very profound reason for that, which we can find explained in the *Brahmanas*:

"Know that *soma*, the food of the gods, is none other than the Moon. When he is not seen that night neither in the East nor West, then he visits this world. And here he enters into the waters and the plants. And since during that night he dwells (*vasati*) here at home (*ama*), that is called *Amavasya*, the New Moon."

Interestingly, according to Vastu Shastra, Northeast of our home is also the best direction to store all healing herbs and medicines, as vital energies of Northeast are said to preserve and improve their healing powers.

Swara of Goddess Citra

Aṁ, the fifteenth "added" *swara* or vowel of Sanskrit alphabet, is associated with Goddess Citra. Its *kala* or quality is a flame. It is a creative spark, which awakens the feeling of new beginning and creation. According to *Agni Purana* it is also connected to Kamadeva or Vedic god of romantic love, as well as god of spring season, which stands for a new beginnings in nature.

Also, according to *Bhuta Damara Tantra*, vowel **aṁ** represents the removal of sorrow (*dukhahāra* and helps to achieve our desires. This differentiates *swara i* (vowel of third lunar day) from **aṁ**, even though both are given the same deity, Kamadeva. *Swara* **aṁ** also represents material benefit or gains.

Sometimes sixteenth vowel **aḥ** is also associated with fifteenth lunar day, especially with *Amavasya*. Differently from *swara* **aṁ**, **aḥ** represents the energy of *moksha* or final release – liberation. *Agni Purana* says that *swara* **aḥ** represents "all that is praiseworthy".

Nakshatras connected to Goddess Citra

Revati nakshatra is connected to *swaras* of Goddess Citra, while Her two arms stand for last two *padas* of Revati nakshatra, as well. Similarly like Revati nakshatra itself, Goddess Citra is all about reaching the final goal: the fullness of Her powers during the Full Moon or the union with Her Beloved on New Moon. It is the last stage and the final destination of Her path, where She finds full completion, *samadhi*. No wonder that Venus, another planet connected to water element, is exalted in Revati nakshatra. Whenever Venus is exalted, it manifests the fullness of Divine Love.

Interestingly, fifteenth lunar day is co-ruled by Saturn in Vedic astrology – although some traditions say that only *Purnima* is ruled by Saturn, while *Amavasya* is ruled by Rahu. Revati nakshatra is also said to be a birth nakshatra of Saturn in *Vayu Purana*. And no wonder: it is Shani, who actually takes care, that we are persistent on our path, and who brings us back to the right path, whenever we go astray, so we can reach our goal. No other planet cares for us and our development as much as Shani does, and no other planet "pushes" us forward with such a dedication. He also shows us the "limits" of the fullness that we can achieve.

Tithi, *vara* and nakshatra resonance

Goddess Citra doesn't really have friends or enemies. Her light shines on everyone, and Her darkness embraces everyone. Therefore there are very few auspicious or inauspicious *yogas* connected with Full Moon or New Moon.

Traditionally it is said that fifteenth lunar day in any of its two forms resonates the best with energies of Thursday, when it forms *siddha yoga* ("combination of accomplishments") or Saturday, when it forms *amrita yoga* ("immortal combination") – as fifteenth lunar day is also co-ruled by Shani. However, combination of Saturday and Full Moon dwelling in Magha nakshatra is said to be fatal according to *Agni Purana*.

Besides that, *Purnima* becomes inauspicious also when it falls on Tuesday and one of the following nakshatras: Ardra, Punarvasu, Jyeshtha, Purvashadha, Uttarashadha, Shravana, Dhanishta or Shatabhisha. It is said that *vinasha yoga* or "combination of destruction" is formed in such a case.

In Vedic month called Shravana, in the end of which Full Moon falls in Shravana nakshatra, *Purnima tithi* becomes *shunya*. Shravana in itself is very emotional and sensitive nakshatra, and when Full Moon additionally is happening there, it additionally agitates the emotional side of this lunar day. This is why this one specific Full Moon in Vedic month can cause the biggest amount of emotional turbulences and confusion. If, additionally, this is happening on Monday, which agitates the lunar energies even more, it causes a dangerous *vinasha yoga* or "combination of destruction".

Purnima or *Amavasya tithis* do not cause, however, *shunya dosha* to any of the nakshatras, similarly like *Chaturti*, *Dashami* and *Chaturdashi*.

YOGAS FORMED WITH PURNIMA

	1	2	3	4	5	6	7
1					siddha		amrita
2					siddha		amrita
3					siddha		amrita
4					siddha		amrita
5					siddha		amrita
6		vinasha			siddha		amrita
7		vinasha			siddha		amrita
8					siddha		amrita
9					siddha		amrita
10					siddha		affliction
11					siddha		amrita
12					siddha		amrita
13					siddha		amrita
14					siddha		amrita
15					siddha		amrita
16					siddha		amrita
17					siddha		amrita
18		vinasha			siddha		amrita
19					siddha		amrita
20		vinasha			siddha		amrita
21		vinasha			siddha		amrita
22		vinasha			siddha		amrita
23		vinasha			siddha		amrita
24		vinasha			siddha		amrita
25					siddha		amrita
26					siddha		amrita
27					siddha		amrita

YOGAS FORMED WITH AMAVASYA

	1	2	3	4	5	6	7
1					siddha		amrita
2					siddha		amrita
3					siddha		amrita
4					siddha		amrita
5					siddha		amrita
6					siddha		amrita
7					siddha		amrita
8					siddha		amrita
9					siddha		amrita
10					siddha		amrita
11					siddha		amrita
12					siddha		amrita
13					siddha		amrita
14					siddha		amrita
15					siddha		amrita
16					siddha		amrita
17					siddha		amrita
18					siddha		amrita
19					siddha		amrita
20					siddha		amrita
21					siddha		amrita
22					siddha		amrita
23					siddha		amrita
24					siddha		amrita
25					siddha		amrita
26					siddha		amrita
27					siddha		amrita

Important rashis for *Purnima* natives

Each *tithi* has a special connection with a number of *rashis*. Understanding those connections can help us not only in understanding our own birth chart on a much deeper level, but in better understanding of the nature of the *tithi* itself. In case of fifteenth lunar day, however, different *rashis* will be important for *Purnima* and different *rashis* will be important for *Amavasya*. Interestingly, the only signs connected to *Purnima* or *Amavasya* will be *rashis* connected either to zodiacal *muladhara chakra* or zodiacal *ajna chakra*. Another interesting thing is that there are no *shunya rashis* for *Purnima* or *Amavasya* – as these lunar days do not make anything "empty". They make everything full.

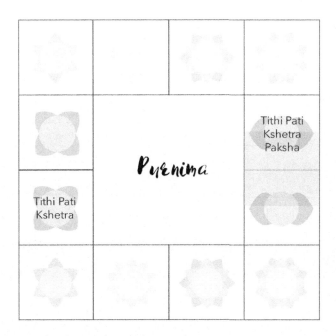

Two *rashis*, which are of great importance for all *Purnima* natives are two movable signs: Cancer and Capricorn. Sign of Capricorn is ruled by the planetary lord of this lunar day (Saturn, *tithi pati kshetra*), while Cancer is the sign opposite to it (*tithi pati kshetra paksha*), which is the sign revealing, where are we heading in life. It is the pathway from zodiacal *muladhara chakra* to zodiacal *ajna chakra* – from the start of *uttarayana* to the beginning of *dakshinayana*, which reveals rising, uplifting and graceful energy of this lunar day. As the process of spiritual growth, however, requires lots of inner transformation, so *Purnima* natives often go through many ups and downs in life, due to water element being so prominent and agitated in their astral body. This is why they usually look mostly for comfort and peace of mind, symbolised by sign of Cancer. The exact house, which becomes sign of Cancer, will additionally reveal, where are they going to seek this peace of mind.

Purnima natives usually have a natural interest in philosophy or spirituality, as well, as Cancer is the sign, in which Jupiter gets exalted. However, they also tend to procrastinate a lot or be a little bit indecisive or insecure in life, as Cancer is also the sign, in which Mars gets debilitated.

Additionally, the space between two signs of Cancer and Leo, right in the middle of zodiacal *ajna chakra* becomes more energised on *Purnima*. The spiritual energy is at its peak on this lunar day – which can either make us feel closer to the Divine, or make us feel more nervous, depending on the state of our mind. This is why my Gurudev, Paramahamsa Vishwananda, highly advised to do OM Chanting (a specific group meditation practice, as practised by ancient *rishis*) on Full Moon days. He said:

"As the Full Moon reacts on the water element, it reacts on the body and the mind. OM Chanting imprints the cosmic sound of OM, making each cell of your body vibrate this cosmic sound. So automatically, in place of going crazy, you feel good! You feel calm, in a meditative mood."

Important rashis for *Amavasya* natives

Two *rashis*, which are of great importance for all *Amavasya* natives, on the other hand, are two fixed signs: Leo and Aquarius. Sign of Aquarius is co-ruled by the planetary lord of this lunar day (Rahu, *tithi pati kshetra*), while Leo is the sign opposite to it (*tithi pati kshetra paksha*), which is the sign revealing, where are we heading in life. As this is a much more materialistic and grounded axis, it also reveals a bit more materialistic side of *Amavasya* natives. As they are born on the day, when Moon is not visible at all, they always have this inner need to step forward and shine their light – to make people actually *see* them. This is why they might often either be leaders or have aspiration to become leaders, which is revealed by sign of Leo being *tithi pati kshetra paksha*.

Additionally, the space between two signs of Capricorn and Aquarius, right in the middle of zodiacal *muladhara chakra* becomes more energised on *Amavasya*. In this exact portion of this two signs dwells Dhanishta nakshatra, the star of ambition. Similarly, people born on *Amavasya* often have many ambitions. Other planetary placements will reveal, whether these ambitions will be of material or spiritual nature.

Sadhana for Goddess Citra

Goddess Citra is mostly pleased with our meditation and fasting. To connect with Goddess Citra on a deeper level, you can either do a meditation of sitting on Her lap, as given by my Gurudev (described in Chapter 24), or colour Her *yantra* and meditate on it, facing Northwest on *Purnima* or Northeast on *Amavasya*. Colouring Sri Yantra, which represents Goddess Tripurasundari Herself and the totality of all Her energies and all Nitya Devis is also extremely auspicious on Full Moon day – when all their energies are shining together. For your *sadhana* you can use one of the two mantras below or one of the affirmations. There are couple of more advanced mantras for worship of Goddess Citra in *Tantraraja*, but they are not supposed to be recited without a guidance of a Guru.

Mantras:

oṁ aiṁ hriṁ śriṁ aṁ citrayai namaḥ
oṁ aiṁ hriṁ śriṁ aṁ purnayai namaḥ

Affirmations:

I allow myself to be full.
I accept the fullness of myself.
I allow myself to see the fullness in all creation.
I allow myself to reach beyond the comfort zone.

Questions for self-analysis

Every lunar day is an opportunity to learn something new about ourselves. Nitya Devis and their wisdom can become our guides on this sacred journey. Questions below can help you in recognising certain "shadow" tendencies in yourself, which may arise on *Purnima* or *Amavasya*. If you were born on this lunar day, these questions might be of big importance for you in life and allow you to face your weaknesses.

- Do I notice the Divine fullness present in every life experience?
- What stops me from manifesting the fullness of my potential?
- Which new ideas would I like to give birth to?
- Am I too focused on myself?
- Am I going too much into any of the extremes?
- Do I control my emotions in a healthy way?
- Can I allow myself to go out of my comfort zone?
- What my potential and my limitations can teach me?
- Where do I really want to go in life?
- What can lead me towards more blissful life?

Yantra of Goddess Citra

CHAPTER 23

YOUR CHART FROM PERSPECTIVE OF TITHIS

Now, when you already got in touch with different lunar phases and their sacred energies, you might be curious, how to apply this knowledge, while reading a chart. There are many ways and methods, how you can approach this topic – some of them easier, and some of them more complex. In this book I will focus mostly on the easiest ways of applying the knowledge about the *tithis*, which I also found to be the most practical in my Vedic astrology practice.

Tithi dosha

Before I read any chart, I usually check if there is any *tithi dosha* in a chart. *Tithi dosha* is produced by unfortunate combination of *tithi*, *vara* and nakshatra. The most common *tithi dosha* is *tattwa dosha*, which is produced when the element of *tithi* and weekday is the same. If, additionally, the element of nakshatra would be the same, this *dosha* or "flaw" will be more severe. *Tithi doshas* are, however, affecting mostly *Jaya* (ether) and *Rikta* (water) *tithi* natives, as during *Nanda* (fire), *Bhadra* (earth) and *Purna* (air) *tithis* some auspicious *yogas* (such as *siddha* or *amrita*) are overriding the negative effect of *tattwa dosha*.

Tithi dosha can be also produced, whenever there is any other inauspicious combination of *tithi*, nakshatra and weekday. Always check the resonance between *tithi*, nakshatra and weekday before reading a chart, as this will affect the person's life greatly. The relationship between the nakshatra lord, *vara* lord and *tithi* lord in a birth chart will reveal additional details about person's life.

Grahana yoga

It is also said that certain planets will naturally cause some problems for natives of certain lunar days. This is called *grahana yoga*, as the *tithi* is eclipsing in a way a positive aspect of this planet. *Saptami tithi* natives may experience certain problems from Rahu (foreign and chaotic energies), *Ashtami tithi* natives may experience certain problems from Jupiter (spiritual authorities, wealth, children, husband, etc.), *Navami tithi* natives may experience certain problems from Mercury (community and communication), *Dashami tithi* natives may experience certain issues from Sun (authorities, confidence, etc.), *Ekadashi tithi* natives may experience certain problems from Mars (stress, fights, anger, nervousness, etc.), *Dvadashi tithi* natives may experience certain problems from the Moon (people around us, mother, etc.), *Chaturdashi tithi* natives may experience certain problems from Ketu (foreign energies, impulsiveness, spirituality, etc.), *Purnima* natives may experience certain problems from Venus (women, wife, love life, etc.) and *Amavasya* natives may experience certain problems from Saturn (older people, ancestors, diseases, etc.). To know more details about how these "problems" are going to manifest, you need to see the exact position of "problematic" planet in the chart of the person and exact role of this planet in a chart. Often it might be quite revealing.

Tithi rashi

Tithi rashi is a very important sign in any chart. The state of this sign will reflect the state of water element in our body, as well as will reveal, from which source are we deriving our peace of mind - and how big is this "water body". Is it just a lake, or the entire ocean? Or maybe it is completely dry? Dry or hot planets, such as Sun, Mars, Ketu or Saturn, won't be very welcome in *tithi rashi*, neither their aspects. Nourishing planets such as Moon, Venus or Jupiter would be excellent. Also, depending, whether it is fixed, dual or movable sign, it will reveal how is, really, our peace of mind and from where do we derive it. Lastly, we would also check the element of this sign, its watery potential, placement of this sign's lord, as well as its position from ascendant and from the Moon. By knowing *tithi rashi* and its state, you will clearly know, which exact qualities of exact Nitya Devis will be the most present in the native.

Determining *tithi rashi* is quite easy, if you have accurate time of birth of the person. If you don't have accurate time, then *tithi rashi* can be even helpful in birth chart rectification in some cases.

To know your *tithi rashi*, you need to know, on which exact degree of your chart, has your *tithi* started. Each *tithi* is 12 degrees long. Now, the only thing you need to calculate is, on which degree of these twelve does your Moon dwell. If it is first degree, then *tithi rashi* would be Aries. If it is second degree, then it will be Taurus. If it is third degree, then Gemini. In this way each of 12 degrees of each *tithi* is assigned to one of the zodiacal signs. Depending on the state of this sign, you will know, how supported is your water element and your entire wellbeing.

12 degree and 1 degree of any *tithi* might be especially problematic and cause some emotional disturbances. Whenever birth *tithi* is exactly on the border or *sandhi* of two *tithis*, the *tithi rashi* would fall in Pisces/Aries *gandanta* – which is the most disturbing from the perspective of *tithi rashi*. Additionally, if this happens on the border between *Purna tithis* (5, 10 and 15) and *Nanda tithis* (6, 11 and 1), this would be emotionally even more disturbing, as the transition from each *Purna tithi* to *Nanda tithi* is called *tithi gandanta* – because it is the transition from one *guna* to another, similarly like in *rashi chakra*. This, however, affects a person much more, when it falls in the portion of *Purna tithi*, when the mind or the Moon is just approaching this zone of transformation. It can produce highly indecissive mind and create many disturbing emotions within a person, which will negatively influence also person's relations, financial flow and feeling of direction in life. Healing one's water element is of great importance for such a person.

Tithi shunya dosha

According to *Garga Samhita*, some *rashis* are also made *shunya* or "empty" by certain *tithis*, as described in the chapters about respective Nitya Devis and their *tithis*. This *rashis* are sometimes called *shunya* ("fruitless"), *dagdha* ("burnt") or *visha* ("poisonous"). The only *tithis*, which don't create any *shunya rashis* are Purnima and Amavasya.

Shunya rashi can make this exact sign in the chart quite weak and vulnerable, and sometimes even malefic. This will also affects this sign's lord. This is one of the many secret reasons, why sometimes, you can see a chart, when some planet or *rashi* seems to have an excellent position, but due to some reason, it fails to give good results to the person. Below you can see the full list of *tithis* and signs (as well as their lords), which they are making *shunya*.

TITHI SHUNYA RASHIS

Tithi	Shunya rashis	Lords of shunya rashis
Pratipad (1)	Libra & Capricorn	Saturn & Venus
Dvitiya (2)	Sagittarius & Pisces	Jupiter
Tritiya (3)	Leo & Capricorn	Sun & Saturn
Chaturti (4)	Taurus & Aquarius	Venus & Saturn
Panchami (5)	Gemini & Virgo	Mercury
Shashti (6)	Aries & Leo	Mars & Sun
Saptami (7)	Cancer & Sagittarius	Moon & Jupiter
Ashtami (8)	Gemini & Virgo	Mercury
Navami (9)	Leo & Scorpio	Sun & Mars
Dashami (10)	Leo & Scorpio	Sun & Mars
Ekadashi (11)	Sagittarius & Pisces	Jupiter
Dvadashi (12)	Libra & Capricorn	Saturn & Venus
Trayodashi (13)	Taurus & Leo	Venus & Sun
Chaturdashi (14)	Gemini, Virgo, Sagittarius, Pisces	Mercury & Jupiter
Purnima / Amavasya (15)	----	----

Unless these signs are occupied by Rahu or Ketu, or unless its lords (Venus or Saturn) are placed 3rd, 6th, 8th or 12th house from ascendant or Moon, or are retrograde, or in conjuction with malefic planet, or, lastly, in nakshatras of Rahu or Ketu, these two signs and houses ruled by those planets won't bring good results for the native. In such a case these signs must be strengthened (by strengthening their lords) to bring good results and remedies must be applied. *Shunya* planets do produce good results, however, when they transit 3rd, 6th, 8th or 12th house from from ascendant or Moon.

Additionally, certain *tithis* except *Chaturti, Dashami, Chaturdashi, Purnima* and *Amavasya* have the power to make some nakshatras *shunya* or fruitless. This can make the manifestation of energy of certain nakshatras a little bit "spoiled", which is why it is important not to plan any important actions on those days. If a person is born on a day like that, then the person must be very mindful about developing the positive qualities of that nakshatra, instead of letting it manifest its lower octave. These *tithis* are causing *shunya dosha* to exact nakshatras:

- **Pratipad:** Uttarashadha
- **Dvitiya:** Anuradha
- **Tritiya:** Uttara Phalguni, Uttarashadha, Uttara Bhadrapada
- **Chaturti:** ---
- **Panchami:** Magha
- **Shashti:** Rohini
- **Saptami:** Hasta, Mula
- **Ashtami:** Purva Bhadrapada
- **Navami:** Krittika
- **Dashami:** ---
- **Ekadashi:** Rohini
- **Dvadashi:** Ashlesha
- **Trayodashi:** Citra, Svati
- **Chaturdashi:** ---
- **Purnima / Amavasya:** ---

This actually reveals, how great is the power of the *tithi* in a birth chart. Even though *tithi* has the power to make certain *rashis* or nakshatras *shunya*, it can never happen the other way around. Certain Vedic months, though, have the power to make not only certain *tithis*, but also certain nakshatras and *rashis shunya*. These *tithis* are not auspicious to take any important action during these exact Vedic months. People born on these exact lunar days in these exact Vedic months can also face certain ups and downs in the sphere of emotions in their life. This is shown below:

- **Caitra:** Ashtami and Ekadashi
- **Vaishakha:** Dvadashi
- **Jyeshtha:** Trayodashi
- **Ashada:** Shashti
- **Shravana:** Purnima
- **Bhadrapada:** Saptami
- **Ashwayuja:** Navami
- **Krittika:** Panchami
- **Margashirsha:** Dvitiya
- **Pushya:** Pratipad
- **Magha:** Chaturti and Dashami
- **Phalguna:** Chaturdashi

Tithi pati

Tithi pati or *Tithesha* is the planetary ruler of a lunar day – in other words: *tithi* lord. Planetary co-rulers, similarly like the directions associated with them, will be revealing us mostly the shadow qualities of each lunar day. Planetary co-rulers in a way "eclipse" the Divine qualities of the *tithi* and its ruling Goddess. When you understand, which exact qualities needed to be overcome in your mind (which is what *tithi* lord is telling you about) in order for the healthy flow of energy to manifest in your life (which is represented by the Goddess of each *tithi*), you can start to manifest the best version of yourself.

Tithi lord or planetary co-ruler reveal us how we utilise the water element or the emotions in our life. The planet, which is your *tithi* lord, becomes the carrier of water element and carrier of emotion in your natal chart. The quality of your emotions or flow in life will depend mostly on the placement of your *tithi* lord. *Tithi* lord present in watery signs (Cancer, Scorpio or Pisces) is excellent and reveals very pleasant emotions. In earthly signs (Taurus, Virgo or Capricorn) the flow of emotions won't be bad either. In airy signs (Gemini, Libra or Aquarius) the natural flow of emotions might be already a bit disturbed. But with *tithi* lord in fiery signs (Aries, Leo or Sagittarius) the person might experience really intense, transformative emotions and certain emotional shocks, as well – especially in the sphere of relationships, as this sphere of our life is mostly affected by the *tithis*. Such person will need to consciously work on uplifting the energies of one's water element with the help of remedies such as keeping one's body well hydrated or getting in touch with the form of Goddess presiding over one's birth *tithi*.

Apart from the sign, occupied by the *tithi* lord, it is always important to check also, if the *tithi* lord has any company or receives any aspects – as it may significantly change the entire story. It is also worthy to check fourth house from the *tithi* lord, as it will reveal our emotional balance – while second house from the *tithi* lord will reveal our hormonal balance. Seventh house from the *tithi* lord will reveal the quality of our relationships with people (especially with our spouse), while twelfth house from the *tithi* lord will reveal our ability to express our *bhakti*, or love for the Divine.

Lunar day	Tithi (Vedic name)	Planetary co-ruler
First	Pratipad	Sun
Second	Dvitiya	Moon
Third	Tritiya	Mars
Fourth	Caturti	Mercury
Fifth	Panchami	Jupiter
Sixth	Shashti	Venus
Seventh	Saptami	Saturn
Eight	Ashtami	Rahu
Ninth	Navami	Sun
Tenth	Dashami	Moon
Eleventh	Ekadashi	Mars
Twelfth	Dvadashi	Mercury
Thirteenth	Trayodashi	Jupiter
Fourteenth	Caturdashi	Venus
Fifteenth	Purnima	Saturn
Fifteenth	Amavasya	Rahu

Tithi pati kshetra & Tithi pati kshetra paksha

This is one genius concept, which allowed me, personally, to date certain most important events in my life, with the help of *Narayana dasha* and *Sudarshan chakra dasha*. It is a beautiful concept, revealing the natural direction, towards which the natives of exact *tithis* are heading. It reveals the desire connected to your birth *tithi*.

Tithi pati kshetra or "field of the lord of the *tithi*" will be *mulatrikona* sign of the lord of this *tithi* for the first 8 *tithis* and the sign, in which another portion of this planet remains (but must be different from its *mulatrikona*) for last 8 *tithis*. *Tithi pati kshetra paksha* will be simply the sign opposite to it – and it will be the sign revealing hidden desire of the *tithi* and the direction towards which it is going in life. In fact, when you know the sign, which is your *tithi pati kshetra paksha*, you can very easily determine in *Narayana dasha* (or any other *Rashi dasha*) such moments in your life, when some major shift will happen – and usually a positive one. The final outcome will be, however, also dependent on the state of that *rashi*.

Tithi	Tithi pati	Tithi pati kshetra	Tithi pati kshetra paksha
Pratipad	Sun	Leo	Aquarius
Dvitiya	Moon	Taurus	Scorpio
Tritiya	Mars	Aries	Libra
Caturti	Mercury	Virgo	Pisces
Panchami	Jupiter	Sagittarius	Gemini
Shashti	Venus	Libra	Aries
Saptami	Saturn	Aquarius	Leo
Ashtami	Rahu	Pisces	Virgo
Navami	Sun	Aries	Libra
Dashami	Moon	Leo	Capricorn
Ekadashi	Mars	Scorpio	Taurus
Dvadashi	Mercury	Gemini	Sagittarius
Trayodashi	Jupiter	Pisces	Virgo
Caturdashi	Venus	Taurus	Scorpio
Purnima	Saturn	Capricron	Cancer
Amavasya	Rahu	Aquarius	Leo

These are just some of the tools, which can help you to read a chart from perpective of the *tithis* and which I found the most helpful in my personal astrology practice. A proper application of those tools can be sometimes very revealing, as anything related to the *tithi* will reveal the inner emotional state of the person, which will influence all one's actions. Whenever you are reading a chart of a person and you sometimes ask yourself, from where certain issues or influences come from, look at the *tithi*; look at the emotion. Sometimes those influences, which are invisible, have the most to say.

Tithis in synastry

Analysing the *tithis* is also greatly helpful in synastry – as *tithis* are all about sacred relationships. After going through this journey with the Moon and familiarising yourself with different manifestations of the Divine Mother presiding over lunar phases, you can already start to feel, why certain *tithis* will "click" very nicely with each other, while other *tithis* won't. Specific *tithis* resonate better with exact elements, *gunas*, nakshatras and weekdays – which is why you will naturally "click" better with people born on the *tithis* of friendly element, nakshatra or weekday. For some *tithis* some other limitations will apply, as well, like the energies of certain planets being specifically disturbing for certain lunar days.

The easiest way to determine, what will be "born" of any of your relations (as this concept doesn't apply only to partnership), you can try a very easy technique. Firstly locate the position of your Sun and Moon, and then locate Sun and Moon in other person's chart. Meditate a little on Sun and Moon in your chart and other person's chart, and try to *feel* or understand through nakshatras, which quality of light the Sun is shining and giving in both charts and how Moon in each chart is modifying this light and receiving it. Sun always shines and always gives; Moon always reflects and always receives. By understanding, which exact quality of Sun are you shining forth, you will easily understand, which kind of light you are shining into the world and what you are giving in all your relations. By understanding the exact quality of your Moon, on the other hand, you get to understand, how you *receive* and welcome things in your life. Combinining both aspects into one allows you to understand, what is the quality of light, which your self is emanating, and how it is modified by the receiving mind.

In synastry, see firstly, what quality is shining through your Sun – and then analyse how it is reflected and received by the Moon of other person. This will show you, what you are bringing into that relationship. If you follow it the opposite way, understanding what quality of light is manifested by other person's Sun and how it is received by your Moon, you will understand, what will you receive in this relationship. Applying to it, additionally, *navatara* system, can help you to determine very accurately, what will be the final outcome of such a relationship.

And, if you wish to go one step further... Calculate the distance between your Sun and other person's Moon, and *vice versa*, and see what kind of *tithi* would be created by such a planetary relationship. *Tithi* calculated from your Sun will indicate what you bring into the life of other person, and how it is received, while *tithi* calculated from the Sun of other person, will reveal, what you receive in this relationship and *how* are you receiving it.

It is also always worthy to check, does the *tithi* of one person cause *shunya dosha* to any of the vital points of another native's chart – such as 1, 5 and 9 house, as well as Moon's nakshatra, ascendant nakshatra or Atma karaka nakshatra. Any such a *dosha* may cause certain dissatisfaction or distance in a relationship – but it doesn't always need to be something very negative.

These are just couple of useful techniques of looking at a chart from a perspective of a *tithi*. But once you really *feel* the *tithis* and start working with them, the possibilities are literally infinite.

If you have a desire to learn more about practical application of the wisdom of the *tithis* in real life and on real birth charts, I have also done an entire course on the mysteries of the lunar phases in Vedic Astrology, as well as series of webinars on Patreon. You will find all the links on the last pages of this book.

CHAPTER 24

SADHANA – PRAYING WITH THE MOON

And so, you went on a journey with the Moon. You travelled with all the Nitya Devis and experienced all their different moods on the way. But... *did you*? Did you really felt the emotion hidden in the heart of each of them? Or did you just try to understand them with the mind?

You might like to remind yourself once again: *tithis* are not about understanding. They are about *feeling*. Even if this book would have thousand pages, these would still be just empty words. What makes this knowledge *real* is your own personal experience.

Start from simple things. Start from just looking around, every single day, and writing down, how the emotions and different aspects of exact *tithi* and exact Nitya Devi manifest in your own life. Every single day one of these Goddesses is trying to teach you something very profound about yourself. After all, they are the guardians of Time, as well as the guardians of Supreme Self, in the form of Lalita Tripurasundari in tantric tradition. Even if they are bringing you some unpleasant vibrations or unpleasant emotions, they are doing it only for your highest good – so you can learn something and evolve. This is why they are the Mothers – because they hold our little self on their lap and carry us through different moments in Time, like a mother would hold a child.

There is one meditation, given by my Gurudev that is particularly dear to my heart. I used to meditate with each of the Nitya Devis in such a way on each of their respective lunar days – and I can tell you that just from this meditation, I have learned *so much*. This is one of the easiest and yet, at the same time, one of the most profound ways to connect to Divine Mother, as well as Her fifteen manifestatons.

Meditation with the Divine Mother

"Close your eyes and imagine yourself sitting on the lap of the Divine Mother. See yourself small sitting in Her lap. Just enjoy being in Her lap. Feel Her motherly love, Her protection.

Feel that you don't need to bother about anything. You are a child – what should you bother about? What should you think about? Just be.

Now talk to the Mother. Talk to the Mother the same way you talk to everybody. Ask Her whatever you want. See and hear Her answering you.

Now, when you have tasted the sweetness of the Mother, know that She is always with you. Ever ready to help you, ever ready to fulfill all your wishes. Don't be shy to ask. Because She is the only one that gives. She has abundance. She has more to give than you can think. So take from the inexhaustible source."

This touching meditation with the Divine Mother was given by my Gurudev on one of his darshans in Poland. It is a truly beautiful meditation, which can help you a lot in healing water element or *tithi* within you – especially if you choose to meditate with the Goddess presiding your birth *tithi*, on exact lunar day ruled by Her. And, if you wish to *really feel* the energy of each *tithi* and connect with them on a much deeper level, try to meditate in such a way with each Nitya Devi on Her exact lunar day – at least for fifteen consecutive days. Just by doing so you will learn more about the *tithis* than you can possibly read in any book.

You can also connect to different *tithis* or Nitya Devis by chanting one of their mantras, at least 108 times, on their respective lunar days. In each of the chapters dedicated to Nitya Devis you will also find most favourite mode of worship for each Goddess, as well as affirmations and questions for self-analysis, which you can use for daily practice. Self-analysis is especially useful for keeping mind under control, as well as analysing how influences of different lunar phases manifest in real life.

Keep in mind, however, that connecting to *tithis* through affirmations or self-analysis is still dwelling on the level of the mind. If you want to reach beyond the duality of the mind, and really *feel* them, meditation, mantra or *yantra* are the best tools for that – as they make your mind focused on something, while keeping it open for new insights.

Yantras of Nitya Devis

Colouring the *yantra* of exact Nitya Devi or meditating with it is one of the best way to connect with this Nitya Devi and one of the best remedies for any *tithi dosha*. Whether you experience *tithi dosha*, weak *tithi rashi* or any other negative influence, which takes its source from your birth *tithi*, your personal *tithi yantra* can be of great help for you. By colouring the exact *yantra*, you will not only heal your *tithi*, but you will also allow its Divine qualities to manifest in much more harmonious way in your life. And even if you do not suffer from any *tithi dosha*, colouring a *yantra* is simply a beautiful experience and a wonderful way to honour Nitya Devis. This is one of the experiences, which I would recommend for everybody to have – especially if you are astrologer yourself or thinking seriously about becoming one. Nothing will give you such a deep understanding of different energies of the *tithis* like the process of colouring their *yantras*.

If you can, find for yourself fifteen days in your schedule and colour one *yantra* a day – each day for different Nitya Devi, according to the lunar day. It is a very fascinating process, which will heal more in you than you can possibly imagine. I have went through this process myself and I cannot even express how much it changed me.

How to work with *yantras*

Yantra literally means "a machine, a device, an instrument". It also means "an amulet" or "a support". All the *yantras* were very carefully designed by the ancient *rishis* of India to support our harmonious connection with the Divine and the world, as well as to protect us from heavier energies and create the sacred space around us.

In our age of Internet and commercialisation, when all the sacred knowledge is wide-spread, easily available and, unfortunately, often abused and unappreciated, we can find all sorts of *yantras*, which we can either print for ourselves or order one from the massive production. And, in our hectic lives, this is often what we do: we want to get the easiest "remedy" possible to find some sort of karmic shortcut in our daily life, hoping that the *yantras* will magically work on their own, like a pill. Yet, in ancient times, it was never just about "getting" the *yantra*. It was never about "using" the Divine energy for our purposes. It was about making a heart connection with the Divine present in that form.

My Gurudev has revealed, that in ancient times, before even undertaking the process of creating any *yantra*, people would fast for as long as 40 days. The process of creation of the *yantra* was a sacred one. Body, mind and spirit needed to be well prepared for that. Body was purified through fasting, mind was purified through chanting the mantras, and spirit was purified through connection with the Divine in meditation. Then, when the time was right and the planetary energies were well aligned with our purpose, the sacred process of drawing or painting the *yantra* was commenced.

In this sacred process, however, it was never about the goal itself. The process was much more important than the end result. I have observed many times, how many inner processes can be triggered just by such a seemingly simple activity as colouring a *yantra*. In this process all our dysharmonious energies are once again aligned to the Higher Harmony of the universe. But, above all, we make a true heart connection to form of the Divine Mother, we are drawing a *yantra* for. We invoke the Divine presence into our inner space, we pay our respect to Her, we worship Her and we embrace Her with Love – at the same time embracing with Love these part of ourselves, which She represents. In itself this is a very profound meditation. Some of the *yantras* (like Sri Yantra), indeed, are said to be so powerful, that just a meditation on them can lead us to enlightenment.

Additionally, my Gurudev had said, that whenever you make a *yantra* with your own hands, it is infinitely more powerful, as it is infused with your bhakti – and any mistake gets automatically rectified by the power of your devotion. Such a *yantra*, which is painted with your love and devotion, in the proper state of body, mind and spirit, with utmost care to even the tiniest detail of this sacred process, is a true tool for self-transformation. Only such a *yantra* can be said to be truly alive.

Yet, there is one more "secret ingredient" that makes the *yantra* really alive and turns it into a generator of positive energy. Similarly like any device needs some sort of fuel or electricity to work, in the same way *yantra* needs to be infused with its respective mantra, so the life can be breathed into it. My Gurudev said, that the *yantra*, which is not activated in such a way is just an ordinary piece of paper. It is our devotion, which keeps the energy within a *yantra* alive.

It is also good to keep in mind, that in ancient times only natural materials were used to create or colour the *yantras*. Colours were always hand-made by the person, who was about to draw or colour the *yantra*. As difficult as it might be in our times, it is very important that we do at least so little to respect our Mother Earth to at least use 100% vegan pencils or paints, not containing any animal products, neither tested on animals. It is my humble request to you, who are reading this book to honour the Divinity of the *yantra* in this way and to make sure that nobody had suffered during the process of you getting your materials for colouring. It is highly disrespectful to the Divine Mother, Shakti Herself to abuse Her children (who are animals and plants, as well) in any way.

Also, if you are not strictly vegetarian, please, follow a strictly vegetarian diet (or, ideally, vegan) during the process of drawing or colouring a *yantra* to pay your respect to Mother Nature.

Step 1: Choosing the right time

To get in tune with the energy of each Nitya Devi, chose Her exact *tithi* for your *sadhana*. It is easier to connect with Nitya Devis at night. If you can choose such a time and can sit in such a way, that you are bathed in moonlight during the entire process, that is even better.

Step 2: Preparation

Preparation for the process of colouring or drawing the *yantras* is a very important part of the process, as well. Ideally, you should fast at least on the day of colouring the *yantra*. If this is not possible for your body, then at least avoid by any means eating any animal products (meat, fish, eggs, gelatine, etc.), as well as garlic and onion, to keep your mind pure and receptive for Divine energies. Also, make sure to prepare as natural colours for painting as possible. By any means they must be 100% vegan, not containing any non-vegan ingredients, neither tested on animals. By colouring the *yantras* of Nitya Devis, you are connecting to Mother Nature Herself – it is essential that you do not disrespect Her other children.

Step 3: Meditation

Before you start to colour your *yantra*, make sure you also meditate a little on exact Nitya Devi, whose energy you are going to invoke. Chant Her mantra at least 108 times before you start the process of colouring the *yantra*. You may also want to meditate with this form of Goddess while doing so. If you can wear the same colour as this Nitya Devi and face the direction connected with this *tithi* in *Kalachakra*, that would be ideal.

Step 4: Colouring

While colouring the *yantra*, always start from *bhupura* (outer border of the *yantra*, symbolising the border of our material perception) and then slowly proceed to the center, layer by layer. You may also want to honour the *shaktis* or powers present in different shapes of the *yantra* by chanting their names, before colouring each respective layer. You may, as well, just chant inwardly the mantra connected to this Nitya Devi during the process of colouring.

Step 5: Activating the yantra

At the end of the process, before proceeding to meditation with the *yantra*, it is always important to activate it first. This is done either by placing your right hand on the yantra or placing the yantra on your heart and chanting the mantra of the exact Nitya Devi for 108 times with devotion, to invoke Her presence.

Step 6: Completing the process

When your *yantra* is already activated, you can place it on its prescribed direction or keep it on your altar or other sacred place. If you don't have such a sacred place, Northeast is a universal direction to keep all the sacred or healing objects in your home (and it is also connected to water element in our home).

Having such *yantra*, which was coloured by you with devotion on exact lunar day is a very precious thing. You can use it as a tool for meditation – just keep your gaze fixed on the *yantra* on Her respective lunar day, and you can inwardly chant Her mantra. This would be greatly healing for your *tithi* and water element within you. If you wish to additionally strengthen your *tithi* or water element, then on exact lunar day governed by the Goddess of your birth *tithi* in *Shukla paksha* (excerpt, if your birth *tithi* is *Amavasya*), place a glass or pot (ideally copper pot) of water on the *yantra* of your Nitya Devi over night, on Northeast of your apartment or, ideally, in the moonlight. Such water will have greatly healing properties, which will be optimal just for you and will help in restoring harmonious vibrations of water element within you. This won't only improve your health, but can powerfully counteract any other side effects of *tithi dosha*, such as problems with relationships, financial flow or feeling of fulfillment in life. I have tested this method several times with different people.

If you don't have a wish to place your coloured *yantra* in any place of the apartment, and you were colouring the yantra just as a form of *sadhana* and a sacred process of connecting to Nitya Devis, you can also burn your *yantra* at the end to complete your intention. If you wish to burn your *yantra* at the end, you can skip Step 5.

Time for your own journey with the Moon

And so, our journey with the Moon is coming to an end. But it never really ends. Once a cycle is completed, another one starts straight away, as evolution is the law of life. Everyday can become for you an opportunity to understand your personal journey with the Moon better and for something new to unfold. You have the knowledge and you have the tools. But now you need to walk on this path on your own.

And I wish you a really amazing journey with the Moon.

ABOUT THE AUTHOR

Achala (Sylwia Mihajlović) is a Jyotishi and an Atma Kriya Yoga teacher from Poland. She offers Atma Kriya Yoga courses in Europe (and recently some other parts of the world), as well as online Jyotish webinars, private tutoring sessions and individual readings based on the art of Vedic astrology. From the moment she started to practice yoga and meditation at the early age of 17, she dedicated her whole life to the path of spiritual development, and became a disciple of Paramahamsa Sri Swami Vishwananda. Author of *Discovering Youniverse* and *Navagraha Yantras*.

If you wish to learn more about the *tithis* directly from Achala, you can join her on bi-monthly webinars about the mysteries of lunar phases (and some other aspects of Vedic Astrology from time to time) by subscribing here and becoming a part of our community: https://www.patreon.com/achala

If you wish to share some of your personal experiences after reading the book or your own observations about lunar phases, which could be helpful for further research, you are encouraged to do so by writing at: info@4harmony.eu

Find out more: http://www.4harmony.eu/

Majority of the quotes of Paramahamsa Sri Swami Vishwananda in this book come from his official Facebook page, where you can receive a daily dose inspiration from enlightened Master:
https://www.facebook.com/ParamahamsaVishwananda/

Printed in Great Britain
by Amazon

25338411R00190